PENGUIN  CLASSICS

PERSONAL NARRATIVE

ALEXANDER VON HUMBOLDT was born on the family estate at Tegel in Berlin in 1769. With his elder brother Wilhelm he was educated by tutors and then at Frankfurt, Göttingen and Hamburg Universities where he studied botany, literature, archaeology, electricity, mineralogy and the natural sciences. In 1790 he travelled abroad and published his first works in botanical and chemical journals. While at Jena he befriended Goethe. He worked in the Prussian Mining Administration until his mother died in 1796. A large inheritance enabled Humboldt to travel; after a few frustrations he was allowed by Charles IV of Spain to travel in the Spanish American colonies at his own expense, with his companion Aimé Bonpland. After five years in the New World (1799–1804) Humboldt settled in Paris to begin publishing his encyclopaedic *Relation historique du voyage aux régions équinoxiales du nouveau continent*, finally completed in thirty volumes in 1834, where the *Personal Narrative* comprised volumes 28 to 30. Humboldt was not only a prominent figure in the Parisian scientific world but also Chamberlain to Friedrich Wilhelm III, and Councillor of State to Friedrich Wilhelm IV. In 1829 he travelled to Russia and Central Asia and published his account in French in 1843. In 1834 he began his comprehensive survey of creation, *Kosmos*, completed posthumously in 1862. He died in 1859, a bachelor, and was buried in the family vault at Tegel, honoured as one of the great speculative scientific travellers of the nineteenth century.

JASON WILSON was born in Mauritius in 1944, was a lecturer at Kings College, London, and is currently Reader in Latin American Literature at University College, London. He has published *Octavio Paz: A Study of his Poetics* (1979), *Octavio Paz* (1986), *An A–Z of Latin American Literature in English Translation* (1989), the *Traveller's Literary Companion to South and Central America* (1993) and essays on W.H. Hudson, Charles Darwin, Julio Cortázar and Latin American poetry. He is currently working on scientific and literary travellers in Latin America.

MALCOLM NICOLSON was born in 1952 and is a Senior Research Fellow in the Wellcome Unit for the History of Medicine, University of Glasgow, having formerly been Wellcome Lecturer in the History of Medicine, University of Edinburgh. A graduate of the University of Aberdeen, he wrote his Ph.D. thesis on the history and sociology of plant ecology in the Science Studies Unit, University of Edinburgh. He has also worked in the University of Canterbury, Christchurch, New Zealand and the Wellcome Institute, London, and is an honorary member of the Department of Science and Technology Dynamics, University of Amsterdam. His main research interest is currently the development of diagnostic practice but he continues to work on the history of ecology and environmental thought.

ALEXANDER VON HUMBOLDT

Personal Narrative

Abridged and Translated with an Introduction by
JASON WILSON

and a Historical Introduction by
MALCOLM NICOLSON

PENGUIN BOOKS

PENGUIN BOOKS

Published by the Penguin Group
Penguin Books Ltd, 27 Wrights Lane, London w8 5tz, England
Penguin Books USA Inc., 375 Hudson Street, New York, New York 10014, USA
Penguin Books Australia Ltd, Ringwood, Victoria, Australia
Penguin Books Canada Ltd, 10 Alcorn Avenue, Toronto, Ontario, Canada m4v 3b2
Penguin Books (NZ) Ltd, 182–190 Wairau Road, Auckland 10, New Zealand

Penguin Books Ltd, Registered Offices: Harmondsworth, Middlesex, England

Relation historique du voyage aux régions équinoxiales du nouveau continent first published 1814–25
This translation published in Penguin Classics 1995

029

Abridgement, translation, introduction and notes copyright © Jason Wilson, 1995
Historical introduction copyright © Malcolm Nicolson, 1995
All rights reserved

The moral right of the translator and the author of the Historical introduction has been asserted

Map on pages vi–vii by Nigel Andrews

Set in 9.75/12.25 pt Monotype Bembo
Filmset by Datix International Limited, Bungay, Suffolk
Printed and bound in Great Britain by Clays Ltd, Elcograf S.p.A.

ISBN-13: 978-0-14-044553-4

www.greenpenguin.co.uk

MIX
Paper from
responsible sources
FSC™ C018179

Penguin Books is committed to a sustainable
future for our business, our readers and our planet.
This book is made from Forest Stewardship
Council™ certified paper.

CONTENTS

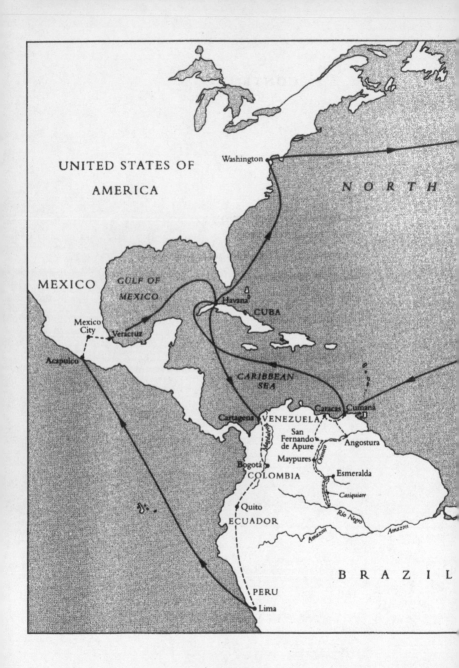

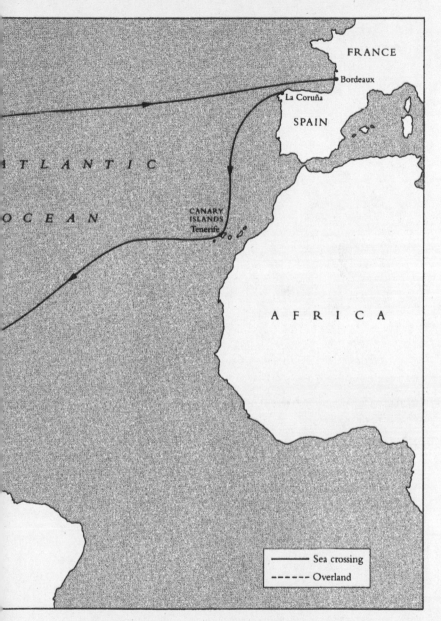

HUMBOLDT'S ROUTE, 1799–1804

HISTORICAL INTRODUCTION

In a few hours we sail round Cape Finisterre. I shall collect plants and fossils and make astronomical observations. But that's not the main purpose of my expedition – I shall try to find out how the forces of nature interact upon one another and how the geographic environment influences plant and animal life. In other words, I must find out about the unity of nature.

Alexander von Humboldt wrote these words on 5 June 1799, sitting in his cabin on the corvette *Pizarro*, in the Spanish port of La Coruña.. He was writing farewell letters to his friends as the ship's company made final preparations for the crossing of the Atlantic. Twenty-nine years old, Humboldt was on the verge of realizing a long cherished ambition – to make a journey of scientific discovery in the New World. On 16 July, he and his travelling companion Aimé Bonpland landed in Cumaná, in what is now Venezuela, to begin their five-year-long exploration of South America.

Humboldt and Bonpland travelled by horseback or on foot, by boat or dugout canoe, over the plains of Venezuela, up and down the Orinoco river, into the Andes, along mountain valleys and passes to Bogotá, Quito and Lima, and then by ship to Mexico. They also made voyages to Cuba and to the United States before returning to Europe in August 1804. The successful completion of this adventurous and arduous expedition secured for Humboldt personal fame and consolidated his international scientific reputation. He and Bonpland had gathered an immense scientific and scholarly harvest on the journey – huge amounts of information on climatology, geology, mineralogy, terrestrial magnetism, plant geography, zoology, political economy and ethnography, as well as thousands of dried plant specimens. Publishing the results of this expedition was to dominate much of Humboldt's remaining career, and to exhaust his private income. The first of a series of thirty volumes appeared in 1807 (or perhaps 1805). The last was not ready until 1834.

Among the more strictly scientific publications of the expedition, Alexander von Humboldt wrote a narrative account of his journey, which he entitled *Relation historique du voyage aux régions équinoxiales du nouveau continent*. It appeared in three volumes between 1814 and 1825. Even at three volumes the *Relation historique* is incomplete – a fourth volume was written but never published. When composing the *Relation historique*, Humboldt sought to encapsulate within the volumes the totality of his experience of South America. He wrote not only for a specialized audience of scientists but for a broader audience of educated lay persons.

The first English translation, *Personal Narrative of Travels to the Equinoctial Regions of America*, appeared between 1814 and 1829. As well as being an entertaining travelogue, the *Personal Narrative* provides a useful and accessible introduction to the character and diversity of Humboldt's scientific, scholarly and aesthetic concerns. Although he made other scientific journeys, notably to Siberia in 1829, Humboldt always regarded the expedition to the Americas as the most important of his travels. In the New World he had visited the tropical zone where plant and animal life displayed the greatest richness and diversity of form. In the *Personal Narrative* we can discern the grand themes that characterized his life's work as a whole – the painstaking empiricism, the remarkable breadth of intellectual interest, the passion for the beauties of nature, and the commitment to a universal science.

Born in 1769, Alexander von Humboldt grew up in what has been termed the 'second great age of discovery'. From his early boyhood his imagination was stirred by accounts of navigation and exploration. In the eighteenth century, however, exploration was no longer simply a matter of travelling to unknown locations. Geographical discovery had become closely wedded to scientific inquiry. Expeditions were generally much better equipped and their members better trained for systematic empirical study than had previously been the case. Where earlier explorers had merely observed, the aim of the new scientific traveller was to record more accurately, to measure more precisely, and to collect more comprehensively. Moreover, in writing the accounts of their travels, many eighteenth-century explorers sought to demonstrate not only scientific accomplishment but also aesthetic sensitivity and literary skill. Humboldt enthusiastically adopted this form of investigatory enterprise. In South America he was to bring it to a new peak of perfection.

The origins of Alexander von Humboldt's style of exploration may, thus, be found within the practices of his eighteenth-century predecessors. For example, one of the early exponents of a more precise and quantitative style of exploration was the French mathematician and naturalist Charles-Marie de La Condamine (1701–74). In 1735 La Condamine sailed to South America as a member of an expedition organized by the Académie Royale des Sciences, the object of which was to ascertain whether the earth was an oblate spheroid, as Isaac Newton had hypothesized. Working over a number of years in the difficult terrain of a high valley in the Andean mountains, near Quito, La Condamine and his companions made detailed and painstaking geometric and astronomical measurements. In 1743 La Condamine began his journey home in the most adventurous way possible, by sailing down the Amazon in a canoe. In the course of his two-month voyage, he continued to take astronomical and topographical measurements, and also observed the use of rubber and cinchona bark by the native Indians. La Condamine's account of his travels, *Relation abrégée d'un voyage fait dans l'intérieur de l'Amérique méridionale*, provided an evocative blend of science and adventure in far-away places. As we shall see, this was a combination that was to be found in Humboldt's own writings, more than half a century later.

In the year of Humboldt's birth, another mathematician and navigator Louis Antoine de Bougainville (1729–1811) completed the first French circumnavigation of the globe. In the course of his voyage, Bougainville discovered new islands, recorded the customs of the Polynesians, and collected many new species of plants and animals. He was, for example, the first to confirm the presence of marsupial mammals in the East Indies. Bougainville's *Voyage autour du monde* appeared in 1771 and quickly became an enormous bestseller. Even more vividly than La Condamine, Bougainville evoked the exotic delights of strange lands and the thrills of geographical and scientific discovery.

Voyage autour du monde was avidly read by the young Humboldt.

It was, however, the three voyages of Captain James Cook (1728–79), between 1768 and 1780, that most brilliantly displayed the potential of the scientific expedition and most directly inspired in Humboldt the ambition to become an explorer himself. The purpose of Cook's first voyage, in the *Endeavour*, was to travel to Tahiti to observe the transit of Venus (its passage across the visible disc of the sun) and, then, to investigate whether a continental land mass existed in the far southern latitudes. In terms of new geographical, astronomical, ethnographic and botanical knowledge, the achievement of the voyage of the *Endeavour* was immense. Cook was a masterly navigator and marine surveyor, and he was accompanied on the voyage by the accomplished naturalists Joseph Banks and Daniel Solander.

On his second voyage, from 1772 to 1775, Cook was accompanied by the German naturalists Johann Reinhold Forster (1729–98) and his son Georg (1754–94). In the Pacific, the Forsters undertook extensive studies in 'physical geography, natural history and ethnic philosophy [anthropology]'. On their return, the elder Forster published *Observations Made during a Voyage round the World*, which was a remarkably broad and systematic account of their investigations, discussing ocean currents, coral reefs and volcanoes, together with a wide range of botanical and ethnographic issues. As well as being an assiduous observer, Forster was an accomplished experimenter, and his research was illuminated by a wide acquaintance with the best science of his day. Forster's work provided one of the most significant models for the Humboldtian style of exploratory science.

Late in life, Humboldt explicitly compared his achievements to those of Cook's voyages. But with one difference – whereas Cook had navigated the oceans, Humboldt had penetrated the continents. However, while undoubtedly following the eighteenth-century model of scientific exploration, Humboldt displayed a broader variety of scientific interests and intellectual concerns than any other explorer before or, indeed, since. To characterize more fully the scope and range of Humboldt's investigatory enterprise, one must look more specifically at his intellectual background in German thought and European science.

*

During the later half of the eighteenth century, profound transformations were taking place in the organization of knowledge and natural inquiry. One of the leading figures within this process of change was the German philosopher Immanuel Kant (1724–1804). In his lectures on 'Physical Geography', Kant expressed profound dissatisfaction with the system of classifying the natural world that had been devised by the Swedish naturalist Carl Linnaeus (1707–78). Linnaeus had named and classified plants according to a relatively small number of features of their external structure. To Kant, a taxonomy produced by such a process was bound to be arbitrary. It was incapable of conveying 'the idea of a whole out of which the manifold character of things is ... derived'. It did not, in other words, convey the richness and complexity of natural phenomena, nor did it sufficiently emphasize the importance of integrative and unifying processes that were not directly visible. Kant maintained that the essential prerequisite of a satisfactory form of natural inquiry was a full description of phenomena as they actually occurred and coexisted in the world.

The German geographers of the late eighteenth and early nineteenth centuries followed Kant in assuming an underlying causal unity of nature, of which the visible forms of things were only one aspect. This idea was linked to a concept of regionality. The earth was one interconnected whole – but it was also conceived of as made up of distinct natural units, of regions. Each natural region was distinctively different in a number of ways from its neighbours. The character of each region was produced by the interrelation of all its phenomena. Thus, the climatic and environmental conditions of a particular place affected everything from the nature of its vegetation to the moral properties of its human inhabitants. As Humboldt was later to put it:

the character of different regions of the earth may depend upon a combination of all these external phenomena ... the outline of mountains and hills, the physiognomy of plants and animals, the azure of the sky, the forms of the clouds and the transparency of the atmosphere ...

The investigations of Johann Reinhold Forster were structured around a strong geographical and regional framework. Forster's regionality, like Kant's, was supported by a theory of environmental influence. Different skies, different climates, different prevailing winds, all helped produce the diversity of forms of vegetation. Moreover, Forster regarded vegetation as one of the aspects of the environment that impinged most directly upon humanity. Plants thus mediated between the physical and the human sphere. To Forster the study of vegetation was therefore a centrally important part of natural inquiry. This was a view that was later to be strongly endorsed by Humboldt.

The son of a minor aristocratic family, Alexander von Humboldt received his early education from a private tutor. However, in his teens he received informal instruction in experimental natural philosophy from the Kantian physician Marcus Herz, and in floristic botany from Karl Ludwig Willdenow, later to become Professor of Natural History at the University of Berlin and one of the leading botanists of the day. Both these men exerted a formative influence upon the fledgling natural philosopher. Humboldt quickly developed his own interests in experimental investigation, and botany, in all its forms, remained a lifelong preoccupation.

In the late eighteenth century, the University of Göttingen was the premier centre for scientific scholarship in Germany. By the 1780s, a distinctive style of natural inquiry had developed at Göttingen, which closely harmonized with many of Kant's philosophical prescriptions. A number of Göttingen professors, including Blumenbach, Zimmermann and Treviranus, embraced Kant's definition of holistic organization and shared the philosopher's concern with the effect of the total environment upon the organism. Blumenbach and Treviranus also sought to identify the recurring structural features that they held to underlie the variety of plant and animal shape and form – another expression of the search for unity in the diversity of nature that was characteristic of German natural philosophy at this time. In 1789 Humboldt began a course of study at the University of Göttingen, studying under Blumenbach among others. Although he remained there for only one year, Humboldt always regarded his time at Göttingen as the most valuable part of his scientific education. Resonances with the concerns of the Göttingen school may be discerned in his mature work.

It was also at Göttingen that Humboldt first met Georg Forster. As noted above, Georg Forster had been with Captain Cook on his second voyage. Like his father, Georg had published an account of the expedition, *Voyage round the World on the Resolution*. While lacking the full systematic treatment and detailed scientific content of Johann Reinhold's *Observations*, Georg's *Voyage* is also a fine example of the late eighteenth-century genre of travel narrative, simultaneously displaying aesthetic sensitivity and broad scientific curiosity. Thus, early in his development as a natural philosopher, Humboldt came under the influence of an experienced practitioner of the art of scientific travelling.

In the spring of 1790 Humboldt and Georg Forster travelled together from Germany, through the Low Countries, to France and England. Their crossing of the Channel was Humboldt's first sea-voyage and it further stimulated his appetite for adventure – as did his meeting in London with another of Cook's former companions, Sir Joseph Banks. Humboldt was shown Banks's herbarium, then the largest in the world, containing many specimens collected in the Pacific.

Shortly after their return to Germany, Georg Forster published a description of their journey, *Ansichten vom Niederrhein von Brabant, Flandern, Holland, England und Frankreich*. This text was acclaimed in literary circles as a major achievement, particularly by the leading Romantics, Goethe and Schiller. The harmonization of scientific investigation with aesthetic awareness that Forster had accomplished was hailed as evidence of a new maturity of attitude among natural philosophers. Here was a demonstration that scientific inquiry need not be cold and unresponsive to the beauties of nature. It could embrace and celebrate the earth in the act of studying it.

As the reader of the *Personal Narrative* will quickly notice, there is much of Georg Forster's exemplar in Humboldt's own travel writing. Both men paid particular attention to the morphology of landscape. Both favoured panoramic description. Both valued scientific accuracy and avidly collected all manner of detail and data. Their empiricism was combined with enthusiastic recording of subjective impressions, aesthetic judgements and emotional responses.

In 1791 Humboldt began a course of training at the Freiberg School of Mines, run by the eminent geologist Abraham Werner. Here Humboldt undertook intensive study of, among other subjects, geology, mineralogy, surveying and mathematics. In his spare time he conducted a series of chemical experiments and investigated the geography and physiology of the local flora. Successful completion of the course at Freiberg qualified Humboldt for a career as a mining inspector, and in 1792 he duly took up his post in the Prussian Department of Mines.

From its base in Berlin, the Department of Mines was responsible for a variety of quarrying and mining operations, involving the extraction of salt, peat, copper and gold, as well as lignite, coal and iron ore. Its possessions were scattered over a wide area, extending into Poland. Humboldt's work as a mining inspector thus provided him with excellent opportunities to gain experience over a considerable range of scientific and survey work. For instance, in June 1792 he was sent to make a report of the geological structure and mining potential of the Fichtel and Franconian hills, and in March of the following year he began a long tour of Austria, Poland and what was to become Czechoslovakia, to investigate techniques of salt production. These tours provided invaluable training for the ambitious scientific traveller. Humboldt's reports, characterized as they are by indefatigable activity and curiosity, by meticulous quantitative observation and the rigorous application of scientific principles, were an important prototype for his later and still more wide-ranging accounts of South and Central America.

While working for the Department of Mines, Humboldt conducted investigations into geological stratification, and the effects of gases on animals – in the course of which he designed improved breathing equipment for miners. In 1795 he made an extensive trip through the Swiss and French Alps during which he learned much about geomagnetism and about the effects of altitude and topography on climate and vegetation. Humboldt also continued to pursue experimental investigations, particularly on 'animal electricity' and magnetism, publishing in 1797 a major work, *Versuche über die gereizte Muskel- und Nervenfaser nebts Vermuthungen über den chemische Process des Lebens in der Thier- und Pflanzenwelt (Experiments on Excited Muscle and Nerve Fibre with Conjectures on the Chemical Process of Life in the Animal and Vegetable World)*. Although Humboldt's theories of the nature of Galvanic phenomena did not achieve the lasting currency of those of his older contemporary, Alessandro Volta, the *Versuche* well displays both his technical skill as an experimenter and his astonishing energy. The results of approximately 4,000 experiments are summarized in 980 pages.

However, probably the most innovative and influential research Humboldt was engaged with, during the early and mid 1790s, was his work on the geography and environmental relations of plants. Humboldt first set out his programme for a new form of plant geography in 1793. In his *Florae Fribergensis specimen*, Humboldt followed Kant in distinguishing between a true history of nature and a mere description of natural objects such as had been provided by the older Linnaean system. No longer should botanists study merely individual species and their outward appearances; no longer should they be preoccupied solely with descriptive taxonomy and nomenclature. To Humboldt, the central concern of the plant geographer ought to be, by contrast, the complex phenomena of vegetation as they occurred in living nature:

Observation of individual parts of trees or grass is by no means to be considered plant geography; rather plant geography traces the connections and relations by which all plants are bound together among themselves, designates in what lands they are found, in what atmospheric conditions they live ... and describes the surface of the earth in which humus is prepared. This is what distinguishes geography from nature study, falsely called natural history ...

Humboldt identified his proposed botanical innovations with changes occurring contemporaneously in other fields of natural inquiry. In particular he associated his programme for plant geography with the new historical geology, or geognosy, proposed by his former teacher Abraham Werner. Werner sought to transcend classical mineralogy – which had concentrated on the study of individual minerals – and to move towards a unified history of the geological structure of the earth. The gist of Humboldt's remarks in the *Florae Fribergensis specimen* was that the new programme to provide a satisfactory history of the earth must encompass not only geological phenomena but biological ones as well. Here his concerns were cognate with those of his mentors in Göttingen:

Geognosy studies animate and inanimate nature . . . both organic and inorganic bodies. It is divided into three parts: solid rock geography, which Werner has industriously studied; zoological geography, whose foundations have been laid by Zimmermann; and the geography of plants, which our colleagues left untouched . . .

This grand vision of a complete historical geography of the earth and all its productions provided a central theme for Humboldt's later work. All his diverse writings were characterized by the desire to create what he termed *la physique générale* – the universal, synthetic science that would comprehend both the unity and the diversity of nature:

This science [*physique générale*], which without doubt is one of the most beautiful fields of human knowledge, can only progress . . . by bringing together of all the phenomena and creations which the earth has to offer. In this great sequence of cause and effect, nothing can be considered in isolation. The general equilibrium, which reigns amongst disturbances and apparent turmoil, is the result of an infinity of mechanical forces and chemical attractions balancing each other out. Even if each series of facts must be considered separately to identify a particular law, the study of nature, which is the greatest problem of *la physique générale*, requires the bringing together of all the forms of knowledge which deal with the modifications of matter.

Exploration was thus, for Humboldt, not merely a matter of adventure. It was an essential part of natural inquiry, a necessary condition of *la physique générale*. Only the traveller could bring 'together of all the phenomena and creations which the earth has to offer'; only the traveller could hope to grasp both the diversity of phenomena and the underlying unity of nature.

As we have seen, the geography of vegetation had a major part to play within this cosmological scheme. In a conception very similar to that of Johann Reinhold Forster, Humboldt regarded the regional distribution of plants both as a direct expression of the physical environment and as a formative influence upon human society. The priority that Humboldt accorded to the study of the living plants in their natural environment further emphasized the requirement that the scholar should also be an explorer. The study of dried specimens in a herbarium, while essential, was not by any means wholly sufficient as a basis for plant geography. The botanist must observe the manner by which different species of plants grow together, and how these groupings change under the influence of altitude, climate and topography. Thus Humboldt wrote that:

rather than discovering new, isolated facts I preferred linking already known ones together. The discovery of a new genus seemed to me far less interesting than an observation on the geographical relations of plants, or the migration , of social plants, and the heights that different plants reach on the peaks of the cordilleras.

It was his work on botany that first brought Humboldt to the personal attention of one of the dominant figures of German Romanticism, Goethe. Famous as a poet and playwright, Goethe was also an accomplished botanist and had written extensively on theories of plant and animal structure. Humboldt's link with Goethe, and with German Romanticism as a whole, is a significant one for it displays that his concerns and interests were far from being narrowly technical or scientific. Like his brother Wilhelm, Alexander was admitted as a young man to the élite German literary circles. He made the acquaintance, for instance, of the poet, playwright and historian, Friedrich Schiller. Humboldt wrote 'The Genius of Rhodes' – an attempt to treat themes from animal chemistry in the form of a poetical allegory – for Schiller's influential periodical *Die Horen*. Although Humboldt was later to have serious disagreements with Schiller, he never repudiated his connections with the German Romantic movement. His friendship with Goethe was a close and enduring one. The German edition of Humboldt's key text, *Essai sur la géographie des plantes*, published in 1807, was dedicated to Goethe. And Humboldt's last and most ambitious major work, *Kosmos*, contains many passages that give high praise to the *Naturphilosophen*. Goethe's influence is acknowledged in the book's introduction and much of the text is redolent of the Romantic tradition. Similar resonances can be readily identified within the *Personal Narrative*.

Humboldt's fraternity with the German Romantic movement is very obvious in the role that he ascribes to aesthetics within natural inquiry. A major problem facing the philosophy of knowledge at the end of the eighteenth century was how human reason, which had only sense data to work with and was thus confined to the scrutiny of external characteristics, could ever come to comprehend the inner realities of things. The Kantian response was to argue that reason simply could never have direct access beyond the phenomena. The best one could hope for was, through establishing systematic interconnections and law-like relationships, to organize natural phenomena into synthetic holistic schema. But not every *Naturphilosophen* was prepared to accept a necessary dichotomy between the understanding of the investigator and the object being investigated. An alternative solution was proposed whereby a theory of aesthetics came to the aid of the theory of rationality. Man's aesthetic sensitivities could, if suitably trained and applied, transcend the limitations of reason, penetrate beyond surface phenomena and, sensuously and intuitively, grasp the underlying unities of nature.

Humboldt is clearly sympathetic to this point of view:

... who is there that does not feel himself differently affected beneath the embowering shade of the beeches grove, or on hills crowned with a few scattered pines, or in the flowering meadow where the breezes murmur through the trembling foliage of the birch? A feeling of melancholy, or solemnity, or of light buoyant animation is in turn awakened by the contemplation of our native trees. This influence of the physical on the moral world – this mysterious reaction of the sensuous on the ideal, gives to the study of nature, when considered from a higher point of view, a peculiar charm which has not hitherto been sufficiently recognized.

At the very least, to Humboldt aesthetic sensitivity was an essential complement to rationality:

With the simplest statements of scientific facts there must ever mingle a certain eloquence. Nature herself is sublimely eloquent. The stars as they sparkle in the firmament fill us with delight and ecstasy, and yet they all move in orbit marked out with mathematical precision.

Natural science, if it was to be true to nature, must be aesthetically satisfactory.

In 1797 Humboldt relinquished his post in the Department of Mines and began to make more concrete plans to realize his ambition to undertake a major journey. In the company of the geologist Leopold Buch, he spent the winter in the Tyrolean Alps taking magnetic, topographical and meteorological measurements. Here Humboldt was deliberately practising the skills in handling instruments that he would need on a scientific expedition, although he had as yet no firm idea where he was to go. From the Tyrol, he went on to Paris, where he soon became immersed in the scientific culture of what was, at this time, the intellectual capital of the world.

With his strongly held liberal principles, Humboldt felt at home in the Paris of the Directorate. There he was able to meet and talk with many of the most famous scientific workers of the day – with the botanists Jussieu and Desfontaines, the zoologists Cuvier and Lamarck, the chemists Chaptal and Fourcroy, and many mathematicians and astronomers including Laplace, Borda and Delambre. Contacts with these men, all leading figures within their respective fields, undoubtedly assisted Humboldt in defining and refining the research agenda of his projected expedition. Borda, for instance, drew Humboldt's attention to important shortcomings in the then current knowledge of the magnetic field of the earth. After his experience in Paris, there could be no doubt that Humboldt would confidently devote himself to the elucidation of the very latest and most intriguing questions of contemporary field science.

In Paris Humboldt also met a hero of his youth – the circumnavigator Louis Antoine de Bougainville, now aged seventy but still active. The French Government were, at this time, planning a new expedition around the world and Humboldt was invited to join the complement. However, financial stringencies forced the postponement of the venture. Humboldt then determined upon a privately financed journey to Africa. With this in view, he and Bonpland travelled over the Pyrenees and into Spain. The journey to Madrid took six weeks. On the way, Humboldt systematically took physical measurements, as a result of which he was able to show conclusively that the interior of Spain was a continuous high plateau. This was a dramatic exemplification of the new discoveries that were within the reach of the meticulous and well-equipped scientific traveller.

In Madrid Humboldt had a remarkable piece of good luck. He was presented at the Spanish Court and told the King of his plans to make a scientific expedition. The Spanish ministers, impressed with Humboldt's reputation as a mining geologist, considered that, if Humboldt were to visit the Spanish possessions, he might make discoveries of economic value. Humboldt and Bonpland were accordingly supplied with royal passports for Spanish America, granting them permission to visit anywhere they wanted and guaranteeing them the assistance of government officials. This was an astonishing privilege to be granted to non-Spaniards since, at this time, the Spanish Imperial territories were virtually closed to foreigners. From then on the destination of Humboldt's expedition was fixed as Spanish America.

This was a very fortunate turn of events since access to the Spanish possessions not only allowed Humboldt to journey to places as exotic as any he could possibly have wished for, it also supplied him with the ideal arena within which to exercise his skills. The vast area of the interior of South America was essentially virgin territory as far as detailed geographical and scientific research was concerned. Virtually no scientific work, apart from the determination of the Imperial boundary, had been undertaken inland from the coast since the expedition of La Condamine, over sixty years earlier. The natural sciences, especially geology, had advanced considerably in the interval. Humboldt was, thus, uniquely privileged in making the first real exploration of one of the earth's major land masses. His journey has been aptly described as 'the scientific discovery of America'.

Upon reading the accounts of earlier expeditions, Humboldt had often regretted that travellers 'seldom possessed a wide enough knowledge to avail themselves of what they saw'. No such criticism could be made of the young man who sat in his cabin on the evening of 5 June 1799, outlining to his friends the programme of inquiry he would seek to follow in South America. Humboldt had prepared himself very conscientiously indeed for his expedition. He was already an accomplished investigator and a proficient experimentalist, more than competent across a range of the major field sciences, well trained in the use of the necessary measuring instruments. He had cultivated a remarkable broad sweep of research interests, embracing the major scientific and intellectual concerns of his day. Nor was his inquiring and synthetic mind by any means confined to narrowly technical issues. Humboldt had praised his former travelling companion Georg Forster as a man who knew 'a little about everything'. But the pupil had surpassed his mentor. Humboldt knew, it might be said, a lot about almost everything that was important to the late eighteenth-century scientist.

The young explorer's material equipment matched the comprehensiveness of his knowledge and skill. With the benefit of a considerable private income, Humboldt had been able to supply himself with a full complement of scientific instruments. The list of equipment purchased by Humboldt for his expedition provides a useful insight into the character of the scientific enterprise he and Bonpland were engaged in. They took with them, among other things such as books and notebooks, chronometers, telescopes, sextants, theodolites, quadrants, a dipping needle, compasses, a magnetometer, a pendulum, several barometers, several thermometers, hygrometers, electrometers, a cynometer (for measuring the blueness of the sky), eudiometers (for measuring the quantity of oxygen in the atmosphere), an apparatus to determine the temperature at which water boils at different altitudes, a rain gauge, galvanic batteries, and reagents for chemical analysis. Even on short canoe trips away from his main base, Humboldt carried a sextant, an artificial horizon, a dip needle, a device for measuring magnetic variation, a thermometer, a barometer and a hygrometer. It is evident that a commitment to painstaking, accurate empirical investigation was a defining feature of Humboldt's scientific enterprise. Everything that could be measured was to be measured.

As Susan Cannon (1978) has pointed out, in the latter half of the eighteenth century the technology of instrument building had made great advances. Measuring equipment became more accurate, more reliable and less cumbersome than had previously been the case. In other words, the sort of very intensive instrumental quantification undertaken by Humboldt would not have been attainable by a traveller much earlier in the century. In pioneering his particular mode of scientific investigation and exploration, Humboldt was thus riding the crest of a wave of technical innovation and improvement.

As we have noted above, Humboldt compared his achievements to those of Cook. While evidently proud of this comparison, Humboldt also maintained that land-based expeditions had considerable advantages over maritime ones. Observations of topographical features taken from ships were often inaccurate. Moreover, the ship-borne explorer was often able to spend only relatively short periods of time ashore. He thus saw only the margins of land masses, and could not hope for the more comprehensive and comparative understanding achievable by those who had penetrated the interior. In the study of geology, geomagnetism, ethnography, botany, zoology and political economy, the sustained contact with his material that the land-based explorer enjoyed would produce a greater scientific harvest.

On the other hand, those undertaking a scientific expedition a large part of which was over land incurred difficulties and inconveniences that the sea-borne explorer did not suffer. Whereas Cook's navigational instruments and Banks's elaborate stock of collecting equipment were easily stored in their relatively commodious and stable ship, Humboldt's *matériel* could only be transported with great difficulty and inconvenience, and at considerable expense. Humboldt and Bonpland often dragged after them a caravan of as many as twenty mules, with Indian handlers. Even when travelling by river boat, they were greatly inconvenienced by the narrowness and instability of the freshwater craft. Under such circumstances, glass specimen jars were frequently broken and mercury barometers had a short life expectancy. If one also bears in mind the inherent dangers of travel in the Tropics, the ever-present hazards of disease, accident or violence, it will be appreciated that the success of Humboldt's expedition to the Americas was achieved only through heroic perseverance in the face of a multitude of difficulties. Its triumphant completion constituted a pioneering demonstration of the feasibility of sustaining long scientific expeditions on land.

Humboldt's commitment to instrumental measurement was not merely a fetish for spurious precision. When accurate figures could not be obtained, he was often prepared to advance an educated guess, as illustrated by his estimates of the human population of the various regions he passes through. To Humboldt, moreover, measurement and quantification were not ends in themselves. They were means towards comprehending the unifying forces of nature. To this end the various readings were tabulated and compared over time and between different sites. As we have seen, Humboldt sought not merely to measure but to generalize.

Despite Humboldt's stress on quantification, he did not hold that progress in the technology of instrumentation had rendered superfluous the recording of subjective impressions. It might be said that, to Humboldt, subjective responses were themselves a sort of instrument – in the sense that aesthetic and emotional reactions to natural phenomena counted as data about these phenomena. For example, the impression different sorts of vegetation made upon the sensitive observer provided a clue as to the particular formative effect that each natural environment had upon human society:

... but the man who is sensitive to the beauties of nature will ... find there the explanation of the influence exerted by the appearance of vegetation over man's taste and imagination. He will take pleasure in examining what is constituted by the 'character' of the vegetation and the variety of sensation it produces in the soul of the person who contemplates it ... What a marked contrast between forests in temperate zones and those of the equator, where the bare slender trunks of the palms soar above the flowered mahogany trees and create majestical portico arches in the sky ... How does this ... appearance of nature, rich and pleasant to a greater or lesser degree, affect the customs and above all the sensibility of people?

On the way to the Americas, the *Pizarro* stopped at Tenerife in the Canary Islands. Humboldt's description of the time he and Bonpland spent on the island provides virtually a replica in miniature of his account of their expedition to South America as a whole. After describing their approach to the port of Santa Cruz, Humboldt supplies a panoramic description of the harbour. Shortly after landing, he expresses delight at seeing plants in their natural habitat that he has previously only seen growing in greenhouses. Throughout his visit, temperature and other meteorological readings are taken continuously. The topography of the island is interpreted from the perspective of 'a geologist who sees the past rather than the present state of nature in everything'. Finely detailed observation of the vegetation leads him to muse over its floristic history, especially in relation to the famous dragon tree, a venerable specimen of which is lovingly described. Examples of the dialect of Spanish spoken in Tenerife are recorded.

At the same time, Humboldt expresses considerable scepticism regarding much of the description of the islands by earlier travellers.

In the Canaries, Humboldt is interested, as always, in the effect that the physical environment exerts upon humanity. He remarks, for example, upon the great clarity of the air:

This transparency may be one of the main reasons for the beauty of tropical scenery; it heightens the splendours of the vegetation's colouring, and contributes to the magical effects of its harmonies and contrasts. If the light tires the eyes during part of the day, the inhabitant of these southern regions has his compensation in a moral enjoyment, for a lucid clarity of mind corresponds to the surrounding transparency of the air.

It was not only the natural environment to which Humboldt was sensitive:

Tenerife ... benefits from a good part of what nature has lavished in the Tropics. Its flora include the beautiful and imposing bananas and palms ... Nowhere else in the world seems more appropriate to dissipate melancholy and restore peace to troubled minds ... These effects are due not only to the magnificent situation and to the purity of the air, but above all to the absence of slavery, which so deeply revolts us.

The highlight of the visit to Tenerife was an expedition to the summit of the island's highest peak – the Pico de Teide, 3,718 metres high. During the climb, Humboldt distinguishes several different strata of volcanic rock formed in chronological sequence. He hypothesizes on the origin of the water vapour issuing from thermal vents, and he compares the shape of the summit to that of other volcanoes he has visited. He notes the altitudinal differentiation of the vegetation on the slopes of the mountain. He records his response to the view from the summit:

A journey to the Tenerife volcano's summit is not solely interesting for the amount of phenomena available for scientific research but far more for the picturesque beauties offered to those who keenly feel the splendours of nature. It is a hard task to describe these sensations for they work on us so much more powerfully the more they are vague. When a traveller must describe the highest peaks, the river cataracts, the tortuous Andes valleys, he risks tiring his readers with the monotonous expression of his admiration. It seems better ... to evoke the particular character of each zone. We get to know the features of each region better the more we indicate its varying characteristics by comparing it with others. This method enables us to discover the sources of the pleasures conferred by the great picture of nature.

The purpose of taking detailed scientific observations in any one locality is to achieve a comparative and general perspective upon natural phenomena in the different regions of the earth. And this comparative understanding must simultaneously be both scientifically and aesthetically satisfactory.

It may seem to the modern reader that Humboldt's commentary on Tenerife – ranging as it does from the reasons for the tastiness of the flesh of the local goats to speculation as to the moral character of the aboriginal inhabitants – is unstructured and rambling. To an extent, this is a perception that was shared by his contemporaries. Humboldt did receive some criticism from reviewers over the unstructured nature of his text and the extent to which he continually digressed from his narrative. But, to a large extent, this opinion is based upon a misunderstanding of Humboldt's intention in writing the *Personal Narrative*. Charles Darwin was more perceptive when he described Humboldt's text as a 'convenient vehicle for miscellaneous discussions'. In modern terms one might conceive of the *Personal Narrative* as being something like a cross between a travel book and an edition of *New Scientist* magazine. Indeed the ever-changing focus of the author's attention, his universal and insatiable curiosity, is one of the peculiar charms of the *Personal Narrative*. One must also remember that, to Humboldt, any lack of coherence in his inquiries might be only a superficial or a temporary shortcoming. As science progressed, as *la physique générale* matured, so the real linkages between apparently disparate phenomena would become more readily perceptible to the natural philosopher.

Throughout Humboldt's and Bonpland's journey in South America we see the same pattern of endless collecting of specimens, careful taking of quantitative data, and recording of aesthetic impressions. In the uncharted interior of the continent Humboldt employs his skill in astronomical observation to making the first reliable maps, notably of the course of the Orinoco. But always the data, whether quantitative or qualitative, are collected so as to lead towards comprehensive descriptions and generalizations about underlying unities:

This site has something wild and tranquil, melancholic and attractive about it. In the midst of such powerful nature we felt nothing inside but peace and repose. In the solitude of these mountains I was less struck by the new impressions recorded at each step than by the fact that such diverse climates have so much in common. In the hills ... palm trees and tree fern grow; in the afternoon, before the rainfalls, the monotonous screaming of the howler monkeys seems like a distant wind in the forests. Despite these exotic sounds, and the strange plant forms and marvels of the New World, everywhere nature allows man to sense a voice speaking to him in familiar terms. The grass carpeting the ground, the old moss and ferns covering tree roots, the torrent that falls over steep calcareous rocks, the harmonious colours reflecting the water, the green and the sky, all evoke familiar sensations in the traveller.

The Humboldtian enterprise is also typified by his response to the earthquake he experienced in Cumaná and to the later one that destroyed a substantial part of the city of Caracas:

I reckoned that it was my duty in this book to record all the data obtained from reliable sources concerning the seismic shocks ... As a historian of nature, the traveller should note down the moment when great natural calamities happen, and investigate the causes and relations, and establish fixed points in the rapid course of time, in the transformations that succeed each other ceaselessly so that he can compare them with previous catastrophes.

Here we can discern both Humboldt's characteristic optimism and his committed philanthropy. Meticulous, painstaking empiricism will ultimately find order in even the most chaotic and destructive of events. Eventually and inevitably humanity would benefit from scientific inquiry.

The published portion of the *Personal Narrative* ends with Humboldt and Bonpland only part way through their American journey. We leave them shortly after their extended visit to Cuba, which supplied the material for one of Humboldt's most influential texts, *Essai politique sur l'île de Cuba*, a pioneering work in what is now called human geography. The narrative does not describe, therefore, one major episode of Humboldt's experience of South America – the attempt he and Bonpland made to climb Mount Chimborazo, an active volcano and the highest peak in the northern Andes. While they did not reach the summit, in ascending to above 6,000 metres they set a mountaineering altitude record that would not be bettered for thirty years.

During their climb, Humboldt and Bonpland ascended from the level of rainforest and human settlement, through the several altitudinal vegetation zones, to the region of permanent snow, taking measurements all the way. On the slopes of the mountain they thus experienced, within a small compass, much of the physical and vegetational diversity of the continent.

In their camp at the foot of the mountain, Humboldt began to compose his *Essai sur la géographie des plantes* (*Essay on the Geography of Plants*), which articulated more fully the programme for plant geography he had first outlined in the *Florae Fribergensis specimen*. It is an indication of the importance Humboldt gave to the *Essai* that he originally intended it as the introduction to all the scientific publications of the expedition. Humboldt's new plant geography was, of course, a thoroughly empirical investigation of the environment of plants. Physical measurements were taken and then correlated with the occurrence of the various types of vegetation. Such correlations would, it was hoped, aid in the discernment of the laws that governed the distribution of vegetation.

However, another of the principal attractions of the study of vegetation was the extent to which the plant geographer shared the interests and joys of the landscape artists. The two approaches to nature were mutually complementary. Humboldt suggested that the pictorial representation of landscape would be improved if the painter studied the classification of plant form developed by the plant geographer:

How interesting and instructive to the landscape painter would be a work that should present to the eye accurate delineation of the . . . principal forms enumerated both individually and in collective contrast! What can be more picturesque than the arborescent ferns, which spread their tender foliage above the Mexican laurel oak! What more charming than the aspect of banana groves, shaded by those lofty grasses, the gaudua and bamboo! It is particularly the privilege of the artist to separate these into groups, and thus the beautiful images of nature . . . resolve themselves beneath his touch . . . into a few simple elements.

In the *Essai* Humboldt sought to define the subject matter of the new form of botanical science and:

to draw natural philosophers' attention to the great phenomena which nature displays in the regions through which I have travelled. It is their whole which I have considered in this essay.

Humboldt's concern with holistic structures and with the unity of landscape is well exemplified by the *Tableau physique des Andes et pays voisins*. This is a large and elaborate engraving, folded within the pages of the *Essai*. It depicts a cross-sectional profile of the Andes from the Atlantic to the Pacific at the latitude of Chimborazo. In this one figure are mapped or tabulated much of the information Humboldt and Bonpland collected in their travels in South America: which plant and animal species live where, where the altitudinal zones of vegetation begin and end, the types of agriculture pursued, the underlying geological structures and rock types, the temperature of the air and its chemical composition, the limit of perpetual snow, and a wide variety of other physical and meteorological data.

The *Tableau*, with its vision of a unified landscape, is a very typical Humboldtian production. Its object was to give, in a single illustration, a complete impression of the unified interrelatedness and complexity of a natural region – the *régions équinoxiales* of South America. Like Chimborazo itself, the *Tableau* encapsulated for Humboldt the totality of the scientific and aesthetic impression made upon him by the Tropics of South America. In a textual, rather than a graphic medium, the *Personal Narrative* had an identical objective.

Upon his return from South America, Humboldt based himself in Paris and set about writing up and publishing the results of his American investigations. He did not seek to live off his reputation as an explorer and adventurer. On the contrary, he continued to play a central role within what was the finest community of scientific workers in Europe. He was, for instance, active in the élite Society of Arcueil, of which Laplace, Berthollet and Gay-Lussac were also members. By the 1820s, Alexander von Humboldt had published several expedition volumes, as well as many shorter publications on a wide variety of subjects. He had become arguably the most famous natural scientist in the world. Distinguished by polymathic learning and a synthetic habit of thought, he bestrode many fields and areas of investigation.

While Humboldt had no students as such, he inspired, either directly or by the example of his published works, a whole generation of younger investigators. As we have noted, his journeys in South America had displayed the feasibility of sustaining a scientific expedition over land, and other travellers quickly followed his example. Many of the early explorers of the western territories of the United States, for example, more or less directly employed the Humboldtian model of quantitative investigation. In Britain his works were eagerly read by, among many others, Charles Lyell and Joseph Hooker. Charles Darwin knew passages of the *Personal Narrative* by heart and yearned to visit the Canary Islands because Humboldt had written so eloquently of Pico de Teide and the dragon tree. When Darwin eventually visited South America, his impressions of the tropical rainforest were partially formed by his prior reading of Humboldt. Interest in Humboldt's travels among English speakers was further stimulated by the publication in 1849 of a translation of his favourite and most popular work, the compilation volume *Ansichten der Natur* (*Views of Nature*), which had originally appeared in 1808. The *Ansichten* contained further vivid description of his explorations and experiences in South America, including the epic ascent of Chimborazo.

Humboldt's impact on the development of the discipline of geography as a whole was profound. His monographs on Cuba and Mexico were the first geographical treatises to incorporate substantial material from natural science, politics and economics. It was not long before similar treatments of other areas by other hands began to appear.

Humboldt exercised his major influence partly through a vast scholarly acquaintance and partly through a voluminous correspondence. He had at his disposal considerable academic patronage, both in

Paris and later in Berlin to where he returned in 1827. How he utilized this patronage to support like-minded younger researchers is exemplified by the career of Franz J.F. Meyen. Meyen was working as a physician until Humboldt secured for him the position of Professor of Botany at the University of Berlin. In both the outline and the detail of his investigations, Meyen closely emulated Humboldt. Between 1830 and 1832, Meyen travelled in the New World and, like his mentor, made both scientific and aesthetic observations on the summits of the Andes. Surviving correspondence between the two men indicates that Humboldt influenced his protégé's travel plans at every stage.

Upon his return from South America, Meyen wrote a book on plant geography, which was one of the earliest and most explicit articulations of the distinctive Humboldtian programme for the new science. *Outlines of the Geography of Plants* was a sustained and sophisticated attempt to correlate the distribution of vegetation with measured physical factors, such as temperature and humidity. Meyen employed the isoline mapping method, which had been developed by Humboldt, to aid this correlation. He also considered the effect of vegetation upon human society and its role within the aesthetic appreciation of nature. Humboldt took great trouble to make Meyen's book known to a wide audience, personally sponsoring a French translation.

While Franz Meyen was undoubtedly one of the most favoured of Humboldt's scientific protégés, many other French, German and Scandinavian botanists benefited similarly from his generosity and personal encouragement. The cumulative effect was that, by the middle of the nineteenth century, the distinctive Humboldtian form of plant geography had become an identifiable and successful specialty within botany. At the end of the century, Humboldtian plant geography provided one of the roots from which the new discipline of plant ecology sprung.

Humboldt exercised similar influence in the physical and earth sciences, notably in his promotion of the study of terrestrial magnetism. He was the principal motivator behind the 'magnetic crusade' of the 1830s that, with the support of several European governments including the British, set up observation stations around the world.

The success of this venture led to similar schemes being proposed for the collection of meteorological data. This observation network is, of course, still with us, much enlarged. To Humboldt must go much of the credit for the establishment of the modern science of climatology.

By the 1840s, however, Humboldt's personal scientific reputation was, to a considerable extent, a victim of his own success in cultivating and stimulating a new generation of research workers. Inevitably, their more advanced investigations quickly made his foundational work seem out of date. This is often the fate of the pioneers of new sciences.

Furthermore, the universalist form of scientific inquiry that Humboldt had proselytized for was, in the changed intellectual climate of the mid nineteenth century, no longer sustainable. One of the distinctive features of Humboldtian science is that it corresponds to none of our modern scientific disciplines or specialties. *La physique générale* was essentially an all-encompassing, comprehensive enterprise. But few, if any, of his followers could be as polymathic or as universal as the great man himself. Reforms in the system of German university education were, moreover, encouraging the division of natural philosophy into more specialized disciplines, closer in character to those we recognize in the twentieth century. Thus, following generations of researchers would increasingly work within institutional and cognitive contexts narrower and more fragmented than those occupied by Humboldt himself. But many of the scientists of the mid and late nineteenth century were Humboldt's intellectual heirs nevertheless, selectively employing the resources presented by his work as they found them applicable within their own individual disciplines. As Susan Cannon (1978) has pointed out, wherever one finds investigations of the geographical distribution of plants and animals, of terrestrial magnetism, meteorology, hydrology, ocean currents, the structures of mountain chains and the orientation of strata, or of solar radiation, one sees something of Humboldt's legacy.

Nor was Humboldt's impact confined to the natural sciences. As we have seen he suggested that landscape painters might benefit from the study of the physiognomy of plants and that they should attempt graphically to delineate the principal vegetational types. This challenge was indeed taken up. Humboldt was himself a competent draftsman and painter, and many artists drew inspiration from his characterizations, either in words or in images, of what was awe-inspiring and picturesque in nature. His descriptive prose was also widely admired, by Balzac and Victor Hugo, among others. For many years, his more accessible texts, such as the *Personal Narrative* and *Ansichten der Natur*, remained popular with the general reading public for their evocative accounts of adventure and far-away places. Whether read as empirical science, as escapist literature, or as a manifesto for the Romantic artist, Humboldt's books were the lens through which much of the nineteenth century saw South America.

Malcolm Nicolson

INTRODUCTION

I

The *Sun* of Monday 1 February 1802 published a note about 'the particulars of the dangers to which Humboldt had been exposed during his world journey'. The newspaper had extended Humboldt's journey to a 'world' one, though Humboldt spent all his five years in the Americas, leaving Spain in 1799 and returning to France in 1804. The word 'dangers' is crucial. Had Humboldt remained in Paris or Berlin and studied the natural sciences he might have achieved some note as a researcher, as an encourager of talent, and as a writer, but he would not have caught the nineteenth-century public's imagination in the way he did. The alliance of danger and science ensured that Humboldt was tested against more than the conventions and securities of the known world that his reading public inhabited. The mystique of 'danger' turns the scientist into a conquistador sallying out into the unknown. The 1802 note in the *Sun* enumerated the perils: rivers infested with crocodiles, wild Indians, severe storms, marauding negro slaves – adventures that have little to do with science. In an autobiographical note written in South America in 1801 Humboldt explained how the prospect of danger had lured him away from a secure home life:

I was spurred on by an uncertain longing for what is distant and unknown, for whatever excited my fantasy: danger at sea, the desire for adventures, to be transported from a boring daily life to a marvellous world.

Elsewhere he wrote: 'I despised anything to do with bourgeois life; that slow rhythm of home life and fine manners sickened me.'

These adolescent longings – *reiselust* – became real. The promise of a life of danger abroad drove Humboldt to try to travel as a naturalist to Egypt, then with Captain Baudin round the world, and finally succeeding with his own self-financed five-year trip to the Spanish

American colonies, accompanied by his secretary, the botanist Aimé Bonpland. It did not matter where Humboldt ended up as long as it was outside Europe, where few scientists had been before. His yearning was grounded on a premise: few scientists had made hazardous voyages inland in tropical America. Only by the risk of travelling could the scientist observe, with his own eyes, and compare; and make the whole earth his laboratory, ensuring that science advanced beyond dogma and hypothesis.

The promise of adventure abroad as a scientist seduced young Charles Darwin who, before the offer to accompany Captain Fitzroy on the *Beagle* as a gentleman naturalist, had read Humboldt thoroughly enough to want to emulate him. Darwin learned Spanish and planned the details of a trip to the Canaries because Humboldt had written so movingly about the Teide volcanic peak and the dragon tree. In a letter (1831) Darwin wrote:

In the morning I go and gaze at Palm trees in the hot-house and come home and read Humboldt: my enthusiasm is so great that I cannot hardly sit still on my chair . . . I will never be easy till I see the peak of Teneriffe and the great Dragon Tree . . .

The same year he wrote to his mentor Henslow: 'I read and reread Humboldt, do you do the same.' Years later in 1865 he recalled: 'Nothing stimulated my zeal so much as reading Humboldt's *Personal Narrative*.' In 1868 he confessed: 'I copied out from Humboldt long passages about Teneriffe.' When Darwin set off on the *Beagle* he travelled with Humboldt's *Relation historique* (in Helen Maria Williams's English translation) on board, knew passages by heart, and read it as he first explored the jungle, sometimes preferring Humboldt to what he actually saw. Glimpsing the Tenerife peak from the *Beagle*, but unable to land, Darwin was 'repeating to myself Humboldt's sublime descriptions'. From Santa Cruz, May 1832, he wrote home to Henslow: 'I formerly admired Humboldt, I now almost adore him; he alone gives any notion of the feelings which are raised in the mind on first entering the Tropics.' Darwin even adopted Humboldt's enthusiastic language (and later reacted against it). He liked the way Humboldt had squeezed exuberant, tropical nature – chaos – into sober prose. In May 1834 he wrote:

Few things give me so much pleasure as reading the *Personal Narrative*; I know not the reason why a thought which has passed through the mind, when we see it embodied in words, immediately assumes a more substantial and true air.

In a letter home to a sister Darwin advised her: 'If you really want to have a notion of tropical countries, *study* Humboldt. – Skip the scientific parts . . .'

Another example of the spell cast by Humboldt's lifetime fame as an adventuring scientist can be gauged by Johann Wolfgang Goethe (1749–1832) who wrote that Humboldt's company was 'exceedingly interesting and stimulating. Within eight days one could learn as much from books as he imparts in an hour.' To Friedrich Schiller, Goethe wrote: 'My natural history studies have been roused from their winter sleep by his presence.' But it was to his biographer Eckerman that Goethe expressed most praise (1826):

Alexander von Humboldt was here this morning for a few hours. What a man he is! I have known him so long, and yet he amazes me all over again. One can truly say that he has no equal in information and lively knowledge. Whatever one touches, he is everywhere at home, and overwhelms one with intellectual treasure.

This 'intellectual treasure' is what Humboldt brought back with him from his experiences in the Americas.

However, Humboldt's reputation did not reach only great scientists like Goethe and Darwin. Humboldt was 'intellectual godfather' to countless young travellers and scientists. Charles Lyell (1797–1875), the influential geologist, wrote in 1823 to his father: 'There are few heroes who lose so little by being approached as Humboldt.' Joseph Hooker (1817–1911), noted botanist, Director of Kew Gardens and confidant to Darwin, mockingly echoed this view of a hero in 1845:

So I went in and saw to my horror a paunchy little German instead of Humboldt. There was no mistaking his head, however, which is exceedingly like all the portraits though now powdered with white. I expected to see a fine fellow, six feet without his boots . . .

But by 1871 Hooker complained about Humboldt's declining reputation in a letter to Darwin: '. . . just as I think Humboldt is underrated nowadays. Well, these were our gods, my friend'. In 1881, again to Darwin, Hooker claimed Humboldt as the originator of a new kind of adventuring scientist: 'I am constrained to regard him as the first of scientific travellers.' Humboldt's fame spread beyond the confines of science. In 1875 the painter Marianne North set off for Tenerife 'to the famous view of the Peak, described so exquisitely by Humboldt' (her paintings can be seen at Kew). The Prussian Prince Maximilian von Wied spent two years in eastern Brazil after befriending Humboldt. Louis Agassiz received a $3,000 grant from Friedrich Wilhelm IV to research in Brazil thanks to Humboldt. W.H. Prescott, the popular historian of the conquest of both Mexico and Peru, wrote to Humboldt in 1843: 'I have been very often guided by the light of your researches.' In France writers and painters like Balzac, Victor Hugo, Chateaubriand, Gérard and Flaubert publicly admired him. The North American transcendental philosopher and poet Ralph Waldo Emerson called Humboldt 'the Encyclopaedia of science'; American painters like Frederick Church and George Catlin travelled to South America thanks to Humboldt (see Katherine E. Manthorne, 1989); Harriet Martineau crowned him as 'the Monarch of science', but it was Lord Byron who, by satirizing him in *Don Juan* (Canto 4, verse 112; 1821), best attests to Humboldt's fame:

> Humboldt, 'the first of travellers', but not
> The last, if late accounts be accurate,
> Invented, by some name I have forgot,
> As well as the sublime discovery's date,
> An airy instrument, with which he sought
> To ascertain the atmospheric state,
> By measuring the intensity of blue.
> Oh Lady Daphne, let me measure you!

The recently independent Spanish American intellectuals and politicians particularly revered Humboldt. Lucas Alamán (1792 1853), Mexican politician and historian, wrote to Humboldt from Mexico in 1824 thanking him for having 'woken his compatriots up from the lethargy in which foreign domination had held them'. Domingo

Faustino Sarmiento (1811–88), Argentine writer and president, thanked Humboldt for being one of the two Europeans (the painter Rugendas was the other) 'who have portrayed America most truthfully'. Simón Bolívar (1783–1830), liberator, summed up the debts to his friend Humboldt: 'Baron Humboldt did more for the Americas than all the conquistadores.' In homage to Humboldt, as Mary Louise Pratt shows (1992), Bolívar also climbed the snowy peak of Chimborazo. Pratt summarizes Humboldt's influence in the Americas: 'Humboldt's writings ... became essential raw material for American and Americanist ideologies forged by creole intellectuals in the 1820s, 1830s and 1840's. D.A. Brading (1991) claims that Humboldt's *Essai politique sur le royaume de la Nouvelle-Espagne* (on Mexico) (1811) continues to be 'an essential text for all students of Mexican history and Spanish imperialism'. The twenty-second edition of the *Dictionnaire universel d'histoire et de géographie* (1871), compiled, by M.-N. Bouillet, outlined Humboldt's astonishing nineteenth-century reputation:

This scientist has renewed the face of science in several ways, above all contributing to the advance of physical geography and botanical geography. Member of all the scientific societies, admitted into the Prussian King's intimacy, becoming his private advisor, sought after by the most eminent men of all the civilized countries, Humboldt has attained all the honours to which a scientist may aspire.

When Humboldt's 17,000-volumed library was sold in London in 1863 it comprised his 181 diplomas and honours awarded. Humboldt's more popular books, the *Relation historique* (1814–25), *Vue des cordillères* (1810) and *Ansichten der Natur* (1808) created a new kind of nineteenth-century hero; the observing, imperturbable scientist living a life of danger denied to his reader. That most of Humboldt's work has long been out of print, and that no twentieth-century translations into English of his voyage exist, testify to the amazing eclipse of a man whom V.S. Pritchett called 'one of the irresistible scientific brains of the late eighteenth century'.

Humboldt's fame has clear roots in the link between his personality and the kind of scientist he became. A bare chronology of his busy and successful official life does not explain this link. For Humboldt scientific discipline insisted on observing and jotting down what is actually seen — 'juger d'après la simple vue' — in order to free perception from dogma. Testing and experimenting ensured that desire and fancy did not distort or exaggerate. In this sense, Humboldt was virtually the first European scientist — with notable exceptions like La Condamine — to scrutinize the interior of South America as if he was seeing it for the first time, suspicious of previous descriptions. Earlier travellers, he insisted, just copied from each other. At the same time, Humboldt brought an intense curiosity to his observations developed thanks to his eclectic scientific formation, and to the Parisian Encyclopaedists he so admired. The result of accurately noting down everything he saw culminated in his life's-work, thirty folio and quarto volumes trying to trap Latin America within covers, in words, pictures and statistics. Here we see how the scientific attitude consciously differed from the 'facile emotionalism' of his friend Chateaubriand because, as Humboldt wrote: 'I have tried to be truthful in my description, scientifically true without going into arid regions of knowledge.'

There is a further link between the way Humboldt presented himself as a public figure in his travel writings with this scientific frame of mind. As a travel writer Humboldt followed the format of La Condamine's 1745 *Voyage sur l'Amazon*, and his friend Georg Forster's 1777 *Voyage round the World on the Resolution*, so that his *Relation historique* became, in Charles Darwin's perceptive insight, a 'convenient vehicle for miscellaneous discussions' where anything whatsoever could be written about, from Aztec ruins to the horrors of slavery, from climbing Chimborazo (then thought to be the highest mountain in the world) to breast-feeding old men, from electric eels to earth-eating jungle Indians. Humboldt achieved this inclusiveness without the intrusion of his own personality. That is, he writes like an observing scientist. After introducing a personal anec- dote he apologized: '(let this appeal to personal feeling be forgiven)'. He only reluctantly referred to himself: 'If I dare resort to my own experience' or 'If I may be permitted personal emotions'. The scientist absented himself from his prose in order to let his reader see directly, as if reading what today we would call a documentary. In order to investigate objective laws — 'pour saisir les lois' — the messy subjectivity of the scientist had to be ignored. In his 1801 autobiographical fragment Humboldt took the deliberate decision 'not to try to describe my agitated life'. Yet, despite this effort at impersonality, privileging what is observed over who is observing, there is something in his persona as it emerged from his writings and reputation that appealed to his reading public. Humboldt could not escape 'expressing' himself, between the lines, as a tone of voice, however assiduously he struggled to avoid his 'I' by referring to himself in the third person as 'the traveller'. Humboldt had established a complex relationship between his personality, his fame and his writing: 'My life is in my written works', he warned future biographers.

Humboldt deliberately suppressed his private life. He burned or destroyed many letters in order to further efface himself from biographers. When his correspondence with his close friend the Republican scientist François Arago (1786–1853) was published in 1860 it caused a scandal; his reading public did not expect such a 'malicious' Humboldt. Early on in his *Relation historique* Humboldt stated that faced by the imposing torrid zone no traveller should talk about the 'détails minutieux de la vie'. Humboldt's reluctance to centre his voyage round his personality is aristocratic; he felt an 'extrême répugnance' at the very thought of writing his travelogue.

The result of this choice is that we learn little about the minute details of Humboldt's or Bonpland's personal lives; about bodily discomforts, fears, homesickness, nightmares, defecation, digestion or perspiration. It is as if Humboldt did not care about such mundane matters. However, this is more than a rhetorical pose: Humboldt survived incredible ordeals – capsizing, attacks, fever, starvation – with barely a comment. His imperturbability suggests a superhuman persona; his travelogue provides a relief from the complaining, self-indulgent grand tourists, and, most important, there is a sacrificial nobility about his call to scientific duty.

Humboldt strove to be a scientist all the time, every day. He was irritated that public curiosity sought out 'la personne des voyageurs' rather than appreciating scientific works. His scientific intentions were 'strangely disfigured' in a pirate travelogue in six volumes made from newspaper accounts, published in Germany under his name. His own strict aim was to be a scientist – 'le but de notre voyage était purement scientifique'. However, science, for Humboldt, meant disclosing the harmonic unity of nature, the 'liens qui unissent tous les phénomènes de la nature'. This Romantic notion of a hidden harmony, banishing evil, had a seductive, therapeutic effect: in Humboldt's own words, studying the occult laws of nature 'dissipates melancholy and restores peace to troubled minds'.

In his travelogue Humboldt digressed scientifically as freely as he wanted once he had banished his interfering subjectivity. This compulsive, wordy digressing is the most noteworthy and prolix trait in Humboldt's scientific persona. He climbed a volcàno, and then, over forty-nine quarto pages, hunted out all references to volcanoes from the ancient Greeks to contemporary travellers, dismissing his reader's boredom, as if human time and narrative economy had little to do with science. No wonder Humboldt never finished his *Relation historique*, or ever found a convenient form for his associative thinking. He, as usual, recognized this trait in himself: 'I was at fault to tackle from intellectual curiosity too great a variety of scientific interests.' Nevertheless, this obsessive attempt to cram everything into a book vividly conveys his personality, as well as his modernity. In 1806 he published in French a second autobiographical fragment, called 'My Confessions', in the form of a letter to the Swiss physicist Marc Auguste Pictet (1752–1825), where he analysed himself as 'anxious, agitated, unable to enjoy anything that I have finished, and never content except when undertaking something new and doing three things at the same time'.

'Agitated' is a telling word that Humboldt applied to himself without revealing the content of this agitation. It is not far-fetched to see his agitation (or neurosis) as a reason for why he sought the mask of scientist. Humboldt confessed to his friend the German mineralogist Johann Karl Freiesleben (1774–1846) about his unhappy childhood 'where I was subjected to a thousand restraints and much self-imposed solitude, and where I was often placed in circumstances that obliged me to maintain a close reserve and to make continual self-sacrifices'. To compensate for this emotional starvation in his childhood Humboldt dedicated himself to learning. He wrote to his tutor J.H. Campe (1746–1818): 'A man should accustom himself to stand alone. Isolation has much in its favour. One learns thereby to search inwardly and gain self-respect without being dependent on the opinions of others.' The most noteworthy trait in Humboldt's growing-up was his relationship with his mother Elizabeth de Colomb, from a French Huguenot background. When she died in 1796 he wrote to Karl Freiesleben: 'She passed away quietly. You know, my dear friend, that my heart could not have been much pained by this event, for we were always strangers to each other.' From this emotional starvation Helmut de Terra (1955), his best biographer in English, adduced Humboldt's therapeutical dependence on a harmonic (mother) nature. Humboldt wrote to Wilhelm, his older brother, from Asia in 1829:

Nature can be so soothing to the tormented mind, a blue sky, the glittering surface of lake water, the green foliage of trees may be your solace. In such company it is even possible to forget the reality of one's personal existence. It lends wings to our feelings and thoughts.

This nature-contemplation was Humboldt's astute way of coping with his agitation.

The mask of scientist also conveniently prevented the public from inquiring into Humboldt's sexuality. From early on Humboldt knew that hard work controlled his libido. In a letter to his friend Wegener he wrote (1789): 'Serious themes, and especially the study of nature, become barriers against sensuality.' As we learn in the *Relation historique*, sensuality is overcome by occupying the mind; science triumphed over any outbursts of lust. According to Fernando Ortiz (1960), the Cuban anthropologist, at least five people in Spanish America claimed Humboldt's paternity. But Humboldt was no womanizer; his perspicacious brother Wilhelm sensed this incapacity to relate to the opposite sex in a letter to his wife: 'Happy he will hardly ever be, and never tranquil, because I cannot believe that any real attachment will steal his heart ... a veil hung over our innermost feelings which neither of us dared to lift.' Two incidents on his Spanish American journey capture Humboldt's repressed sexuality. Madame Fanny Calderón de la Barca reports in her *Life in Mexico* (letter of 5 January 1840) that *la güera* (fair) Rodriguez, 'celebrated by Humboldt as the most beautiful woman he had seen in the whole course of his travels', took Humboldt to visit a nopal (cactus) plant-ation. When he had first set eyes on her he had cried out '*Válgame Dios!* Who is that girl?' and then remained constantly in her company. But Madame Calderon de la Barca adds that he was 'more captivated it is said, by her wit than by her beauty', and then conventionally guessed that Humboldt was more fascinated by flirting with the fair woman than by studying all the 'mines or mountains, geography or geology'. A similar asexual attraction determined Humboldt's interest in Rosita Montúfar of Quito, with whom he was reputed to have fallen in love. However, he was more interested in her brother Carlos Montúfar, who joined the expedition at Humboldt's expense. Charles Minguet has even suggested that Humboldt destroyed the already written and ready-for-press fourth volume of his *Relation historique* to avoid a scandal about having chosen young Carlos Montúfar over a poor but brilliant scientist, Francisco José de Caldas (1771–1816), recommended by the botanist Celestino Mutis in Bogotá. Science was a male world; it was natural for Humboldt to surround himself with other male scientists in austere working conditions. Yet sometimes these friendships crossed the barriers of male friendships. Helmut de Terra quotes a letter from Humboldt to an early friend Reinhard Haeften (1797): 'My love for you is not just friendship, or brotherly love – it is veneration, childlike gratefulness, and devotion to your will as my most exalted law.' This kind of adoration led Humboldt to have intense male-scientific relationships with François Arago, Louis Joseph Gay-Lussac and many others. Was Humboldt just a prudent bachelor apt to romanticize male-scientific friendships so that one biographer could label this 'latent homosexuality' (Helmut de Terra, 1955)? Or were his relations with his friends 'without any sexual overtones' (L. Kellner, 1963)? In Gabriel García Marquez's novel *El general en su laberinto* (1989) Simón Bolívar meets a nomadic German who tells indecent stories about Humboldt's 'shameless pederasty'. Whether a deviant sexuality lurked behind Humboldt's confessed agitations is guesswork.

Humboldt's admiration for the French Revolution and his detesta-tion of slavery further reveal his personality. These passions are linked because slavery was abolished when the Constituent Assembly adopted the Declaration of the Rights of Man in August 1789. At the end of his life, despite his official status as Chamberlain to the Prussian King Friedrich Wilhelm IV, Humboldt wrote to his intimate friend the scientist and Republican Arago: 'You know the colour of my opinions which have not varied since 1789.' In a letter to his friend the German writer Karl Varnhagen von Ense he wrote (1853): 'I, who remember 1789, and have shared in its emotions!' In the company of his friend Georg Forster Humboldt first visited Paris in July 1790, and wrote then that 'I carried sand' (to help build the Temple of Liberty) and that the 'spectacle of the Parisians . . . flutters in my mind like a dream'. He confessed in *Kosmos* (1845–62) years later that he and Forster 'held the same political views'. Forster, a 'jacobin allemand', was sent as a deputy to the National Assembly in Paris when Mayence became united with France. He died in Paris in 1794. In order to travel abroad Humboldt had at first wanted to join Captain Baudin's world tour financed by the Directorate in Paris. In letters back home from South America to French scientific friends he adopted the new revolutionary calendar (used between 1793 and 1805). In all his letters to his companion Aimé Bonpland he signed Alexandre Humboldt, suppressing the baronetcy. In February 1852 he wrote to Varnhagen von Ense:

It has ever been my opinion, that even the wildest Republic can never do as great and lasting injury to the intellectual progress of mankind, and to its consciousness of its inherent titles of honour, as *le régime de mon oncle, le despotisme éclairé*.

He was in his own words 'a Republican at heart'.

Humboldt approved the Revolution's desire to make everybody 'tu'; to substitute trousers for breeches, and natural, uncombed hair for wigs, and he thrilled to the 'popular emotion of fraternity'. But above all Humboldt supported the abolition of slavery. In the *Relation historique* Humboldt affirmed: 'Slavery is no doubt the greatest evil that afflicts human nature.' The influence of the French Revolution left a Gallic mark on Humboldt's beliefs and actions: he remained a revolutionary, a rationalist, a materialist and an atheist. The French poet Lamartine detected these allegiances: 'You will not find God's name in his work because Humboldt belonged to those scientific materialists who, not daring to negate God's existence publicly, kept silent.' His silence kept many disciples guessing. Humboldt was probably, like his father, a mason.

Despite his secret political colours it is noteworthy that while in the Spanish American colonies on the eve of their respective independences from Spain, Humboldt never publicly fomented revolution. He was extremely careful not to criticize the Spanish Crown, the Church or the missions. He even dedicated his *Essai politique sur le royaume de la Nouvelle-Espagne* (1811) to the Spanish Monarch Charles IV. Charles Minguet (1969) rightly associates Humboldt's political views with Spain's *ilustrados*, or progressive liberals, and their belief in enlightened, slow reform under a monarchy. This middle position allowed Humboldt to work for the Prussian King and hold on to his youthful revolutionary fervours in Paris. His later comments on how science had been stifled by Spain's fanaticism and superstition, and how missions had been hostile to progress, must be seen in the context of 1815 when the Republican ideal was maintained solely in the emergent Spanish American nations. Humboldt's, and especially Bonpland's, encouraging of young radical Spanish Americans in the 1800s, like Simón Bolívar, Andrés Bello, Servando de Mier, Francisco Antonio de Zea, Manuel Palacio and others, obviously contributed to his later fame when these revolutionaries and their ilk came to power.

Evidence of Humboldt's exalted public persona can be gauged through the differences between his actual physique – Helmut de Terra (1955) describes Humboldt as 'five feet eight inches tall, light brown hair, gray eyes, large nose, rather large mouth, well-formed chin, open forehead marked by smallpox' – and the countless representations of Humboldt – nearly all imaginary – in the Tropics. *Humboldt and Bonpland on the Orinoco*, after Kellner (1963), has a Byronic Humboldt with neat curly hair standing placidly with a telescope in his hand, the image of male desirability. In 1806 Friedrich Georg Weitsch portrayed Humboldt turning to the viewer, sitting in neat, clean clothes with an orchid in his hand and a manuscript (or plant-drying equipment?) on his knees, as if about to give us a lecture. The real Humboldt was well evoked in 1822 by his disciple, the French geologist and explorer J.B. Boussingault (1802–67) who refers to his smallpox (caught in Cartagena), and to his right hand, paralysed by rheumatism from sleeping rough in the humid Orinoco. When Humboldt wanted to write or shake hands he used his left hand to raise his semi-paralysed one. In 1822 Humboldt still dressed in the fashions of the Directorate; blue suit, gold buttons, yellow waistcoat, striped trousers, campaign boots, white tie and floppy hat. He refused to live in luxurious chambers as befitted the King's Chamberlain. His spartan study contained only a simple bed, four wicker chairs and a pine table on to which he wrote his calculations. When the table was covered with his graffiti a carpenter would come and plane them off. This monastic austerity described by Boussingault can be set against another detail that seizes Humboldt's reality, namely that he so adored everyday life in the Tropics that he insisted his rooms in Berlin remained constantly heated at 70 °F.

II

In his laconic 1801 autobiographical fragment – on the top of which he wrote 'never publish' – Humboldt traced his yearning to experience tropical jungle – 'the Torrid Zone' – back to his studying botany with the German botanist Karl Willdenow (1765–1812), and especially to his relationship with the radical naturalist Georg Forster (1754–94) who had accompanied Cook on his second world trip (1772). In Humboldt's eulogy of Forster's qualities there is a hint of a self-portrait:

The English lack the capacity to understand what could be called Forster's many-sided intellect and genius. They look for a precise poetic talent, a deep knowledge. Only a few of them can appreciate a mixture of everything, a man who knows a little about everything . . .

He adds: 'What was great and rare in young Forster was his way of philosophizing about natural history.' If this characterization applies to Humboldt himself, he inherited it from the mood of the times, especially the *Sturm-und-Drang* stress on emotion and tears as part of the process of understanding nature. At the end of his 1801 autobiography he confessed that he often cried without knowing why. He even

wanted to dedicate his Spanish American works to the radical drama-
tist Friedrich Schiller, close friend to the Humboldt brothers. In 1794
he had written to Schiller attacking the present day 'archivists' of
nature, for he sought, like Schiller, a more 'elevated' and harmonious
view of nature derived from 'the diverse impressions of joy and
melancholy that the world of plants creates in sensitive men'. He
clearly owed his integrated view of nature as an interlocking whole to
Goethe – his notions of *urform*, *urpflanze* and *urtier* – who in 1807
defined nature as:

Every one thing exists for the sake of all things and all for the sake of one; for
the one is of course the all as well. Nature, despite her seeming diversity, is
always a unity, a whole . . . a relationship to the rest of the system.

This all-embracing or holistic view of nature stimulated Humboldt's
interest in several branches of science, such as astronomy, botany,
geology, anthropology, linguistics, as strands in a system converging
to a unified view of nature. In 1806 Humboldt wrote to Schiller's
sister-in-law Karoline von Wolzogen (1763–1847): 'The sense of the
great influence of Jena pursues me everywhere, as Goethe's ideas
about nature had so moved me, and so to speak, given me new
organs.' Humboldt's debt to Goethe points to Goethe's patron Duke
Charles Augustus who, in Jena, had Fichte, Hegel, Schelling, Schlegel
(to whom Humboldt gave all his notes on indigenous languages in
Spanish America) and Schiller teaching at the university between
1787 and 1806 (with Herder near by at Weimar).

Humboldt's work on geology affords a good example of his
scientific formation. He studied first under Abraham Gottlieb Werner
(1749–1817), adopting Werner's Neptunist theory, which, crudely
put, claimed that rocks were the product of sedimentation, as seen in
Humboldt's 1790 essay (see my chronology). After many years actually working in and inspecting mines, and five years in the Americas
studying volcanoes at first hand, Humboldt became a Vulcanist. In
fact his empirical view that volcanoes should be grouped along
underground fissures was quite original. Humboldt was aware that he
was not a geologist. He wrote to Marc Auguste Pictet: 'I am self-
taught in almost all the sciences with which I am now exclusively
occupied.' He lamented not having read the Scottish geologist James

Hutton (1726–96) before setting off for the Spanish American colonies. Later, Darwin complained that Humboldt's geology was 'funny stuff', but Humboldt was always thorough, and empirical, though not strong on theory.

Just as crucial as the influence of Jena was the liberating example of Jean-Jacques Rousseau. From *A Discourse on Inequality* (1755) Humboldt learned about natural equality, and about reading the book of nature, 'which never lies'. Rousseau embodied the 'cry of nature' in the decimated South American Caribs. He postulated that travel, especially to Spanish America, was the best way to learn and 'shake off the yoke of national prejudices'. Rousseau's notion that 'happiness is less an affair of reason than of feeling' catches an important aspect of Humboldt's scientific attitudes. If we link Rousseau to the abolition of slavery, then the famous opening sentence from *The Social Contract* (1762): 'Man was born free, and he is everywhere in chains,' voiced Humboldt's passions; the whole section on slavery and freedom – 'to renounce freedom is to renounce one's humanity' – underpins Humboldt's own thinking. In 1806 Humboldt wrote in French an autobiographical life summary with the give-away title 'My Confessions'. Even closer to Humboldt was Rousseau's disciple the writer Bernardin de Saint-Pierre (1737–1814). In his later *Kosmos* (1845–62) Humboldt recalled travelling up the Orinoco to the Casiquiare – and thus proving what had been only speculation before about a natural river passage joining the Orinoco and Amazon river systems – with a copy of Saint-Pierre's ill-fated romance *Paul et Virginie* (1787), which he read aloud to his companion Aimé Bonpland during a thunderstorm. Humboldt praised this novel 'for the wonderful truth with which [it] paints the power of nature in the tropical zone'. In the *Relation historique* we learn that Humboldt admired Saint-Pierre 'because he knew nature not as a scientist, but because he felt it in all its harmonious links'.

Humboldt chose Paris to publish his American writings on his return because Paris was the scientific capital of the world, where scientists were most free to speculate; in Paris he met Dominique François Arago (who became an intimate friend), Georges Cuvier, Geoffroy Saint-Hilaire, Louis Antoine de Bougainville, Jean Baptiste Lamarck, Pierre Simon de Laplace (to whom he dedicated his travelogue) and many others. He corresponded with the politically persecuted Swiss scientist Augustin de Candolle, who had praised Humboldt in the preface to his *Species* (1818). These freethinking *idéologues* link directly back to Diderot and the Encyclopaedists, as Charles Minguet (1969) has argued; a tradition that endowed Humboldt with his 'empirisme raisonné'. For example, Humboldt's view of nature shares its tenets with Lamarck's 'transformisme' and that harmonious balance of nature's 'rapports' (a key Humboldtian term) seen as a whole. Both men, in L.J. Jordanova's words (1980), dealt with biological adaptation, 'not conflict and competition'. Equally Humboldt shared Georges Cuvier's stress on 'facts' and laws against the idealist German *Naturphilosophie*. In fact it would be hard to trace Humboldt's scientific ideas; living in Paris he had to relate to shifting centres of intellectual power in the scientific community. When Louis Agassiz arrived in Paris, his biographer Edward Lurie (1960) writes, 'there was only one person in all Paris who equalled Cuvier in power, political influence, and commanding rank in natural history – Alexander von Humboldt'. This prestige is reflected in Humboldt's position in the scientific society (studied by Maurice Crosland, 1967) that the chemist Claude Louis Berthollet organized in his country retreat at Arcueil. The fifteen members comprised the Parisian scientific élite (Laplace, Arago, Gay-Lussac, etc.), with Humboldt the only foreigner, the only noble, and lacking the strict professional training of his colleagues, and this honour despite Bonaparte's suspicion that Humboldt was a Prussian spy. Humboldt read the first paper presented at Arcueil, on terrestrial magnetism, in 1807, a second on plant geography in 1809, and a third on isothermal lines in 1817. In May 1837 Humboldt wrote to Varnhagen von Ense: 'Fortunately, the great French world is free from the petty jeering and fault-finding which reign paramount in Berlin and Potsdam, where empty-headed folk keep pecking for months together at a caricature drawn by their own feeble imagination.' To the Swiss scientist Marc Auguste Pictet in 1806 Humboldt justified his Gallic eclecticism: 'It is said that I am busy with too many things at the same time, from botany to astronomy to comparative anatomy. I answer: can you prohibit a man's desire to know, to understand everything around him?' The best image of Humboldt in Paris comes from Louis Agassiz's centenary address (1869). Agassiz accompanied Humboldt to Cuvier's famous lectures in the Collège de France when Cuvier was trying to demolish Geoffroy Saint-Hilaire's defence of Goethe's 'unity of structures in the bony frame of all the vertebrates'. Humboldt would whisper his criticisms 'seeing more clearly than Cuvier himself the logic of his investigations' for 'whatever deficiencies Goethe's doctrine of unity might contain, it must be essentially true, and Cuvier ought to be its expounder instead of its opponent'. Humboldt dedicated the 1811 edition of his *Recueil d'observations de zoologie et d'anatomie comparée* to the powerful Georges Cuvier who contributed a section on axolotls, thanking Humboldt for 'cette honorable association'.

It was also in this revolutionary and scientific Paris that Humboldt found his travelling companion the botanist Aimé Goujaud Bonpland (1773–1858), whom he met in 1798 at the Hotel Boston where both lodged. They were due to join Captain Baudin's Directorate-financed world tour but war with Austria intervened. After a fruitless wait in Marseille, hoping to join Napoleon in Egypt, they travelled together to Spain, and then to Spanish America. All Bonpland's expenses were met by Humboldt. In the Spanish Government passport he was Humboldt's 'ayudante', or secretary. During the five-year voyage Bonpland seems to have been as sturdy, meticulous and 'heroic' as Humboldt himself, though he rarely emerges from anonymity in Humboldt's *Relation historique*. They shared scientific and political passions. Back in Paris from their five-year expedition Bonpland reluctantly wrote one of the thirty volumes dedicated to their voyage, though Humboldt placed his name on all the works.

Aimé Bonpland was born on 28 August 1773 at La Rochelle, the son of a surgeon. In 1791 he was in Paris studying anatomy. In 1794 he joined the navy, but was back in Paris a year later studying zoology and botany with Lamarck and Antoine Laurent de Jussieu (brother to Joseph who had travelled with La Condamine to South America from 1735 to 1744). On his return to France in 1804 after the five-year trip, Bonpland helped Humboldt with the writing of the massive *Voyage aux pays équinoxiales*. In 1808 he was appointed botanist (Intendant) at Empress Joséphine's Malmaison, helping her lay out the garden. He wrote a *Description des plantes rares cultivées à Malmaison et à Navarre* (1813–17) (with fifty-four plates by Redouté). In 1810 he met a widow, one of Joséphine's childhood friends, married her in 1813, and lived to regret it. After Joséphine's death in May 1814 Bonpland resigned from his post.

His later life is dramatic. He longed to return to a freer life in South America, and escape an unhappy marriage. At first he thought of joining Simón Bolívar, who had made him a tempting offer. But the Argentine radical Bernardino de Rivadavia invited him out to Buenos Aires. While out botanizing and studying the yerba maté plant Bonpland was arrested for settling on disputed land, and for growing the monopolized yerba maté, by troops of the Paraguayan dictator Dr Francia, and kept prisoner from 1821 to 1831, working in Santa María for nine years. Back in Argentina and living on farms on the Uruguay river, he continued to send boxes of botanical specimens to the Paris museum, and towards the end of his life helped organize a small natural history museum in Corrientes. He died in March 1858 on his *estancia*, and was buried in Paso de los Libres (for further details on Bonpland see Jason Wilson, 1994).

Glimpses of Bonpland's personality are rare. In a letter to his brother soon after their arrival at Cumaná Humboldt wrote about the thrill of being in the New World: 'Bonpland assured me that he would go stark mad if the excitement didn't stop soon.' More moving is Humboldt's caring for Bonpland's fate after his release from captivity in Paraguay. He wrote to François Guizot (25 May 1833), the French politician and historian, thanking him for having got Bonpland the *Légion d'honneur*. He had also written to the King. Humboldt managed to get Bonpland a pension of 3,000 francs a year by donating his herbarium to the Jardin des Plantes. He adds: 'I let my collection go to be useful to my friend. I now do not possess even a blade of grass, not one reminder of Chimborazo!'

Originally Bonpland was to have written up the botanical discoveries. But the *Nova Genera et species plantarum* was delegated to the German botanist Carl Sigismund Kunth (1788–1850) because Bonpland 'did not like the drudgery of studying species in herbarium and laboratory'. Kunth took twenty-two years to complete the work. As early as 1806 (in a letter from Berlin) Humboldt was worried that

Bonpland might return to Latin America, and invited him, all expenses paid, to Berlin, to 'eat cakes' and meet Wilhelm. In a letter to Bonpland from Rome Humboldt joked about the writing of their voyage. Bonpland had been proof-reading for only he was 'capable of properly reading my rough draft'. By 1810 Humboldt was begging Bonpland to work harder on the manuscripts for 'the high importance of science, for your own reputation, and for what you agreed with me in 1798'. By 1818 Humboldt complained that he had no news of Bonpland in Buenos Aires, swore his constant and affectionate devotion, and described how he was getting Bonpland elected to the Parisian Académie Royale des Sciences as a corresponding member (duly carried out in 1819). In 1852 the Académie Royale des Sciences in the name of Cuvier wrote Bonpland a letter congratulating him as the 'first to investigate the culture of maté and to try to improve it in a scientific manner'.

III

The Spanish Crown had zealously kept foreigners out of its colonies, especially heretical scientists. Between La Condamine's 1735 journey and Humboldt's 1799 one, no permission had been granted to any foreign scientist to investigate the interior of the continent. Science was alien to Spanish culture. Humboldt had been jeered in Spain when he set up his measuring instruments; earlier La Condamine had suffered similar hostilities in Quito. Humboldt was denied permission to travel to the Portuguese colonies because his scientific ideas proved too subversive. The scientist was not welcome. That Humboldt was reputed to be a radical, lifetime admirer of the French Revolution, an abolitionist, did not help. After his five-year journey the Spanish American independence turmoils again made it hard for foreigners to travel through the continent. Between 1823 and 1840 no foreigner could travel in Brazil. It meant that Humboldt was the sole source of information over a long period, and he conditioned, in M. Deas's words (1980), 'the way in which nineteenth-century Europe viewed Latin America'.

Scientifically speaking Latin America was virgin land. It had not been named and mapped by Europeans; thousands of species awaited their proper scientific tags; rivers, mountains, the climate, the population, all this and more awaited quantification. In an 1812 introduction to his *Relation historique* Humboldt recognized that he had travelled 'across regions which for centuries have remained virtually unknown to most European nations, even to Spain itself'. He often called Spanish American nature 'neuf et merveilleux'. The hinterlands had not changed since before the conquest. He and Bonpland collected their booty of forty-two cases and over 6,000 dried plant species (he collected over 60,000 plants, but all the animal and bird skins rotted) in order to give European scientists access to this unknown land. For Humboldt the scientist South America was still a New World waiting to be discovered. Robin Furneaux (1969) summarizes: 'His must be regarded as the first truly scientific inquiry into South America. For thoroughness, perseverance, curiosity, courage and sheer force of intellect it is unlikely ever to be surpassed.'

Science in Humboldt's terms was 'pure', but his writings were misappropriated by more commercially minded men. The obsession with gold and mines haunted Humboldt and Bonpland as they travelled about. After publishing his statistical study of New Spain (Mexico) in 1811 (see my chronology) Humboldt was horrified that his section on gold mines was printed separately and used to attract British investors in Mexico. He was appalled that one of his maps was copied without his permission by a Mr Arrowsmith in 1805. He has often been accused of justifying Imperial greed (see Juan A. Ortega y Medina (1960) and L. Kellner (1963) for further details). Recently Mary Louise Pratt (1992) accused Humboldt of stimulating interest in Pacific guano, which led to a boom and even war between Chile and Peru.

Humboldt and Bonpland left La Coruña on 5 June 1799 and returned to Bordeaux on 3 August 1804, having spent over five years in the Americas. As can be seen on the map provided the explorers moved inland through present-day Venezuela to the Brazilian border, Colombia, Ecuador, Peru, Cuba and Mexico. Throughout this long trip Humboldt and Bonpland never ceased taking notes and collecting, and never lost their enthusiasm. Before arriving at Cumaná Humboldt wrote to the mineralogist Johann Karl Freiesleben: 'What happiness is approaching! My head is giddy with joy! ... What a treasure of observations I will be able to make concerning the construction of the earth!' By 25 January 1800, after only seven months in Spanish America, Humboldt and Bonpland had dried over 4,000 plants and discovered over 800 new species for European science, yet their aim was always to observe, not collect. From Cuba Humboldt wrote in a letter (21 February 1801) to his brother: 'I was born for the Tropics, and have never felt so constantly well.' By February 1801 he had classified over 12,000 plants. How far away he was from his European base can be seen from the fact that up to 21 September 1801 he had not received one letter from Europe. In November 1802 he could still boast to the astronomer Jean Baptiste Delambre that he was visiting countries 'never seen by naturalists before'. At sea, near Bordeaux, and nearly home after five years, Humboldt's tone does not alter: 'I am returning with thirty-five cases filled with botanical, astronomical and geological treasures.' The difficulties of sending his specimens home cannot be exaggerated. Humboldt had to divide his herbals into three lots. One collection he sent to England and Germany, another to Cádiz and France, and a third remained in Havana. He lost one lot, and all Bonpland's insects. In a public library in Philadelphia Humboldt read in a newspaper: 'Arrival of Monsieur de Humboldt's manuscripts at his brother's house in Paris by way of Spain.' Humboldt's typical reaction: 'I could scarcely suppress an exclamation of joy.' But if the voyage lasted over five years, that was nothing compared to the labour of writing it, which lasted twenty-seven years from 1808 to 1834.

Humboldt's nineteenth-century prestige depended as much on the writing of his books as on the voyage itself. The publication of his *Voyage aux régions équinoxiales du nouveau continent, fait en 1799, 1800, 1801, 1802, 1803 et 1804* began in Paris, in French, in 1805 (there is confusion over this date, 1807 may be more realistic), and ended in 1834 after the thirty folio and quarto volumes had been published. There are the four volumes prepared by Bonpland on tropical plants gathered in Mexico; more famous volumes like the *Atlas pittoresque du voyage* with its sixty-nine plates made from Humboldt's own sketches (vols. 15 and 16, 1810), which Humboldt saw as the companion volume to his narrative *Relation historique*; a fascinating study of historical geography (vol. 17, 1814–34); his *Essai politique sur le royaume de la Nouvelle-Espagne* (vols. 25 and 26, 1811); and his equally famous plant geography (vol. 27, 1805). Volumes 28 to 30 were what I have called his *Personal Narrative*, titled in French the *Relation historique du voyage aux régions équinoxiales du nouveau continent*, which came out in 1814, 1819 and 1825. This was supposed to be the popularizing part of his massive publication, dealing with the actual journey, sometimes taking the form of a diary. However, it ends in March 1801 with the explorers halfway up the Magdalena river in Colombia. I have already noted that Humboldt had the fourth volume ready for publication but ordered it destroyed. According to Miguel Wionczek (1977) the thirteen diary volumes in French of Humboldt's 1799–1804 journey remained unedited in the Staatsbibliothek in what was East Berlin. The volumes corresponding to his travels in Ecuador and Peru were edited by Margot Faak (1986), and parts of his later journeys to Quito, Peru and up Chimborazo appeared in his 1808 *Ansichten der Natur*, published in German and French simultaneously. The *Relation historique* was translated three times into English in the nineteenth century.

The writing of these thirty volumes ruined Humboldt. According to the biographer L. Kellner (1963), the printing and engraving cost £24,000 and the paper £4,800 but it sold at the prohibitive price of £383 for an unbound copy and £412 for a bound copy. Louis Agassiz noted in 1869 that the price of his American works was $2,000, twice the price of the French Government's publication on Egypt, which had cost about $800,000 to produce. Charles Minguet (1969) calculated that of the 90,000 thaler Humboldt inherited from his mother in 1796 he spent 40,000 on his five-year trip and 100,000 on publishing his work. Economic needs forced him to work for the Prussian kings as Chamberlain. But finance was not the only bother. Humboldt wrote to Augustin de Candolle, the eminent botanist, in 1812: 'I am still working on that interminable journey and it bores me terribly' – and he still had some twenty years to go. Earlier in 1805 he wrote to Cotta, his German publisher: 'you can imagine how hard it is to write up the manuscripts from five years of travel'.

Humboldt was quite clear as to his authorial intentions. To Boussingault he wrote in 1822: 'If my work has any merit it is for the overall views that link the formation of the two hemispheres; it is the first essay of this kind.' Humboldt aimed to interest any 'educated man' of 'good taste', and not just specialists. He sought 'educated but unscientific readers for the fascination of the discovery of scientific truths'. As I have already quoted, he was aware that his style of writing differed from that of Forster and Chateaubriand, for he attempted to write truthfully, and scientifically, 'without going into arid regions of knowledge'. Elsewhere he added: 'The charlatanry of mere literature will thus be combined with utility.'

However, all Humboldt's commentators and biographers agree that his work can be clinical, even dull; he digresses at will, ignoring the reader's impatience. His intimate friend the scientist François Arago hit the nail on the head: 'Humboldt, you really don't know how to write a book. You write endlessly, but what comes out of it is not a book, but a portrait without a frame.' Was Humboldt just too busy and sociable to dedicate himself to writing? He himself thought this:

If I only knew how to describe adequately how and what I felt, I might, after this long journey of mine, really be able to give happiness to people. The disjointed life I lead makes me feel hardly certain of my way of writing . . .

He thought the failure of his style had something to do with his digressive manner of thinking: 'one must bring order into one's ideas and suppress what is extraneous to the principal point. And that is what I cannot do'. In a letter to Varnhagen von Ense in 1834 he enumerated further faults in his style: 'The besetting sins of my style are an unfortunate propensity to poetical expressions, a long participial construction, and too great concentration of various opinions and sentiments in the same sentence.' It is as if he wanted to cram into language everything he had observed and pondered over in South America, a Mallarméan dream of shrinking the world into a book. Humboldt blamed himself: 'I was at fault to tackle from intellectual curiosity too great a variety of scientific interests.' But the most lucid reason for Humboldt's faults are analysed psychologically in his autobiography of 1806, 'My Confessions', where he described himself as:

anxious, agitated, unable to enjoy anything that I have finished, and never content except when undertaking something new and doing three things at the same time. It is in this mood of moral anxiety, a consequence of my nomadic life, that you must find the causes of the defects in my work. I have done more good through what I have communicated, through the ideas that I have awoken in others, than in my own published works.

There are further explanations. As a stylistic exercise Humboldt intended to both instruct and move his reader for his version of Romantic science linked the observer to the observed through feeling and emotions. Humboldt was an able sketcher and painter; the words 'charm' and 'picturesque' epitomized his conventional stylistic intentions. Through static word-pictures he wanted his readers to see and feel awe; that is, to react aesthetically, but it involved difficulties in the actual writing, rather than in the therapeutic meditating on nature, which Humboldt did not really overcome. Confronting his reader with the unknown, with 'grandeur' and 'marvel' – key Humboldtian words – meant finding adequate words. Humboldt admitted his inadequacy when referring to the Tenerife volcano: 'It is a hard task to describe these sensations for they work on us so much more powerfully the more they are vague.'

Something must be said about Humboldt's choice of French for writing his works. During his five years abroad Humboldt had occasion to speak German only twice. By 1800 he spoke Spanish fluently, despite calling it 'my Prussian Castilian'. By February 1801 he claimed he knew Spanish as if it was his mother tongue. He wrote the first draft of the *Essai politique sur le royaume de la Nouvelle-Espagne* in Spanish, and on 20 August 1800 he wrote a report for the Captain-General of Venezuela in Spanish. In fact he enjoyed speaking Spanish. He found the *criollos* (creoles, or American-born Spaniards) and mestizos (half-castes of creole and Indian parentage) of the Spanish colonies simple, without pretensions. He loved their generosity and hospitality. In 1800 he wrote to Baron Forell, Saxon Ambassador in Madrid: 'On returning to Europe I will very reluctantly de-Spanishify myself.' He pitted these uneducated but straightforward colonists against the over-sophisticated, devious Europeans who justify unethical behaviour with philosophical maxims. He liked their way of life so much that in 1822 he planned to return to the Tropics and Mexico and live in 'América libre'. But Humboldt spoke to Bonpland in French, wrote his diary notes during the journey in French, and corresponded with many French scientists. By choosing to publish in Paris he was obliged to write in French.

His French is curiously flat, scientific and modern. I was struck by the disparity between the English of his nineteenth-century translators and his French. Helen Maria Williams's seven-volumed translation (*Personal Narrative of Travels to the Equinoctial Regions of the New Continent, during the Years 1799–1804*, 1814–29) was the fruit of collaborating with Humboldt himself who 'corrected many of my errors', which led to a faithful version close to his French except when Humboldt enthused – then his translator interpreted and exaggerated. Helen Maria Williams said of Humboldt: 'while he appears only to address himself to our reason, he has the secret of awakening the imagination, and of being understood by the heart'. Her translation plays on this appeal to the heart, and becomes, in her own words, 'an imperfect copy of a sublime model'. 'Wild' nature becomes 'wild and stupendous nature'; 'high Alps' become 'lofty chain of the Alps'; a 'dark curtain of mountains' becomes a 'vast and gloomy curtain of mountains'; 'destroyed' continents becomes continents 'rent asunder'; 'so much does he love liberty' becomes 'so sacred to his soul is liberty'. In these random examples my literal translation of Humboldt's French appears first. Caroline Darwin accused her brother Charles of reading so much Humboldt that his phraseology made use of 'flowery French expressions' instead of his own 'simple straightforward and far more agreeable style', confusing the translation with Humboldt's original and cool French.

In 1851 Thomasina Ross published a corrective translation also titled *Personal Narrative of Travels to the Equinoctial Regions of the New Continent*, in three volumes, which reads more plainly. She complained that Helen Maria Williams's version 'abounds in foreign terms of expression', but she has simply edited it, many of the expressions being identical. She still indulges in period flavour. Humboldt's 'triste' becomes 'gloomy'; a bird that has a 'chant le plus agréable' becomes 'the most heart-soothing song'; 'qui s'occupe' becomes 'devoted to'; 'le gazon court et serré' becomes 'the short-swarded turf'; and all in a few pages. Only from these poeticized translations can we see what Darwin meant by Humboldt's style as a 'rare union of poetry with science'.

As a propagandist for his harmonic view of science Humboldt had to engage and flatter his public. Leonard Darwin described the tone of his father's prose – trying to account for his popularity – as that of a 'courteous gentleman', talking patiently to his readers, a tone that the poet Osip Mandelstam defined as 'scientific conversation'. The non-scientific reader is not excluded, or patronized. The same applies to Humboldt's tone of voice. He allows his reader to accompany him like another silent Bonpland, and participate in his endless curiosity about the physical world. Science could still be grasped by the educated general public. Humboldt did not hide behind jargon, or mathematics. His discourse is accessible, pleasing, patient and polite. Humboldt wanted to gently educate and convince his reader; let him share his appreciation of the magic, charm, mysteries and sublimities of nature. Science was morally uplifting.

IV

Humboldt modestly summarized his scientific achievements to his friend Leopold Buch (1774–1853), the geologist: 'I have a very good idea how much I owe to a combination of fortunate circumstances, to influential friends, to a moderate mixture of miscellaneous knowledge and keenness of observation.' He wrote to his confidant François Arago: 'I have observed a great many things as I am not without ability but I have achieved nothing.' Goethe claimed that Humboldt owed his success to 'good ordinary sense, much energy, and persever-ance'. Despite his disclaimer Humboldt did achieve a wide variety of triumphs, both insignificant and important, which I have summarized from various sources as follows.

For example, in geology he was the first to observe 'reverse polarity in magnetism', and he coined the term 'magnetic storm'. He discovered the decrease in the earth's magnetic force from the poles to the equator. He also invented the term 'jurassic', and propagated the notion of 'seismic waves'. He was the first to show that Latin America was not a young continent geologically speaking. He grouped volcanoes along vast subterranean lines, and demonstrated the igneous formation of rocks. In botany, Humboldt was the first to systematically tabulate plant life in connection with meteorology and geography, and instigated plant geography as a scientific discipline, especially in his beautiful botanical map in which growth of particular plants is related to temperature and altitude. In his writings he was the first to enumerate the plants native to America before the conquest (manioc, yucca, maize, potato, sweet potato, tomato, peanut, pepper, vanilla, cocoa, avocado, pineapple, etc.). He achieved all this despite the botanist Robert Brown's complaint that his work 'contains but little matter wrapt up in his usual declamatory nonsense' (see D.J. Mabberley, 1985).

Humboldt was the first to bring clinical reports of the poison curare back to Europe. He also sent guano back to Europe for chemical analysis, leading to the guano fertilizer boom. With his detailed drawings, Humboldt was the first European to discuss and speculate on Aztec art, including the Aztec calendar, or sun stone. In relation to the Indian population of the New World he was the first, in 1825, to seriously calculate the total population of the Spanish American colonies (17,785,000, with 13,509,000 coloured, 3,276,000 white and 150,000 Spanish born). In fact he was the first to objectively report on the American Indians, calculating the Indian population before the conquest as 250,000 in Hispaniola in 1492, down to 500 in 1538. He discovered Aztec manuscripts, or codices, and speculated on the Asian origins of American Indians.

Humboldt was equally important in geography. His 'isothermal lines' led to a way of comparing climatic conditions across different countries. He discovered that the 'interior of Spain forms a high plateau', and confirmed that the Casiquiare channel joined the Orinoco and Amazon river systems. He worked out why America was called America (from a 1509 map by a Martius Ilacunylus). He was the first to plan the Panama canal, prepare a general map of Mexico and Cuba based on astronomical observations, and draw generally reliable and beautiful maps of the Orinoco and Magdalena rivers. As is recognized by its name, he was the first to measure the cold coastal current off western South America. Indeed, Humboldt single-handedly integrated America into world geography.

As a historian Humboldt was the first European to write a 'tableau objectif' of the conquest of America, including many documents on Columbus, in his still untranslated *Histoire de la géographie du nouveau monde* (1814–34). He dissipated the legend of Spanish cruelty, and could be said to have been the first European to observe in detail, with statistics, a colonial world.

For some thirty years Humboldt also held the world altitude record after climbing 19,700 feet up Chimborazo, not finally climbed until 1880 by Edward Whymper. He was also the first to have climbed the La Silla above Caracas.

As a writer, Humboldt's popular scientific travelogue, the *Relation historique*, created a new genre, as Victor W. von Hagen (1949) has shown, explicitly followed by Charles Darwin, Henry Bates, Thomas Belt, A.R. Wallace and Louis Agassiz through to Redmond O'Hanlon today. About Humboldt Darwin wrote: 'You might truly call him the parent of a grand progeny of scientific travellers, who, taken together, have done much for science.' In assessing his debt to Georg Forster Humboldt also described his own place as a travel writer: 'With him began a new era of scientific travels. Georg Forster was the first to describe with charm the varying stages of vegetation, the climatic conditions, the nutrients in relation to the customs of people in different localities.'

Finally Humboldt foreshadowed a tradition where writing – cutting generically across travelogues, novels, anthropology and the social sciences – is the means of appropriating Latin America's chaotic reality, not to colonize it, but to understand it by accurately reporting. Juan Bautista Alberdi, future Argentine President, wrote to Justo José de Urquiza, Argentine President, recommending that German Burmeister, one of Humboldt's disciples, be invited out to Argentina, claiming that people like Humboldt (and Burmeister) 'let us know about the riches that we possess unconsciously'. The premise behind this verbal naming and taming of Latin American nature is that only science trains the mind to notice reality. For Humboldt the discipline of science 'brings you closer to reality'. It is for this reason that Simón Bolívar famously said: 'Humboldt was the true discoverer of America because his work has produced more benefit to our people than all the conquistadores.'

In preparing this edition of Humboldt's travels I decided to concentrate on the traveller and his actual impressions. Today we read Humboldt for the breadth and freshness of his wide-ranging mind. The Humboldt to recover for the closing of the twentieth century is the one who criticized Hegel to his friend Varnhagen von Ense in terms that define Humboldt at his best:

But to a man like me – spellbound, insect-fashion, to earth and the endless variety of natural phenomena which it contains – a dry theoretical assertion of utterly false facts and views about America and the Indian world is enslaving and oppressive.

A closer guide to what to omit in my selection was Humboldt himself who checked the second German translation from the French of his *Relation historique*, and wrote a prologue on 28 March 1859, six weeks before he died, where he advised his German translator to avoid summaries and to eliminate digressions and strictly scientific details, though I have not always concurred with the actual cuts in Dr Adalbert Plott's version of Hermann Hauff's translation from Humboldt's French, *Von Orinoko zum Amazonas: Reise in die Aquinoktial: Gegenden des Neuen Kontinents*, especially as it ends earlier than the full French edition (on 24 November 1800, not in March 1801).

The first volume of the original edition was published in 1814 by F. Schoell, dedicated to P.J. de la Place (that is, Laplace, 1749–1827), the French mathematician and astronomer who briefly became Interior Minister during the Revolution, and counted 643 quarto pages. The second volume came out with Maze also in Paris in 1819 with 722 pages, and the third and last volume was published by J. Smith in London and Paris in 1825 with 632 pages – in total some 1,997 pages, which I have edited down to 300 (Alain Gheerbrant edited Humboldt's journal down to 459 pages in 1961; Charles Minguet edited it down to 143 pages in 1980). I have attempted to give a representative flavour of Humboldt's style and mind, resisting turning him into a magical realist, so that the man continuously dipping his thermometer into water, and locating his position by stars at night, and speculating on Indian languages, and complaining of mosquitoes, comes directly through to his reader today. I have also resisted turning his matter-of-fact French into a racier English.

Finally, concerning Humboldt's own texts, his quotations from Spanish are often at odds with current Spanish (inconsistencies with accents, using x for j), and there are times when Humboldt is not consistent with spelling – *vijaho* and *vijao*, Father Cereso and Father Cerezo, Jolokiano and Iolokiano, Portobello and Porto Bello, *tutuma* and *tutumo* – just as he indiscriminately uses metres, toises and feet.

Jason Wilson, London 1994

ACKNOWLEDGEMENTS

Alexander von Humboldt wrote fluently in German, Spanish and French, and spoke excellent English; he was a polymath, and travelled extensively. It would need another Humboldt to encompass such a life and its works. Most commentators have taken specialized aspects of Humboldt, and dealt uniquely with that aspect. It is for this breadth of concern that any work on Humboldt must be based on secondary material in all the languages that Humboldt himself spoke. It is notable, for example, that the research done on Humboldt in Spanish around his Cuban, Colombian, Venezuelan, Peruvian and Mexican visits is not usually included in studies emanating from Britain. Many people have assisted me over the years, without in any way being responsible for the final work.

I would like to thank Andrea Wilson, Adrienne Lee, Anthony Edkins, the late Harold Blakemore, and Malcolm Deas for help with snippets of information; Dr David Knight, whose helpful report picked out many flaws; Alan Ross for first publishing my Humboldt writings in the *London Magazine* in 1987, and especially Paul Keegan for commissioning the project for Penguin, and Sarah Coward, astute copy-editor who combed the manuscript for inconsistencies. However, any errors remain mine.

ALEXANDER VON HUMBOLDT:
A CHRONOLOGY FROM 1769 TO 1859

1769   Friedrich Wilhelm Heinrich Alexander von Humboldt –
        known as Alexander – is born on 14 September at the
        family estate in Tegel, near Berlin, into a wealthy Prussian
        family – second son to Alexander Georg von Humboldt,
        Chamberlain to the Imperial Prince, and Marie Elizabeth de
        Colomb, of French and Scottish Protestant descent. His elder
        brother Wilhelm was born on 22 June 1767. The two
        brothers are brought up together at Tegel, and share the
        same tutors, the first of which is J.H. Campe, a keen
        geographer (and translator of *Robinson Crusoe*).

1779   Father dies, and G.J.C. Kunth, a formative influence as
        tutor, is made trustee. The Humboldt brothers and tutor
        move to Berlin and meet, among others, the composer
        Mendelssohn's family.

1787   Begins studying at Frankfurt University, and is particularly
        enthusiastic about botany classes with Karl Ludwig
        Willdenow.

1789   At Göttingen University studying literature, archaeology,
        electricity and the natural sciences. Sets off around Germany
        on the first of his travels.

1790   Travels abroad with Georg Forster (1754–94) who had ac-
        companied Captain Cook on his second voyage around the
        world, and whose *Voyage round the World on the Resolution*
        (London, 1777) was extremely influential on Humboldt.
        They visit Holland, England (where Humboldt meets Caven-
        dish and Sir Joseph Banks in Soho Square) and France,
        where they spend a week in Paris helping to carry sand to
        build the Temple de la Liberté. Forster publishes his account
        of their journey, *Ansichten vom Niederrhein von Brabant,*

Flanden, Holland, England und Frankreich, while Humboldt publishes his first work in botanical and chemical journals, as well as a mineralogical treatise.

1791   Finishes his studies in Hamburg. Returns to Berlin and further botanical excursions with Willdenow. Joins the Freiberg School of Mines, where he studies with Abraham Werner, leader of the Neptunist school in geology.

1792   Joins Department of Mines of the Prussian Government and travels around inspecting mines.

1793   Appointed Superintendent of Mines in Franconia, and founds free miners' school in Steben. Publishes *Florae Fribergensis specimen*.

1794   Appointed Councillor of Mines. Meets Goethe in Jena. Publishes *Aphorismen aus der Chemischen Physiologie de Pflanzen*.

1795   Travels to Switzerland and Italy. With his brother he begins his Galvanistic experiments.

1796   Comes into his fortune with his mother's death. Long estranged from her, however, he does not grieve. Retires from the Prussian mining administration and decides to fulfil his yearning for travel far abroad. In many senses his multi-disciplinary studies up to 1796 can be seen as his preparations for a world tour.

1797   Lives in Jena, studying astronomy, chemistry, botany and mineralogy, and often visits Goethe. His old tutor Kunth divides up family inheritance and Humboldt receives 312,000 French gold francs, or 90,000 thaler (German silver coin). Publishes a study of muscular irritations and travels to Vienna. Plans a trip to Brazil, and another with Lord Bristol to Egypt – both fail. Before leaving for Paris, he visits the Tyrolean Alps with the geologist Leopold Buch, where they spend the winter taking magnetic, topographical and meteorological measurements.

1798   Back in Paris he is accepted on Captain Baudin's world voyage – which is constantly delayed. Meets future travelling companion Aimé Bonpland (1773–1858), a doctor and botanist. They travel together to Marseille and wait in vain for a boat; then move on through Spain to Madrid. After meeting Charles IV at Aranjuez Humboldt is given special permission to explore the hinterlands of Spanish America. This was to be the first foreign expedition since La Condamine's fateful trip (1735–44), and the last for many years, due to the independence wars.

1799 On 5 June Humboldt and Bonpland leave La Coruña on the corvette *Pizarro*. Reach Tenerife on 19 June, and on 21 June climb the Teide peak. Reach Cumaná on 16 July where they stay for several months, taking short excursions to the Araya peninsula, the Chaima Indian missions, the Caripe convent and the Guácharo caves. Leave for Caracas on 18 November.

1800 Stay in Caracas until 7 February when they set off for the Orinoco. Reach San Fernando across the llanos on 27 March. Ascend the Apure river to the cataracts and arrive at San Fernando de Atabapo on 24 April. After entering the Temi river they cross land at Pimichín (6 May) and reach the Casiquiare on 12 May. Drifting downstream to the Orinoco they reach Angostura (today Ciudad Bolívar) on 13 June. Altogether they spend seventy-five days on the rivers, covering 2,250 kilometres. Recover from malaria and leave for New Barcelona on 10 July. Arrive back in Cumaná and leave for Cuba on 24 November, arriving at Havana on 19 December.

1801 Leave Cuba on 5 March after excursions around Havana. Reach Cartagena on 30 March, ascend Magdalena river to Honda, arriving at Bogotá on 6 July, where they meet Spain's greatest botanist José Celestino Mutis (1732–1808). Finally leave Bogotá on 8 September to rejoin Captain Baudin by travelling over land to Quito.

1802 Arrive at Quito on 6 January and stay until 9 June. Humboldt tries to climb Chimborazo and reaches 19,700 feet, the world record at the time. Begins to take notes for *Essai sur la géographie des plantes*. Arrive in Lima on 2 September to learn that Captain Baudin has sailed round the Cape of Good Hope.

1803 Leave Guayaquil for Acapulco on 3 January, arriving there on 15 February and in Mexico City on 11 March, where they stay until 13 May. In Mexico Humboldt meets the viceroy, and visits mining areas of Guanajuato. Climbs the Jorulla volcano on 19 October.

1804 Leave Veracruz for Cuba on 7 January, remaining there until 29 April; this visit supplying Humboldt with the material for his *Essai politique sur l'île de Cuba*. Reach Philadelphia on 20 May. Humboldt befriends President Thomas Jefferson in Washington. Finally leave the New World on 30 June, arriving in Bordeaux on 3 August and in Paris on 25 August. Humboldt meets Bolívar and Napoleon (who dislikes him and thinks him a Prussian spy) in Paris, and befriends the young scientist Louis Joseph Gay-Lussac (1778–1850).

1805 Humboldt begins work on his South American travels. Visits his brother Wilhelm in Rome and climbs Vesuvius. After nine years' absence he returns to Berlin and is nominated Court Chamberlain to the Prussian King, Friedrich Wilhelm III.

1807–27 Lives on and off in Paris, publishing, at his own expense, thirty folio and quarto volumes *Voyage aux régions équinoxiales du nouveau continent, fait en 1799, 1800, 1801, 1802, 1803 et 1804*. (The last volume is published in 1834.) In 1808 he publishes simultaneously in French and German his own favourite (and most popular) book, *Ansichten der Natur*. Publishes *Essai politique sur le royaume de la Nouvelle-Espagne* in 1811. Leaves Paris in 1827 to settle in Berlin. Begins the public lectures that would culminate in *Kosmos*.

1829 Sets off on his last great journey, to Russia and Central Asia.

1835 His brother Wilhelm dies.

1840 Appointed Councillor of State by new Prussian King, Friedrich Wilhelm IV.

1843 Publishes his Asian travel book, also in French, *Recherches sur les chaînes de montagnes et la climatologie comparée*, in three volumes.

1845 Starts to publish *Kosmos* in German (the last volume of which appeared posthumously in 1862).

1859 Dies on 6 May. Buried in family vault at Tegel with his brother and sister-in-law.

FURTHER READING

ON HUMBOLDT

Ludmilla Assign (ed.), *Letters of Alexander von Humboldt, Written between the Years 1827 and 1858 to Varnhagen von Ense* (London, 1860).

Angel Bedoya-Maruri, *Alexander von Humboldt: Modelo en la lucha por el progreso y la liberación de la humanidad. Memorial. Bicentenario de su nacimiento* (Berlin, 1969).

Douglas Botting, *Humboldt and the Cosmos* (London and New York, 1973) (reviewed by V.S. Pritchett in *The Complete Essays* (London, 1991)).

Karl Bruhns, *Alexander von Humboldt: Eine Wissenschaftliche Biographie*, 2 vols. (Leipzig, 1872).

M.D. Deas and R.A. McNeil (eds.), *Europeans in Latin America: Humboldt to Hudson* (Oxford, 1980).

Margot Faak, *Alexander von Humboldt: Reise auf dem Rio Magdalena, durch die Anden und Mexico* (Berlin, 1986).

Alain Gheerbrant (ed.), *Voyages aux régions équinoxiales du nouveau continent fait en 1799 et 1800 par A. de Humboldt* (Paris, 1961).

Wolfgang-Hagen Hein (ed.), *Alexander von Humboldt: Life and Work* (Ingelheim am Rein, 1987).

L. Kellner, *Alexander von Humboldt* (Oxford, 1963).

Charles Minguet, *Alexandre de Humboldt: Historien et géographe de l'Amérique espagnole (1799–1804)* (Paris, 1969).

— (ed.), Alexander von Humboldt, *Cartas americanas* (Caracas, 1980) (superseding E.T. Hamy's *Lettres américaines* (Paris, 1904)).

— (ed. and intro.), Alexander von Humboldt, *Voyages dans l'Amérique équinoxiale*, 2 vols. (Paris, 1980).

Fernando Ortiz (intro.), Humboldt, *Ensayo político sobre la isla de Cuba* (Havana, 1960).

Kurt Schleucher, *Alexander von Humboldt: Der Mensch, der Forscher, der Schriftsteller* (Berlin, 1988).

Henry Stevens, *The Humboldt Library: A Catalogue of the Library of Alexander von Humboldt, with a Bibliography and Biographical Sketch* (London, 1863).

Helmut de Terra, *Humboldt: The Life and Times of Alexander von Humboldt (1769–1859)* (New York, 1955).

ON THE SCIENTIFIC BACKGROUND

Louis Agassiz, *Address Delivered on the Centennial Anniversary of the Birth of Alexander von Humboldt* (Boston, 1869).

Susan Cannon, *Science in Culture: The Early Victorian Period* (New York, 1978).

Maurice Crosland, *The Society of Arcueil: A View of French Science at the Time of Napoleon I* (London, 1967).

Andrew Cunningham and Nicholas Jardine (eds.), *Romanticism and the Sciences* (Cambridge, 1990) (with useful reading lists).

L.J. Jordanova, *Lamarck* (Oxford, 1980).

Edward Lurie, *Louis Agassiz: A Life in Science* (Chicago, 1960).

D.J. Mabberley, *Jupiter Botanicus: Robert Brown of the British Museum* (Braunschweig, 1985).

D.R. Oldroyd, *Darwinian Impacts: An Introduction to the Darwinian Revolution* (Milton Keynes, 1980).

Dorinda Outram, *Georges Cuvier: Vocation, Science and Authority in Post-Revolutionary France* (Manchester, 1984).

William T. Stearn (ed.), *Humboldt, Bonpland, Kunth and Tropical American Botany* (Stuttgart, 1968).

Donald Worster, *Nature's Economy: The Roots of Ecology* (New York, 1979).

GENERAL BACKGROUND ON SCIENTIFIC TRAVELLERS IN THE NEW WORLD

Max Biraben, *German Burmeister: Su vida, su obra* (Buenos Aires, 1968).

D.A. Brading, *The First America: The Spanish Monarchy, Creole Patriots and the Liberal State (1492–1867)* (Cambridge, 1991).

Iris H.W. Engstrand, *Spanish Scientists in the New World: The Eighteenth-Century Expeditions* (London, 1981).

Robin Furneaux, *The Amazon: The Story of a Great River* (London, 1969).

Edward J. Goodman, *The Explorers of South America* (New York, 1972).

Victor W. von Hagen, *The Green World of the Naturalists: A Treasury of Five Centuries of Natural History in South America* (New York, 1948).

— *South America Called Them: Condamine, Humboldt, Darwin, Spruce* (London, 1949).

Katherine E. Manthorne, *Tropical Renaissance: North American Artists Exploring Latin America (1833–1879)* (Washington, 1989).

José Antonio Maya, *Celestino Mutis y la expedición botánica* (Madrid, 1986).

Juan A. Ortega y Medina, *Humboldt desde México* (Mexico, 1960).

Oscar Rodriguez Ortiz (ed.), *Imágenes de Humboldt* (Caracas, 1973).

Mary Louise Pratt, *Imperial Eyes: Travel Writing and Transculturation* (London and New York, 1992).

Jason Wilson, 'The Strange Fate of Aimé Bonpland', *London Magazine* (April–May 1994), pp. 36–48.

Miguel S. Wionczek, *El Humboldt venezolano* (Caracas, 1977).

Personal Narrative

of Travels to the Equinoctial Regions of America

CONTENTS

Contents

HUMBOLDT'S INTRODUCTION

Twelve years have elapsed since I left Europe to explore the interior of the New Continent. From my earliest days I was excited by studying nature, and was sensitive to the wild beauty of a landscape bristling with mountains and covered in forests. I found that travelling out there compensated for a hard and often agitated life. But pleasure was not the only fruit of my decision to contribute to the progress of the physical sciences. For a long time I had prepared myself for the observations that were the main object of my journey to the torrid zone. I was equipped with instruments that were easy and convenient to use, made by the ablest artists, and I enjoyed the protection of a government that, far from blocking my way, constantly honoured me with its confidence. I was supported by a brave and learned friend whose keenness and equanimity never let me down, despite the exhaustion and dangers we faced.

Under such favourable circumstances, and crossing regions long unknown to most European nations, including Spain itself, Bonpland and I collected a considerable number of materials, which when published may throw light on the history of nations, and on our knowledge about nature. Our research developed in so many unpredictable directions that we could not include everything in the form of a travel journal, and have therefore placed our observations in a series of separate works.

Two main aims guided my travels, published as the *Relation historique*.[1] I wanted to make known the countries I visited, and to collect those facts that helped elucidate the new science vaguely named the Natural History of the World, Theory of the Earth or Physical Geography. Of these two aims, the second seemed the more important. I was passionately keen on botany and certain aspects of zoology, and flattered myself that our researches might add some new species to those already known. However, rather than discovering new, isolated facts I preferred linking already known ones together. The discovery of a new genus seemed to me far less interesting than an observation on the geographical relations of plants, or the migration of social plants, and the heights that different plants reach on the peaks of the cordilleras.

The natural sciences are connected by the same ties that link all natural phenomena together. The classification of species, which we should consider as fundamental to botany, and whose study has been facilitated by introducing natural methods, is to plant geography what descriptive mineralogy is to the rocks that form the outer crust of the earth. To understand the laws observed in the rocks, and to determine the age of successive formations and identify them from the most distant regions, a geologist should know the simple fossils that make up the mass of mountains. The same goes for the natural history that deals with how plants are related to each other, and with the soil and air. The advancement of plant geography depends greatly on descriptive botany; it would hinder the advancement of the sciences to postulate general ideas by neglecting particular facts.

Such considerations have guided my researches, and were always present in my mind as I prepared for the journey. When I began to read the many travel books, which form such an interesting branch of modern literature, I regretted that previous learned travellers seldom possessed a wide enough knowledge to avail themselves of what they saw. It seemed to me that what had been obtained had not kept up with the immense progress of several sciences in the late eighteenth century, especially geology, the history and modifications of the atmosphere, and the physiology of plants and animals. Despite new and accurate instruments I was disappointed, and most scientists would agree with me, that while the number of precise instruments multiplied we were still ignorant of the height of so many mountains and plains; of the periodical oscillations of the aerial oceans; the limit of perpetual snow under the polar caps and on the borders of the torrid zones; the variable intensity of magnetic forces; and many equally important phenomena.

Maritime expeditions and voyages round the world have rightly conferred fame on naturalists and astronomers appointed by their governments, but while these distinguished men have given precise notions of the coasts of countries, of the natural history of the ocean and islands, their expeditions have advanced neither geology nor general physics as travels into the interior of a continent should have. Interest in the natural sciences has trailed behind geography and nautical astronomy. During long sea-voyages, a traveller hardly ever sees land; and when land is seen after a long wait it is often stripped of its most beautiful products. Sometimes, beyond a sterile coast, a ridge of high mountains covered in forests is glimpsed, but its distance only frustrates the traveller.

Land journeys are made very tiresome by having to transport instruments and collections, but these difficulties are compensated by real advantages. It is not by sailing along a coast that the direction, geology and climate of a chain of mountains can be discovered. The wider a continent is the greater the range of its soil and the richness of its animal and vegetable products, and the further the central chain of mountains lies from the ocean coast the greater the variety of stony strata that can be seen, which reveal the history of the earth. Just as every individual can be seen as particular, so can we recognize individuality in the arrangement of brute matter in rocks, in the distribution and relationships of plants and animals. The great problem of the physical description of the planet is how to determine the laws that relate the phenomena of life with inanimate nature.

In trying to explain the motives that led me to travel into the interior of a continent I can only outline what my ideas were at an age when we do not have a fair estimate of our faculties. What I had planned in my youth has not been completely carried out. I did not travel as far as I had intended when I sailed for South America; nor did it give me the number of results I expected. The Madrid Court had given me permission in 1799 to sail on the Acapulco galleon and visit the Philippine Islands after crossing its New World colonies. I had hoped to return to Europe across Asia, the Persian Gulf and Baghdad. With respect to the works that Bonpland and I have published, we hope that their imperfections, obvious to both of us, will not be attributed to a lack of keenness, nor to publishing too quickly. A determined will and an active perseverance are not always sufficient to overcome every obstacle.

Having outlined the general aim, I will now briefly glance at the collections and observations we made. The maritime war during our stay in America made communications with Europe very uncertain and, in order for us to avoid losses, forced us to make three different collections. The first we sent to Spain and France, the second to the United States and England, and the third, the most considerable, remained constantly with us. Towards the end of our journey this last collection formed forty-two boxes containing a herbal of 6,000 equinoctial plants, seeds, shells and insects, and geological specimens from Chimborazo, New Granada and the banks of the Amazon, never seen in Europe before. After our journey up the Orinoco, we left a part of this collection in Cuba in order to pick it up on our return from Peru and Mexico. The rest followed us for five years along the Andes chain, across New Spain, from the Pacific shores to the West Indian seas. The carrying of these objects, and the minute care they required, created unbelievable difficulties, quite unknown in the wildest parts of Europe. Our progress was often held up by having to drag after us for five and six months at a time from twelve to twenty loaded mules, change these mules every eight to ten days, and oversee the Indians employed on these caravans. Often, to add new geological specimens to our collections, we had to throw away others collected long before. Such sacrifices were no less painful than what we lost through accidents. We learned too late that the warm humidity and the frequent falls of our mules prevented us from preserving our hastily prepared animal skins and the fish and reptiles in alcohol. I note these banal details to show that we had no means of bringing back many of the objects of zoological and comparative anatomical interest whose descriptions and drawings we have published. Despite these obstacles, and the expenses entailed, I was pleased that I had decided before leaving to send duplicates of all we had collected to Europe. It is worth repeating that in seas infested with pirates a traveller can only be sure of what he takes with him. Only a few duplicates that we sent from America were saved, most fell into the hands of people ignorant of the sciences. When a ship is held in a foreign port, boxes containing dried plants or stones are merely forgotten, and not sent on as indicated to scientific men. Our geological collections taken in the Pacific had a happier fate. We are indebted for their safety to the generous work of Sir Joseph Banks, President of the Royal Society of London, who, in the middle of Europe's political turmoils, has struggled ceaselessly to consolidate the ties that unite scientific men of all nations.

The same reasons that slowed our communications also delayed the publication of our work, which has to be accompanied by a number of engravings and maps. If such difficulties are met when governments are paying, how much worse they are when paid by private individuals. It would have been impossible to overcome these difficulties if the enthusiasm of the editors had not been matched by public reaction. More than two thirds of our work has now been published. The maps of the Orinoco, the Casiquiare and the Magdalena rivers, based on my astronomical observations, together with several hundred plants, have been engraved and are ready to appear. I shall not leave Europe on my Asian journey before I have finished publishing my travels to the New World.

In our publications Bonpland and I have considered every phenomenon under different aspects, and classed our observations according to the relations they each have with one another. To convey an idea of the method followed, I will outline what we used in order to describe the volcanoes of Antisana and Pichincha, as well as Jorullo, which on the night of the 20th of September 1759 rose 1,578 feet up from the plains of Mexico. We fixed the position of these remarkable mountains in longitude and latitude by astronomical observations. We took the heights of different parts with a barometer, and determined the dip of the needle and magnetic forces. We collected plants that grew on the slopes of these volcanoes, and specimens of different rocks. We found out the exact height above sea-level at which we made each collection. We noted down the humidity, the temperature, the electricity and the transparency of the air on the brinks of Pichincha and Jorullo; we drew the topographical plans and geological profiles of these volcanoes by measuring vertical bases and altitude angles. In order to judge the correctness of our calculations we have preserved all the details of our field notes.

We could have included all these details in a work devoted solely to volcanoes in Peru and New Spain. Had I written the physical description of a single province I could have incorporated separate chapters on geography, mineralogy and botany, but how could I break the narrative of our travels, or an essay on customs and the great phenomena of general physics, by tiresomely enumerating the produce of the land, or describing new species and making dry astronomical observations? Had I decided to write a book that included in the same chapter everything observed from the same spot, it would have been excessively long, quite lacking in the clarity that comes from a methodical distribution of subject matter. Despite the efforts made to avoid these errors in this narration of my journey, I am aware that I have not always succeeded in separating the observations of detail from the general results that interest all educated minds. These results should bring together the influence of climate on organized beings, the look of the landscape, the variety of soils and plants, the mountains and rivers that separate tribes as much as plants. I do not regret lingering on these interesting objects for modern civilization can be characterized by how it broadens our ideas, making us perceive the connections between the physical and the intellectual worlds. It is likely that my travel journal will interest many more readers than my purely scientific researches into the population, commerce and mines in New Spain.

After dividing all that belongs to astronomy, botany, zoology, the political description of New Spain, and the history of the ancient civilizations of certain New World nations into separate works, many general results and local descriptions remained left over, which I could still collect into separate treatises. I had prepared several during my journey; on races in South America; on the Orinoco missions; on what hinders civilization in the torrid zone, from the climate to the vegetation; the landscape of the Andes compared to the Swiss Alps; analogies between the rocks of the two continents; the air in the equinoctial regions, etc. I had left Europe with the firm decision not to write what is usually called the historical narrative of a journey, but just to publish the results of my researches. I had arranged the facts not as they presented themselves individually but in their relationships to each other. Surrounded by such powerful nature, and all the things seen every day, the traveller feels no inclination to record in a journal all the ordinary details of life that happen to him.

During my navigation up the South American rivers, and over

land, I had written a very brief itinerary where I described on the spot what I saw when I climbed the summit of a volcano or any other mountain, but I did not continue my notes in the towns, or when busy with something else. When I did take notes my only motive was to preserve those fugitive ideas that occur to a naturalist, to make a temporary collection of facts and first impressions. But I did not think at the time that these jotted-down notes would form the basis of a work offered to the public. I thought that my journey might add something to science, but would not include those colourful details that are the main interest in journeys.

Since my return the difficulties I experienced trying to write a number of treatises and make certain phenomena known have overcome my reluctance to write the narrative of my journey. In doing this I have been guided by a number of respectable people. I realized that even scientific men, after presenting their researches, feel that they have not satisfied their public if they do not also write up their journal.

A historical narrative covers two quite different aims: whatever happens to the traveller; and the observations he makes during his journey. Unity of composition, which distinguishes good work from bad, can be sought only when the traveller describes what he has seen with his own eyes, and when he has concentrated on the different customs of people, and the great phenomena of nature, rather than on scientific observations. The most accurate picture of customs is one that deals with man's relationships with other men. What characterizes savage and civilized life is captured either through the difficulties encountered by a traveller or by the sensations he feels. It is the man himself we wish to see in contact with the objects around him. His narration interests us far more if a local colouring informs the descriptions of the country and its people. This is what excites us in the narrations of the early navigators who were driven more by guts than by scientific curiosity and struggled against the elements as they sought a new world in unknown seas.

The more travellers research into natural history, geography or political economy, the more their journey loses that unity and simplicity of composition typical of the earlier travellers. It is now virtually impossible to link so many different fields of research in a narrative so that what we may call the dramatic events give way to descriptive passages. Most readers, who prefer to be agreeably amused to being solidly instructed, gain nothing from expeditions loaded with instruments and collections.

To give some variety to my work I have often interrupted the historical narrative with straightforward descriptions. I begin by describing the phenomena as they appeared to me, then I consider their individual relations to the whole.

I have included details about our everyday life that might be useful to any who follow us in the same countries. I have retained only a few of those personal incidents that offer no interest to readers, and amuse us only when well written.

Concerning the country I have travelled through, I am fully aware of the great advantages enjoyed by those who travel to Greece, Egypt, the banks of the Euphrates, and the Pacific Islands over those who travel to America. In the Old World the nuances and differences between nations form the main focus of the picture. In the New World, man and his productions disappear, so to speak, in the midst of a wild and outsize nature. In the New World the human race has been preserved by a few scarcely civilized tribes, or by the uniform customs and institutions transplanted on to foreign shores by European colonists. Facts about the history of our species, different kinds of government and monuments of art affect us far more than descriptions of vast emptinesses destined for plants and wild animals.

If America does not occupy an important place in the history of mankind, and in the revolutions that have shattered the world, it does offer a wide field for a naturalist. Nowhere else does nature so vividly suggest general ideas on the cause of events, and their mutual inter-relationships. I do not mean by this solely the overpowering vegetation and freshness of organic life, the different climates we experience as we climb the cordilleras and navigate those immense rivers, but also the geology and natural history of an unknown continent. A traveller can count himself lucky if he has taken advantage of his travels by adding new facts to the mass of those previously discovered!

Connected by the most intimate bonds of friendship over the five years of our travels (and since then), Bonpland and I have jointly published the whole of our work.[2] I have tried to explain what we both observed but, as this work has been written from my notes on the spot, all errors that might arise are solely mine. In this introduction I would also like to thank Gay-Lussac and Arago, my colleagues at the Institute, who have added their names to important work done, and who possess that high-mindedness which all who share a passion for science should have. Living in intimate friendship I have consulted them daily on matters of chemistry, natural history and mathematics.

Since I have returned from America one of those revolutions that shake the human race has broken out in the Spanish colonies, and promises a new future for the 14 million inhabitants spread out from La Plata to the remotest areas in Mexico. Deep resentments, exacerbated by colonial laws and maintained by suspicious policies, have stained with bloodshed areas that for three centuries once enjoyed not happiness but at least uninterrupted peace. Already in Quito the most educated citizens have been killed fighting for their country. While writing about certain areas I remembered the loss of dear friends.[3]

When we reflect on the great political upheavals in the New World we note that Spanish Americans are in a less fortunate position than the inhabitants of the United States, who were more prepared for independence by constitutional liberty. Internal feuds are inevitable in regions where civilization has not taken root and where, thanks to the climate, forests soon cover all cleared land if agriculture is abandoned. I fear that for many years no foreign traveller will be able to cross those countries I visited. This circumstance may increase the interest of a work that portrays the state of the greater part of the Spanish colonies at the turn of the nineteenth century. I also venture to hope, once peace has been established, that this work may contribute to a new social order. If some of these pages are rescued from oblivion, those who live on the banks of the Orinoco or Atabapo may see cities enriched by commerce and fertile fields cultivated by free men on the very spot where during my travels I saw impenetrable jungle and flooded lands.

Paris, February 1812.

CHAPTER I

*Preparations – Departure from Spain – Landing at
the Canary Islands*

From my earliest days I felt the urge to travel to distant lands seldom visited by Europeans. This urge characterizes a moment when our life seems to open before us like a limitless horizon in which nothing attracts us more than intense mental thrills and images of positive danger. I was brought up in a country that has no relations with either of the Indies, and I lived in mountains far from the sea and famous for their working mines, yet I felt an increasing passion for the sea and a yearning to travel far overseas. What we glean from travellers' vivid descriptions has a special charm; whatever is far off and suggestive excites our imagination; such pleasures tempt us far more than anything we may daily experience in the narrow circle of sedentary life. My taste for botanizing and the study of geology, with the chance of a trip to Holland, England and France accompanied by Georg Forster, who was lucky enough to travel with Captain Cook on his second world tour, helped determine the travel plans I had been hatching since I was eighteen years old. What attracted me about the torrid zone was no longer the promise of a wandering life full of adventures, but a desire to see with my own eyes a grand, wild nature rich in every conceivable natural product, and the prospect of collecting facts that might contribute to the progress of science. Personal circumstances prevented me from carrying out these absorbing plans, and for six years I had the leisure to prepare myself for the observations I would make in the New World by travelling through several European countries and exploring the Alps, whose structure I would later compare with the Andes between Quito and Peru.

During that time a voyage to explore the Pacific was being planned in France, under the direction of Captain Baudin.[4] The early plan was daring and grand, and would have been better entrusted to a more enlightened man. The idea was to travel across the Spanish colonies in South America from the mouth of the River Plate to the kingdom of Quito and the Panama isthmus. The two corvettes would then proceed to New Holland through the Pacific archipelagoes, stopping at Madagascar and returning home round the Cape of Good Hope. I had arrived in Paris when the preparations for the voyage had just begun. I had little faith in Captain Baudin's character as he had given me cause to be suspicious in the Viennese Court when charged to accompany one of my friends to Brazil, but as I could never with my own resources have afforded such a far-reaching expedition, nor visited such a beautiful part of the earth, I decided to risk taking part in the expedition. I got permission to embark with my instruments on one of the corvettes destined for the Pacific, and I did this on the agreement that I could leave Captain Baudin whenever it suited me. Michaux, who had visited Persia and parts of North America, and Bonpland, who became and remained a close friend, were also to accompany this expedition as naturalists.

I met the Swedish Consul Skiöldebrand, who passed through Paris on his way to embark in Marseille on a mission to bring gifts to the Dey of Algiers. That respectable gentleman had lived for a long time on the African coast and, as he was well known in the Algerian Court, could get me authorization to visit the Atlas mountains. Every year he despatched a ship to Tunis, which brought pilgrims to Mecca, and he promised to let me go to Egypt that way. I did not hesitate to seize that chance and was convinced I could carry out the plan I had hatched before my arrival in France. Up until then no geologist had ever explored the high mountain ranges that in Morocco reach the perpetual snows. I quickly completed my collection of instruments and obtained books that dealt with the countries I was to visit. I said goodbye to my brother, whose example and advice had helped guide my thinking. He approved of my motives for wanting to abandon Europe; a secret voice told me we would see each other again. I left Paris eager to embark for Algeria and Egypt, and chance – so often playing a decisive role in human lives – had it that I would see my brother again after returning from the Amazon and Peru, without putting a foot on African soil.

The Swedish frigate that was to convey Skiöldebrand to Algeria was expected at Marseille towards the end of October. Bonpland and

I rushed there in case we arrived late and missed the boat. We did not predict the new set-backs that were soon to crop up.

Skiöldebrand was as impatient as we were to reach his destination. Several times a day we would climb the Notre-Dame de la Garde mountain, which dominated a wide stretch of the Mediterranean. Every sail that appeared on the horizon excited us. But after two months of waiting we heard through the newspapers that the Swedish frigate had been badly damaged in a storm off Portugal, and had put into Cádiz to refit. Private letters then confirmed this news; the *Jaramas* (as it was called) would not reach Marseille before the spring.

We did not feel like prolonging our stay in Provence until the spring. The countryside, and especially the climate, were a delight, but the sight of the sea continuously reminded us of the failure of our plans. During a trip we made to Hyères and Toulon we came across the frigate *La Boudeuse*, bound for Corsica, which had been under the command of Bougainville[5] during his world voyage. This famous navigator had been particularly kind to me during my stay in Paris while I prepared to join Captain Baudin. I cannot describe the impression that this ship, which had carried Commerson to the Pacific, had on me. There are moments in our lives when painful feelings mingle with our experiences.

We resolved to spend the winter in Spain, hoping to embark from Cartagena or Cádiz in the spring, if the political situation in the east permitted this. We crossed the kingdoms of Catalonia and Valencia to reach Madrid. On the way we visited the ruins of Tarragona and ancient Saguntum. From Barcelona we made an excursion to Montserrat, whose elevated peaks are inhabited by hermits. The contrast between luxuriant vegetation and desolate, bare rocks forms a peculiar scenery.

Arriving at Madrid I soon congratulated myself on my decision to visit the peninsula. Baron de Forell, Saxon Ambassador to the Spanish Court, received me in a friendly way that greatly favoured my project. To his knowledge of mineralogy he added a great interest in the progress of science. He let me know that under the patronage of an enlightened minister, Don Mariano Luis de Urquijo, I might be permitted to make a journey to the interior of Spanish America, at my own expense. After all the set-backs I had suffered I did not hesitate to take up this suggestion.

In March 1799 I was presented at the Court of Aranjuez and the King received me graciously. I explained the motives that prompted me to undertake a journey to the New World and the Philippines, and presented a memoir of my plans to the Secretary of State. Señor de Urquijo supported my petition and overcame every obstacle in my, path, proceeding with commendable generosity given I had no personal relationship with him. The zeal with which he helped me can be due only to his love for science.

I obtained two passports; one from the Secretary of State, the other from the Council of the Indies. Never before had such concessions been granted to a traveller, and never had the Spanish Government shown such confidence in a foreigner. To waylay all the possible reservations that the viceroys and captain-generals might raise concerning the nature and finality of my work, it said in my safe conduct from the First Secretary of State that 'I was authorized to freely use my physical and geodesical instruments, that in all the Spanish possessions I could make astronomical observations, measure the height of mountains, collect whatever grew on the ground, and carry out any task that might advance the Sciences.'⁶

For the past year so many obstacles had crossed my path that I could hardly believe that at last my innermost desires would be fulfilled. We left Madrid in the middle of May and crossed Old Castile and the kingdoms of León and Galicia to La Coruña, where we were to embark for the island of Cuba. The winter had been long and hard but now, during our journey, we enjoyed the mild temperatures of spring that in the south usually begin in March or April. Snow still covered the tall granitic peaks of the Guadarrama but in the deep Galician valleys, which reminded me of the picturesque scenery of Switzerland and the Tyrol, the rocks were covered in flowering cistus and arborescent heaths. The traveller is happy to quit the Castilian plains devoid of vegetation and their intense winter cold and summers of oppressive heat.

The First Secretary of State had particularly recommended Brigadier Rafael Clavijo, recently appointed Inspector General of Maritime Couriers. This officer advised us to board the corvette *Pizarro*, bound for Havana and Mexico. This light frigate was not famed for its sailing speed, although during its long journey from the River Plate it had luckily just escaped English men-of-war. Clavijo sent instructions to the *Pizarro* to authorize the loading of our instruments, and to allow us to carry out atmospheric tests during the sea-voyage. The captain was ordered to stop at Tenerife and remain there as long as was needed for us to visit the port of Orotava and climb the Pico de Teide.

The harbours of Ferrol and La Coruña both communicate with the same bay, so a ship driven by foul weather towards the coast may anchor in either, according to the wind. Such an advantage is invaluable where the sea is almost always rough, as it is between Capes Ortegal and Finisterre, the promontories Trileucum and Artabrum of ancient geography. A narrow passage, flanked by perpendicular granite rocks, leads to the extensive bay of Ferrol. No port in Europe offers such an extraordinary anchorage, from its very inland position. The narrow and tortuous passage by which vessels enter this port has been opened, either by the pounding of waves or the reiterated shocks of very violent earthquakes. In the New World, on the coasts of New Andalusia, the Laguna del Obispo is formed exactly like the port of Ferrol. The most curious geological phenomena are often repeated at immense distances on the surface of different continents; and naturalists who have examined different parts of the globe are struck by the extreme resemblances observed in the fracturing of coasts, in the sinuosities of the valleys, in the appearance of mountains, and in their distribution by groups. The accidental concurrence of the same causes must everywhere have produced the same effects; and amidst the variety of nature an analogy of structure and form is observed in the arrangement of inanimate matter, as well as in the internal organization of plants and animals.

The moment of leaving Europe for the first time is impressive. We vainly recall the frequency of communications between the two worlds; we vainly reflect how, thanks to the improved state of navigation, we may now cross the Atlantic, which compared to the Pacific is but a shortish arm of the sea; yet what we feel when we begin our first long-distance voyage is none the less accompanied by a deep emotion, unlike any we may have felt in our youth. Separated from the objects of our dearest affections, and entering into a new life, we are forced to fall back on ourselves, and we feel more isolated than we have ever felt before.[7]

A thick fog that hid the horizon warned us at last – to our delight – that the weather was changing. On the evening of the 4th of June the north-east wind, so constant on the Galician coast at this time of year, began blowing. On the 5th the *Pizarro* set sail, despite the news, which had reached the watch-tower at Sisarga a few hours previously, that an English squadron was bound for the Tagus river mouth. Those who came to watch our corvette weigh anchor warned us by shouting that within three days we would be captured and would have to follow our ship into Lisbon. This forecast worried us.

By two in the afternoon the *Pizarro* was under sail. The channel that ships follow to leave the port of La Coruña is long and narrow. As it opens towards the north, and as the wind blew against us, we had to tack eight times, three of which were useless. We manoeuvred very clumsily, and once dangerously, as the current dragged us close to some reefs against which waves noisily broke. We stared at the San Antonio castle where the luckless Malaspina[8] fretted in a State prison. At this moment of leaving Europe to visit those countries this illustrious traveller had so fruitfully visited, I would rather have thought about something less sad.

At half past six we passed the Tower of Hercules, which acts as the La Coruña lighthouse, at the top of which a coal light has been kept burning from remote times to guide ships. At around nine we spotted the light of a fisherman's hut at Sisarga, the last we would see on the European coast. Soon distance weakened that feeble light, which we began to confuse with stars on the horizon, but our eyes refused to stop staring at it. These impressions are never forgotten by those who begin a long ocean journey at an age when their feelings remain vivid and profound. So many memories are awoken in our imagination by a dot of light in a dark night, flickering on and off above the rough waves, signalling our home land!

At sunset on the 8th of June the look-out sighted from his crow's-nest a British convoy sailing along the coast towards the south-east. To avoid it we altered our course during the night. We were also given orders not to put our lights on in the great cabin so that we would not be seen from afar. We constantly had to use dark-lanterns to make our observations of the sea's temperature, or read the markings on our astronomical instruments. In the torrid zone, where twilight lasts a few minutes, we were condemned to inaction, in similar circumstances, from six in the evening. For me this was particularly irritating as I have never suffered from seasickness and no sooner am I on board than I feel the urge to work more than ever.[9]

From La Coruña to the 36th degree of latitude we had scarcely seen any living creature apart from sea swallows and a few dolphins. We searched in vain for seaweed and molluscs. On the 11th of June we were struck by a curious sight that later we would see often in the Pacific. We reached a zone where the sea seemed covered with an enormous amount of jellyfish. The boat could hardly move, though the jellyfish floated towards the south-east four times faster than the current. This procession lasted some forty-five minutes; then we saw a few scattered and exhausted ones struggling to follow the main bunch, as if tired of their journey.

Between Madeira and the African coast we were almost becalmed, which suited me perfectly as I could carry out my magnetic experiments. We never tired of admiring the magnificent nights; nothing approaches the clarity and serenity of the African sky. We were struck by the extraordinary number of shooting stars that crossed the night sky. The further south we advanced, the more we saw, especially near the Canary Islands. When we were about 40 leagues east of Madeira, a common swallow (*Hirundo rustica*) landed on the topmast. It was so exhausted we easily caught it. What drives a bird so far off its course at such a calm time of year?

The *Pizarro* had orders to anchor off the island of Lanzarote, one of the seven large Canary Islands, to find out if the English were still blockading the Santa Cruz bay. From the 15th we were dubious about which route to follow. Finally, on the 16th, at two in the afternoon, we sighted land, which looked like a little cloud stuck on the horizon. At five, with the sun very low, we could clearly see the island of Lanzarote before us.

The current dragged us towards the coast with more force than was safe. As we advanced we saw first the island of Fuerteventura, famous for the many camels that live there, and then later the small island of Lobos, in the channel that separates Fuerteventura from Lanzarote. We spent the night on deck; the moon illumined the island's volcanic peaks, whose slopes, covered in ash, shone like silver.

The night was beautifully serene and fresh; although we were only a short distance from the African coast and the limit of the torrid zone, the thermometer recorded only 18 °C. It seemed as if the phosphorescence of the sea heightened the mass of light diffused in the air. After midnight great black clouds rose behind the volcano and intermittently covered the moon and the beautiful Scorpion constellation. On the shore we saw lights move in all directions; probably fishermen getting ready for work. During the voyage we had been reading the ancient Spanish navigators, and those moving lights reminded us of Pedro Gutiérrez,[10] Queen Isabel's page, who saw similar lights on Guanahani Island on the memorable night the New World was discovered.

The island of Lanzarote used to be called Titeroigotra. When the Spaniards arrived its inhabitants differed from those on the other islands by their superior culture. They built their houses with cut stones while the Guanches of Tenerife lived in caves like troglodytes. At that time a strange custom – repeated only in Tibet – prevailed. A woman had several husbands, who each took it in turn to exercise the rights of the head of the family. Each husband was known as such during a lunar month; then another took his place while he returned to being a servant in the house. In the fifteenth century the island of Lanzarote consisted of two states separated by a wall; a kind of monument, which outlives national enmities, found also in Scotland, Peru and China.

Guessing from some signs on an old Portuguese map, the captain of the *Pizarro* thought we were opposite a small fort built north of Teguise, the capital of Lanzarote. Mistaking some basaltic crags for a castle he saluted it properly by hoisting the Spanish flag and sending a boat with an officer to the supposed fort to find out if the English were lurking in these waters. We were not a little surprised to discover that the land we took for the coast of Lanzarote was the small island of Graciosa, and that for several leagues around there was not a sound of life.

We took the opportunity to use the boat to survey the land around the large bay. No words can evoke the feelings of a naturalist who first steps on soil outside Europe. So many objects call for his attention that it is hard to order his impressions. At each step he thinks he is coming across something new, and in his excitement he does not recognize things that commonly feature in botanical gardens and natural history collections. Two hundred yards off the coast we saw a man fishing with a rod. We turned the boat towards him but he fled and hid behind a rock. It took our sailors some effort to capture him. The sight of the corvette, the thunder of our cannons in such a solitary place – possibly visited only by pirates – the launching of our boat, all this terrified the poor fisherman. He informed us that the island of Graciosa on which we had landed was separated from Lanzarote by a small channel called El Río. He offered to guide us to Los Colorados harbour to find out about the blockade at Tenerife but, when the man assured us that for weeks he had not seen any ships out at sea, the captain decided to set sail for Santa Cruz.

We re-embarked at sunset and set sail, but the breeze was too weak to enable us to follow our route to Tenerife. The sea was calm; a reddish haze covered the horizon, seeming to magnify everything. In such solitudes, surrounded by so many uninhabited islands, we savoured the view of such a grandiose and wild nature. The black mountains of Graciosa had perpendicular walls some 500 to 600 feet high. Their shadows, projected across the sea, made the scene gloomy. The basalt rocks stuck out of the water like the ruins of a vast building. Their existence reminded us of that bygone age when underwater volcanoes gave birth to new islands, or destroyed continents. Everything around us spoke of destruction and sterility; yet beyond this scene the coast of Lanzarote seemed more friendly. In a narrow gorge, between two hills crowned with scattered trees, you could see some cultivated land. The last rays of sun lit up the ripe corn, ready for harvesting. Even the desert is animated when you see some trace of man's work in it.

On the morning of the 18th the wind freshened a little and we managed to pass through the channel. We lost sight of the small islands of Alegranza, Montaña Clara and Graciosa, which appear to have been inhabited by the Guanches. People visit them now only to gather archil,[11] but this is less sought after since so many north European lichens yield better dyes. Montaña Clara is noted for its beautiful canary-birds. There are also goats, proof that the interior of the island is not as desolate as the coast we had seen.[12]

CHAPTER 2

Stay at Tenerife — Journey from Santa Cruz to Orotava —
Excursion to the top of the Pico de Teide

From the time we left Graciosa the sky remained so consistently hazy that despite the height of the mountains of Gran Canaria we did not make out the island until the evening of the 18th. It is the granary of the archipelago of the Fortunate Islands and, remarkably for an area outside the Tropics, there are two wheat harvests a year, one in February, the other in June. Gran Canaria has never been visited before by a geologist, yet it is worth observing because its mountains differ entirely from those of Lanzarote and Tenerife.

On the morning of the 19th of June we caught sight of the point of Naga, but the Pico de Teide remained invisible. Land stood out vaguely because a thick fog effaced the details. As we approached the natural bay of Santa Cruz we watched the mist, driven by wind, draw near. The sea was very rough, as it usually is in this place. After much sounding we anchored. The fog was so thick that visibility was limited to a few cables' length. Just as we were about to fire the customary salute the fog suddenly dissipated and the Pico de Teide appeared in a clearing above the clouds, illuminated by the first rays of sun, which had not reached us yet. We rushed to the bow of the corvette not to miss this marvellous spectacle, but at that very same moment we saw four English warships hove to near our stern, not far out in the open sea. We had passed them closely by in the thick fog that had prevented us from seeing the peak, and had thus been saved from the danger of being sent back to Europe. It would have been distressing for naturalists to have seen the Tenerife coasts from far off and not to have been able to land on soil crushed by volcanoes. We quickly weighed anchor and the *Pizarro* approached the fort as closely as possible to be under its protection. Here, two years before in an attempted landing, Admiral Nelson lost his arm to a cannon-ball. The English ships left the bay; a few days earlier they had chased the packet-boat *Alcudia*, which had left La Coruña just before we did. It had been forced into Las Palmas harbour, and several passengers were captured while being transferred to Santa Cruz in a launch.

The location of the town of Santa Cruz is similar to La Guaira, the busiest port in the province of Caracas. The heat is excessive in both places, but Santa Cruz is sadder. On a deserted sandy beach, houses of a dazzling white with flat roofs and windows without panes lie close to a rocky cliff stripped of vegetation. A fine stone quay and public walk planted with poplars are the only attraction in that monotonous picture. From Santa Cruz the peak seems far less picturesque than it does from the port of Orotava. There a smiling and richly cultivated plain contrasts with the wild appearance of the volcano. From the groves of palm and banana trees on the shore to the region of strawberry trees, laurels and pine the volcanic rock is covered with luxuriant vegetation. It is easy to see why the inhabitants of the beautiful climates of Greece and Italy thought they had discovered one of the Fortunate Isles on the western part of Tenerife. The eastern Santa Cruz side is everywhere marked with sterility.

After answering tiresome questions about political events from those who came on board, we landed. The boat was straightaway sent back to the ship in case the surf, which in this bay is dangerous, should crush it against the wharf. Our attention was first caught by a tall woman, of a brownish complexion and badly dressed, called the *capitana*. She was followed by several other women, equally badly dressed. They tried to board the *Pizarro* but were refused. In this harbour, frequented by Europeans, licentiousness seems to be quite ordered. The *capitana* is chosen by her companions, she ensures that no injuries are done to sailors, and then sends them back on board at the right time. Officers seek her out if they think one of their crew might be hiding on land to desert later.

When we stepped into the streets of Santa Cruz the heat was suffocating, though the thermometer recorded only 25 °C. After breathing sea air for such a long time one suffers on land, not because the air contains more oxygen at sea but because it is less charged with the gases emanating from rotting animal and vegetable substances.

Santa Cruz, the Añaza of the Guanches, is a pretty town of some 8,000 people. I was not struck by the vast number of monks that travellers always find in the Spanish possessions, nor shall I bother to describe the churches, the Dominican library with its meagre 200 tomes; nor the quay where people meet in the evening to enjoy the fresh air, nor the famous 30-foot-high monument in Cararra marble dedicated to Our Lady of Candelaria in memory of the virgin's miraculous appearance in 1392 in Chimisay, near Güimar. The port of Santa Cruz is in fact a great caravanserai on the route to America and India. Every traveller who writes his adventures begins by describing Madeira and Tenerife, though the natural history of these islands remains quite unknown.

The recommendations from the Madrid Court assured us that we were always well received in all the Spanish possessions. The Captain-General immediately gave us permission to visit the island. Colonel Armiaga, in command of an infantry regiment, warmly welcomed us to his house. We did not tire of admiring the banana trees, the papaw trees, the *Poinciana pulcherrima* and other plants usually seen only in greenhouses.

Although the captain of the *Pizarro* had orders to remain long enough at Tenerife to allow us to climb the peak, snow permitting, he let us know that the English ships' blockade meant that we could not count on a stay of more than four or five days. So we hurried to the port of Orotova on the western slope of the volcano where we hoped to find guides. Nobody in Santa Cruz had ever climbed to the summit of the mountain.

On the 20th of June, before sunrise, we set off for the Villa de Laguna, some 350 toises[13] above Santa Cruz harbour. The narrow and tortuous path leading to La Laguna climbs along a torrent, which in the rainy season turns into fine cascades. Near the town we met some white camels, barely laden. These animals are mainly used to transport goods from the customs house to the merchants. Camels are not numerous in Tenerife, while in Lanzarote and Fuerteventura there are thousands.

As we approached La Laguna the air cooled. This sensation delighted us as we found the air in Santa Cruz asphyxiating. As we tend to feel disagreeable sensations more strongly, we felt the change in temperature more as we returned from La Laguna to the port, as if we were approaching the mouth of a furnace.

The perpetual cool that prevails in La Laguna makes the city the favourite home for the inhabitants of the Canaries. The residential capital of Tenerife is magnificently placed in a small plain surrounded by gardens at the foot of a hill crowned with laurel, myrtle and strawberry trees. It would be a mistake to rely on some travellers who believe the town lies by a lake. The rain sometimes forms an enormous sheet of water, and a geologist who sees the past rather than the present state of nature in everything would not doubt that the whole plain was once a great lake, now dried up. La Laguna has fallen from its opulence since the erupting volcano destroyed the port of Garachico and Santa Cruz became the trading centre of the island. It has no more than 9,000 inhabitants, with nearly 400 monks distributed in six convents, though some travellers insist half the population wear cassocks. Numerous windmills surround the city, a sign that wheat is cultivated in this high country. The Guanches called wheat at Tenerife *tano*, at Lanzarote *triffa*; barley in Gran Canaria was called *aramotanoque*, and at Lanzarote *tamosen*. The flour of roasted barley (*gofio*) and goat's milk constituted the main food of these people about whose origins so many systematic fables have been written.

Many chapels, called *ermitas* by the Spaniards, surround La Laguna. Built on hillocks among evergreen trees, these chapels add a picturesque effect to the countryside. The interior of the town does not correspond at all to its outskirts. The houses are solid, but very ancient, and the streets sad. A botanist should not complain of the age of these houses for the roofs and walls are covered with *Sempervivum canariensis* and the pretty trichomanes, mentioned by every traveller. The plants are watered by the abundant mists.

The ground of the island rises to form an amphitheatre and, as in Peru and Mexico, contains in miniature all the possible climates, from African heat to alpine cold.[14] The mean temperatures of Santa Cruz, the port of Orotava, Orotava itself and La Laguna form a descending series. In southern Europe the change of seasons is too strongly felt to offer the same advantages. Tenerife on the other hand, on the threshold of the Tropics and a few days' journey from Spain, benefits from a good part of what nature has lavished in the Tropics. Its flora include the beautiful and imposing bananas and palms. He who is able to feel nature's beauty finds in this precious island a far more effective remedy than the climate. Nowhere else in the world seems more appropriate to dissipate melancholy and restore peace to troubled minds than Tenerife and Madeira. These effects are due not only to the magnificent situation and to the purity of air, but above all to the absence of slavery, which so deeply revolts us in all those places where Europeans have brought what they call their 'enlightenment' and their 'commerce' to their colonies.

The valley of Tacoronte leads one into a delicious country glowingly spoken of by all travellers. In the Tropics I found places where nature is more grand and richer in its varieties; but after crossing the Orinoco, the Peruvian cordilleras and the valleys of Mexico I admit that I have never seen a more attractive, more harmonious view in the distribution of greenery and rocks than the western coast of Tenerife.

The sea coast is fringed with date and coconut palms; above them groups of banana trees stand out from the dragon trees whose trunks are often rightly compared to snakes' bodies. The hills are covered in vines, which grow over high stakes. Orange trees loaded with blossom, myrtle and cypress surround chapels raised devotedly by the islanders on cleared hilltops. Land is divided by hedges made of agave and cactus. Innumerable cryptogamous plants, predominantly fern, cover the walls moistened by small clear-water springs. In winter when the volcano is covered with snow and ice this place enjoys an eternal spring. In summer, as the evening falls, a sea breeze freshens the air. The coastal population is very dense and appears to be even greater because the houses and gardens are scattered, increasing the picturesque aspect. Unhappily, the wealth of the inhabitants does not correspond with hard work or with nature's richness. Those who work the land are not its owners; the fruit of their labour belongs to the nobility and the feudal system that for so long was the shame of Europe and still prevents the people's progress here.

On our way to the port of Orotava we passed through the pretty villages of Matanza and Victoria. These names are found together in all the Spanish colonies and contrast in an ugly way with the peaceful feelings those countries inspire. Matanza signifies slaughter, and the word alone recalls the price at which victory was won. In the New

World it generally indicates the defeat of the Indians; at Tenerife the village of Matanza was built in a place where the Spaniards were defeated by the Guanches, who were soon sold as slaves in Europe.[15]

By the morning of the 21st of June we were on our way to the volcano's summit. The day was not fine and the peak's summit, generally visible from Orotava from sunrise to ten at night, was covered in cloud. What links an excursion to the peak with similar ones to Chamonix or Etna is that one is obliged to follow guides, and sees only what has already been seen and described by previous travellers.

From a distance Villa de la Orotava pleases because of the many streams running down the main streets. The Agua Mansa spring, trapped in two large reservoirs, turns several mills and is then released in the nearby vineyards. The climate in the town is even more refreshing than in the port as a strong wind always blows from ten in the morning onwards. Because of the altitude water evaporates in the air and frequently precipitates to make the climate misty. The town lies 160 toises above sea-level; which is 200 toises lower than La Laguna; it was noted that plants flower a month later here.

Orotava, the ancient Taoro of the Guanches, lies on an abrupt slope of a hill. The streets seemed deserted; the houses solidly built but melancholic; they nearly all belong to a nobility accused of being too proud, presumptuously calling itself the Twelve Houses. We passed along a high aqueduct lined with luxuriant fern, and visited many gardens where northern European fruit trees grow along with orange, pomegranate and date trees. Even though we knew about Franqui's dragon tree[16] from previous travellers, its enormous thickness amazed us. We were told that this tree, mentioned in several ancient documents, served as a boundary mark and already in the fifteenth century was as enormous as it is today. We calculated its height to be about 50 to 60 feet; its circumference a little above its roots measured 45 feet. The trunk is divided into many branches, which rise up in the form of a chandelier and end in tufts of leaves similar to the Mexican yucca.

This tree, which grows only in cultivated areas in the Canaries, Madeira and Porto Santo, presents a curious phenomenon in plant migration. In Africa it has never been found in a wild state, and its country of origin is East India. How has this tree become acclimatized in Tenerife? Did the Guanches have contact with nations originally from Asia?

From Orotava, along a narrow and stony path through a beautiful chestnut forest (*el monte de castaños*), we reached an area covered with brambles, laurels and arboreal heaths. The trunks of the latter grow to an extraordinary size and their mass of flowers contrasts agreeably with the abundant *Hypericum canariensis*. We stopped under a solitary pine to fill up with water. This place commanded a magnificent panorama over the sea and the western part of the island.

We continued to climb from this pine to the crater of the volcano without crossing one valley, for the ravines do not merit this name. To the eyes of a geologist the whole of the island is one mountain whose oval base is prolonged to the north-east and in which several systems of volcanic rock, formed in different periods, may be distinguished.

Above the region of arborescent heaths, called Monte Verde, lies the region of ferns. Nowhere else have I seen such a profusion of pteris, blechnum and asplenium. The roots of the *Pteris aquilina* serve as food for the inhabitants of Palma and Gomera; they grate it to a powder and mix in a bit of barley flour, which when boiled is called *gofio*. The use of such a primitive food is proof of the misery of the peasants of the Canary Islands. Monte Verde is scored by several small and arid ravines. Above the zone of ferns we reached a juniper and pine wood, severely punished by storms.

We spent nearly two and a half hours crossing this plain, which is nothing but an immense sea of sand. Despite the altitude the thermometer indicated 13.8 °C in the evening, 3.7 °C higher than at noon. We suffered continuously from the pumice-stone dust. In the midst of this plain are tufts of broom, *Spartium nubigenum*. This beautiful shrub grows to a height of some 9 feet and is covered with aromatic flowers with which the goat hunters we met in our path decorated their hats. The dark, chestnut-coloured goats of the peak are supposed to be very tasty as they eat the leaves of this plant, and have run wild in these wastes from time immemorial.

As far as the rock of Gayta, that is, up to the beginning of the great retama plain, the Tenerife peak is covered in beautiful vegetation, with no traces of recent devastations. But hardly have you entered the plain littered with pumice-stone than the countryside changes dramatically; at every step you trip over enormous obsidian blocks thrown down by the volcano. Everything here betrays a deep solitude. A few goats and rabbits are the only signs of life in this high plain. From up here the island becomes an immense heap of burned matter surrounded by a narrow fringe of vegetation.

Above the region of *Spartium nubigenum* we passed through narrow defiles and small, old ravines cut by rainwater to a higher plateau and then on to the place where we intended to spend the night, some 1,530 toises above the coast. This place is called Estancia de los Ingleses (English Halt) because most of the travellers who have scaled the peak have been English. Two protruding rocks form a kind of cave, which offers shelter from the wind. This point, higher than the summit of Canigou, can be reached on mule: many a curious traveller hoping to reach the crater's edge from Orotava have had to wait here. Despite it being summer and there being a blue African sky above us that night we froze; the thermometer dropped to 5 °C. Our guides lit a bonfire with dried retama branches. Without a tent or coats, we had to lie down on calcinated scree, and the flames and smoke that the wind drove ceaselessly towards us made it an extremely uncomfortable night. We had never spent a night so high up and I had no idea that we would soon live in cities higher than the summit of this volcano. The further the temperature plummeted, the thicker the clouds round the peak grew. A strong north wind dissipated them; at intervals the moon appeared, its white disk shining against a blue backdrop. With the volcano in sight, that night scene was truly majestic. Suddenly the peak would disappear completely in the mist, then it would reappear worryingly close, casting its shadow over the clouds below us like some monstrous pyramid.

Around three in the morning, lit by the dismal light of a few pine torches, we set off for the summit of the Piton. We began the ascent from the northern side, which is extremely steep. After two hours we reached a small plateau, named Alta Vista because of its height. The *neveros*, those natives who collect ice and snow to sell in the nearby towns, reach as far as this point. Their mules, better trained to climb than those hired by travellers, reach Alta Vista. The *neveros* then have to carry the collected snow on their shoulders as they go down. Beyond this point the *malpaís* begins. This term, in use in Mexico, Peru and all places where there are volcanoes, refers to regions stripped of vegetation and covered in lava fragments.

We turned to the right to visit the ice cave situated at 1,728 toises, just under the perpetual snow altitude limit. During winter the grotto fills with ice and snow and, as the sun's rays do not penetrate its interior, summer heat is unable to melt the frozen water.

Day was breaking when we left the ice cave. A layer of white fleecy cloud blocked out the lower regions of the surrounding islands. The clouds were spread out so uniformly and in such a flat way that they looked like an immense plain covered in snow. The colossal pyramid of the peak, the volcanic summits of Lanzarote, Fuerteventura and La Palma stuck up like reefs above a sea of fog. Their dark colour contrasted vividly with the whiteness of the clouds.

We were forced to cut our own track across the *malpaís*. The slope is very steep, and the volcanic blocks slipped under our feet. The rubble on the peak's summit has sharp edges and leaves gaps into which explorers risk falling up to their waists. Unfortunately the laziness and bad temper of our guides made this ascent more difficult. They were despairingly phlegmatic. The night before they had tried to convince us not to pass beyond the limit of the rocks. Every ten minutes they would sit down to rest; they threw away pieces of obsidian and pumice-stone that we had carefully collected. Finally we realized that none of them had ever visited the volcano's summit before.

After three hours' walking we reached a small plain called La Rambleta at the far end of the *malpaís*; from its centre rises the Piton or Sugar Loaf. From the Orotava side this mountain resembles those pyramids with steps found in Féjoun or Mexico. Here we found the air holes that locals call the Nostrils of the Peak (Narices del Pico). Hot watery vapours seep out at regular intervals from cracks in the rock, and the thermometer marked 43.2 °C. I cannot, however, accept the daring hypothesis which states that the Nostrils of the Peak are vents of an immense apparatus of distillation whose lower part is situated below sea-level. Since we have been studying volcanoes with more care, and since innate love for all that is marvellous is less common in geological books, doubts have been expressed about these constant and direct links between sea water and volcanic fire. There is a far simpler explanation of this phenomenon. The peak is covered with snow part of the year; we found snow still around on the Rambleta plain. This led us to conclude that the Tenerife peak, like the Andes and Manila islands' volcanoes, are filled with filtered water. The watery vapours emitted by the Nostrils and cracks of the crater are those same waters heated.

We had yet to climb the steepest part of the mountain, the Piton, which forms the summit. The slope of this small cone, covered with volcanic ashes and fragments of pumice-stone, is so steep that it would have been impossible to reach the top had we not been able to follow an old lava current that seemed to have flowed down from the crater and whose remains have defied the ravages of time. The debris forms a wall of scoria, which reaches into the loose ash. We climbed to the Piton by clinging to this sharp-edged scoria, which, worn down by the weather, often broke off in our hands. It took us half an hour to reach the top, though it was only some 90 toises above us.

When we reached the Piton's summit we were surprised to find that there was barely enough room to sit down comfortably. We faced a small circular wall of porphyritic lava, with a base of pitch-stone, which prevented us from seeing the interior of the crater called La Caldera or the Cauldron. The wind blew so hard from the west that we could scarcely stand on our feet. It was eight in the morning and we were frozen though the temperature was just above freezing-point. We had become accustomed to heat, and the dry wind increased the sensation of cold.

The brink of the crater does not resemble any of the other volcanoes I have visited, such as Vesuvius, Jorullo or Pichincha. On the peak the wall, which surrounds the crater like a parapet, is so high that it would not let you reach La Caldera were it not for a breach on the eastern side caused by a very ancient lava overflow. We climbed down through this gap to the bottom of the elliptical funnel.

The external edges of La Caldera are almost perpendicular, rather like the Somma seen from the Atrio del Cavallo. We got to the bottom of the crater following a trail of broken lava from the eastern breach of the wall. We only felt the heat above the crevices, which exhaled watery vapours with a strange buzzing sound. Some of these crevices can be found on the outside of the crater, on the external parapet that surrounds it. A thermometer placed inside one of them rose suddenly from 68 °C to 75 °C. This would have risen higher, but we had to pull the thermometer out to prevent our hands from being burned. It might be thought that these vapours, which escape in puffs of air, contain muriatic or sulphuric acids, but when condensed they had no particular taste. Experiments showed that these chimneys exhale pure water only.

While on the spot I sketched a view[17] of the crater's interior edge as it is seen on the descent through the eastern wall's breach. Nothing is more striking than the superimposition of these lava strata, which reveals similar sinuosities to the calcareous rock of the Alps. These enormous ledges, sometimes horizontal and sometimes sloping or undulating, reminded us that long ago the entire mass had flowed, and that a combination of disruptive causes determined a particular flow. The crest of the wall exhibits the same strange ramifications we find in coke. The northern edge is the highest. Towards the southwest the wall has considerably subsided and an enormous amount of scoria seems glued to the outer edge. On the west the rock is perforated, and through a wide opening you can see the sea and horizon. Perhaps the force of the steam broke through here just when the lava overflowed from the crater.

The bottom of the crater is reached with danger. In a volcano such as Vesuvius, whose main activity is directed towards the summit, the depth of the crater varies with each eruption, but at the Tenerife peak the depth appears to have remained unchanged for a long time. Judging from what I could see, the actual site of the crater is properly speaking a solfatara; an area for interesting but not striking observations. The majesty of the site is due more to its height above sea-level, to the profound silence of these elevated regions, and to the immense space over which the eye ranges from the mountain's summit.

A journey to the Tenerife volcano's summit is not solely interesting for the amount of phenomena available for scientific research but far more for the picturesque beauties offered to those who keenly feel the splendours of nature. It is a hard task to describe these sensations for they work on us so much more powerfully the more they are vague. When a traveller must describe the highest peaks, the river cataracts, the tortuous Andes valleys, he risks tiring his readers with the monotonous expression of his admiration. It seems better suited to my intentions in this narrative of my journey to evoke the particular character of each zone. We get to know the features of each region better the more we indicate its varying characteristics by comparing it with others. This method enables us to discover the sources of the pleasures conferred by the great picture of nature.

Travellers know by experience that views from the summits of high mountains are neither as beautiful, picturesque, nor as varied as those from the heights of Vesuvius, Righi or the Puy-de-Dôme. Colossal mountains such as Chimborazo, Antisana or Monte Rosa compose such a huge mass that the richly cultivated plains are seen only at a great distance where a bluish and watery tint spreads over the landscape. The Tenerife peak, due to its narrow shape and local position, combines the advantages of the less high summits with those of the very high. From its top we can see not only the sea to the horizon, but also the forests of Tenerife and the inhabited coastal strips, which seem so close that their shapes and tones stand out in beautiful contrasts. It could be said that the volcano crushes the little island that serves as its base, and that it shoots up from the depths of the seas to a height three times higher than cloud level in summer.

Seated on the crater's external edge we turned our eyes towards the north-east where the coasts are decorated with villages and hamlets. At our feet masses of mist, continually tossed about by the winds, changed shape all the time. A uniform layer of cloud between us and the lower regions of the island had been pierced here and there by wind currents sent up from the heated earth. The Orotava bay, its vessels at anchor, the gardens and vineyards round the town, appeared in an opening that seemed to enlarge all the time. From these solitary regions our eyes dived down to the inhabited world below; we enjoyed the striking contrasts between the peak's arid slopes, its steep sides covered with scoriae, its elevated plains devoid of vegetation, and the smiling spectacle of the cultivated land below. We saw how plants were distributed according to the decreasing temperatures of altitudes. Below the peak lichens begin to cover the scorious and polished lava; a violet (*Viola cheiranthifolia*) similar to the *Viola decumbens* climbs the volcano's slopes up to 1,740 toises above all other herbaceous plants. Tufts of flowering broom decorate the valleys hollowed out by the torrents and blocked by the effects of lateral eruptions. Below the retama lies the region of ferns, and then the arborescent heaths. Laurel, rhamnus and strawberry-tree woods grow between the scrub and the rising ground planted with vines and fruit trees. A rich green carpet extends from the plain of brooms and the zone of alpine plants to groups of date palms and banana trees whose feet are bathed by the ocean.

The apparent proximity of the hamlets, vineyards and coastal gardens from the summit is increased by the surprising transparency of the air. Despite the great distance we could not only pick out the houses, the tree trunks and the sails on the vessels, but also the vivid colouring of the plain's rich vegetation. The Pico de Teide is not situated in the Tropics, but the dryness of the air, which rises continuously above the neighbouring African plains and is rapidly blown over by the eastern winds, gives the atmosphere of the Canary Islands a transparency which not only surpasses that of the air around Naples and Sicily, but also of the air around Quito and Peru. This transparency may be one of the main reasons for the beauty of tropical scenery; it heightens the splendours of the vegetation's colouring, and contributes to the magical effects of its harmonies and contrasts. If the light tires the eyes during part of the day, the inhabitant of these southern regions has his compensation in a moral enjoyment, for a lucid clarity of mind corresponds to the surrounding transparency of the air.

Despite the heat the traveller feels under his feet on the brink of the crater, the cone of ashes remains covered with snow for several months. The cold, angry wind, which had been blowing since dawn, forced us to seek shelter at the foot of the Piton. Our hands and feet were frozen, while our boots were burned by the ground we walked on. In a few minutes we reached the foot of the Sugar Loaf, which we had so laboriously climbed; our speed of descent was in part involuntary as we slipped down on the ashes. We reluctantly abandoned that solitary place where nature had magnificently displayed herself before us. We deluded ourselves that we might again visit the Canary

Islands, but this, like many other plans, has never been carried out.

We crossed the *malpaís* slowly; for it is hard to walk securely on lava fragments. Nearer the Station of the Rocks the path down was extremely difficult; the short thick grass was so slippery that we were constantly forced to lean our bodies backwards in order not to fall. In the sandy plain of retama the thermometer rose to 22.5 °C; this heat seemed suffocating after the cold we had suffered on the summit. We had no more water; our guides had not only secretly drunk our small supply of malmsey wine but had also broken our water jugs.

In the beautiful region of the arborescent erica and fern we at last enjoyed some cool breezes, and we were wrapped in thick clouds, stationary at some 600 toises above sea-level.

Near the town of Orotava we came across great flocks of canaries. These birds, well known in Europe, were in general uniformly green; some had a yellowish tinge on their backs; their song was the same as that of the domesticated canary. It has been noted that those canaries captured in the island of Gran Canaria, and in the islet of Monte Clara, near Lanzarote, have a louder, more harmonious call. In every zone, among birds of the same species, each flock has its peculiar call. The yellow canaries are a variety now breeding in Europe; those we saw in cages had been bought at Cádiz and other Spanish ports. But the bird from the Canary Islands that has the most agreeable song is unknown in Europe. It is the *capirote*, which has never been tamed, so much does he love his freedom. I have enjoyed his sweet and melodious warbling in a garden in Orotava, but have never seen him close enough to judge what family he belongs to. As for the parrots supposedly seen during Captain Cook's stay at Tenerife, they never existed but in the narratives of some travellers who have copied from each other.

Towards sunset we reached the port of Orotava where we received the unexpected news that the *Pizarro* was not to sail until the 24th or 25th. Had we been warned of this delay we would have prolonged our stay on the peak, or made another journey to the volcano of Chahorra. The following day we visited the outskirts of Orotava and enjoyed the pleasant company that Cologan's house offered. We noticed that Tenerife had attractions not only for those who busy themselves with natural history; we found in Orotava several people who had a taste for literature and music, bringing their European sophistication with them to these distant islands. In this respect, with the exception of Havana, the Canary Islands bore no resemblance to any other Spanish colonies.

On the eve of Saint John's Day we were present at a country party in Little's garden. This gentleman, who greatly helped the Canarians during the last wheat famine, has cultivated a hill covered with volcanic debris. In this delicious place he has installed an English garden from which there is a magnificent view of the peak, of the villages along the coast, and of the island of Las Palmas on the edge of the great ocean. That view can only be compared to the views of Genoa and Naples bays; but Orotava is far superior to both in terms of the grandeur of its masses and the richness of its vegetation. As night fell the volcano's slopes presented us with a wonderful spectacle. Following a custom introduced by the Spaniards, though it dates back to remotest times, the shepherds lit the fires of Saint John. The scattered masses of fire and columns of smoke driven by the wind stood out from the deep green of the forests lining the peak. The shepherds' distant yells of joy were the only sounds that broke the silence of that night in those solitary places.[18]

Before we leave the Old World to cross over into the New there is a subject I must speak about because it belongs to the history of man, and to those fatal revolutions that have made whole tribes disappear from the earth. We ask in Cuba, in Santo Domingo and in Jamaica, where are the primitive inhabitants of these countries? We ask at Tenerife, what has become of the Guanches whose mummies alone, buried in caves, have escaped destruction? In the fifteenth century almost all the mercantile nations, especially the Spaniards and the Portuguese, sought slaves on the Canary Islands, as later they did on the Guinea coast. Christianity, which originally favoured the freedom of mankind, served later as a pretext for European cupidity.

A short time after the discovery of America, when Spain was at the zenith of her glory, the gentle character of the Guanches was the fashionable topic, just as in our times we praise the Arcadian innocence of the Tahitians. In both these pictures the colouring is more vivid than true. When nations are mentally exhausted and see the seeds of depravity in their refinements, the idea that in some distant region infant societies enjoy pure and perpetual happiness pleases them.

CHAPTER 3

*Crossing from Tenerife to the coasts of South America – Sighting
of Tobago – Arrival at Cumaná*

On the evening of the 25th of June we left Santa Cruz and set our
course for South America. A strong north-westerly was blowing and
tight, sharp waves were caused by strong currents. We soon lost sight
of the Canary Islands above whose high peaks a reddish mist appeared;
only the Pico de Teide reappeared briefly from time to time as the
wind dispersed the clouds surrounding the peak. For the first time we
realized how deeply we are stirred by the sight of land situated on the
limits of the torrid zone, where nature appears so opulent, grandiose
and marvellous. We had stayed at Tenerife for a few days only, yet we
left the island feeling we had lived there for a long time.

The sea-crossing from Santa Cruz to Cumaná, the most eastern
part of the New Continent, was indescribably beautiful. We cut the
Tropic of Cancer on the 27th and, despite the *Pizarro* not being a fast
sailer, took only twenty days to cover the 900 leagues that separate
the African coast from the New World. Some land birds, blown out
to sea by the strong wind, followed us for a few days.

We followed the same route as Columbus had taken on his first
voyage out to the Antilles. It is well known that during the crossing
from Santa Cruz to Cumaná, or from Acapulco to the Philippines,
sailors barely have to worry about working the sails. We crossed the
ocean as if descending a river, and would have been in no greater
danger if we had made the voyage in an open boat.

The further we left the African coast behind the weaker the wind
became: it was often completely calm for hours, followed regularly
by electrical phenomena. Thick black perfectly shaped clouds formed
in the east; it seemed as if a squall might force us to fasten the topsail;
then the wind would rise again, a few large raindrops would fall, and
the storm would vanish without a single clap of thunder. It is thanks
to these squalls alternating with dead calms that you are able to cross

the ocean from the Canaries to the West Indies during June and July.

Nothing equals the beauty and mildness of a tropical ocean's climate. While the trade wind blew strongly the thermometer remained steadily at 23 °C or 24 °C by day, and 22 °C to 22.5 °C by night. What a contrast between the tempestuous seas of the northern latitudes and those regions where the peace of nature is never disturbed! If the return journey from Mexico or South America was as quick and agreeable as the outgoing one the number of Europeans settled in the colonies would be considerably less than it is at the present. The seas that surround the Azores and Bermudas, which you cross when returning to Europe, are oddly called by Spaniards El Golfo de las Yeguas (Gulf of Mares). Settlers who are not used to the sea and who have lived isolatedly in Guianan forests, or in the savannahs of Caracas, or in the mountains of Peru, fear this gulf more than people fear Cape Horn. They exaggerate the dangers of a journey that is treacherous only in winter. They postpone this dangerous return year after year until death surprises them still planning.

To the north of the Cape Verde Islands we found great masses of floating seaweeds. They were the tropical sea-grape variety (*Fucus natans*), which grow on rocks below sea-level from the equator to the 40th degree of latitude. These seaweeds seem to indicate the presence of currents. These scattered weeds should not be confused with those banks of weeds that Columbus compared to great meadows, which terrified the crew of the *Santa María* on the 42nd degree of latitude.

From the 22nd degree of latitude the surface of the sea was covered with flying fish (*Exocoetuus volitans*); they threw themselves 12, 15 and even 18 feet into the air and fell on deck. I do not hesitate to speak on a subject as common in travelogues as dolphins, sharks, seasickness and the phosphorescence of the ocean. There is nothing that does not interest a naturalist as long as he makes a detailed study. Nature is an inexhaustible source of study, and as science advances so new facts reveal themselves to an observer who knows how to interrogate her.

I have mentioned flying fish in order to draw the attention of naturalists to the extraordinary size of their natatory bladder. As this bladder takes up more than half the fish's body volume it probably contributes to its lightness. One could say that this reservoir of air is more adapted for flying than swimming. Flying fish, like almost all animals with gills, enjoy the possibility of breathing for a long time with the same organs both in air and in water. They pass much of their time in the air, although flying does not make them less wretched. If they leave the sea to escape from the voracious dolphin they meet frigate-birds, albatrosses and other birds in the air, which seize them in mid-flight. Thus, on the Orinoco banks, herds of capybara (*Cavia capybara*) rush from the water to escape crocodiles and fall prey to jaguars waiting for them on the banks. I doubt that flying fish leap from the water solely to escape their predators. Like swallows they shoot forward in thousands in straight lines, always against the waves. In our climate, by a clear-water river struck by the sun's rays, we often see single fish, with no reason to fear anything, leap into the air as if they enjoyed breathing air. Why aren't these games more frequent and prolonged with flying fish who, thanks to their pectoral fins and extreme lightness, fly easily in the air?

On the 1st of July we came across the wreck of a sunken ship. We could distinguish its mast covered in floating seaweed. In a zone where the sea is perpetually calm the boat could not have sunk. Perhaps its remains came from the northerly stormy area and were dragged there by the extraordinary whirling of the Atlantic Ocean in the Southern hemisphere.

On the 3rd and 4th of July we crossed that part of the Atlantic Ocean where charts indicate the Maelstrom; at night we changed course to avoid the danger, though its existence is as dubious as that of the isles of Fonseco and Saint Anne.[19] The old charts are filled with rocks, some of which really exist, though most are due to optical illusions, which are more frequent at sea than on land.

From the time we entered the torrid zone we never tired of admiring, night after night, the beauty of the southern sky, which as we advanced further south opened up new constellations. A strange, completely unknown feeling is awoken in us when nearing the equator and crossing from one hemisphere to another; the stars we have known since infancy begin to vanish. Nothing strikes the traveller more completely about the immense distances that separate him from home than the look of a new sky. The grouping of great stars, some scattered nebulae that rival the Milky Way in splendour, and regions that stand out because of their intense blackness, give the southern sky its unique characteristics. This sight strikes the imagination of those who even, without knowledge of the exact sciences, like to stare at the heavens as if admiring a lovely country scene, or a majestic site. You do not have to be a botanist to recognize immediately the torrid zone by its vegetation. Even those with no inkling of astronomy know they are no longer in Europe when they see the enormous constellation of the Ship or the brilliant Clouds of Magellan rise in the night sky. Everything on earth and in the sky in the tropical countries takes on an exotic note.

On the night of the 4th of July, at about the 16th degree of latitude, we saw the Southern Cross clearly for the first time; it appeared strongly inclined and shone intermittently between clouds. When flashes of lightning passed across its centre it shone with a silvery light. If a traveller may be permitted to speak of his personal emotions, I will add that on that night I saw one of the dreams of my earliest youth come true.

When we first glance at geographical maps, and read the narratives of navigators, we feel a special charm for certain countries and climates, which we cannot explain when older. These impressions exercise a considerable hold over what we do in life, and we instinctively try to connect ourselves with anything associated with these places. When I first studied the stars to identify them I was disturbed by a fear unknown to those who love sedentary life. It was painful to me to have to renounce the hope of seeing the beautiful constellations near the South Pole. Impatient to explore the equatorial regions I could not raise my eyes to the sky without dreaming of the Southern Cross and remembering a passage from Dante.[20] Our joy over discovering the Southern Cross was vividly shared by those sailors who had lived in the colonies. In the solitudes of the oceans you wave at a star as if it is a friend you haven't seen for ages. Portuguese and Spaniards are particularly susceptible to this feeling; religious sentiments attach them to a constellation whose shape recalls the sign of the faith planted by their ancestors in the deserts of the New World.

That the Cross is nearly perpendicular when it passes the meridian is known to all who inhabit the Tropics. It has been observed at which hour of the night, in different seasons, the Cross is erect or inclined. How often have we heard our guides exclaim in the savannahs of Venezuela or in the desert stretching from Lima to Trujillo, 'Midnight is past, the Cross begins to bend!' How those words reminded me of that moving scene where Paul and Virginie,[21] seated near the source of the river Lataniers, chat together for the last time, and where the old man, at the sight of the Southern Cross, warns them that it is time to separate!

The last days of our crossing were not as peaceful as the mild climate and calm ocean had led us to hope. We were not disturbed by the dangers of the deep, but by the presence of a malignant fever that developed as we approached the West Indies. Between the overcrowded decks the heat was unbearable; the thermometer stayed at 36 °C. Two sailors, several passengers and, strangely, two blacks from the Guinean coast and a mulatto child were attacked by an illness that threatened to turn into an epidemic. The symptoms were not as serious in all the sick; but some of them, even among the most robust, became delirious on the second day and lost all body strength. With that indifference which on passenger ships affects everything that is not to do with the ship's movements and speed, the captain did not for a moment think of applying the simplest remedies. He did not fumigate. A phlegmatic and ignorant Gallician surgeon prescribed bleedings, attributing the fever to what he called the heat and corruption of blood. There was not an ounce of quinine on board and we, on boarding, had forgotten to bring a supply, more concerned for our instruments than for our health as we had not predicted that a Spanish ship would be without this Peruvian bark febrifuge.

On the 8th of July a sailor, near death, recovered his health in circumstances worthy of relating. His hammock had been strung in such a way that between his face and the ceiling there was not more than 10 inches. In such a position it was impossible to administer the sacraments; according to the custom on Spanish ships the Last Sacrament has to be brought down lighted by candles, followed by the crew. For this reason they had to take the sailor to a more airy place near the hatchway where they had made a little berth with flags and canvas. The man would stay there until his death. But hardly had he passed from an asphyxiating, noxious and humid atmosphere to the open air than he gradually began to recover from his lethargy. His convalescence began the day they moved him out from the middle deck. As is common in medicine the same facts are quoted in support of diametrically opposed systems; this recovery confirmed our doctor's ideas about bleeding and evacuation. We soon felt the fatal effects of this treatment and longed to reach the coast of America.

The pilots trusted the ship's log more than my time-keeper,[22] and smiled at my prediction that we would soon sight land, sure that we still had two to three days of sailing. It was with great satisfaction that on the 13th, at about six in the morning, high land was seen through the mist by someone from the mast. A strong wind blew and the sea was very rough. Every now and then heavy drops of rain fell. Everything pointed to a difficult situation. The captain intended to pass through the channel that separates the islands of Tobago and Trinidad and, knowing that our corvette was slow to turn, feared the south wind and the approach to the Boca del Dragón.

The island of Tobago presents an extremely picturesque scene. It is a heap of rocks skilfully cultivated. The dazzling whiteness of the rocks stands out from the green of the scattered trees. High cylindrical cacti crown the mountain tops and give a peculiar quality to the tropical countryside. Just this sight tells the traveller that he is looking at the American coast, because the cacti are as unique to the New World as heaths are to the Old.

We had left doubled the northern cape of Tobago and the small island of Saint Giles when the look-out pointed out the presence of an enemy squadron. We immediately changed course and the passengers began to fret as many of them had invested small fortunes in goods to sell in the Spanish colonies. The squadron did not appear to move and soon we saw that the look-out had confused ships with an isolated reef.

The epidemic on board the *Pizarro* spread rapidly as soon as we neared the coast of Terra Firma.[23] By night the thermometer regularly marked 22 °C or 23 °C, by day it rose to 24 °C and 27 °C. Congestion in the head, extreme dryness of skin and the failing of all strength became alarming symptoms but, having reached the end of the voyage, we flattered ourselves that the sick would recover their health as soon as we landed them on Margarita Island or at Cumaná harbour, both known for their salubrity.

This hope was not totally justified. The youngest passenger attacked by the malignant fever was unluckily the only victim. He was a nineteen-year-old Asturian, the only son of a widow without means. Several circumstances made the death of this sensitive and mild-tempered youth moving. He had embarked against his will; his mother, whom he hoped to help through his work, had sacrificed her tenderness and own interests in order to assure the fortune of her son in the colonies, helping a rich cousin in Cuba. The luckless youth had fallen from the start into a total lethargy, with moments of delirium, and died on the third day. Yellow fever, or black vomit as it is called at Veracruz, does not carry off the sick so frighteningly quickly. Another Asturian, even younger than he, never left his bedside and, more remarkably, never caught the illness. He was following his compatriot to Cuba, to be introduced into his relation's house, on whom they had based all their hopes. It was desperate to see this young man abandon himself to deep grief and curse the advice of those who had sent him to a distant land, alone and without support.

We were all on deck sunk in sad thoughts. There was no doubt that the fever raging on board had taken a pernicious turn. Our glances were fixed on a deserted mountainous coast, intermittently lit by the moon. The calm sea shone with a feeble phosphorescence. We heard only the monotonous cries of large sea birds seeking the shore. A deep calm reigned in these lonely places, but nature's calm contrasted with the painful feelings agitating us. Towards eight that night the dead man's knell was tolled; at this lugubrious signal the sailors stopped work and kneeled in short prayers in a touching ceremony, which, recalling the times when the early Christians saw themselves as members of the same family, brought us together in a common sorrow. At night the young Asturian's corpse was carried to the bridge, and the priest arranged to delay dropping him into the sea until dawn, according to the Roman Catholic rite. Everybody mourned the bad luck of this young man who but a few days before had seemed so fresh and healthy.

The passengers on board the *Pizarro* who had not yet noticed the symptoms of this malady[24] decided to leave the ship at the first port of call and await the arrival of another mail-boat to continue on to Cuba and Mexico. They felt the between decks were infected, and though it had not been proved that the fever was contagious I thought it more prudent to disembark at Cumaná. It would have been a pity to put into port at Cumaná and La Guaira without penetrating into a land so little explored by naturalists.

The decision we took on the night of the 14th of July had a happy influence on the direction of our travels. Instead of weeks, we spent a year in this part of the world. Had not the fever broken out on board the *Pizarro* we would never have explored the Orinoco, the Casiquiare and the frontiers with the Portuguese possessions on the Río Negro. We perhaps also owed to this circumstance the good health we enjoyed for such a long period in the equinoctial regions.

It is well known that during the first months that Europeans are exposed to the burning heat of the Tropics they live in great danger. The ease of acclimatization seems to be in the inverse ratio of the difference between the mean temperature of the torrid zone and that of the native country of the settler because the irritability of the organs and their vital actions are powerfully modified by the atmospheric heat. We were lucky enough for recently disembarked Europeans to spend that dangerous period in Cumaná, a very hot but dry place celebrated for its salubrity.

At around eleven in the morning we caught sight of a low-lying island with large sand dunes. We did not see any sign of life or farming through the telescope. Here and there rose the cylindrical cacti in the form of candelabra. The ground, devoid of vegetation, seemed to ripple due to the intense refraction of the sun's rays through the air above an intensely heated surface. All over the world deserts and beaches look like rough seas from the effect of mirage.

The sight of such a flat land did not match the ideas we had formed about the island of Margarita. While we tried hard to match what we saw with what appeared on our map a look-out sighted some small fishing-boats. The captain of the *Pizarro* called them with a cannon shot: but this signal is useless in places where the weak confront the strong only to be crushed. The boats escaped to the west. The coasts from a distance are like clouds, where each observer sees the form of the objects that occupy his imagination. Our readings on the chronometer contradicted our maps, and we were lost in useless conjectures. Some took dunes for Indian huts, and pointed out the place where the fort of Pampatar was situated; others saw herds of goats common in the dry valleys of Saint John; or the high mountains of Macanao, partly hidden by clouds. The captain decided to send a pilot ashore, and the men prepared to lower the longboat.

As we were about to go ashore we saw two pirogues sailing along the coast. The captain hailed them with a second burst of cannon fire, and though we hoisted the Spanish colours they drew near defiantly. Their pirogues, like all those used by Indians, were cut from one tree trunk. In each canoe there were eighteen Guaiquerí Indians, naked to the waist and very tall. They looked very muscular, with a skin colour between brown and coppery red. From afar, sitting still and standing out against the horizon, they could be taken for bronze statues. Their appearance did not correspond with the traits and extreme weakness described by previous travellers.

When we were close enough to the pirogues to shout to the Indians in Spanish they lost their suspicion and boarded. They informed us that the low-lying island opposite was called Coche, and had never been inhabited. Spanish ships sailing in from Europe usually sailed further north between this island and Margarita to take a coastal pilot aboard at Pampatar.

The Guaiquerí belong to a tribe of civilized Indians inhabiting the coast of Margarita and the surroundings of the town of Cumaná. They enjoy several privileges because they remained faithful to the Castilians from earliest times. Also the King names them in some decrees as 'his dear, noble and loyal Guaiquerías'. Those manning the two pirogues had left Cumaná harbour at night. They were searching for building timber from the cedar forests (*Cedrela odorata*, Linn.) that stretch from Cape San José beyond the mouth of the Carupano river. They offered us fresh coconuts and stunningly coloured fish from the *Chaetodon* genus. What riches these poor Indians held in their pirogues! Huge *vijao* (*Heliconia bihai*) leaves covered bunches of bananas; the scaly cuirass of an armadillo (*Dasypus*, *cachicamo*); the fruit of the calabash tree (*Crescentia cujete*), used by the Indians as a cup, quite common in European cabinets, vividly reminded us that we had reached the longed-for torrid zone.

The chief of one of the pirogues offered to stay on board to guide us as a coastal pilot. He was a most trustworthy Guaiquerí; a keen observer, and led by a genuine thirst for learning he had studied the produce of the sea and land around him. It was fortunate that the first Indian we met on arrival was a man whose knowledge was to prove extremely helpful for our journey's objectives. With great pleasure I record his name as Carlos del Pino, who accompanied us for sixteen months up and down the coast, and into the interior.

Towards evening the captain weighed anchor and sailed west. Soon we came within sight of the little island of Cubagua, now entirely deserted but once famous for its pearl fisheries. There the Spaniards, immediately after Columbus's and Ojeda's journeys, had built a city called Nueva Cádiz, of which there is now not a trace. At the beginning of the sixteenth century Cubagua pearls were known in Seville, Toledo and the great fairs at Augsburg and Bruges. Nueva Cádiz had no water, so it had to be conveyed there from the Manzanares river. For some reason this water was thought to cause eye diseases.

The wind hardly blew so the captain thought it safe to tack until dawn. He did not dare enter Cumaná harbour at night. An unfortunate incident that occurred a year before justified his prudence. A mail-boat had anchored without lighting its poop lanterns; it was taken for an enemy and fired on by the fort. A cannon-ball ripped the captain's leg off and he died a few days later in Cumaná.

We spent part of the night on deck as the Indian pilot entertained us with stories about the plants and animals of his land. We learned with great satisfaction that a few leagues from the coast there was a mountain range, inhabited by the Spaniards, where it was quite cold, and that in the plains there were two kinds of very different crocodile (*Crocodilus acutus* and *C. bava*), as well as boas, electric eels (*Gymnotus electricus, temblador*) and various species of jaguar. Though the words *bava, cachicamo* and *temblador* were entirely unknown to us the naïve descriptions of the forms and habits of the animals allowed us to identify them easily. Nothing excites a naturalist's curiosity more than marvellous tales of a country he is about to explore.

At dawn on the 16th of July 1799 we saw the green, picturesque coast. The mountains of Nueva Andalucía, hidden in clouds, bordered the horizon. The city of Cumaná, with its fort, stood in coconut groves. At nine in the morning, after forty-one days at sea, we anchored in the harbour. The sick crawled on deck to comfort themselves with the vision of a land where they hoped they would be cured.[25]

CHAPTER 4

First stay in Cumaná — The Manzanares river banks

Our eyes were fixed on groups of coconut trees that bordered the river whose trunks, which were more than sixty feet high, dominated the landscape. The plain was covered with thickets of cassia, capers and arborescent mimosa, which, similar to Italian pines, spread their branches out like parasols. The pinnated leaves of the palms stood out against the blue sky, in which there was not a trace of mist. The sun was climbing rapidly towards its zenith; a dazzling light spread through the atmosphere on to the whitish hills covered in cylindrical cacti, as well as the becalmed sea and the shores populated with pelicans (*Pelicanus fuscus*, Linn.), flamingoes and herons. The intense luminosity of the day, the vivid colours and forms of the vegetation, the variegated plumage of the birds, all bore the grand seal of tropical nature.

The town of Cumaná, capital of New Andalusia, lies a mile from the landing-stage or the *boca* battery where we stepped ashore after crossing the bar of the Manzanares river. We had to traverse a vast plain (*el salado*) between the Guaiquerí dwellings and the coast. The reverberation from the parched land increased the intense heat. The thermometer, plunged into the white sand, reached 37.7 °C. The first plant we gathered from American soil was the *Avicennia tomentosa* (*Mangle prieto*), which scarcely reaches 2 feet high here. This shrub, with the sesuvium, the yellow gomphrena and the cacti, covered a ground saturated with soda salts; they belong to the scant social plants like European heaths, and in the torrid zone thrive only on the seashore and high in the Andean plateaux.

The Indian pilot led us across his garden, which seemed more a copse than cultivated land. As proof of the land's fertility he showed us a silk-cotton tree (*Bombax heptaphyllum*) whose trunk measured nearly 2.5 feet in diameter after only four years' growth. However, I think the Indian's estimate of the tree's age was somewhat exaggerated. Still on the Cumaná beach, in the Guaiquerí's garden, we saw for the first time a *guama* (*Inga spuria*) loaded with flowers, remarkable for the length and silvery brilliance of their numerous stamen. We passed the neatly arranged streets of the Indian quarters, bordered with small new houses of attractive design. This part of the town has just been rebuilt after the earthquake a year and a half before our arrival that destroyed Cumaná. Hardly had we crossed the wooden bridge over the Manzanares river, full of *bavas* or small crocodiles, than we saw traces of that terrible catastrophe everywhere; new buildings rose over the ruins of the old.

The *Pizarro*'s captain accompanied us to the provincial governor's residence to present Don Vicente Emparán with our passports granted by the First Secretary of State. He received us with that frankness and simplicity that have always characterized the Basques. Before he was appointed governor of Portobello and Cumaná he distinguished himself as a captain in the Royal Navy. His name evokes one of the most notable and distressing episodes in the history of naval warfare. After the last break between Spain and England two of Governor Emparán's brothers, outside Cádiz, attacked each other's ships, thinking the other was the enemy. The battle was ferocious and both ships sunk at almost the same time. Only a few of the crew were saved, and the two brothers realized their mistake just before dying.

The Governor of Cumaná expressed great satisfaction at our decision to remain awhile in New Andalusia, a province scarcely known in Europe at the time, not even by name, and whose mountains and numerous river banks afford a naturalist a wonderful field for observations. The governor showed us cottons dyed with indigenous plants and beautiful furniture carved from local wood. He was interested in all branches of natural philosophy, and to our amazement asked us if we thought that the atmosphere in the beautiful tropical sky contained more nitrogen than that in Spain, or if the speed with which iron oxidated was due to the greater humidity shown by the hair hygrometer. The name of his native country pronounced on a distant shore could not please the ears of a traveller more than hearing the words 'nitrogen', 'oxidation of iron' and 'hygrometer'. We knew, despite the court orders and recommendations of an influential minister, that we would face innumerable unpleasant incidents if we did not manage to make good relations with those ruling these immense lands. Sr Emparán was far too enamoured of the sciences to think it odd that we had come so far to collect plants and determine specific places from astronomical observations. He did not suspect any other motives than those that figured in our safe conducts, and the proof of public esteem he gave us throughout our stay in his territory contributed to giving us a warm welcome in all the South American countries.

At nightfall we ordered our instruments to be disembarked; and to our relief none had been damaged. We hired a spacious and well-situated house for our astronomical observations. When the sea wind blew we enjoyed the cool air. The windows did not have glass panes, nor the paper squares that replace glass in most Cumaná houses. All the passengers on the *Pizarro* left the ship, but those with the malignant fever recovered very slowly. Some were still terribly pale and emaciated after a month of illness, despite the care lavished on them by their compatriots. In the Spanish colonies the hospitality is such that a European who arrives without money or recommendations is almost sure to find help should he disembark sick in any port. Catalans, Galicians and Basques maintain an intense trade with America, where they form three distinct bodies, and exercise a great influence on the customs, industry and commerce of the colonies. The poorest inhabitant of Sitges or Vigo may be assured of being received in the house of a Catalan or Galician merchant (*pulpero*[26]) whether in Chile or Mexico or the Philippines. I have witnessed moving examples where strangers are looked after assiduously for years. Some may say that hospitality is no virtue in a land with such a magnificent climate, with plenty of food, and where indigenous plants supply efficient medicines, and a sick person finds necessary refuge in a hammock under a covering. But does not the arrival of a stranger in a family imply more work? Are not the proofs of disinterested sympathy, the spirit of sacrifice in the women, the patience that long convalescence requires, worthy of note? It has been observed that, with the exception of some populated cities, hospitality has not really decreased since the arrival of the Spanish settlers in the New World. It distresses me to think that this change will happen as the colonial population and industry progress rapidly, and that the state of society that we have agreed to call advanced civilization might banish 'the ancient Castilian frankness'.

The hill of calcareous rocks on which Cumaná stands, once an island in an ancient gulf, is covered with candle-like cacti and opuntia, some of the most arresting reaching as much as 30 to 40 feet high, with their trunks branching out like candelabra and covered in lichen. Near Maniquarez, at Punta Araya, we measured a cactus (*Tuna macho*) whose trunk had a circumference of 1.54 metres. Europeans who do not know opuntia apart from those in hothouses will be surprised to learn that the wood of this plant hardens extraordinarily with age, that for centuries it resists both air and humidity, and that the Cumaná Indians use it for making oars and door-frames. Cumaná, Coro, Margarita Island and Curaçao are the places in South America where the nopals thrive most. Only after a long stay could a botanist write a monograph on the genus *Cactus*.

One place where spiky cacti of great size grow together is almost impossible to walk through. These areas, known as *tunales*, not only prevent bare-chested Indians from entering, but also anyone fully dressed. During our solitary walks we tried several times to penetrate the *tunal* that crowns the hill with the fort, along which runs a path. There we found thousands of examples of this strange plant. At times nightfall surprised us as there is no twilight. Then this place becomes dangerous, for the rattlesnake (*Crotalus cumanensis*), the coral and other poisonous snakes seek out these hot places to deposit their eggs in the sand.

The *tunal* is considered here and everywhere in the Spanish colonies as crucial to military defence; and when earthworks are raised the engineers propagate the thorny opuntia, as they keep crocodiles in the ditches. In regions where nature is so fertile, man uses the carnivorous reptile and a plant with an armour of thorns to his advantage.

The San Antonio fort, where the Castilian flag is hoisted on feast days, stands at some 30 toises above sea-level. From its bare calcareous site it dominates the town, and seen from sea as you enter the port it looks very picturesque. It is a wonderful place to enjoy the sunset and view the gulf as a fresh sea breeze reaches it.

The town of Cumaná itself stretches from the San Antonio fort to the small Manzanares and Santa Catalina rivers. The delta formed by the former is fertile, covered with mammees, sapotas (*achra*), banana trees and other plants cultivated by the Indians in their *charas*.[27] The town boasts no buildings of particular interest, and the frequency of earthquakes prevents such plans.

The outlying area of Cumaná is as densely populated as the old town. This includes Los Cerritos, where we met with attractive tamarind trees, San Francisco to the south-east, and the place where the Guaiquerí live. The name of this tribe was quite unknown before the conquest. The Indians who use this name used to belong to the Warao who still inhabit the marshy area of the Orinoco delta. Some old men assured me that the language of their ancestors was a Warao dialect, but in Cumaná and Margarita not one Indian has spoken anything but Castilian for over a century.

The word 'Guaiquerí', like the words 'Peru' and 'Peruvian', owes its origin to a simple mistake. When Christopher Columbus's companions reached Margarita Island, on whose northern tip these Indians still live, they found several Indians fishing with harpoons, throwing these sharp-pointed sticks tied with string at the fish. Columbus's men asked the Indians in the Haitian language what their name was, but the Indians thought the foreigners referred to their harpoons made of the hard and heavy wood of the macana palm and answered: 'Guaike, guaike', meaning 'pointed stick'. These Guaiquerí are an intelligent and civilized tribe of fishermen, notably different from the wild Guarano from the Orinoco who build their houses up in the mauritia palm trees.

The beach near the mouth of the small Santa Catalina river is lined with mangrove trees (*Rhizophora mangle*); but these mangroves (*manglares*) are not extensive enough to affect the salubrity of Cumaná's air. Otherwise the plain is partly bare and partly covered with tufts of plants including the *Avicennia tomentosa*, the *Scoparia dulcis*, a shrub-like mimosa with very sensitive leaves,[28] and especially cassias, so many of which can be found in South America that on our travels we gathered more than thirty new species.

On leaving the Indian suburbs and climbing the river towards the south we reached a little wood of cacti, and then a marvellous place shaded by tamarind trees, brazilettos, bombax and other trees remarkable for their leaves and flowers. Here the soil is rich enough for pasturing, and among the trees there are dairies built of reeds. The milk is kept fresh not in the calabashes, which are made of thick ligneous fibres, but in porous earthenware pots from Maniquarez. A prejudice current in northern countries led me to believe that cows in the torrid zone did not give buttery milk. However, during my stay in Cumaná, and especially while on a trip through the vast plains of Calabozo, covered in grasses and sensitive plants, I learned that European cows adapt perfectly to extreme heat provided they are given water and good fodder.

As the inhabitants of Cumaná prefer the freshness of the sea breeze to forests their favourite walk is along the open shore. The Castilians, accused of not being fond of trees or birdsong, have transported these tastes and prejudices into their colonies. In Terra Firma, Mexico and Peru it is rare to see a native plant a tree just to get some shade, and, excepting the great capitals, tree alleys are almost unknown. The arid plain of Cumaná provides an extraordinary phenomenon after violent rainstorms. After being drenched with rain the earth is heated by the sun and gives off that musky smell common to many different tropical animals like the jaguar, the small tiger-cat, the capybara (*Cavia capybara*), the gallinazo vulture (*Vultur aura*), the crocodile, viper and rattlesnake. These gases seem to emanate from mould containing innumerable reptiles, worms and insect remains. I have seen Indian children from the Chaima tribe pick out 18-inch millipedes from the earth and eat them.

The waters of the Manzanares river are very clear and do not resemble at all the Manzanares river in Madrid, made to seem even more narrow by its sumptuous bridge. It springs, like all the rivers of New Andalusia, from the llanos (plains) known as the plateaux of Jonoro, Amana and Guanipa. The construction of a dyke to irrigate the land has been several times proposed to the government, but without success for, despite the apparent sterility, the land is extremely productive wherever heat and humidity meet.

The banks of the Manzanares are very attractive, shaded by mimosas, erythrinas, ceibas and other gigantic trees. A river whose temperature descends during the floods to as low as 22 °C when the air is 30 °C to 35 °C is a blessing in a country where the heat is excessive all year round and one wants to bathe several times a day. Children spend a good part of their lives in this water; everybody, including the richest women, knows how to swim. In a country where people live so close to nature the most important question people ask each other on first meeting is whether the river water is fresher than it was the day before. There are several ways of bathing. Each evening we visited a group of respectable people in the Guaiquerí suburb. In the moonlight they would install chairs by the water; men and women were lightly dressed as if at European spas, and would spend hours smoking cigars and chatting with their families and strangers, according to the habits of the place, about the dryness, the heavy rains and the excessive luxury of Caracas and Havana ladies. Nobody worried about the small but rare crocodiles that approach humans without attacking, although dolphins swim upstream and scare bathers by spouting water.

Cumaná harbour has an anchorage in which all the fleets of Europe would fit. The whole of the Gulf of Cariaco, which is about 35 miles long and 6 to 8 miles wide, offers excellent anchoring. The hurricanes of the West Indies are never felt in this region, and you can sail about in an open boat. I have spent some time describing the location of Cumaná because it seemed important to make the place that has seen so many tremendous earthquakes known.

The city, dominated by the fort, lies at the foot of a hill without greenery. Not one bell-tower nor one dome attract the traveller from afar; just a few tamarind trees and coconut and date palms stand out above the flat-roofed houses. The surrounding plains, especially near the sea, appear sad, dusty and arid, while fresh, luxuriant vegetation marks out the winding river that divides the city from its outskirts and the European settlers from the copper-coloured Indians. The isolated, bare and white San Antonio mountain, with its fort, reflects a great mass of light and heat: it is made of breccia, whose strata contain fossil marine life. Far away towards the south you can make out a dark curtain of mountains. They are the high calcareous New Andalusian alps, topped with sandstone and other recent geological formations. Majestic forests cover this inland mountain chain linked along a forested valley with the salty, clayey and bare ground around Cumaná. In the gulf and on its shores you can see flocks of fishing herons and gannets, awkward, heavy birds, which, like swans, sail along the water with their wings raised. Nearer the inhabited areas, you can count thousands of gallinazo vultures, veritable flying jackals, ceaselessly picking at carcasses. A gulf whose depths contain hot thermal springs divides the secondary from the primary and schistose rocks of the Araya peninsula. The two coasts are bathed by a calm blue sea lightly rippled by a constant breeze. A dry, pure sky, only lightly clouded at sunset, lies above the sea, over a peninsula devoid of trees and above the Cumaná plains, while one sees storms building up and bursting into fertile downpours around the inland mountain peaks.

Another characteristic common to both the New Andalusian coast and Peru is the frequency of earthquakes and the limits nature seems to have prescribed for these phenomena. In Cumaná we ourselves felt violent seismic shocks; they were still rebuilding the ruined houses and so we were able to gather detailed information on the spot about the terrible catastrophe of the 14th of December 1797. These notions will be the more interesting as earthquakes have been considered up to now less from a physical and geographical point of view than from the way they disastrously affect the population and well-being of society.

On the Cumaná coast and on Margarita Island most share the opinion that the Gulf of Cariaco was formed as a consequence of a fracturing of the territory and a flooding from the sea. The memory of this powerful cataclysm had been preserved by the Indians up to the fifteenth century, and it is said that by Christopher Columbus's third voyage the Indians still talked about it as recent. In 1530 the inhabitants of the Paria and Cumaná coasts were terrified by new shocks. The sea flooded the land and a huge crack was created in the Cariaco mountains and in the gulf of the same name. A great body of salt water, mixed with asphaltum, burst out of the micaceous schist. At the end of the sixteenth century earthquakes were very common and, according to tradition, the sea flooded the shore several times, rising some 90 to 100 feet above normal. The inhabitants fled to the San Antonio hills, and to the hill where the San Francisco convent stands today.

Because there are no records kept in Cumaná, and thanks to the persistent destructive activity of the termites, the white ants, no documents older than 150 years remain in the archives, thus making it hard to know the exact dates for the earlier earthquakes. We know only that 1766 was most fatal for the settlers and most remarkable for the natural history of the country. There had been a drought for over fifteen months when on the 21st of October 1766 the city of Cumaná was completely destroyed. Every year that date is celebrated by a religious service and a solemn procession. All the houses collapsed in a few minutes, and every hour for fourteen months tremors were felt. In several areas in the province the earth opened up and vomited out sulphureous water. During 1766 and 1767 the Cumaná inhabitants camped out in the streets and began rebuilding only when the tremors slowed down to a few a mon*'.. While the earth continually rocked it felt as if the air was about to dissolve into water. Formidable rainstorms swelled the river; the year was extraordinarily fertile, and the Indians, whose frail shacks survive the most violent earthquakes, celebrated with dances of joy following an ancient superstition about the destruction of the old world and the birth of a new one.

According to tradition, during the quake of 1766 the earth moved in simple horizontal waves; only on the fatal day of the 14th of December did the earth rise up. More than four fifths of the city was completely destroyed, and the shock, accompanied by a loud subterranean noise, resembled the explosion of a mine placed deep in the ground. Fortunately the main shocks were preceded by light undulations thanks to which most of the inhabitants were able to reach the streets, and only a few who hid in the church died. It is generally believed in Cumaná that the worst earthquakes are preceded by weak oscillations in the ground, and by a humming that does not escape the notice of those used to this phenomenon. In those desperate moments you heard people everywhere shouting 'Misericordia! Tiembla! Tiembla!' ('Mercy! The earth is trembling!') The most faint-hearted attentively observe the dogs, goats and pigs. These last, with their acute sense of smell, and skill in poking around in the earth, give warnings of approaching dangers with frightened screams.

In Cumaná, on San Francisco hill with its convent, an intense stink of sulphur was smelled on the 14th of December 1797 half an hour before the great catastrophe. In this same place the underground noise was loudest. At the same time flames were seen on the Manzanares river banks near the Capuchin hospital, and in the Gulf of Cariaco near Mariguitar. This phenomenon, so strange in non-volcanic countries, happens frequently in the calcareous mountains near Cumanacoa, in the Bordones river valley, on Margarita Island and on the plains of New Andalusia. On these plains the sparks of fire rose to a considerable height and were seen for hours in the most arid places. Some asserted that when the ground through which the inflammable substances rose was examined not the smallest crack was found. This fire, which recalls the springs of methane or the Salse of Modena and the will-o'-the-wisp of our marshes, does not burn the grass. The people, though less superstitious here than in Spain, call these reddish flames by the odd name of The Soul of the Tyrant Aguirre; imagining that the ghost of Lope de Aguirre,[29] harassed by remorse, wanders over these countries sullied by his crimes.

We will not continue to describe in detail the local changes produced by the different earthquakes of Cumaná. In order to follow our original plan we shall try to generalize our ideas, and include in one section everything that relates to these frightening and difficult-to-explain phenomena. If men of science who visit the Alps of Switzerland or the coasts of Lapland should broaden our knowledge about glaciers and the aurora borealis, then a traveller who has journeyed through Spanish America should mainly fix his attention on volcanoes and earthquakes. Every part of the earth merits particular study. When we cannot hope to guess the causes of natural phenomena, we ought at least to try to discover their laws and, by comparing numerous facts, distinguish what is permanent and constant from what is variable and accidental.

The great earthquakes, which appear between long series of slight shocks, do not happen regularly at Cumaná. We have seen them take place at intervals of eighty, a hundred and sometimes less than thirty years, while on the Peruvian coasts, for example at Lima, a certain regularity has marked the complete ruin of the city. The local belief in this uniformity has luckily aided public tranquillity and encouraged industry. Most admit that a long period of time elapses before the same causes act with the same energy. But such reasoning counts only if the shocks are considered as a local phenomenon, and if one supposes that great catastrophes are caused at one particular place.

When new buildings are raised on the ruins of the old we learn from those who refuse to rebuild that the destruction of Lisbon on the 1st of November 1755 was soon followed by a second and no less fatal quake on the 31st of March 1761.

A very ancient belief, still commonly held at Cumaná, Acapulco and Lima, establishes a perceptible connection between earthquakes and the state of the atmosphere that precedes these phenomena. On the coasts of New Andalusia people are alarmed when, in excessively hot weather and after long droughts, the breeze suddenly drops and the clear, cloudless sky turns reddish near the horizon. However, this way of predicting earthquakes is very uncertain, for when we gather together all the meteorological variations in times of earthquakes we find that violent shocks take place equally in dry and wet weather, whether when a cool wind blows or during a dead and suffocating calm. From the great number of earthquakes that I have witnessed on both sides of the equator, on the continent and at sea, on coasts and 2,500 toises high, it appears to me that the oscillations are quite independent of the previous state of the atmosphere. This opinion is shared by many educated people in the Spanish colonies whose experience of earthquakes, if not as extensive as mine, covers more years. Against this, scientific observers in Europe, where earthquakes are rare compared to America, tend to admit some close connections between the undulations of the ground and certain meteors that appear as if by chance at the same time. In Italy, for example, the sirocco and earthquakes are suspected to have some link; and in London, the frequency of shooting stars and those southern lights that have since often been observed by Dalton were considered as forerunners of those shocks felt from 1748 to 1756.

In the Tropics on those days when the earth is shaken by violent shocks the regularity of the barometer is not disturbed. I have verified this observation at Cumaná, at Lima and at Riobamba. Scientific observers should note this, for on Santo Domingo, in the town of Cape François, it has been asserted that a water barometer sank 2.5 inches just before the earthquake of 1770. It has also been related that a chemist, at the time of Oran's destruction, fled with his family a few minutes before the earthquake because he had noticed that the mercury in his barometer had sunk in an extraordinary manner. I do not know whether to believe his story. But as it is practically impossible to examine the variations of the weight of the atmosphere during the shocks, we must be satisfied with observing the barometer before and after.

We cannot question that the earth, when split open and shaken by shocks, sometimes emits gaseous substances into the atmosphere in places remote from active volcanoes. At Cumaná, as we have already observed, flames and vapours mixed with sulphureous acid rise from the most arid soil. In other parts of the same province the earth throws up water and petroleum. At Riobamba, a muddy, inflammable mass, called *moya*, issues from crevices that close up again and pile up into hills. Seven leagues from Lisbon, near Colares, during the terrible earthquake of the 1st of November 1755, flames and a column of thick smoke rose up from the rock face of Alvidras and, according to some witnesses, from the depths of the sea. This smoke lasted several days and was thicker when the underground noises accompanied the strongest tremors.

I am inclined to think that nothing escapes from the shaken earth during earthquakes and that when gases and steam are seen they precede as often as they follow or accompany the shocks. This last circumstance probably explains the mysterious influence in equinoctial America of earthquakes on the climate and seasons of rains and droughts. If the earth acts only on the air at the moment of shock we can see why a perceptible meteorological change so rarely predicts one of these great revolutions of nature.

The hypothesis that during the Cumaná earthquakes elastic fluids escape from the earth's surface seems confirmed by the dreadful noise heard during the shocks near the wells in the plain of Charas. Water and sand are sometimes thrown 20 feet high. Similar phenomena did not escape the ancients' notice in areas of Greece and Asia Minor, in caves, crevices and underground rivers. Nature, in its uniform progress, everywhere gives birth to the same ideas concerning the causes of earthquakes, and man, forgetting the measure of its force, tries to diminish the effect of underground explosions. What the great Roman naturalist Pliny said about how wells and caves are the cause is repeated by the most ignorant Indians of Quito when they show travellers the *guaicos*, or crevices, of Pichincha.

The underground noise so frequently heard during earthquakes is not usually related to the strength of the shocks. At Cumaná the noise constantly preceded the shocks, while at Quito, and recently at Caracas and in the West Indies, a noise like the discharge of a battery of guns was heard a long time after the shocks had ended. A third kind of phenomenon, and the most remarkable of all of them, is the rolling of those underground thunders that last several months without being accompanied by the slightest tremors.

In every country subject to earthquakes the spot where the effects are most clearly felt, probably due to a particular disposition of the stony strata, is selected as the cause and focus of the shocks. Thus, at Cumaná, the hill of the San Antonio castle, especially where the San Francisco convent stands, is thought to contain an enormous amount of sulphur and other inflammable matter. We forget that the speed with which the undulations are propagated across great distances, even across the ocean, proves that the centre of action is very remote from the earth's surface. For this same reason earthquakes are not confined to certain types of rock, as some naturalists claim, for tremors pass through all kinds of rock. If I remain faithful to my own experiences I can here cite the granites of Lima and Acapulco, the gneiss of Caracas, the mica-slate of the Araya peninsula, the primitive schist of Tepecoacuilco in Mexico, the secondary limestones of the Apennines, Spain and New Andalusia, and finally the trappean porphyries of the provinces of Quito and Popayan. In these different places the ground is frequently shaken by the most violent shocks, but sometimes, in the same rock, the upper strata form invincible barriers to the propagation of the waves. In Saxony mines we have seen miners rush up frightened by oscillations that were not felt on the earth's surface.

If, in regions remote from each other, primitive, secondary and volcanic rocks conduct in equal ways the earth's convulsive movements, we have also to admit that within very limited areas certain classes of rock do not propagate shocks. At Cumaná, for example, before the great catastrophe of 1797, earthquakes were felt only along the southern calcareous coast of the Gulf of Cariaco as far as the town of the same name, while in the Araya peninsula and at the village of Maniquarez the ground did not move at all. The inhabitants of this northern coast composed of mica-slate built their huts on solid earth, and a gulf some 3,000 to 4,000 toises wide separated them from a plain covered with ruins and overturned by earthquakes. This security, based on the experience of several centuries, no longer exists, because since the 14th of December 1797 new underground communications have opened up. At the present moment the Araya peninsula is not only subject to the same shaking as at Cumaná, but the mica-slate promontory has become a particular centre of tremors.

In New Andalusia, as well as in Chile and Peru, shocks follow the shore line and hardly extend inland. This circumstance indicates, as we shall soon show, an intimate connection between the causes that produce earthquakes and volcanoes. If the earth were most shaken on coasts because they are the lowest part of the land, why do we not feel equally strong oscillations on those vast savannahs or plains scarcely 8 to 10 toises above sea-level?

The earthquakes at Cumaná are connected with those of the West Indies, and it has even been suspected that they are somehow connected with the volcanic activity of the Andean cordilleras. On the 4th of February 1797 the ground of the province of Quito suffered such a destructive upheaval that nearly 40,000 natives died buried in the ruins of their houses, sucked into crevices or drowned in suddenly formed lakes. At the same time, the inhabitants of the eastern Antilles were alarmed by shocks that lasted for eight months when the volcano of Guadeloupe threw out pumice-stone, ashes and gusts of sulphureous gases. This eruption of the 27th of September, during which constant underground roaring was heard, was followed on the 14th of December by the great Cumaná earthquake. Another volcano in the West Indies, at Saint Vincent, has recently given a fresh example of these extraordinary connections. This volcano has not been active since 1718, and it burst out again in 1812. The complete ruin of Caracas preceded this explosion by thirty-four days, and violent waves were felt both on the islands and on the coasts of Terra Firma.

It has long been noted that the effects of great earthquakes extend much further than phenomena arising from active volcanoes. In studying the physical revolutions of Italy and carefully examining the series of eruptions of Vesuvius and Etna, we can see scarcely any sign of simultaneous action, despite their proximity. But it is a fact that at the last two destructions of Lisbon (1755 and 1761) the sea was violently stirred as far away as Barbados in the New World, more than 1,200 leagues from Portugal.

Several facts seem to prove that the causes that produce earthquakes are connected with those that cause volcanic eruptions. The linking of these causes, already known by the ancients, struck Europeans again when America was discovered. This discovery not only brought new objects to satisfy man's curiosity, but also new ideas about physical geography, about the varieties of human species, and about the migrations of tribes. It is impossible to read the narratives of the first Spanish travellers, especially the Jesuit Acosta's,[30] without realizing the happy influence that the appearance of this great continent, the study of its marvellous nature, and the contact with men of different races has exerted on the progress of knowledge in Europe. The germ of a great number of physical truths can be found in these sixteenth-century works, and this germ would have given fruit had it not been crushed by fanaticism and superstition.

We learned at Pasto that the column of thick black smoke that, in 1797, issued from the volcano near the shore for several months, disappeared at the very moment when, 60 leagues south, the towns of Riobamba, Hambato and Tacunga were destroyed by an enormous shock. Thus, sitting in the interior of a burning crater near those hillocks formed by scoriae and ashes, we feel the ground move several seconds before each eruption takes place. We observed this phenomenon at Vesuvius in 1805 while the mountain threw out scoriae at white heat; we witnessed the same thing in 1802 on the brink of the immense crater of Pichincha, but this time only gases came out.

Everything in earthquakes seems to indicate the action of elastic fluids seeking an outlet to spread into the atmosphere. Often on the Pacific coast the action is almost immediately communicated from Chile to the Gulf of Guayaquil, some 600 leagues distant. Remarkably the shocks seem to be stronger the further the country is from the active volcano. The granitic mountains of Calabria, covered with very recent breccias, the calcareous chain of the Apennines, the country of Pignerol, the coasts of Portugal and Greece, those of Peru and Terra Firma, all show striking proof of this claim. The earth, we might say, is shaken with greater force in proportion to the smaller number of funnels communicating the surface to caverns deep inside. At Naples and at Messina, at the foot of Cotopaxi and of Tungurahua, earthquakes are dreaded only if gases and flames do not burst out of the crater. The great catastrophes of Riobamba and Quito have led several well-informed people to think that this unfortunate country would be less often disturbed if the underground fires could break the porphyritic dome of Chimborazo and turn this gigantic mountain into an active volcano. Throughout the ages, similar facts have led to identical hypotheses. Like us, the Greeks attributed the ground's undulations to the tensions of elastic fluids, and quoted in support of their argument the fact that tremors on Elba ceased when a crevasse opened on the Levantine plain.

We have tried to collect at the end of this chapter the general phenomena of earthquakes in different climates. We have shown that subterranean gases are subjected to the same laws as those in the atmosphere. We have avoided discussing the nature of the chemical agents that cause the great earthquakes and volcanoes. It is sufficient to note that these causes are hidden at immense depths, and that we must seek them in what we call primitive rocks, perhaps below the earthy, and oxidized, crust, in the abysses that hold the metalloidal bases of silex, lime, soda and potash.

The phenomena of volcanoes and earthquakes have recently been seen as the effects of voltaic electricity, developed by a particular disposition of heterogeneous strata. It cannot be denied that when violent shocks often follow each other the electricity in the air increases the moment the ground is most shaken. But in order to explain this phenomenon it is not necessary to state a hypothesis which directly contradicts everything that has already been observed concerning the structure of our planet and the disposition of its strata.

CHAPTER 5

The Araya peninsula – Salt marshes – Ruins of
the Santiago fort

We spent the first weeks of our stay in Cumaná testing our instruments, botanizing in the nearby countryside, and investigating the traces of the earthquake of the 14th of December 1797. Dazzled by the sheer amount of different objects we found it awkward to stick to a systematic way of studying and observing. If everything that we saw around us excited us, our instruments in their turn awoke the curiosity of the local inhabitants. The numerous visitors disturbed us; in order not to disappoint all those who seemed so pleased to see the spots of the moon through Dollond's telescope,[31] the absorption of two gases in a eudiometrical tube, or the effects of galvanism on the motions of a frog, we had to answer many obscure questions and repeat the same experiments for hours.

This same situation repeated itself over the five years of our journey whenever we settled down in a place where people knew we had microscopes, telescopes and electrical apparatus. This was all the more tiresome as those who visited us held confused notions of astronomy or physics, two sciences that in the Spanish colonies are called by the bizarre name of new philosophy, *nueva filosofía*. The half-scientific looked at us scornfully when they heard we had not brought with us books like Abbé Pluche's *Spectacle de la nature* or Sigaud la Fond's *Cours de physique* or Valmont de Bomare's Dictionary. These, along with Baron Bielfeld's *Traité d'économie politique*, are the foreign works most admired in Spanish America. No one is deemed learned who cannot quote from them in translation. Only in the great capitals are the names of Haller, Cavendish and Lavoisier replacing those who have been famous for over fifty years.

Our house in Cumaná was magnificently situated for observing the sky and meteorological phenomena; on the other hand, during the day, we witnessed scenes that disgusted us. A part of the great plaza is surrounded with arcades above which runs a long wooden gallery, common to all hot countries. This is where the slaves brought from Africa were once sold. Of all European countries Denmark was the first and for ages the only government to abolish the slave-trade; yet the first slaves we saw here were transported by a Danish slave-ship. What silences the speculations of vile interest in its struggle with the duties of humanity, national honour and the laws of the fatherland?

The slaves put up for sale were young people from fifteen to twenty years old. Every morning they were given coconut oil to rub into their bodies to make their skin black and shiny. All the time buyers would approach and, examining their teeth, would calculate their age and health; they forced open their mouths just as if dealing with horses at market. This debasing custom dates back to Africa as is faithfully shown in a play by Cervantes who, after a long captivity with the Moors, outlined the sale of Christian slaves in Algiers.[32] It is distressing to think that still today in the Spanish West Indies slaves are branded with hot irons to identify them in case they escape. This is how one treats those 'who save other men from the labour of sowing, working in the fields and harvesting'.[33]

The deep impression caused by our first sight of a slave sale in Cumaná was alleviated somewhat by the relief of finding ourselves with a people and on a continent where this spectacle is very rare, and the number of slaves, in general, insignificant. In 1800 there were not more than 600 slaves in the two provinces of Cumaná and New Barcelona, while the total population reached around 110,000. The trade in African slaves, never favoured by the Spanish Crown, has dwindled to almost nothing on these coasts where, in the sixteenth century, it reached a terrifying figure.

Our first excursion was to the Araya peninsula and those regions formerly so infamous for slave-trading and pearl fishing. On the 19th of August, at about two in the morning, we embarked on the Manzanares river, near the Indian settlement. Our main objectives on this short trip were to visit the ruins of the ancient Araya fort, the salt works and the mountains that form the narrow Maniquarez peninsula where we hoped to carry out some geological research. The night was deliciously cool, swarms of luminous insects (*Elater noctilucus*) shone in the air, on the ground covered with sesuvium, and in the mimosa (*Lampyris italica*) thickets bordering the river. We know how common glow-worms are in Italy and all southern Europe, yet the picturesque effect they produce cannot compare with these innumerable scattered and moving lights, which embellish the tropical nights all over the plains, repeating the spectacle of the stars in the sky on the ground.

Descending the river we passed the plantations or *charas* where negroes had lit bonfires for their fiestas. A light billowing smoke rose above the palm-tree tops, giving a reddish colour to the moon's disk. It was a Sunday night and the slaves danced to the monotonous and noisy music of guitars. A fundamental feature of the black African races is their inexhaustible store of vitality and joy. After working painfully hard all week, they prefer to dance and sing on their fiesta days rather than sleep for a long time. We should be wary of criticizing this mixture of thoughtlessness and frivolity for it sweetens the evils of a life of deprivations and suffering!

The boat in which we crossed the Gulf of Cariaco was very spacious. They had spread large jaguar skins out so that we could rest at night. We had been scarcely two months in the torrid zone, and already our organs were so sensitive to the slightest temperature changes that cold stopped us sleeping. To our surprise we saw that the thermometer marked 21.8 °C. This fact is familiar to those who have lived long in the Indies. During our stay at Guayaquil in January 1803, we watched the Indians cover themselves and complain of the cold when the temperature sank to 23.8 °C, while they suffocated with heat at 30.5 °C. A difference of 6 °C or 7 °C was sufficient to cause the opposite sensations of cold and heat. At Cumaná, during heavy showers, people in the streets are heard to complain 'Qué hielo! Estoy emparamado,'[34] though the thermometer exposed to the rain sinks only to 21.5 °C.

At about eight in the morning we landed at Araya point, near the new salt works. A solitary house (La Ranchería de la Salina Nueva) stood in the middle of an arid plain, next to a battery of three cannons, sole defence on this coast since the destruction of the Santiago fort. The salt-works' inspector spends his life in a hammock from where he passes on his orders to his workers, and a 'king's launch' (*la lancha del rey*) brings him his supplies from Cumaná every week. It is astonishing that a salt works which once made the English, Dutch and other powerful maritime countries jealous did not lead to the founding of a village or even a farm. Only a few miserable Indian fishermen's huts exist at the tip of Araya point.

The abundance of salt contained in the Araya peninsula was known to Alonso Niño when, following the tracks of Columbus, Ojeda and Amerigo Vespucci, he visited these countries in 1499. Though the Indians of South America consume the least salt of any people on the globe because they eat mainly vegetables, it appears that the Guaiquerí dug into the clayey and muriatic soil of Punta Arena for salt. The Spaniards, established first at Cubagua, then on the Cumaná coasts, worked the salt marshes from the beginning of the sixteenth century. As the peninsula had no settled population the Dutch availed themselves of the natural riches of a soil that to them seemed common property. In our days, each colony has its own salt works. Navigation has so improved that merchants in Cádiz can send salt, at little expense, from Spain to cure meat in Montevideo or Buenos Aires, some 1,900 leagues away. These advantages were unknown at the time of the conquest. Colonial industry has made so little progress that Araya salt was carried to Cartagena and Portobello.[35] In 1605 the Madrid Court sent armed ships to expel the Dutch by force. The Dutch continued furtively to gather salt until a fort was built in 1622 near the salt works, which became known as Santiago fort, or the Real Fuerza de Araya. These great salt mines are laid down on the oldest Spanish maps. In 1726 a violent hurricane destroyed the Araya salt works and made the expensively built fort useless. This sudden hurricane was very rare in a region where the sea is generally as calm as the water of our large rivers; the high waves penetrated far inland and transformed the salty lake into a gulf several miles long. Since then there have been artificial deposits or vasets to the north of the chain of hills that separate the fort from the northern coast of the peninsula.[36]

Having examined the salt works and finished our geodesical observations, we left at dusk with the intention of spending the night in an Indian hut near the ruins of the Araya fort. We sent our instruments and provisions on ahead as the extreme heat and irradiation from the ground so exhausted us that we only felt like eating in the cool of night and early morning. Going southward, we crossed first the bare plain covered in salty clay, and then two chains of hills formed with sandstone between which there was a lagoon. Night surprised us while following a narrow path bordered on one side by the sea, and on the other by a wall of perpendicular rock. The tide was rising fast, and at each step narrowed the path. When we reached the foot of the old Araya fort we saw before us a natural picture that was melancholic and romantic. Yet neither the freshness of the dark jungle nor the grandeur of the plants could enhance the beauty of the ruins. These ruins stand on a bare, arid hill, with nothing but agave, columnar cacti and thorny mimosa, and seemed less like the work of men than masses of rock torn apart during the early revolutions of the earth.

We wanted to linger and admire the superb spectacle, and to observe the setting of Venus, whose disc appeared now and then between the broken fragments of the fort; but our mulatto guide was parched with thirst and insistently begged us to return. For a long time he had thought that we were lost, and, trying to scare us, he talked of the dangers of tigers and rattlesnakes. It is true that venomous reptiles are very common near the fort, and that a few days before two jaguars had been killed near the entrance to the village of Maniquarez. Judging by the skins we saw they could not be much smaller than tigers from India. We vainly tried to calm our man by telling him that those animals do not attack humans on a coast where goats offer copious prey: but we had to give in and retrace our steps. When we had been walking for three quarters of an hour along a beach covered by high tide we met the negro who was carrying our food; on seeing that we had not returned he had got worried and set out to find us. He led us through a wood of nopal cacti to the hut of an Indian family. We were received with that frank hospitality common in these lands to people from all social classes. From the outside the hut where we slung our hammocks looked very clean. Inside we found fish, bananas and other edibles, and, something that in this arid zone is far more appreciated than delicious food, excellent fresh water.

At dawn the next day we realized that the hut where we had spent the night formed part of a group of huts situated on the banks of a salt lake. They are the few remains left of a considerable village formed long ago around the fort. The ruins of the church were half buried in sand and covered with brushwood. When in 1762 the Araya fort was completely dismantled, to save the expense of maintaining a garrison, the Indians and other coloured residents who lived around about emigrated one by one to Maniquarez, Cariaco and the Guaiquerí suburb at Cumaná. Only a few remained in the wild and desolate village, deeply attached to their native land. These poor people live from fishing on the coast and in neighbouring shoals rich in fish. They seemed content with their fate and found it strange that I asked them why they had no gardens to cultivate nutritious plants. 'Our gardens,' they replied, 'lie on the other side of the strait; we bring fish to Cumaná and they give us cassava, bananas and coconuts in return.' This economic system, which flatters laziness, is followed at Maniquarez and throughout the Araya peninsula. The principal wealth of these inhabitants consists of large, beautiful goats. They move freely about like the goats on the Tenerife peak; they are completely wild, and are branded like the mules because it would be difficult to recognize them from their colour or spots. These fawn goats do not vary in colour like domestic ones. When a settler out hunting shoots a goat that is not his, he brings it to whichever neighbour it belongs to.

Among the mulattos whose huts surround the salt lake we found a shoemaker of Castilian descent. He received us with that gravity and self-sufficiency characteristic in those countries where the people feel they possess some special talent. He was stretching the string of a bow, and sharpening arrows to shoot birds. His trade of shoemaking could not be very lucrative in a country where the majority go barefoot; and he complained that the expense of European gunpowder reduced him to using the same weapons as the Indians. He was the sage of this place; he understood the formation of salt through the influence of the sun and full moon, the symptoms of earthquakes, the marks by which gold and silver mines are found, and the structure of medicinal plants, which he divided, like everybody in South America, into hot and cold. Having collected local traditions he gave us some curious accounts of the pearls of Cubagua, objects of luxury, which he treated with contempt. To show how familiar he was with the Bible he liked quoting Job, who preferred wisdom to all the pearls of

· the Indies. His philosophy was limited to the narrow circle of his vital needs. All he wanted was a strong ass to carry a load of bananas to the loading-wharf.

After a long speech on the vanity of human greatness he pulled a few small opaque pearls from out of his leather pouch and forced us to accept them, making us note down on our writing tablets that a poor shoemaker of Araya, white and of noble Castilian race, had given us something that, across the ocean,[37] was thought of as very precious.

The pearl-oyster (*Aviculidae, Meleagrina margaritifera,* Cuvier) abounds on the shoals that extend from Cape Paria to Cape La Vela. The islands of Margarita, Cubagua, Coche, Punta Araya and the mouth of the Hacha river were as famous in the sixteenth century as the Persian Gulf and the island of Taprobana were to the ancients.

Benzoni[38] relates the adventure of one Louis Lampagnano, to whom Charles V granted the privilege of proceeding with five caravels to the Cumaná coasts to fish for pearls. The settlers sent him back with the bold message that the Emperor, too liberal with what was not his own, had no right to dispose of the oysters living at the bottom of the sea.

The pearl fisheries diminished rapidly towards the end of the sixteenth century, and had long ceased by 1683. The industrious Venetians who imitated fine pearls perfectly, and the growing popularity of cut diamonds, made the Cubagua fisheries less lucrative. At the same time the oysters became scarcer, not because, according to popular legend, they were frightened by the sound of oars and moved away, but because the rash gathering of thousands at a time stopped them propagating themselves. To form an idea of the destruction of the shells caused by the divers, we must remember that a boat collects in two to three weeks more than 35,000 oysters. The animal lives but nine to ten years, and only in its fourth year do pearls begin to show. In 10,000 shells there is often not a single pearl of value.

On the morning of the 20th the son of our host, a young, robust Indian, led us to the village of Maniquarez, passing through Barigon and Caney. It was a four-hour walk. Because of the reverberation of the sun's rays on the sand the thermometer remained at 31.3 °C. The cylindrical cacti along the path made the landscape green, but without freshness or shade. We had walked barely a league when our guide decided, at every opportunity, to sit down and rest. When we got near to Casas de la Vela he even tried to lie down in the shade of a beautiful tamarind tree, to await nightfall. We observed this characteristic trait whenever we travelled with Indians; it has given rise to the most mistaken ideas about the physical constitutions of different races. The copper-coloured Indian, who is more used to the burning heat of these regions than a European, complains more because nothing stimulates his interest. Money is no bait, and if he is tempted by gain he repents of his decision as soon as he starts walking. This same Indian, who would complain when we loaded him with a box filled with plants while herborizing, would row his canoe against the strongest current for fourteen or fifteen hours in order to be back home.

We examined the remarkably solid ruins of Santiago. The 5-foot-thick walls of freestone have been toppled over by mines; but we still found huge sections with scarcely a crack in them. Our guide showed us a cistern (*el aljibe*), 30 feet deep, which though damaged furnishes water to the inhabitants of the Araya peninsula. This cistern was finished in 1681. As the basin is covered with an arched vault the excellent water remains very cool. Crossing the arid hills of Cape Cirial we detected a strong smell of petroleum. The wind blew from the place where the springs of petroleum, mentioned by the first chroniclers,[39] are to be found.

The Maniquarez potteries, famous from time immemorial, are a specialized industry completely run by Indian women. They work with the same method that was used before the conquest. This reveals both the infancy of this craft and that immobility of manners so characteristic of American Indians. Three hundred years have not sufficed to introduce the potter's wheel to a coast not more than forty days' sailing from Spain. The Indians have a vague idea that something of the sort exists, and surely would adopt one should it be shown to them. The quarries where they extract their clay lie half a league to the east of Maniquarez. This clay is produced by the decomposition of a mica-slate stained red by iron oxide. The Indian women prefer the part most loaded with mica; and very skilfully shape vessels of 2 to 3 feet in diameter with regular curves. As they do not know how to use kilns they place scrub from desmanthus, cassia and arborescent capparis around the pots and bake them in the open air.

At Maniquarez we met some creoles who had been hunting at Cubagua. Deer of a small variety abound in this uninhabited island, and one person may kill three or four a day. I do not know how these animals got to the island as chroniclers mention only the great amount of rabbits. The *venado* of Cubagua belong to one of those numerous species of small American deer long confused under the vague name of *Cervus mexicanus*. In the plains of Cari we were shown something very rare in these hot climates, a completely white deer. Albino varieties are found in the New Continent even among tigers. Azara[40] saw a completely white-skinned jaguar.

The most extraordinary, even most marvellous, object on the Araya coast is what the people call the 'eye stone' (*piedra de los ojos*). This calcareous substance is the subject of many conversations as it is, according to Indian science, both stone and animal. It is found in the sand, where it is motionless: but if it is picked up and placed on a polished surface, for example a pewter or pottery plate, it begins to move if you drip some lemon juice on it. If it is then placed in the eye this supposed animal will expel any other foreign substance that may accidentally get in there. At the new salt works, and in the village of Maniquarez, hundreds of eye stones were offered to us, and the Indians pressed us to test them with lemon juice. They wanted to put sand in our eyes to convince us of the virtues of this remedy. Very quickly we saw that these 'stones' are the thin and porous valves of diminutive univalve shells. They have a diameter of some 1 to 4 lines, with one surface plane, the other convex. These calcareous coverings effervesce with lemon juice and start moving as the carbonic acid is formed. When placed in eyes, these eye stones act as tiny round pearls and seeds, used by the Indians of America to stimulate the flow of tears. These explanations did not satisfy the inhabitants of Araya. For man nature seems more grand the more it is mysterious, and the physics of the people rejects any simple explanation.

Along the southern coast, east of Maniquarez, three strips of land run out to sea. In these parts the seabed is made of mica-slate, and from these orogenic rock formations, some 26 metres from the coast, issues a spring of petroleum whose smell reaches far inland. We had to wade into the water up to our waists to observe this interesting phenomenon. The waters are covered with zostera, and in the centre of a large bank of these plants you see a clear round patch, about 3 feet in diameter, across which float masses of *Ulva lactuca*. It is here that the springs are found. The bed of the bay is covered with sand, and the transparent and yellow petroleum resembles naphtha itself, bursting out in jets, accompanied by air bubbles. When we trod down the bottom with our feet we saw how these little springs changed place. The naphtha covers the sea for more than 1,000 feet from the shore line.

After exploring the outskirts of Maniquarez, we embarked in a fishing-boat for Cumaná. Nothing confirms how calm the sea is here as much as the tiny, badly kept boats with their one tall sail. Though we had picked the least damaged boat it leaked so much that the pilot's son had to continually bale out the water with a *tutumo*, or shell of the fruit of the *Crescentia cujete* (or calabash). In the Gulf of Cariaco, especially north of the Araya peninsula, canoes laden with coconuts often capsize because they sail too near the wind and against the waves. These accidents inspire fear only in those travellers who do not swim well; for when a pirogue is manned by an Indian fisherman and his son, the father turns the pirogue round and bales out the water while the son swims around, gathering all the coconuts. In less than a quarter of an hour the pirogue is sailing again without the Indian, with his boundless impassivity, having once complained.

The inhabitants of Araya, whom we visited a second time when returning from the Orinoco, have not forgotten that their peninsula is one of the places most anciently populated by the Castilians. They like talking about the pearl fisheries, the ruins of the Santiago fort, which they hope will be rebuilt one day, and all that they call the ancient splendour of these countries. In China and Japan inventions are called recent if they are more than 2,000 years old: in the European colonies an event seems extremely ancient if it is three centuries old, dating back to the discovery.

This absence of memories, which characterizes these new people in the United States of America and in the Spanish and Portuguese possessions, is worthy of attention. It is not only distressing to the traveller, who becomes deprived of the pleasures of the imagination, it also influences the bonds that tie a settler to the land he inhabits, the form of the rocks around his hut, the trees shading his cradle.

Most of these modern colonies are founded in a zone where the climate, the produce, the sky and landscape, all differ completely from Europe. The settler vainly tries to name the mountains, rivers and valleys with names that recall his motherland; these names soon lose their charm, and mean nothing to later generations. Under the influence of an exotic nature new habits are born for new needs; national memories are slowly effaced, and those remembered, like ghosts of our imaginations, are not attached to any time or place. The glories of Don Pelayo or the Cid Campeador have penetrated the forests and mountains of America; people sometimes pronounce these famous names, but they seem to come from an ideal world, from vague, fabulous times.

Moreover, the American colonies are founded in countries where the dead leave barely any trace of their existence. To the north of Gila river, on the banks of the Missouri, and in the Andean plain, traditions date back only a century. In Peru, Guatemala and Mexico, ruins, historic paintings and sculptured monuments attest, it is true, to ancient Indian civilizations, but throughout an entire province only a few families have precise notions about Inca history or Mexican princesses. The Indian has kept his language, his customs and national character; but the loss of *quipus*[41] and symbolic paintings, the introduction of Christianity, and other factors, have made the historic and religious traditions vanish. On the one hand the European settler scorns everything to do with the defeated Indians. Placed between memories of the metropolis and the actual country he was born in, he looks to both indifferently; in a climate where the equality of the seasons makes the succession of years almost indifferent he lives only for the pleasures of the moment and rarely looks to the past.

CHAPTER 6

Mountains of New Andalusia – Cumanacoa valley – Cocollar summit – Chaima Indian missions

Our first excursion to the Araya peninsula was followed by another more important and instructive one to the mountain missions of the Chaima Indians. Such a variety of objects attracted our attention. We found ourselves in a country bristling with forests on our way to visit a convent shaded by palm trees and arborescent ferns in a narrow valley which was deliciously fresh, despite being in the middle of the torrid zone. In the surrounding mountains there are caves inhabited by thousands of nocturnal birds; and, what struck our imagination more than all the marvels of the physical world, even further up we found a people until recently still nomadic, hardly free from a natural, wild state, but not barbarians, made stupid more from ignorance than from long years of being brutalized. What we knew about history increased our interest in these people. The promontory of Paria was what Columbus first saw of this continent; these valleys ended there, devastated first by the warlike, cannibalistic Caribs, then by the mercantile and orderly European nations. If the Spaniards visited these shores it was only to get, either by violence or exchange, slaves, pearls, gold and dye-woods; they tried to dignify their motives for such an insatiable greed with the pretence of religious zeal.

The treatment of the copper-coloured Indians was accompanied by the same acts of inhumanity that later were meted out to the black Africans, with the same consequences of making both conquered and conquering wilder. From that time wars between the Indians became more common; prisoners were dragged from the interior to the coasts to be sold to whites who chained them to their boats. Yet the Spaniards at that period, and long after, were one of the most civilized nations of Europe. The light that art and literature shed over Italy was reflected on every nation whose language stemmed from the same source as that of Dante and Petrarch. One might have expected a general sweetening of manners as the natural consequence of this noble awakening of the mind, this soaring of the imagination. But across the seas, wherever the thirst for riches led to the abuse of power, the nations of Europe have always displayed the same characteristics. The noble century of Leo X was marked in the New World by acts of cruelty that belonged to a barbaric past.

The missionaries' privilege was to console humanity for a part of the evils committed by the conquistadores; to plead the cause of the Indians before kings, to resist the violence of the *comendadores*, and to gather nomadic Indians into small communities called missions[42] to help agriculture progress. And so, imperceptibly, following a uniform and premeditated plan, these vast monastic establishments were formed into extraordinary regimes, always isolating themselves, with countries four or five times larger than France under their administration.

But these institutions, useful at first in preventing the spilling of blood and establishing the basis of society, have become hostile to progress. The effect of their isolation has been such that the Indians have remained in the same state as they were found before their scattered huts were grouped around missions. Their number has considerably increased but not their mental development. They have progressively lost that vigour of character and natural vivacity which everywhere comes from independence. By subjecting even the slightest domestic actions to invariable rules the Indians have been kept stupid in an effort to make them obedient. Their subsistence is more certain, and their habits more pacific, but subject to constraints and the dull monotony of the missions. They show by their gloomy and abstracted looks that they have not sacrificed freedom for comfort without regret.

At five in the morning on the 4th of September we set out for the missions of the Chaima Indians and the high mountains crossing New Andalusia. Because of the road's extreme difficulties we had been advised to reduce our equipment as much as we could. Two mules sufficed to carry our provisions, our instruments and the paper necessary to dry plants. Our box contained a sextant, a dipping needle, an instrument to determine magnetic variation, thermometers and Saussure's hygrometer.[43] Choosing the instruments caused us most problems on the short journeys.

The morning was deliciously cool. The road, or rather path, that led to Cumanacoa follows the right bank of the Manzanares river, passing the Capuchin hospital situated in a small wood of lignum vitae and caper trees. After leaving Cumaná we reached the San Francisco hill during twilight and enjoyed an extensive view of the sea, the plain covered with golden-flowered bera (*Palo sano, Zygophyllum arboreum*), whose flowers smell of vanilla, and the Brigantín mountains.

At the Divina Pastora hospice the path turns to the north-east along a stretch without trees, formerly levelled by the waters. There we found not only cacti, tufts of cistus-leaved tribulus and the beautiful purple euphorbia, cultivated in Havana gardens under the odd name of *Dictamno real*, but also the avicennia, the allionia, the sesuvium, the thalinum and most of the portulaceous plants that grow on the banks of the Gulf of Cariaco. This geographical distribution of plants appears to designate the limits of the ancient coast and to prove that the hills along the southern side, which we were following, once formed islands separated from the continent by an arm of the sea.

After walking for two hours we reached the foot of the high inland mountain chain. There new rock formations begin, and with them another kind of vegetation. Everything seems more grand and picturesque. The soil, rich in springs, is furrowed by streams in every direction. Gigantic trees, covered with lianas, rise from the ravines; their black bark, burned by the sun and oxygen, contrasts with the fresh green of the pothos and dracontium, whose tough, shiny leaves reach as much as 2 metres in length.

We passed some huts inhabited by mestizos. Each hut stands in the centre of an enclosure containing banana trees, papaw trees, sugar cane and maize. The small extent of cultivated land might surprise us until we recall that an acre planted with bananas produces nearly twenty times as much food as the same space sown with cereals. In Europe our wheat, barley and rye cover vast spaces of land; in general arable lands border each other wherever inhabitants live on wheat. It is different in the torrid zone where man obtains food from plants that yield more abundant harvests more quickly. In these favoured climates the immense fertility of the soil corresponds to the heat and humidity. A large population can be fed from a small plot of land covered with banana, cassava, yams and maize. The isolation of huts dispersed in the forest indicates to the traveller how fertile nature is.

In Europe we calculate the number of inhabitants of a country by the extent of cultivation; in the Tropics, in the warmest and most humid parts of South America, very populated areas seem deserted because man cultivates but a small number of acres to feed himself. Without neighbours, virtually cut off from the rest of mankind, each family forms a different tribe. This isolated state retards the progress of civilization, which advances only as society becomes more populated and its connections more intimate and multiplied. But, on the other hand, solitude develops and strenghtens liberty and independence; and has fed that pride of character which distinguishes the Castilian race.

For these reasons land in the most populated areas of tropical America still seems wild; a quality lost in temperate climates by the cultivation of wheat. Within the Tropics agriculture occupies less land; man has not extended his empire, and he appears not as the absolute master who alters the soil at his will but as a transient guest who peacefully enjoys the gifts of nature. There, near the most populated cities, land remains bristling with forests or covered with a tangle of plants, untouched by plough. Spontaneous vegetation still predominates over cultivated plants, and determines the aspect of nature. If in our temperate regions the cultivation of wheat contributes to the spreading of a dull uniformity over the cleared land, we cannot doubt that, even with an increasing population, the torrid zone will keep its majesty of plant life, those marks of an untamed, virgin nature that make it so attractive and picturesque.

As we entered the jungle the barometer showed that we were gaining altitude. Here the tree trunks offered us an extraordinary view: a gramineous plant with verticillate branches[44] climbs like a liana to a height of 8 to 10 feet, forming garlands that cross our path and swing in the wind. At about three in the afternoon we stopped on a small plain known as Quetepe, some 190 toises above sea-level. A few huts stand by a spring whose water is known by the Indians to be fresh and healthy. We found the water delicious. Its temperature was only 22.5 °C while the air was 28.7 °C.

From the top of a sandstone hill overlooking the Quetepe spring we had a magnificent view of the sea, Cape Macanao and the Maniquarez peninsula. From our feet an immense jungle stretched out as far as the ocean. The tree-tops, intertwined with lianas and their long tufts of flowers, formed an enormous green carpet whose dark tint increased the brilliancy of the light. This picture struck us more powerfully as it was the first time we had seen tropical vegetation. On the Quetepe hill, under the *Malpighia cocollobaefolia*, with its hard coriaceous leaves, we collected our first melastoma, especially that beautiful species that goes under the name of *Melastoma rufescens*, among thickets of *Polygala montana*. Our memory of this place will remain with us for a long time; the traveller pleasurably remembers those places where for the first time he finds a plant family never seen before in its wild state.

Further to the south-west the soil turns dry and sandy. We climbed a relatively high range that separates the coast from the great plains or savannahs bordering the Orinoco. That section of the mountains through which the road to Cumanacoa leads is devoid of vegetation and falls steeply both to the south and north. It has been called Imposible because this impenetrable mountain ridge would offer a refuge to the inhabitants of Cumaná during a hostile invasion. We reached the top just before sunset. I scarcely had the time to take a few horary angles with my chronometer to calculate the geographic longitude of the place.

The view from Imposible is even more beautiful and extensive than that from the tableland of Quetepe. With our naked eyes we could easily pick out the flattened top of the Brigantín, whose exact geographic position must be verified, the landing-place and Cumaná outer harbour. The rocky coast of Araya stretched out before us. We were particularly struck by the extraordinary structure of the harbour known as Laguna Grande, or Laguna del Obispo. A vast basin, surrounded by high mountains, communicates with the Gulf of Cariaco via a narrow canal along which only one boat at a time may pass. With our eyes we traced the sinuosities of this arm of sea, which has dug a bed like a river between perpendicular rocks stripped of vegetation. This extraordinary view reminded us of the fantastic landscape that Leonardo da Vinci painted in the background of his famous portrait of Mona Lisa.

We spent the night in a house occupied by a military post of eight soldiers under a Spanish sergeant. It was a hospice, built next to a powder-magazine. The summit of Imposible, as far as I could make out, was covered with a sandstone rich in quartz, without fossils. Here, as on the neighbouring hills, the strata are lined regularly along a north-north-east, south-south-west axis.

The *llaneros*, or inhabitants of the llanos (plains), send their products – maize, hides and cattle – to Cumaná harbour by the road over Imposible. We saw Indians or mulattos with mules coming towards us, rapidly moving in single file.

Several parts of the vast forests that surround the mountains were on fire. The reddish flames, half hidden by clouds of smoke, stunned us. The inhabitants set fire to the forests to improve their pasturage and to destroy the shrubs that choke the scant grass. Enormous forest fires are also caused by the carelessness of the Indians who forget to put out their camp fires. These accidents have diminished the old trees along the Cumaná–Cumanacoa road, and inhabitants have justly noticed that aridity has increased all over the province, not only because the land has more crevices from earthquakes, but also because it is less forested than it was before the conquest.

We left Imposible on the 5th of September before dawn. The descent is very dangerous for the pack-animals; the path is only some 15 inches wide, with precipices on either side. In 1796 a useful plan to build a road from the village of San Fernando to the mountain was conceived. A third of this route had already been finished, but unfortunately it ran only from the plain to the foot of Imposible. Work was halted for one of those reasons that makes all attempts at improvement in the Spanish colonies fail. Several authorities wanted to assume the rights of running the works. The people patiently paid their tolls for a route that did not exist until the Cumaná governor put an end to this abuse. As we descended we noticed that alpine limestone reappeared under the sandstone. As the strata generally incline to the south and south-east many springs well up along the southern side of the mountain. In the rainy season these springs become torrents that rush down under the hura, the cuspa and the silver-leafed cecropia, or trumpet trees.

The cuspa, common enough around Cumaná and Bordones, is still an unknown tree to European botanists. For a long time it was used only for building houses. Since 1797, under the name of the cascarilla or bark tree (cinchona), it has become rather famous. Its trunk barely reaches 15 to 20 feet high. Its thin, pale yellow bark is an excellent febrifuge. It is even more bitter than the bark of the real cinchona, but less disagreeable. Cuspa is administered with great success in both alcoholic extracts and watery infusions for both intermittent and malignant fevers.[45]

When we left the ravine that descends from the Imposible we entered a thick jungle cut by numerous rivers, which we easily forded. In the middle of the forest, on the banks of the Cedoño river, as well as on the southern slopes of the Cocollar, we found wild papaw and orange trees with large, sweet fruit. These are probably the remains of some *conucos*, or Indian plantations, because the orange is not a native tree; neither are the banana, papaw, maize, cassava and so many other useful plants whose countries of origin are unknown, though they have accompanied man in his migrations from remotest time.

When a traveller recently arrived from Europe steps into South American jungle for the first time he sees nature in a completely unexpected guise. The objects that surround him only faintly bring to mind those descriptions by famous writers of the banks of the Mississippi, of Florida and of other temperate regions of the New World. With each step he feels not at the frontiers of the torrid zone but in its midst; not on one of the West Indian Islands but in a vast continent where everything is gigantic; mountains, rivers and the masses of plants. If he is able to feel the beauty of landscape, he will find it hard to analyse his many impressions. He does not know what shocks him more: whether the calm silence of the solitude, or the beauty of the diverse, contrasting objects, or that fullness and freshness of plant life in the Tropics. It could be said that the earth, overloaded with plants, does not have sufficient space to develop. Everywhere tree trunks are hidden behind a thick green carpet. If you carefully transplanted all the orchids, all the epiphytes that grow on one single

American fig tree (*Ficus gigantea*) you would manage to cover an enormous amount of ground. The same lianas that trail along the ground climb up to the tree-tops, swinging from one tree to another 100 feet up in the air. As these parasitical plants form a real tangle, a botanist often confuses flowers, fruit and leaves belonging to different species.

We walked for hours in the shade of these plant vaults that scarcely let us catch glimpses of the blue sky, which appeared to be more of a deep indigo blue because the green, verging on brown, of tropical plants seemed so intense. A great fern tree (perhaps *Aspidium caducum*) rose above masses of scattered rock. For the first time we saw those nests in the shape of bottles or small bags that hang from the lower branches. They are the work of that clever builder the oriole, whose song blends with the noisy shrieking of parrots and macaws. These last, so well known for their vivid colours, fly around in pairs, while the parrots proper fly in flocks of hundreds. A man must live in these regions, particularly the hot Andean valleys, to understand how these birds can sometimes drown the noise of waterfalls with their voices.

About a league from San Fernando village we left the jungle. A narrow winding path led to open but extremely humid country. In a more temperate climate this region would have been a vast meadow of grass and reeds: but here the ground was packed with aquatic plants with lanceolate leaves, especially basil plants among which we recognized the magnificent flowers of the costus, thalia and heliconia. These succulent plants reach some 8 to 10 feet high; in Europe their bunching together would be considered a small wood.

Near San Fernando the evaporation caused by the sun's rays was so intense that, although lightly dressed, we soon became as soaked as if we had had a steam bath. Along the road a kind of bamboo (*Bambusa gadua*[46]) that the Indians call *iagua* or *gadua* grows to a height of some 40 feet. It is hard to imagine anything more elegant than this arborescent grass. The form and disposition of its leaves give it a lightness that contrasts agreeably with its height. The smooth and shiny trunks of the *iagua* generally lean towards the river banks, swaying at the slightest breeze. However tall canes (*Arundo donax*) may grow in southern Europe they cannot compare with the arborescent grasses; and if I dare resort to my own experience I would say that the bamboo and fern tree are, of all tropical vegetation, what strikes the traveller's imagination most.

The bamboo-lined road led us to the small village of San Fernando, located in a narrow plain, surrounded by steep calcareous cliffs. It was the first mission we visited in America. The houses, or rather shacks, of the Chaima Indians are scattered about, and are without vegetable gardens. The straight narrow streets cut each other at right angles. The thin irregular walls are made of clay and bound with lianas. The monotony of the houses, the serious and taciturn aspect of the inhabitants and the extreme cleanliness inside their homes reminded us of the establishments of the Moravian Brethren.[47] Each family cultivates the *conuco de la comunidad*, which is outside the village, as are their own individual vegetable plots. Adults of both sexes work there an hour in the morning and an hour in the evening. In the missions near the coast, the communal garden is nearly always planted with sugar cane or indigo and run by the missions. Their product, if the law is strictly followed, can be used only for the upkeep of the church and the purchase of whatever the priests may need. San Fernando's great square, in the centre of the village, contains the church, the missionary's house and the modest building that goes pompously under the name of 'king's house' (*casa del rey*). This is the official hostel for travellers and, as we often confirmed, a real blessing in a land where the word 'inn' is unknown. These *casas del rey* can be found all over Spanish colonies, no doubt imitating the Peruvian *tambos* established by Manco Capac's laws.[48]

The syndic in Cumaná had recommended us to the missionaries who run the Chaima Indian mission. This recommendation was all the more useful to us as the missionaries, zealous for the purity of their parishioners' morals, and wary of the indiscreet curiosity of strangers, tended to apply an ancient rule of their order according to which no white secular person could remain more than one night in an Indian village. In general, to travel agreeably in Spanish missions it would not be wise to trust solely to the passport issued by the Madrid Secretary of State: you must arm yourself with recommendations from the ecclesiastical authorities, especially the custodians of convents, or the generals of orders residing in Rome, who are far more respected by missionaries than bishops. Missions have become, in reality, a distinct, almost independent, hierarchy, despite being primitive or canonical institutions.

The missionary in San Fernando was an Aragonese Capuchin, well advanced in years but very strong and lively. His obesity, his good humour and his interest in battles and sieges contradicted the ideas held in northern countries concerning the melancholic reveries and contemplative life of missionaries. Though extremely busy organizing the slaughter of a cow for the following day he received us good-naturedly, and let us hang our hammocks in a gallery of his house. Sitting in his redwood armchair most of the day without doing anything, he complained of what he called the laziness and ignorance of his countrymen. He asked us thousands of questions about the real purpose of our journey, which to him seemed hazardous and quite useless. Here, as on the Orinoco, we grew weary of the lively curiosity manifested by Europeans in the middle of American jungles for the wars and political storms in the Old World.

Our missionary, however, seemed quite satisfied with his situation. He treated the Indians well; his mission prospered, and he enthused about the water, the bananas and the milk of this place. The sight of our instruments, our books and dried plants made him smile sarcastically; and he acknowledged with the naïvety peculiar to the inhabitants of these countries that his greatest pleasure in life, even including sleep, was eating good beef, *carne de vaca*; thus does sensuality triumph when there is nothing to occupy the mind. Our host often enjoined us to visit the cow he had bought, and the following day, at dawn, we could not avoid watching his cow being slaughtered in the manner of the country, that is, cutting its hamstrings before plunging a long knife into the vertebra of its neck. Disgusting as this was, it did teach us about the immense skill of the Chaima Indians, who, numbering eight, managed to cut the animal up into little pieces in less than twenty minutes.

The road from San Fernando to Cumanacoa passes through small plantations in a humid, open valley. We forded numerous streams. In the shade the thermometer did not rise above 30 °C, but we were exposed to the sun's rays because the bamboos along the path gave only a feeble shade and we suffered a lot from the heat. We passed through the village of Arenas, inhabited by Indians of the same race as those at San Fernando. But Arenas is no longer a mission, and the Indians, governed by a regular priest, are less naked and more civilized. Their church is known in the area for the primitive paintings on its walls. A narrow frieze encloses pictures of armadillos, caymans, jaguars and other New World animals.

Francisco Lozano, a labourer who lived in this village, presented a curious physiological phenomenon that struck our imagination, but did not contradict any laws of organic nature. This man breast-fed a child with his own milk. When the mother fell ill, the father, to pacify the child, took it to bed and pressed it to his nipples. Lozano, then thirty-two years old, had never noticed before that he had milk, but the irritation of the nipple sucked by the child caused liquid to accumulate. The milk was thick and very sweet. The father, astonished at how his breasts increased, suckled his child two or three times a day for five months. He attracted his neighbours' attention but, unlike someone living in Europe, never thought of exploiting this curiosity. We saw the certificate, drawn up on the spot, that attested this remarkable fact; eyewitnesses are still living. We were assured that during the breast-feeding the child received no other food but his father's milk. Lozano, away from Arenas when we visited, came to see us at Cumaná, accompanied by his son of already thirteen or fourteen. Bonpland carefully examined the father's breasts and found them wrinkled, like those of a woman who has suckled.[49]

Cumanacoa was founded in 1717 by Domingo Arias on his return from an expedition to the mouth of the Guarapiche river, undertaken in an attempt to destroy a settlement of French pirates. The new town was first called Baltasar de las Arias but the Indian name Cumanacoa prevailed; as did Caracas over Santiago de Leon, still to be found on our maps.

The plain, or rather tableland, on which Cumanacoa stands is only 104 toises above sea-level, three or four times lower than the inhabitants of Cumaná, who have an exaggerated view of how cold it is up there, think it is. The climatic difference between the two neighbouring towns is due less to the height of one of them than to local weather conditions. Among these causes are the proximity of the jungle, the frequency of rivers falling down narrow valleys, the amount of rain and those thick fogs that block out sunlight. The cool climate surprises us all the more because, as in the town of Cartago, at Tomependa on the Amazon, as in the Agarua valleys west of Caracas, very great heat is felt though the height varies between 200 and 480 toises above sea-level. In plains, as well as on mountains, isothermal lines are not constantly parallel to the equator or the surface of the earth. Meteorology's great problem will be to determine the direction of these lines and variations due to local causes, and to discover the constant laws in the distribution of heat.

The port of Cumaná lies some 7 leagues from Cumanacoa. It hardly ever rains in the former place, while in the latter the rainy season lasts seven months. In Cumanacoa the dry season stretches from the winter solstice to the spring equinox. Sporadic showers are common in April, May and June; then a drought begins again until the summer solstice or the end of August. Then the rainy season proper starts and lasts until November, and water pours down in torrents from the sky.

Our first day in the missions corresponded to the first day of the rainy season. Every night a thick mist covered the sky like a uniform veil; only through clearings did I manage to make any observations of the stars. The thermometer marked between 18.5 °C and 20 °C, which in this zone, and for a traveller arrived from the coast, appeared rather cold. In Cumaná I never saw the thermometer go lower than 21 °C. The hottest hours are from midday to three in the afternoon when the thermometer rises to 26 °C or 27 °C. During the hottest hour of the day, two hours before the sun passes over the meridian, a storm regularly built up and then exploded. Thick black low clouds dissolved in rain; the downpour lasted two to three hours while the thermometer sunk to 5 °C or 6 °C. At about five the rain stopped, the sun appeared just before sunset, and the hygrometer moved towards the point of dryness; by eight or nine at night we were again enveloped in a thick mist. These different changes follow successively – we were assured – day after day for months, yet not the slightest breeze was felt.

The vegetation in the plain surrounding the city is monotonous, although remarkably fresh due to the humidity. Its principal feature is an arborescent solanum, the *Urtica baccifera*, which reaches 40 feet tall, and a new species of the *Guettarda* genus. The ground is very fertile and could be easily watered if irrigation ditches were dug from the numerous rivers that do not dry up all year round. The most precious product in the zone is tobacco; it is solely to this plant that the small, badly built city owes its meagre fame. Since the introduction of the royal monopoly (Estanco Real de Tabaco) in 1799 the cultivation of this plant in the Cumaná province is limited almost exclusively to the Cumanacoa valley. This monopolistic farming system is deeply hated by the people. The entire tobacco harvest has to be sold to the government, and to prevent or limit smuggling tobacco was concentrated in only one place. Inspectors travel the country burning plantations found outside the authorized zone, and inform against those wretches who dare to smoke their own home-made cigars. These inspectors are mostly Spaniards, as insolent as those doing the same job in Europe. This insolence has greatly contributed to the maintenance of the hatred between the colonies and the metropolis.[50]

After tobacco the most important product of the Cumanacoa valley is indigo, whose intense colour makes it the equal of Guatemalan indigo. All the indigo factories that we visited are constructed along the same principles. Two vats, where the plants 'rot', are placed together. Each one measures 15 feet square and 2.5 feet deep. From these upper vats the liquid passes into beaters where the water-mill is placed. The axle-tree of the great wheel crosses the two beaters. It is nailed with ladles, fixed to long handles, for the beating. From another percolating vat the coloured starch passes to the drying-boxes, spread on planks of Brazil-wood on small wheels so that they can be pushed under a roof in case of sudden rain. These sloping and low roofs give the drying-boxes the appearance of hothouses from a distance. In the Cumanacoa valley the fermentation of the plant takes place amazingly quickly; usually it does not take longer than four or five hours. This can be attributed to the humidity and the absence of sun during the plant's development.

The Cumanacoa plains, scattered with farms and tobacco plantations, are surrounded by mountains, which are higher in the south. Everything suggests that the valley is an ancient seabed. The mountains that once formed its shores rise vertically from the sea. When excavating foundations near Cumanacoa, beds of round pebbles mixed with small bivalve shells were found. According to many reliable people two enormous femur bones were discovered, about thirty years ago. The Indians took them, as do people today in Europe, for giant's bones, while the semi-educated country people, who try to explain everything, seriously claimed that they are nature's sports, not worthy of consideration. They were probably the gigantic femur of elephants of a vanished species.

We frequently visited a small farm called the Conuco de Bermúdez, situated opposite the Cuchivano crevice. In its moist soil grow bananas, tobacco and several species of cotton trees, especially the one whose cotton is wild nankeen yellow, so common on Margarita Island. The owner told us that the ravine was inhabited by jaguars. These animals spend the day in caverns and prowl around human settlements at night. If well fed they reach some 6 feet in length. A year before, one of these cats had devoured a farm horse. In clear moonlight he dragged his prey across the savannah to the foot of an enormous ceiba. The neighing of the dying horse woke up the farm slaves. Armed with lances and machetes[51] they rushed out in the middle of the night. The jaguar, stretched over its victim, waited quietly, and was killed only after a long and stubborn fight. This fact, and many others verified on the spot, prove that the great jaguar of Terra Firma (*Felis onca*), like the jaguarete of Paraguay and the Asian tiger, does not run away when attacked by man, and is not scared by the number of his enemy. Naturalists today know that Buffon[52] completely failed to recognize the greatest of American cats. What this famous writer says about the cowardice of tigers in the New World relates to the small ocelots (*Felis pardalis*). In the Orinoco, the American jaguar sometimes leaps into the water to attack Indians in their canoes.

Opposite Bermúdez's farm two spacious caves open out of Cuchivano's crevice. At times flames, which can be seen from great distances, burst out. They illuminate the surrounding mountains, and from the mark left on the rocks by these burning gases we could be tempted to believe they reach some 100 feet high. During the last violent Cumaná earthquake this phenomenon was accompanied by long, dull, underground noises.

During a herborizing trip to Rinconada, we tried vainly to penetrate into the crevice. We wanted to closely study the rocks inside that seemed to cause those extraordinary fires. The thickness of the vegetation with its tangle of liana and thorny plants blocked the way. Fortunately the inhabitants of the valley took an active part in our researches, not out of fear of a volcanic eruption, but because their imagination was struck by the idea that the Risco de Cuchivano contained a gold mine. They would not listen to our explanation that there could be no gold in secondary limestone; they wanted to know 'what the German miner thought about the richness of the vein'. Since the times of Charles V and the government of the Welscrs, the people of Terra Firma have retained a belief that Germans know all about exploiting mines. No matter where I was in South America, as soon as people knew where I had been born they brought me mineral samples. In the colonies all the French are doctors, and all Germans miners.

The farmers and their slaves cut a path through the jungle to the first Juagua river waterfall, and on the 10th of September we made our excursion to the Cuchivano crevice. Entering the cave we saw a disembowelled porcupine and smelled the stink of excrement, similar to that of European cats, and knew that a jaguar had been near by. For safety the Indians returned to the farm to fetch small dogs. It is said that when you meet a jaguar in your path he will leap on to a dog before a man. We did not follow the bank of the torrent, but a rocky wall overhanging the water. We walked on a very narrow ledge along the side of a precipice with a drop of some 200 to 300 feet. When it narrowed, so that we could not walk along it any further, we climbed down to the torrent and crossed it on foot, or on the backs of slaves, to climb up the other side. Climbing is very tiring, and you cannot trust the lianas, which, like thick rope, hang from tree-tops. Creepers and parasites hang loosely from the branches they grip; their stalks together weigh a lot, and if you slip and grab one of the lianas you risk bringing down a tangle of green branches. The vegetation became impenetrable the more we advanced. In some places the roots of trees grew in the existing cracks between strata and had burst the calcareous rock. We could hardly carry the plants we picked at each step. The canna, the heliconia with pretty purple flowers, the costus and other plants from the *Amomum* genus reach here the height of 8 to 10 feet. Their tender, fresh green leaves, their silky sheen and the extraordinary development of their juicy pulp contrast with the brown of the arborescent ferns whose leaves are so delicately jagged. The Indians made deep incisions in the tree trunks with their long knives to draw our attention to the beauty of the red- and gold-coloured woods, which one day will be sought after by our furniture makers. They showed us a plant with composite flowers that reaches some 20 feet high (*Eupatorium laevigatum*), the so-called 'Rose of Belveria' (*Brownea racemosa*), famous for the brilliance of its purple flowers, and the local 'dragon's blood', a species of euphorbia not yet catalogued, whose red and astringent sap is used to strengthen the gums. They distinguished species by their smell and by chewing their woody fibres. Two Indians, given the same wood to chew, pronounced, often without hesitation, the same name. But we could not take advantage of our guides' wisdom, for how could they reach leaves, flowers and fruit[53] growing on branches some 50 to 60 feet above the ground? We were struck in this gorge by the fact that the bark of the trees, even the ground, were covered in moss and lichen.

The supposed gold mine of Cuchivano, which was the object of our trip, was nothing but a hole that had been cut in one of the strata of black marl, rich in pyrites. The marly stratum crosses the torrent and, as the water washes out metallic grains, the people imagine that the torrent carries gold because of the brilliancy of the pyrites. We were told that after the great earthquake of 1765 the Juagua river waters were so filled with gold that 'men came from great distances and unknown countries' to set up washing places on the spot. They disappeared over night, having collected masses of gold. Needless to add that this is a fable. Some direct experiments made with acids during my stay at Caracas proved that the Cuchivano pyrites are not at all auriferous. My disbelief upset our guides. However much I said and repeated that from the supposed gold mine the most that could be found was alum and sulphate of iron, they continued to gather secretly all the pyrite fragments they saw sparkling in the water. The fewer mines there are in a country, the more the inhabitants hold exaggerated ideas about how easily riches are extracted from the depths of the earth. How much time was lost during our five-year voyage exploring ravines, at the insistence of our hosts, where pyrite strata have for centuries been called by the pretentious name of *minas de oro!* We have smiled so often seeing men of all classes – magistrates, village priests, serious missionaries – all grinding amphibole or yellow mica with endless patience, desperate to extract gold by means of mercury! This rage for searching for mines amazed us in a climate where the earth needs only to be slightly raked in order to produce rich harvests.

After more tiring climbing, and soaked from crossing the torrent so often, we reached the foot of the Cuchivano caverns. A wall of stone rises perpendicularly 800 toises up. In a zone where the fertility of nature everywhere hides the ground and rocks, it is rare to see a great mountain revealing naked strata in a perpendicular section. In the middle of this unfortunately inaccessible cutting, the two caverns open out in the form of a crevice. We were assured that nocturnal birds, the same as those that lived in the Cueva del Guácharo at Caripe, lived there.

We rested at the foot of the caverns from which the flames have issued more and more frequently as the years have passed. Our guides and the farmer, equally familiar with the local terrain, discussed, in the manner of the creoles, the dangers to which Cumanacoa might be exposed if the Cuchivano became an active volcano and 'se veniesse a reventar' (might explode). It was obvious to them that since the great earthquakes of Quito and Cumaná in 1797 New Andalusia was every day more and more undermined by subterranean fires. They cited the flames that had been seen coming out of the ground at Cumaná, and the tremors in places where there had not been any before. They remembered that in Macarapán sulphureous smells had been noted over the last months. We were struck by these facts on which they had based their predictions, which nearly all turned out to be true. In 1812 enormous damage was done in Caracas, proof of the incredible instability of nature in the north-east of Terra Firma.

On the 12th we continued our journey to the Caripe monastery, centre of the Chaima Indian missions. Instead of the direct road, we chose the one that passes by the Cocollar[54] and Turimiquiri mountains. We passed the little Indian village of Aricagua, pleasantly located in wooded hills. From there we climbed up hill for four hours. This part of the route is very tiring; we crossed the Pututucuar, whose river bed is packed with blocks of calcareous rock, twenty-two times. When we had reached the Cuesta del Cocollar, some 2,000 feet above sea-level, we saw, to our surprise, that the jungle of tall trees had vanished. Then we crossed an immense plain covered in grass. Only mimosas, with hemispheric tops and trunks some 4 to 5 feet in diameter, break the desolate monotony of the savannahs. Their branches are bent towards the ground, or spread out like parasols.

After climbing the mountain for a long time we reached the Hato de Cocollar on a small plateau. This is an isolated farm on the crest of the tableland. We rested here in this lonely spot for three days, well looked after by its owner Don Mathias Yturburi from Biscay, who had accompanied us from Cumaná harbour. We found milk and excellent meat thanks to the rich grassland, and above all a wonderful climate.

From that high point, as far as the eye could see, there was only naked savannah; tufts of trees were scattered about in small ravines and, despite the apparent uniformity of the vegetation, we found a great number of extremely interesting plants. Here I shall limit myself to citing a magnificent lobelia with purple flowers (*Lobelia spectabilis*), the *Brownea coccinea*, which reaches almost 100 feet high, and above all the *pejoa* (*Gaultheria odorata*), famous in the country because when crushed between your fingers it gives off a delicious aroma. What enchanted us most about this solitary place was the beauty and silence of the nights. The owner stayed up with us; he seemed delighted that Europeans recently arrived in the Tropics never tired of admiring the fresh spring air enjoyed in these mountains when the sun sets.

Our host had visited the New World with an expedition that was set up to fell wood for the Spanish navy on the Paria Gulf shore. In the vast jungle of mahogany, cedar and Brazil-wood that borders the Caribbean Sea they wanted to select the largest trees, shape them in a rough way for the building of ships, and send them every year to the dockyard at Cádiz. White, unacclimatized men could not support the hard work, the heat, or the effect of the noxious air from the jungle. The same winds that are loaded with the perfume of flowers, leaves and wood also bring, so to speak, the germs of disease into our organs. Destructive fevers carried off not only the ship carpenter but also those who managed the business; so this bay, which the early

Spaniards called Golfo Triste on account of the gloomy and wild aspect of its coasts, became the graveyard of European seamen.

Nothing can compare to the majestic tranquillity of the stars in the sky in this solitary place. At nightfall, when we stared at the point where the horizon meets the meadows on this gently rolling plain, it seemed, as later in the Orinoco steppes, as if we were seeing the surface of an ocean supporting the starry vault. The tree at whose feet we sat, the luminous insects dancing in the air, the shining constellations of the Southern hemisphere, everything reminded us that we were far from our homeland. And if, in the middle of this exotic nature, the sound of cow bells or the bellowing of a bull came from the small valleys, memories of our native land were suddenly awoken. It was as if we heard distant voices echoing across the ocean, magically carrying us from one hemisphere to another. How strangely mobile is man's imagination, eternal source of his joys and pains!

In the cool of dawn we set off to climb the Turimiquiri. This is the name given to the Cocollar peak, which forms one large mountain range with the Brigantín, called before by the Indians Sierra de los Tageres. We travelled a part of the way on the horses that run free on the savannahs, but are used to being saddled. Even when they look heavily laden they climb the slipperiest slopes with ease. Wherever the sandstone appears above ground the land is even and forms small plateaux succeeding each other like steps. Up to 700 feet, and even further, the mountain is covered with grass. On the Cocollar the short turf begins to grow some 350 toises above sea-level, and you continue to walk on this grass up to 1,800 toises high; above those strips of grassy land you find, on virtually inaccessible peaks, a little forest of cedrela, javillo (*Hura crepitans*) and mahogany. Judging by local conditions, the mountainous savannahs of the Cocollar and Turimiquiri owe their existence to the destructive custom of Indians burning the woods to make pasture land. Today, after a thick tangle of grass and alpine plants have been covering the ground for over three centuries, seeds of trees cannot root themselves in the ground and germinate, despite the wind and the birds that continually bring them from the distant jungle.

The climate of these mountains is so mild that at the Cocollar farm cotton trees, coffee trees and even sugar cane grow with ease. The

Turimiquiri meadows lose their richness the higher they are. Wherever scattered rocks cast shade, lichen and various European mosses grow. *Melastoma guacito* (*Melastoma xanthostachyum*) and a shrub (*Palicourea rigida, chaparro bova*) whose large, leathery leaves rustle like parchment in the breeze rise here and there on the savannah. But the main attraction in the grass is a liliaceous plant with a golden-yellow flower, the *Marica martinicensis*.

The rounded Turimiquiri summit and the sharp peaks, or cucuruchos, stand out, covered with jungle where many tigers live and are hunted for the beauty of their skin. We found that this grassy summit stood at 707 toises above sea-level. A steep rocky ridge going west is broken after a mile by an enormous crevice that descends to the Gulf of Cariaco. In the place where the mountain ridge should have continued two mamelons or calcareous peaks rise, with the more northern one the highest. It is the Cucurucho de Turimiquiri proper, considered to be higher than the Brigantín, well known to sailors approaching the Cumaná coast.

On the 14th of September we descended the Cocollar towards the San Antonio mission. The road passes at first through savannahs strewn with huge calcareous blocks, and then enters a thick jungle. Having crossed two steep passes we saw before us a pretty valley, some 5 to 6 leagues long from east to west. Here lie the San Antonio and Guanaguana missions. The first is famous for its little brick church, with two towers and Doric columns, in a tolerable style. The prefect of the Capuchins finished building it in less than two summers, despite using only Indians from his village. The moulding of the capitals on the columns, the cornices and the frieze, decorated with suns and arabesques, were all modelled from clay mixed with ground brick. The provincial governor disapproved of such luxury in a mission and the church remained unfinished, much to the regret of the fathers. The Indians in San Antonio did not complain at all, indeed they secretly approved the governor's decision, as it favoured their natural laziness.

I stayed in the San Antonio mission long enough to open the barometer and take some measurements of the sun's altitude. The great square lies 216 toises above Cumaná. Beyond the village we crossed the Colorado and Guarapiche rivers, both of which rise in the

Cocollar mountains and meet lower down in the east. The Colorado has a very fast current and its mouth is wider than the Rhine; the Guarapiche, joining the Areo river, is more than 25 fathoms deep. On their banks grow a beautiful grass (*lata o caña brava*), which I drew[55] two years later as I ascended the Magdalena river, whose silver-leafed stalks reach 15 to 20 feet. Our mules could hardly move through the thick mud along the narrow and flat road. Torrents of rain fell from the sky and turned the jungle into a swamp.

Towards evening we reached the Guanaguana mission, situated at about the same height as the village of San Antonio. We really had to dry ourselves. The missionary received us very cordially. He was an old man who seemed to govern the Indians intelligently. The village has been in this place for only thirty years – before it lay more to the south, against a hill. It is astonishing how easily Indian villages are moved about. In South America there are villages that in less than fifty years have changed places three times. Indians feel bound to the land with such weak ties that they indifferently accept orders to demolish their houses and build them again elsewhere. A village changes its site like a military camp. As long as there are clay, reeds, palm tree and heliconia leaves around they finish rebuilding their huts in a few days. These compulsory changes often have no other motive than the whim of a missionary who, recently arrived from Spain, fancies that the site of the mission is feverish, or not sufficiently exposed to the wind. Whole villages have been transported several leagues just because a monk did not like the view from his house.

Guanaguana still does not have a church. The old priest, who had lived for more than thirty years in the American jungles, pointed out that the community's money, meaning the product of the Indians' work, should first be spent on building the missionary house; secondly on building a church; and lastly on their clothes. He seriously insisted that this order could not be altered on any account. The Indians can wait their turn as they prefer walking around completely naked to wearing the scantiest clothes. The spacious padre's house had just been finished and we noted with surprise that the terraced roof was decorated with a great number of chimneys that looked like turrets. Our host told us that this was done to remind him of his Aragonese winters, despite the tropical heat. The Guanaguana Indians grow cotton for themselves, the church and the missionary. The produce is supposed to belong to the community; it is with this communal money that the needs of the priest and altar are looked after. They have simple machines that separate the seed from the plant. Wooden cylinders of tiny diameter between which the cotton passes are activated, like a spinning-wheel, by pedals. However, these primitive machines are very useful and other missions are beginning to imitate them. But here, as in all places where nature's fertility hinders the development of industry, only a few hectares are converted into cultivated land, and nobody thinks of changing that cultivation into one of alimentary plants. Famine is felt each time the maize harvest is lost to a long drought. The Guanaguana Indians told us an amazing story that happened the year before when they went off with their women and children and spent three months *al monte*, that is, wandering about in the neighbouring jungle and living off juicy plants, palm cabbages, fern roots and wild fruit. They did not speak of this nomadic state as one of deprivation. Only the missionary lost out because his village was left completely abandoned, and the community members, when they returned from the woods, appeared to be less docile than before.

The beautiful Guanaguana valley stretches towards the east, opening into the Punzera and Terecen plains. We would have liked to visit those plains to explore the petroleum springs that lie between the Guarapiche and Areo rivers, but the rainy season had started, and every day we had problems trying to dry and preserve our plant collections. Near Punzera we saw little bags woven in silk hanging from the lower branches of the savannah trees. It is the *seda silvestre*, or wild silk of the country, which has a lovely sheen but is rough to the touch. The moth that weaves these cocoons is perhaps the same as the one in the Guanajuato and Antioquia provinces that also makes a wild silk. In the beautiful Punzera forests grow two trees that are called *curucay* and *canela*; the first because it yields a resin much sought after by the *piaches*, or Indian sorcerers; the second because its leaves smell like proper cinnamon from Ceylon.

After struggling a while with our plan to descend the Guarapiche river to the Golfo Triste, we took the direct road to the mountains. The Guanaguana and Caripe valleys are separated by an embankment or calcareous ridge fámous for miles around for its name Cuchilla de Guanaguana. We found this way tiring because we still had to climb the cordilleras, but it is by no means as dangerous as they claim in Cumaná. In many places the path is no more than 14 or 15 inches wide; the mountain ridge it follows is covered with a short slippery grass; its sides are both very steep and the traveller who fell could roll some 700 to 800 feet down over that grass. However, the mountain has abrupt slopes, not precipices. The local mules are so sure-footed that they inspire confidence. They behave just like mules from Switzerland or the Pyrenees. The wilder a country, the more acute and sensitive is instinct in domestic animals. When the mules glimpse a danger they stop and turn their heads from right to left and raise and lower their ears as if thinking. They delay making up their minds, but always choose the right course of action if the traveller does not distract them or make them continue. In the Andes, during journeys of six and seven months, in mountains furrowed with torrents, the intelligence of horses and beasts of burden develops in a surprising way. You often hear mountain people say: 'I will not give you a mule with a comfortable gait, but the one that reasons best (*la más racional*).' This popular expression, the result of long experiences, contradicts far more convincingly than speculative philosophy those who claim that animals are simply animated machines.

CHAPTER 7

The Caripe convent – The Guácharo cave – Nocturnal birds

An alley of avocado trees led us to the Aragonese Capuchins' hospice. We stopped in front of a Brazil-wood cross, surrounded with benches on which the sick monks sit and say their rosaries, in the middle of a spacious square. The convent backs on to an enormous perpendicular wall of rock, covered with thick vegetation. Dazzling white stone appears every now and then through the foliage. It would be hard to imagine a more picturesque place. Instead of European beeches and maples you find here the imposing ceiba trees and the *praga* and *irasse* palms. Numerous springs bubble out from the mountainsides that encircle the Caripe basin and whose southern slopes rise to some 1,000 feet in height. These springs issue mainly from crevices or narrow gorges. The humidity they bring favours the growth of huge trees, and the Indians, who prefer solitary places, set up their *conucos* along these ravines. Banana and papaw trees grow around groves of arborescent ferns. This mixture of wild and cultivated plants gives a special charm to this place. From afar, on the naked mountainside, you can pick out the springs by the thick tangles of vegetation, which at first seem to hang from the rock, and then, as they descend into the valley, follow the meandering streams.

We were received with eagerness by the monks of the hospice. The father superior was away but, notified of our departure from Cumaná, he had taken great pains to ensure our comfort at the convent. There was an inner cloister, typical of all Spanish monasteries. We used this enclosed space to install our instruments and get them working. In the convent we discovered a varied company; young monks recently arrived from Spain before being sent out to different missions, while old, sick missionaries recuperated in the healthy air of the Caripe hills. I was lodged in the father superior's cell, which had a notable library. To my surprise I found Feijóo's *Teatro crítico*, the *Lettres édifiantes*, and

L'abbé Nollet's *Traité d'électricité*. Science has progressed to even the American jungles. The youngest of the Capuchin monks had brought with him a Spanish translation of Chaptal's treatise on chemistry,[56] which he intended to study in the isolation of the mission where he was to be abandoned on his own for the rest of his days. I doubt that the desire to learn can be kept alive in a young monk isolated on the banks of the Tigre river; but what is certain, and an honour to the spirit of this century, is that during our long stay in South American missions we never saw the least sign of intolerance.

Experience has shown that the mild climate and light air of this place are very favourable to the cultivation of the coffee tree, which, as is known, prefers altitudes. The Capuchin father superior, an active, educated man, introduced this new plant into the province. Before, indigo was cultivated in Caripe, but this plant, which needs plenty of heat, gave off so little dye that its cultivation had to be stopped. In the communal *conuco* we found many culinary plants, maize, sugar cane and a large area of coffee trees promising a rich harvest. In Caripe the *conuco* looks like a large, beautiful garden: Indians are obliged to work there every morning from six to ten. The Indian *alcaldes* (or magistrates) and *alguaciles* (or bailiffs) watch over these tasks. They are the high functionaries, who alone have the right to carry a walking-stick, and are appointed by the convent superiors. They are extremely proud of their status. Their pedantic and taciturn seriousness, their cold and mysterious air, and the zeal with which they fulfil their role in the church and communal assemblies make Europeans smile. We were still unaccustomed to these nuances of Indian temperament, found equally on the Orinoco, in Mexico and in Peru, among people totally different from each other in customs and language. The *alcaldes* came to the convent every day, less to deal with the monks about mission matters than to learn about the health of those travellers who had just arrived. As we gave them brandy, they visited us more than the monks thought proper.

Apart from its exceptionally fresh climate the Caripe valley is also famous for the great *cueva*, or Guácharo grotto.[57] In a country so given to the marvellous, a cave that gives birth to a river, and is inhabited by thousands of nocturnal birds whose fat is used for preparing the food in the monastery, becomes an unending topic of discussions and arguments. Hardly has a foreigner disembarked at Cumaná than he hears such talk about the Araya eye stones, the Arenas father who breast-fed his child, and the Guácharo grotto said to be several leagues long, that he soon gets fed up. A keen interest in nature is maintained everywhere where society has no life, or lives in sad monotony, and things are seen in simple ways that do not stimulate curiosity.

The cave, known by the Indians as a 'mine of fat', is not in the Caripe valley itself, but some 3 leagues to the west-south-west. On the 18th of September we set out for that sierra, accompanied by the *alcaldes* and the majority of the monks. A narrow path led us first for an hour and a half south through an attractive plain covered with beautiful grass; then we turned west and ascended a rivulet that issues from the cave mouth. We followed this for three quarters of an hour, sometimes walking in the shallow water, or between the water and the rocky walls on very slippery and muddy ground. Many earthfalls and uprooted tree trunks, over which the mules laboured, and creeping plants made this stretch very tiring. We were surprised to find here, at barely 500 toises above sea-level, the cruciferous plant *Raphanus pinnatus*.

At the foot of the tall Guácharo mountain, and only 400 steps from the cave, we still could not make out its entrance. The torrent flows from a ravine, cut by the waters, under a ledge of rocks that blocks out the sky. The path follows the winding rivulet. At the last bend you suddenly come across the enormous grotto opening. This is an imposing scene, even for those used to the picturesque higher Alps. I had seen the caves of the Derbyshire peaks where, lying flat on a boat, we went down an underground stream under an arch 2 feet high. I had visited the beautiful grotto of Treshemienshiz in the Carpathian mountains, and the Hartz and Franconia caves, which are vast cemeteries with bones of tigers and hyenas, and bears as large as horses. Nature in every zone follows immutable laws in the distribution of rocks, mountains and dramatic changes in the planet's crust. Such uniformity led me to expect that the Caripe caves would not differ from what I had previously seen in my travels. The reality far exceeded my expectations.

The Guácharo cave is pierced into the vertical rock face. The entrance opens towards the south. Gigantic trees grow above the rock that serves as roof to the grotto. The mammee tree and the genipap (*Genipa americana*), with its large shiny leaves, raise their branches towards the sky while those of the courbaril and the *poro*, or coral tree, stretch out to form a thick, green vault. Pothos with succulent stems, oxalises and orchids with strange shapes grow in the driest cracks in the rocks, while climbing plants, swaying in the wind, knot themselves into garlands at the cave entrance. Among these we saw a violet-blue jacaranda, a dolichos with purple flowers, and for the first time, that stunning solandra (*Solandra scandens*) with its orange flower and fleshy tube some 4 inches long.

However, this luxuriant vegetation does not only embellish the outer vault but also reaches into the vestibule of the grotto. We saw, to our surprise, that superb heliconias 18 feet tall, with banana-tree type leaves, *praga* palms and arborescent arums bordered the rivulet's banks right into the cave. Vegetation penetrates inside the Caripe cave some thirty to forty paces. We measured the way in by means of a cord, and went about 430 feet without needing to light torches. Daylight reaches this place because the cave forms one single gallery that stretches south-east to north-west. In the spot where light begins to fail we heard the hoarse screams of the nocturnal birds that, according to the Indians, live only in these underground caves.

The *guácharo* is about the size of our chickens, with the mouth of our goatsuckers and the gait of vultures, with silky stiff hair around their curved beaks. The plumage is of a dark bluish-grey with small streaks and black dots; great white patches in the shape of a heart, bordered with black, mark its wings, head and tail. Its eyes are wounded by daylight; they are blue and smaller than those of the goatsuckers or flying frogs. The wing-span, seventeen or eighteen quill feathers, is 3.5 feet. The *guácharo* leaves the cave at nightfall when there is a moon. It is the only grain-eating nocturnal bird that we know of to date; the structure of its feet shows that it does not hunt like our owls. It eats hard seed, like the nutcracker (bullfinch). The Indians insist that the *guácharo* does not chase beetles or moths like the goatsucker. It is sufficient to compare their beaks to be convinced that they lead completely different lives.

It is difficult to give an idea of the dreadful noise made by thousands of these birds in the darkness of the cave. It cannot be compared to the noise of those crows who live together in nests in our northern pine forests. The *guácharo's* piercing scream reverberates against the rocky vault and echoes in the depths of the cave. The Indians showed us their nests by tying torches on to long poles. They were some 50 to 60 feet above us in holes riddling the ceiling in the form of funnels. The further we penetrated into the cave with our copal torches the more the frightened birds screamed. If for a few moments the din around us quietened we heard the plaintive cry of other nesting birds in other parts of the cave. It was as if differing groups answered each other alternatively.

The Indians enter the caves once a year near midsummer with poles to destroy most of the nests. Several thousand birds are killed; the older ones hover over their heads to defend their young, screaming horribly. The young, called *los pollos del guácharo*, fall to the ground and are cut open on the spot. Their peritoneum is loaded with fat; a layer of fat reaches from the abdomen to the anus, forming a kind of wad between the bird's legs. During this period, called the *cosecha de la manteca* (oil harvest) in Caripe, the Indians build palm-leaf huts near the entrance and in the cave vestibule itself. We could see their remains. With a brushwood fire they melt the fat of the young birds just killed and pour it into clay pots. This fat is known as butter or *guácharo* oil; it is semi-liquid, clear and odourless, and so pure that it lasts for a year without going rancid. In the Caripe convent kitchen they only use fat from this cave, and the food never had a disagreeable taste or smell thanks to this fat.

The race of *guácharo* would long ago have become extinct had not diverse circumstances combined to preserve them. The superstitious Indians rarely dare to penetrate deep into the grotto. It appears that these birds also nest in other nearby caves inaccessible to man. Perhaps this great cave is repopulated by colonies coming from smaller ones because the missionaries assured us that these birds had not diminished in numbers. When the gizzards of the young birds in the cave are opened they contain all kinds of hard and dried fruits, which, under the name of *semilla del guácharo*, are a famous remedy against intermittent fevers. The adult birds carry these seed to their young. They are carefully collected and sent to the sick at Cariaco.

We entered into the cave following the rivulet, some 28 to 30 feet wide. We walked along the banks as far as the calcareous incrustations allowed us; frequently, when the current slipped between high clusters of stalactites, we were forced to walk along the river bed, only 2 feet deep. To our surprise we learned that this underground stream is the source to the Caripe river and becomes navigable for canoes a few leagues from here, after joining the Santa María river. Along the underground rivulet banks we found a quantity of palm-tree wood, remains of trunks used by Indians to climb to the cave's ceiling when searching for nests. The rings formed from the traces of the leaf stems are used as a perpendicular ladder.

The Caripe grotto measures exactly 472 metres and keeps the same width and height of 60 to 70 feet all through. It was difficult to persuade the Indians to penetrate any further into the grotto than where they usually went to collect the fat. We needed the padres' authority to make them go as far as the point where the ground rises suddenly at a 60-degree angle and where the rivulet forms a small underground cascade. This cave, home of nocturnal birds, is for the Indian a mystical place; they believe that the souls of their ancestors live in its depths. Man – they say – should fear these places not illumined by the sun (*zis*) or moon (*nuna*). To join the *guácharos* is synonymous with joining your ancestors, that is, to die. For this reason, the magicians (*piaches*) and the poisoners (*imorons*) cast their nocturnal spells to call up the supreme evil spirit Ivorokiamo. Thus, all over the earth similarities may be found in the early fictions of people, especially those concerning the two principles ruling the world: the abode of souls after death, the happiness of the virtuous and the punishment of the guilty. The most different and barbarous languages present a certain number of similar images because they have the same source in the nature of our intelligence and our sensations. Darkness is everywhere connected with death.

At the point where the river becomes an underground cascade, the ground located near the opening is covered in greenery and looks extremely picturesque. You can see the outside from the far end of the straight gallery, some 240 toises away. Stalactites hanging from the ceiling, like floating columns, stand out from this green background. We shot our guns aimlessly in the dark wherever the screaming birds or the beating of wings made us suspect their nests lay ahead. Bonpland at last managed to kill two *guácharos* dazzled by our torches. This is how I was able to sketch this bird, up to now completely unknown to naturalists. We struggled to climb the rise from which the rivulet fell. We saw that the grotto narrowed; its height shrunk to 40 feet as it followed a north-east direction, parallel to the Caripe valley.

In this part of the cavern the rivulet deposits blackish earth, a mixture of silex, clay and vegetable detritus. We walked in thick mud to a place where, to our shock, we discovered underground vegetation. The seeds that the birds bring into the grotto to feed to their chicks germinate wherever they fall on to earth covering the calcareous incrustations. Blanched stalks with rudimentary leaves rose to some 2 feet. It was impossible to identify the plants as the absence of light had completely transformed their form, colour and aspect. These traces of plant life in the dark struck the Indians, usually so stupid and difficult to impress. They examined the plants in a silence inspired by a place they fear. You could have said these pale, deformed, underground plants seemed like ghosts banished from the earth's surface. For me, however, they recalled one of the happiest days of my youth when during a long stay at the Freiberg mines I began my research into the effects of blanching plants.

Despite their authority the missionaries could not persuade the Indians to go any further on into the cavern. The lower the vault the more piercing the screaming of the *guácharos* became. Thanks to the cowardice of our guides we had to retreat. We found that a bishop of Saint Thomas of Guiana had gone further than us. He had measured 2,500 feet from the mouth to where he stopped, but the cavern went further. The memory of this feat was preserved in the Caripe convent, without precise dates. The bishop had used torches made from white Castile wax, while we had torches made of tree bark and resin. The thick smoke from our torches in the narrow underground passage hurt our eyes and made breathing difficult.

We found our way out by following the rivulet. Before daylight dazzled our eyes we saw the river water outside the grotto sparkle among the foliage. It looked like a painting, with the cave opening as a frame. Once outside we rested by the stream. We could hardly believe that this cave had remained unknown in Europe. The *guácharos* should have made it far more famous. The missionaries had ordered a meal to be prepared at the entrance. Banana and *vijao* (*Heliconia bihai*) leaves served as a tablecloth, following the custom of the country.[58]

CHAPTER 8

*Departure from Caripe – The mountain and valley of Santa
María – The Catuaro mission – Cariaco harbour*

Days passed quickly in the Capuchin convent in the Caripe mountains, despite our simple but monotonous life. From sunrise to sunset we toured the forests and mountains near by looking for plants, and have never collected so many. When the heavy rain stopped us travelling far we visited Indian huts and the communal *conuco*, or attended the nightly meetings when the *alcaldes* handed out the work for the following day. We did not return to the convent until bells called us for meals in the refectory with the monks. At dawn we sometimes accompanied them to the church to attend *doctrina*, that is, religious classes for Indians. It was hard explaining dogma to people who hardly knew Spanish. The monks are almost completely ignorant of the Chaima Indian language, and the resemblance of sounds between the languages muddles the poor Indians so that strange ideas arise. One day we witnessed a missionary struggling to explain to his class that *invierno*, winter, and *infierno*, hell, were not the same thing, but as different as hot and cold. The Chaima Indians know winter only as the rainy season, and imagine that 'the white's hell' is a place where the evil are exposed to horrific rainstorms. The missionary lost his temper, but it was useless; the first impression caused by the almost identical words persisted; in the Indians' minds the images of rain and hell could not be separated.

After spending the whole day outdoors, we wrote down our observations in the convent at night, and dried our plants and sketched what we thought were new species. Unfortunately the misty sky of a valley where the forests give off an enormous amount of water into the air was not favourable for astronomic observations. The only annoyance experienced in the Caripe valley was the impossibility of observing stars due to the sky being continuously covered. I spent part of every night waiting for the moment when a star might be visible between clouds. I often shivered with cold, though the thermometer only sank to 16 °C.

This site has something wild and tranquil, melancholic and attractive about it. In the midst of such powerful nature we felt nothing inside but peace and repose. In the solitude of these mountains I was less struck by the new impressions recorded at each step than by the fact that such diverse climates have so much in common. In the hills where the convent stands palm trees and tree fern grow; in the afternoon, before the rainfalls, the monotonous screaming of the howler monkeys seems like a distant wind in the forests. Despite these exotic sounds, and the strange plant forms and marvels of the New World, everywhere nature allows man to sense a voice speaking to him in familiar terms. The grass carpeting the ground, the old moss and ferns covering tree roots, the torrent that falls over steep calcareous rocks, the harmonious colours reflecting the water, the green and the sky, all evoke familiar sensations in the traveller.

The natural beauties of the mountains absorbed us so completely that we did not notice we were becoming a weight on our good and hospitable padres. Their provisions of wine and wheat bread were small, and both are considered real luxuries in these lands, so it inhibited us to think that our hosts deprived themselves on our account. Our ration of bread had been reduced to one quarter, yet the cruel rains delayed our departure for two days. How long that delay seemed; we dreaded the bell that called us for a meal!

We left finally on the 22nd of September, with four mules carrying our instruments and plants. Leaving the Caripe valley we first crossed a chain of hills running north-east from the convent. The road was uphill across a wide savannah towards the tableland of Guardia de San Agustín. We waited there for the Indian who carried our barometer. We stood at 533 toises above sea-level. The savannahs, or natural grasslands, excellent pasture for the monastery cows, were totally devoid of trees and shrubs. It is the kingdom of the monocotyledonous plants, with only a few maguey (*Agave americana*), whose flowers rise some 26 feet above the grass. On the high tableland of Guardia we felt we had been carried to an ancient lake flattened by the prolonged effect of the waters. You think you can recognize the curves of the ancient shore, the prominent tongues of land, the steep cliffs forming islands. Even the distribution of flora seems to refer to that primitive state. The bottom of the basin is a savannah, while its edges are covered with tall trees. It is sad that a place so favoured by its climate, and fit for wheat, should be totally uninhabited.

Leaving the tableland of Guardia we descended to the Indian village of Santa Cruz. First we reached a steep, extremely slippery slope that the missionaries strangely named Bajada del Purgatorio, or Descent of Purgatory. It consists of eroded slaty sandstone, covered with clay; the slope seems terribly steep. To go down, the mules draw their hind legs to their forelegs, lower their rumps and trust their luck sliding downhill. The rider has nothing to fear as long as he drops the reins and leaves the mule alone. From here to the left we saw the great pyramid of Guácharo. This calcareous peak looks very picturesque, but we soon lost it to view when we entered the thick jungle known as Montana de Santa María. We spent seven hours crossing it. It is hard to imagine a worse path; a veritable ladder, a kind of gorge where, during the rainy season, torrent water rushes down the rocks step by step. The steps are from 2 to 3 feet high. The hapless animals first have to calculate how to pass their loads between the tree trunks, and then jump from one block to another. Scared of slipping they wait a few moments, as if studying the terrain, and then draw their four legs together like wild goats do. If the mule misses the nearest rock it sinks deep into the soft ochre clay that fills in the gaps between the rocks. When there are no rocks, the rider's feet and the mule's legs are supported by a tangle of enormous tree roots. The creoles have faith in the skill and instinct of their mules and remain in the saddle during the long dangerous descent. We preferred to dismount because we feared fatigue less than they do, and were more prepared to travel slowly as we never stopped collecting plants and examining the rocks.

The jungle that covers the steep slope of the Santa María mountain is one of the densest I have ever seen. The trees are amazingly tall and thick. Under the dark green and matted canopy of leaves it always seems far darker than under our pine, oak and beech woods. Despite the temperature, it would seem that the air cannot absorb all the water emanating from the ground, the leaves and trunks of the trees with their tangle of orchids, peperomias and other succulent plants.

Mixed with the aromatic smells given off by the flowers, fruit and even wood there was something of our misty autumn forests. Among the majestic trees that reach 120 to 130 feet high our guides pointed out the *curucay*, which yields a whitish, liquid resin with a strong odour. The Cumanagoto and Tagire Indians used to burn it before their idols as incense. The young branches have an agreeable taste, though somewhat acid. Apart from the *curucay* and the enormous trunks of the hymenaea, from 9 to 10 feet in diameter, we noticed, above all others, the dragon (*Croton sanguifluum*), whose dark purple resin flows from its white bark; as well as the medicinal *calahuala* fern, and the *irasse*, *macanilla*, corozo and *praga* palm trees. This latter gives a tasty 'heart of palm' that we sometimes ate at the Caripe convent. These palm trees with pinnate and thorny leaves contrast pleasingly with the tree ferns. In the Caripe valley we discovered five new species of tree fern, while in Linnaeus's time botanists had not even found four in both continents.

We observed that fern trees are usually far rarer than palm trees. Nature has limited them to temperate, humid and shady places. They shun the direct rays of the sun and while the *pumos*, corypha of the steppes, and other American palms prefer the naked, burning plains these tree fern, which seen from afar look like palms, maintain the character and habits of cryptogams. They prefer solitary places, shade, humidity and damp. Sometimes you find them on the coast, but only when protected by thick shade.

As we descended the Santa María mountain fern trees became rarer and palms more frequent. Nymphales, the beautiful large-winged butterflies that fly at prodigious heights, became more and more common. Everything suggested that we were near the coast in a zone whose average temperature ranged between 28 °C and 30 °C.

The weather was cloudy, threatening one of those cloudbursts during which some 1 to 1.5 inches of rain may fall in a day. The sun shone on the tree-tops and, although we were not exposed to the rays, the heat was asphyxiating. Thunder rolled at a distance. The clouds hovered over the peaks of the high Guácharo chain, and the plaintive howling of the araguatoes, heard so often in Caripe at sunset, announced the imminent storm. For the first time we had an opportunity to see those howler monkeys that belong to the family

Alouatta (*Stentor*, Geoffroy), whose different species have long been confused by zoologists close at hand. While the small American sapajous, who imitate sparrow song with a whistle, have a simple, thin tongue bone, the large monkeys, the alouates and spider monkeys (*Ateles*, Geoffroy), have a tongue that rests on a large bony drum. The sad howling typical of the araguato is produced by air penetrating violently into this drum. I sketched these organs[59] on the spot as they are not well known to European anatomists. If you think about the size of the alouatta's bony box and the number of howler monkeys that can gather in one tree in the Cumaná and Guianan jungles, you will be less surprised by the force and volume of their united voices.

The araguato, which the Tamanaco Indians call *aravata* and the Maypures *marave*, resembles a bear cub. From the top of its small and pointed head to the beginning of its prehensile tail it measures 3 feet; its coat is thick and reddish-brown; even its breasts and belly are covered in pretty fur. The araguato's face is blackish-blue, with wrinkled skin. Its beard is longish, and although its facial angle is no more than 30 degrees there is as much humanity in its look and facial expressions as in the marimonda (*Simia belzebuth*) and the capuchin (*Simia chiripotes*) of the Orinoco.

The araguato of the Caripe region is a new species of the genus *Stentor* that I named *Simia ursina*. I prefer this name to the one referring to its colour. Its eyes, voice and gait make it appear sad. I have seen young araguatoes brought up in Indian huts. They never play like the little sagoins. Their seriousness was described naïvely by Lopez de Gomara at the start of the sixteenth century: 'The aranata of the Cumaneses has the face of a man, the beard of a goat, and a serious bearing, *honrado gesto*.' The closer they resemble man the sadder monkeys look.

We stopped to observe the howler monkeys, which move in lines across the intricate branches linking the jungle trees in packs of thirty and forty. While watching this new spectacle we met a group of Indians on their way to the Caripe mountains. They were completely naked, like most Indians in these lands. Behind them came the women, laden with heavy packs, while all the men and boys were armed with bows and arrows. They walked in silence, staring at the ground. We would have liked to ask them if the Santa Cruz mission, where we hoped to spend the night, was far off. We were exhausted, and thirsty. The heat was increasing as the storm approached, and we had not found any springs. As the Indians invariably answered *si padre* and *no padre* we thought they understood a little Spanish. In their eyes every white is a monk, a padre. In the missions the colour of the skin characterizes the monk more than the colour of his habit. When we asked those Indians if Santa Cruz was far off they answered *si* or *no* so arbitrarily that we could make no sense of their answers. This made us angry, for their smiles and gestures showed that they would have liked to direct us as the jungle became thicker and thicker. We had to leave them; our guides, who spoke the Chaima language, lagged behind as the loaded mules kept falling into ravines.

After travelling several hours downhill over scattered blocks of stone we suddenly found we had reached the end of the Santa María jungle. As far as our eyes could see a vast plain spread out, its grass revived by the rainy season. Looking down on to the tree-tops it seemed as if we were looking at a dark green carpet below us. The jungle clearings seemed like huge funnels in which we recognized the delicate pinnate leaves of the *praga* and *irasse* palms. The countryside is extremely picturesque due to the Sierra of Guacharo whose northern slopes are steep and form a rocky wall some 3,000 feet high. There is little vegetation on this wall, so you can follow the calcareous strata. The peak itself is flat.

The savannah we crossed to reach the Indian village of Santa Cruz is made up of various very flat plateaux lying one above another. This geological phenomenon seems to show that they were once basins where water poured from one to the other. On the spot where we last saw the limestone of the Santa María jungle we found nodules of iron ore, and, if I was not mistaken, a bit of ammonite, but we could not detach it. The Santa Cruz mission is situated in the middle of the plain. We reached it as night fell, half dead with thirst as we had been eight hours without water. We spent the night in one of those *ajupas* known as 'kings' houses', which serve as *tambos* or inns for travellers. As it was raining there was no chance of making any astronomical observations so, on the next day, the 23rd of September, we set off for the Gulf of Cariaco. Beyond Santa Cruz thick jungle reappears. Under tufts of melastoma we found a beautiful fern, with leaves similar to the *osmunda*, which belonged to a new genus (*Polybotria*) of the polypodiaceous order.

The Catuaro mission is situated in a very wild place. The church is surrounded by tall trees. At night jaguars hunt the Indians' chickens and pigs. We lodged in the priest's house, a monk of the Observance congregation, to whom the Capuchins had given this mission because they did not have enough priests in their own community. He was a doctor in theology, a little, dried-up and petulant man. He entertained us with stories about the trial he had had with the superior of his convent, with the enmity of his brothers and the injustice of the *alcaldes*, who, ignoring his privileges, once threw him in jail. Despite these set-backs he had conserved an unfortunate liking for what he called metaphysical questions. He wanted to know what I thought of free will, of how to raise the soul from the prison of the body, and, above all, about animal souls. When you have crossed a jungle in the rainy season you do not feel like these kind of speculations. Besides, everything about this little Catuaro mission was odd, even the priest's house. It had two floors, and had become the object of a keen rivalry between secular and ecclesiastical authorities. The priest's superior found it too luxurious for a missionary, and wanted the Indians to demolish it; the governor opposed this strongly, and his will prevailed.

There we met the district *corregidor*, Don Alejandro Mejía, an amiable and well-educated man. He gave us three Indians who would cut us a path through the jungle with machetes. In this country, where people rarely travel, the vegetation is so fertile that a man on horseback can barely make his way along the jungle paths tangled with liana and branches during the rainy season. To our great annoyance the Catuaro missionary insisted on leading us to Cariaco, and we could not decline his offer. He told us a dreadful story. The independence movement, which had nearly broken out in 1798, had been preceded and followed by trouble among the slaves at Cariaco. An unfortunate negro had been condemned to death and our host was going to Cariaco to give him some spiritual comfort. How tedious this journey became. We could not escape talking about 'the necessity of slavery, the innate wickedness of the blacks, and how slavery benefited Christians'!

The road through the Catuaro jungle resembles the descent through the Santa María mountain; the difficult parts are given odd names. You follow a narrow channel, scooped out by torrents and filled with a fine, sticky clay. In the steep parts the mules sit on their rumps and slide downhill. This descent is called Saca Manteca because the consistence of the mud is like butter. There is no danger in this descent as the mules are very skilled at sliding.

In Cariaco we found most of the inhabitants in their hammocks, ill with intermittent fevers that in autumn become malignant and lead to dysentery. If you think how extraordinarily fertile and humid the plain is, and of the amount of vegetation that rots there, it is easy to understand why the atmosphere here is not as healthy as it is at Cumaná. In the torrid zone the amazing fertility of the soil, the frequent and prolonged rainy season, and the extraordinary opulence of the vegetation are advantages outweighed by a climate dangerous for whites.

The fevers reigning in Cariaco forced us, to our regret, to shorten our stay there. As we were still not completely acclimatized, the inhabitants to whom we had been recommended warned us not to delay. In the town we met many people who, through a certain ease of behaviour, or through being more broad-minded and preferring a United States type government, revealed that they were in contact with foreigners. For the first time we heard the names of Franklin and Washington enthusiastically pronounced. With these shows of enthusiasm we heard complaints about the present state of New Andalusia, exaggerated enumerations of their natural wealth, and passionate and impatient hopes for a better future. This state of mind struck a traveller who had been witness to the great political upheavals in Europe.

We embarked at dawn hoping to cross the Gulf of Cariaco in a day. The sea is no rougher than any of our great lakes when a breeze blows. From the Cumaná wharf the distance is only 3 leagues. Leaving the small town of Cariaco behind us we went west towards the Carenicuar river, which, straight as an artificial canal, runs through gardens and cotton plantations. On the banks of the river we saw Indian women washing clothes with the fruit of the *parapara* (*Sapindus saponaria*). They say that this is very rough on their hands. The bark of this fruit gives a strong lather, and the fruit is so elastic that when thrown on to stone it bounces three or four times to the height of 6 feet. Being round, it is also used to make rosaries.

Once on board we had to contend with strong winds. It poured with rain, and near by thunder rolled. Flocks of flamingoes, egrets and cormorants flew past towards the shore. Only the alcatras, a large kind of pelican, continued to fish calmly in the gulf. We were eighteen on board, and the narrow pirogue, overloaded with sugar cane and bunches of bananas and coconuts, could hardly hold our instruments. The edge of the boat barely stood above the water-line.

Adverse winds and rain forced us to go on shore at Pericantral, a small farm on the southern coast of the gulf. The whole of this coast, covered in beautiful vegetation, is completely uncultivated. Only some 700 people live here, and, excepting in the village of Mariguitar,[60] we saw only coconut plantations, which produce oil for the people.

We did not leave the Pericantral farm until dark. We spent a very uncomfortable night in the narrow, overloaded pirogue. At three in the morning we found ourselves at the mouth of the Manzanares river. As the sun rose we saw the *zamuro* vultures (*Vultur aura*) perched in flocks of forty and fifty in the coconut palms. To sleep, these birds line up together on branches like fowl, and are so lazy that they go to sleep ages before sunset and do not wake up until the sun is up. It seems as if the trees with pinnate leaves share this laziness with the birds. The mimosas and tamarinds close their leaves when the sky is clear some twenty-five to thirty-five minutes before sunset, and in the morning do not open them again until the sun is high up.

CHAPTER 9

Physical constitution and customs of the Chaima Indians
– Their language

In the chronicle of our journey to the Caripe missions I did not wish to insert general considerations concerning the customs, languages and common origins of the different Indian tribes populating New Andalusia. Now, having returned to my starting-point, I will place in one section matters that concern the history of human beings. As we advance further into the interior of the continent this subject will become even more interesting than the phenomena of the physical world.

In the mountainous regions we have just crossed, Indians form half the population of the provinces of Cumaná and New Barcelona. Their number can be calculated at some 60,000, of which some 24,000 live in New Andalusia. The Indians of Cumaná do not all live in the mission villages. Some are dispersed around the cities, along the coasts, attracted by fishing, and some in the small farms on the llanos or plains. Some 15,000 Indians, all belonging to the Chaima tribe, live in the Aragonese Capuchin missions we visited. However, their villages are not as densely populated as in New Barcelona province. Their average population is only 500 to 600, while more to the west, in the Franciscan missions of Piritu, there are Indian villages with up to 3,000 inhabitants. If I calculated the Indian population in the provinces of Cumaná and New Barcelona to be some 60,000 I included only those living on Terra Firma, not the Guaiquerí on Margarita Island, nor the great number of independent Guaraunos living in the Orinoco delta islands. Their number is estimated, perhaps exaggeratedly, at some 6,000 to 8,000. Apart from Guaraunos families seen now and then in the marshes (Los Morichales), which are covered with moriche palms, for the last thirty years there have been no wild Indians living in New Andalusia.

I use the word 'savage' grudgingly because it implies a cultural difference between the tamed Indians living in missions and the free ones, which belies the facts. In the South American jungles there are Indian tribes who live peacefully in villages under their chiefs, who cultivate banana trees, cassava and cotton in large areas of land, and weave their hammocks with cotton fibres. They are not more barbarous than the naked Indians of the missions who have learned to make the sign of the cross. In Europe it is a common fallacy to assume that all Indians who are not tamed are nomadic hunters. In Terra Firma agriculture was known long before the arrival of the Europeans, and today is still practised between the Orinoco and Amazon rivers in jungle clearings never visited by missionaries. What the missionaries have achieved is to have increased the Indians' attachment to owning land, their desire for secure dwelling places, and their taste for more peaceful lives. It would be accepting false ideas about the actual condition of South American Indians to assume that 'Christian', 'tamed' and 'civilized' were synonymous with 'pagan', 'savage' and 'free'. The tamed Indian is often as little a Christian as the free Indian is an idolater. Both, caught up in the needs of the moment, betray a marked indifference for religious sentiments, and a secret tendency to worship nature and her powers.

If the independent Indians have almost disappeared over the last century in those areas north of the Orinoco, it must not be concluded that fewer Indians exist at present than in the time of the bishop of Chiapas, Bartolomeo de las Casas. I have already proved in my work on Mexico how mistaken it is to assume the destruction and diminution of Indians in the Spanish colonies, as Ulloa has written 'Es cosa constante irse disminuyendo por todas partes el numero de los Indios' (There is everywhere a constant decrease in the number of Indians). There are still more than 6 million copper-coloured races in both Americas, and though countless tribes and languages have died out it is beyond discussion that within the Tropics, where civilization arrived with Columbus, the number of Indians has considerably increased.[61]

As the missionaries struggle to penetrate the jungles and gain the Indian land, so white colonists try, in their turn, to invade missionary land. In this long-drawn-out struggle the secular arm continually tends to take over those Indians tamed by the missions, and missionaries are replaced by priests. Whites and mestizos, favoured by *corregi-*

dores, have established themselves among the Indians. The missions are transformed into Spanish villages and the Indians soon forget even the memory of their own language. So civilization slowly works its way inland from the coast, sometimes hindered by human passions.

In the New Andalusia and Barcelona provinces, under the name of the Gobierno de Cumaná, there are more than fourteen tribes: in New Andalusia reside the Chaimas, the Guaiquerí, the Pariagotos, the Quaquas, the Araucans, the Caribs and the Guaraunos; in the province of New Barcelona, the Cumanagotos, the Palenques, the Caribs, the Piritus, the Tomuzas, the Topocuares, the Chacopotes and the Guarives. Nine to ten of these tribes consider themselves to be of entirely different races. Of the remaining tribes, the most numerous are the Chaimas in the Caripe mountains, the Caribs in the southern savannahs of New Barcelona, and the Cumanagotos in the Piritu missions. Some Guarauno families live on the left shore of the Orinoco where the delta begins, under missionary discipline. The most common languages are those of the Guaraunos, the Caribs, the Cumanagotos and the Chaimas.

The Indians in the missions dedicate themselves to agriculture, and, apart from those who live in the high mountains, all cultivate the same plants; their huts are arranged in the same manner; their working day, their tasks in the communal *conuco*, their relationship with the missionaries and elected functionaries, all run along fixed rules. However, we observe in the copper-coloured men a moral inflexibility, a stubbornness concerning habits and customs, which, though modified in each tribe, characterize the whole race from the equator to Hudson's Bay and the Strait of Magellan.

In the missions there are a few villages where families belong to different tribes, speaking different languages. Societies composed of such heterogeneous elements are difficult to govern. In general, the padres have settled whole tribes, or large parts of them, in villages not far from each other. The Indians see only those of their own tribe, for lack of communication and isolation are the main aims of missionary policy. Among the tamed Chaimas, Caribs and Tamanacs racial characteristics are retained if they are allowed to keep their respective languages. If man's individuality is reflected in his dialects, then these in their turn influence thoughts and feelings. This intimate link between language, national character and physical constitution ensures the differences and idiosyncrasies of the tribes, which in turn constitutes an unending source of movement and life at the mental level.

Missionaries have managed to rid the Indians of certain customs concerning birth, entering puberty and burying the dead; they have managed to stop them painting their skin or making incisions in their chins, noses and cheeks; they have banished the superstitious ideas that in many families are passed down mysteriously from father to son; but it was far easier to suppress practices and memories than it was to replace the old ideas with new ones. In the missions the Indian has a far more secure life than he had before. He is no longer a victim of the continuous struggle between man and the elements, and he leads a more monotonous and passive life than the wild Indian, but he is also less likely to animate his own spiritual development. His thinking has not increased with his contact with whites; he has remained estranged from the objects with which European civilization has enriched the Americas. All his acts seem dictated exclusively by wants of the moment. He is taciturn, without joy, introverted and, on the outside, serious and mysterious. Someone who has been but a short time in a mission could mistake his laziness and passivity for a meditative frame of mind.

I shall begin with the Chaimas, of whom some 15,000 live in the missions we visited. Their territory stretches over the high mountain range of the Cocollar and the Guácharo, the banks of the Guarapiche, the Colorado river, the Areo and the Caño de Caripe. According to a statistical survey made with great care by a father superior in the Aragonese Capuchin mission of Cumaná, nineteen mission villages, the oldest dating back to 1728, held 1,465 families, and a total of 6,433 people. From 1730 to 1736 the population was diminished by the ravages of smallpox, always more fatal for the copper-skinned Indians than for the whites.

The Chaimas are usually short and thickset, with extremely broad shoulders and flat chests, and their legs are rounded and fleshy. The colour of their skin is the same as that of all American Indians from the cold plateaux of Quito to the burning jungles of the Amazon.

Their facial expression is not hard or wild but rather serious and gloomy. Their foreheads are small and barely salient, which is why in various languages of their territory they say about a beautiful woman that 'she is fat, with a narrow forehead'; their eyes are black, deep set and very elongated. The Chaimas, and all South American Indians, resemble the Mongols in the shape of their eyes, their high cheekbones, their straight and smooth hair, and an almost total absence of beard; yet they differ in the form of their noses. These are rather long and broad at the nostril, which opens downwards like a Caucasian nose. Their mouths are wide, with full lips but not fleshy, and frequently show their good nature. Between the nose and mouth are two furrows that diverge from the nostrils to the corners of the mouth. The chin is very small and round; the jaws very strong and wide.

The Chaimas have attractive white teeth like all who lead a very simple life, but not as strong as negro teeth. The early explorers noted their custom of blacking their teeth with plant juices and quicklime; today this custom has disappeared. I doubt whether the custom of blacking their teeth had anything to do with odd ideas about beauty or a remedy against toothache. It could be said that Indians do not know toothache, and Spaniards who live in the Tropics do not suffer from this pain either.

Like all the Indian tribes that I know the Chaimas have small, slender hands. Contrary to this, their feet are large, and their toes remain extremely mobile. All the Chaimas resemble each other, as if they were all related, and this is all the more evident because between twenty and fifty years old, age is not indicated by wrinkling skin, white hair or body decrepitude. When you enter a hut it is hard to differentiate a father from a son, one generation from another. I think that this family resemblance has two different causes: the local position of the Indian villages, and the lack of intellectual culture. Indian nations are subdivided into an infinity of tribes, all hating each other, and never allied even if speaking the same language or living on the same river or nearby hill. This characteristic is preserved in the missions where marriages are made only within tribes. This blood link that unites a whole tribe is naïvely illustrated by those Spanish-speaking Indians who designate members of the same tribe as *mis parientes* (my relatives).

The Indians of the missions, remote from all civilization, are influenced solely by physical needs, which they satisfy very easily in their favourable climate, and therefore tend to lead dull, monotonous lives, which are reflected in their facial expressions.

The Chaimas, like all semi-wild people in hot climates, show a great aversion to clothes. In the torrid zone the Indians are ashamed – so they say – to wear clothes, and if they are forced to do so too soon they rush off into the jungle in order to remain naked. Despite the efforts of the monks the Chaima men and women walk around naked in their houses. When they go into villages they put on a kind of cotton shirt, which hardly reaches to their knees. Sometimes we met Indians outside the mission grounds, during a rainstorm, who had taken their clothes off and rolled them under their arms. They prefer to let the rain fall on their naked bodies than letting it wet their clothes. The older women hid behind trees and burst into loud fits of laughter when they saw us pass by fully dressed.

Chaima women are not pretty according to our ideas of beauty; however, the girls have a sweet, melancholic look, which softens their often hard and wild mouths. They wear their hair in two plaits and do not paint their skin; in their extreme poverty they use no ornaments apart from shell, bird-bone and seed necklaces and bracelets. Both women and men are very muscular, though plump and round. I saw no Indian with any natural deformity. In the wild state, which is a state of equality, nothing can induce a man to marry a deformed or ill woman. Such a woman, if she survives the accidents of life, dies childless.

The Chaimas hardly have any hair on their chins, like the Tongouses and other Mongolic races. They pluck out the few hairs that grow. In general it is erroneous to say that they cannot grow beards, because they pluck them out – though even without that custom, they would be mostly smooth-faced.

The Chaimas lead an extremely monotonous life. They go to bed regularly at half past seven in the evening, and get up long before dawn, at about half past four. Every Indian has a fire next to his hammock. Women suffer the cold greatly; I have even seen a woman shiver at church when the temperature was above 18 °C. Their huts are very clean. Their hammocks and reed mats, their pots full of cassava or fermented maize, their bow and arrows, all are kept in perfect order. Men and women wash every day, and as they walk around naked do not get as dirty as people who wear clothes. Apart from their village hut they also have in the *conuco*, next to a spring or at the entrance to a small valley, a hut roofed with palm- or banana-tree leaves. Though life is less comfortable in the *conuco* they prefer living there as much as possible. I have already alluded to their irresistible drive to flee and return to the jungle. Even young children flee from their parents to spend four or five days in the jungle, feeding off wild fruit, palm hearts and roots. When travelling through the missions it is not rare to find them empty as everyone is either in their garden or in the jungle, *al monte*. Similar feelings account for civilized people's passion for hunting: the charm of solitude, the innate desire for freedom, and the deep impressions felt whenever man is alone in contact with nature.

Among the Chaimas, as among all semi-barbarous people, the state of women is one of privation and suffering. The hardest work falls to them. In the evening when we saw the Chaimas return from their gardens the men carried only their machetes to cut their way through the undergrowth. The women walk loaded with bananas, a child in their arms and two others sometimes perched on top of their load. Despite this social inequality South American Indian women seem, in general, happier than North American ones. In the missions men work in the fields as much as women.

Nothing matches the difficulty that Indians have in learning Spanish. As long as they are distanced from white men they have an aversion to be called civilized Indians or, as the missions call them, *indios muy latinos*. But what struck me most, not only among the Chaimas, but among all the isolated missions that I later visited, was the extreme difficulty they have in co-ordinating and expressing the simplest ideas in Spanish, even if they know the meaning of the single words and sentences.

You would think their mental stupidity greater than that of children when a white asks them questions about objects that have surrounded them since birth. Missionaries assured us that this is not due to timidity, and that among the missionary Indians in charge of public works this is not an innate stupidity but a block they have concerning the mechanisms of a language so different to their mother tongue.

The Indians affirmed or denied whatever pleased the monks, and laziness, accompanied by that cunning courtesy common to all Indians, made them sometimes give the answers suggested by the questions. Travellers cannot be wary enough of this over-obliging approbation when they want to find out what Indians think. To test an Indian *alcalde* I asked him 'if he did not think that the Caripe river that comes from the Guacharo caves might not return there by some unknown entrance after climbing up the hill'. He looked as if he gave it serious thought for a while and answered in support of my theory: 'If it did not do this how else is there always water in the river?'

The Chaimas have extreme difficulty in coping with numerical relationships. I did not meet one who could tell me whether he was eighteen or sixty years old. The Chaima language has words to express high numbers, but few Indians know how to use them. As they need to count the more intelligent ones count in Spanish up to thirty or forty, and even that seems a great mental strain. In their own language they cannot count up to six. Since European savants have dedicated themselves to the study of the structure of American languages we cannot attribute the imperfection of a language to what appears to be the stupidity of a people. We recognize that everywhere languages offer greater richnesses and more nuances than can be supposed from the lack of culture of the people speaking them.

The American languages have a structure so different from Latin that the Jesuits, who look carefully to anything that might favour a quick establishing of missions, introduced the richer Indian languages, especially Quechua and Guarani, instead of Spanish, to their converts because these languages were systematic and already widespread. They tried to substitute these poorer, coarser dialects with irregular constructions. They found this substitution easy; Indians from different tribes docilely learned them, and these languages became a medium of communication between missionary and Indian. Through these languages the Jesuits found it easier to link the various tribes until then separated from each other by language.

In America, from the Eskimos to the Orinoco banks, from the burning plains to the icy Strait of Magellan, mother tongues, quite different in terms of their roots, share the same physiognomy. We recognize striking analogies in grammatical structure, not only in the more learned languages like that of the Incas, the Aymara, the Guaranu, Cora and Mexican, but also in the more primitive ones. It is thanks to this structural analogy rather than words in common that the mission Indian learns another American language more easily than a metropolitan one. In the Orinoco jungle I have met the dullest Indians who speak two or three languages.

If the Jesuit system had been followed, languages that cover a large amount of the continent would have become almost general. In Terra Firma and on the Orinoco, Carib and Tamanaco alone would be spoken, and in the south and south-west, Quechua, Guarani, Omagua and Araucan. By appropriating these languages with regular grammatical forms, the missionaries would have had a more intimate contact with their Indians. The numberless difficulties arising from missions with a dozen different tribes would have vanished with the confusions of their languages, and the Indian, by preserving an American language, would have retained individuality and national identity.

At the Capuchin hospice in Caripe I collected, with Bonpland's help, a small list of Chaima words. The three languages most common in this province are Chaima, Cumanagoto and Carib. Here they have been seen as separate languages and a dictionary of each has been compiled for mission use. The few grammars printed in the seventeenth century passed into the missions and have been lost in the jungle. Damp air and voracious insects (termites known as *comején*) make preserving books in these hot lands almost impossible, and they are soon destroyed.

On the right bank of the Orinoco, south-east of the Encaramada mission, 100 leagues from the Chaimas, live the Tamanacos. Despite the distance and numerous local obstacles it is clear that Chaima is a branch of Tamanaco. I discovered the link between these languages years after my return to Europe when I compared data collected in a grammar book of an old missionary on the Orinoco, printed in Italy.[62]

CHAPTER 10

Second stay in Cumaná – Earthquakes – Extraordinary meteors

We stayed another month at Cumaná. The river journey we intended to take up the Orinoco and the Río Negro demanded all kinds of preparation. We had to choose the easiest instruments to carry on narrow canoes; we had to provide ourselves with the funds for a ten-month trip inland across a country without communications with the coast. As astronomic determination of places was the main aim of our undertaking I did not want to miss the solar eclipse that would be visible at the end of October. I chose to wait until then in Cumaná where the sky is usually beautiful and clear. It was too late to reach the Orinoco river banks, and the high Caracas valley offered less favourable chances due to the mists that gather round the neighbouring mountains. Having precisely fixed the Cumaná longitude I had a starting-point for my chronometric determinations, the only ones I could count on when usually I did not remain long enough to take lunar distances or to observe Jupiter's satellites.

A dreadful accident almost made me put off my Orinoco journey, or postpone it for a long time. On the 27th of October, the night before the eclipse, we were strolling along the gulf shore as usual, to take some fresh air and observe high tide. Its highest point in this area was no more than 12 to 13 inches. It was eight at night and the breeze had not begun. The sky was overcast and during this dead calm it was extremely hot. We were crossing the beach that separates the landing-stage from the Guaiquerí Indian village. I heard somebody walking behind me; as I turned I saw a tall man, the colour of a mulatto, and naked to the waist. Just above my head he was holding a macana, a huge stick made of palm-tree wood, enlarged at the end like a club. I avoided his blow by leaping to the left. Bonpland, walking at my right, was less lucky. He had noticed the mulatto later than I had; he received the blow above his temple and fell to the ground. We were alone, unarmed, some half a league from any houses, in a vast plain bordered by the sea. The mulatto, instead of attacking me, turned back slowly to grab Bonpland's hat, which had softened the blow and fallen far from us. Terrified at seeing my travelling companion on the ground and for a few seconds unconscious I was worried only about him. I helped him up; pain and anger doubled his strength. We made for the mulatto who, either due to that cowardice typical of his race or because he saw some men far off on the beach, rushed off into the *tunal*, a coppice of cacti and tree aviccenia. Luck had him fall as he was running, and Bonpland, who had reached him first, began fighting with him, exposing himself to great danger. The mulatto pulled out a long knife from his trousers, and in such an unequal fight we would surely have been wounded if some Basque merchants taking the fresh air on the beach had not come to our aid. Seeing himself surrounded the mulatto gave up all idea of defending himself: then he managed to escape again and we followed him for a long time through the thorny cacti until he threw himself exhausted into a cow shed from where he let himself be quietly led off to prison.

That night Bonpland had a fever; but being brave, and gifted with that good character which a traveller should rank higher than anything else, he took up his work the next morning. The blow from the macana reached the crown of his head; he felt it for two to three months, up to our stay in Caracas. When he bent down to pick up plants he was several times made dizzy, which made us worry that some internal damage might have been done. Luckily our fears had no base and these alarming symptoms slowly vanished. The Cumaná inhabitants showed us the greatest kindness. We discovered that the mulatto came from one of the Indian villages round the great Maracaibo lake. He had served on a pirate ship from the island of Santo Domingo and, after a quarrel with the captain, had abandoned ship on the Cumaná coast. Why, after knocking one of us down, did he then try to steal a hat? In an interrogation his answers were so confused and stupid that we were unable to clear this matter up.

Despite Bonpland's tiresome accident I found myself the next day, the 28th of October, at five in the morning, on the roof terrace of our house, preparing to observe the eclipse. The sky was clear and beautiful. The crescent of Venus and the constellation of the Ship, so dazzling because of the proximity of their enormous nebulae, were soon lost by the rays of the rising sun. I congratulated myself for such a fine day, as during the last weeks storms had built up regularly in the south and south-east two or three hours after the sun passed the meridian and had prevented me setting the clocks with the corresponding heights. At night one of those reddish vapours, which hardly affect the hygrometer in the lower levels of the atmosphere, covered the stars. This phenomenon was all the more extraordinary as in previous years it often happened that for three or four months one did not see the least trace of cloud or vapour. I observed the complete progress and end of the eclipse.

The days before and after the eclipse were accompanied by strange atmospheric phenomena. We were in the season called winter here, that is, when clouds build up and release short stormy downpours. From the 10th of October to the 3rd of November the horizon is covered over each night by a reddish mist, quickly spreading across the sky-blue vault in a more or less thick veil. When this reddish mist lightly covered the sky not even the brightest stars could be seen even at their highest points. They twinkled at all altitudes as if after a rainstorm.

From the 28th of October to the 3rd of November the reddish mist was thicker than usual: at night the heat was stifling yet the thermometer did not rise beyond 26 °C. The sea breeze, which usually refreshed the air from eight to nine at night, was not felt at all. The air was sweltering hot, and the dusty, dry ground started cracking everywhere. On the 4th of November, around two in the afternoon, extraordinarily thick black clouds covered the tall Brigantín and Tataraqual mountains, and then reached the zenith. At about four it began to thunder way above us without rumbling; making a cracking noise, which often suddenly stopped. At the moment that the greatest electrical discharge was produced, twelve minutes past four, we felt two successive seismic shocks, fifteen seconds from each other. Everybody ran out into the street screaming. Bonpland, who was examining some plants, leaning over a table, was almost thrown to the floor, and I felt the shock very clearly in spite of being in my hammock. The direction of the earthquake was from north to south, rare in Cumaná.

Some slaves drawing water from a well, some 18 to 20 feet deep next to the Manzanares river, heard a noise comparable to artillery fire, which seemed to rise up out of the well; a surprising phenomenon, though quite common in American countries exposed to earthquakes.

A few minutes before the first shock there was a violent gust of wind, accompanied by flashes of lightning and large raindrops. The sky remained covered; after the storm the wind died down, staying quiet all night. The sunset was extraordinarily beautiful. The thick veil of clouds tore open into strips just above the horizon, forming shreds, and the sun shone at 12 degrees of altitude against an indigo-blue sky. Its disc appeared incredibly swollen, distorted and wavy at its edges. The clouds were gilded, and clusters of rays coloured like the rainbow spread in every direction from its centre. A great crowd had congregated in the main square. This phenomenon, the accompanying earthquake, thunder rolling as the earth shook, and that reddish mist lasting so many days were blamed on the eclipse.

Hardly twenty-two months had passed since a previous earthquake had nearly destroyed the city of Cumaná. The people regard the reddish mist veiling the sky and the absence of a sea breeze at night as infallible ill omens. Many people came to see us to ask if our instruments predicted any further quakes. Their anxiety increased greatly when on the 5th of November, at the same time as the day before, there was a violent gust of wind, accompanied by thunder and a few raindrops. But no shock was felt.

The earthquake of the 4th of November, the first I had experienced, made a great impression on me, heightened, perhaps accidentally, by remarkable meteorological variations. It was also a movement that went up and down, not in waves. I would never have thought then that, after a long stay in Quito and on the Peruvian coast, I would get as used to these often violent ground movements as in Europe we get used to thunder. In Quito we never considered getting out of bed when at night there were underground rumblings (*bramidos*), which seemed to announce a shock from the Pichincha volcano. The casualness of the inhabitants, who know that their city has not been destroyed in three centuries, easily communicates itself to the most frightened traveller. It is not so much a fear of danger as of the novelty of the sensation that strikes one so vividly when an earthquake is felt for the first time.

When shocks from an earthquake are felt, and the earth we think of as so stable shakes on its foundations, one second is long enough to destroy long-held illusions. It is like waking painfully from a dream. We think we have been tricked by nature's seeming stability; we listen out for the smallest noise; for the first time we mistrust the very ground we walk on. But if these shocks are repeated frequently over successive days, then fear quickly disappears. On the Peruvian coasts we got as used to the earth tremors as sailors do to rough waves.

The night of the 11th was cool and exceptionally beautiful. A little before dawn, at about half past two in the morning, extraordinarily luminous meteors were seen. Bonpland, who had got up to get some fresh air in the gallery, was the first to notice them. Thousands of fire-balls and shooting stars fell continually over four hours from north to south. According to Bonpland, from the start of this phenomenon there was not a patch of sky the size of three quarters of the moon that was not packed with fire-balls and shooting stars. The meteors trailed behind them long luminous traces whose phosphorescence lasted some eight seconds.

Almost all Cumaná's inhabitants witnessed this phenomenon as they got up before four in the morning to go to first mass. The sight of these fire-balls did not leave them indifferent, far to the contrary; the older ones recalled that the great 1766 earthquake was preceded by a similar manifestation.[63]

CHAPTER II

Journey from Cumaná to La Guaira – The road to Caracas –
General observations on the provinces of Venezuela – Caracas

Crossing from Cumaná to La Guaira by sea our plan was to stay in Caracas until the end of the rainy season; from there we would go to the great plains, the llanos, and the Orinoco missions; then we would travel upstream on the great river from south of the cataracts to the Río Negro and the Brazilian frontier, and return to Cumaná through the capital of Spanish Guiana, called Angostura[64] or Straits. It was impossible to calculate how long this journey of some 700 leagues would take in canoes. On the coasts only the mouth of the Orinoco is known. No trading is carried out with the missions. What lies beyond the plains is unknown country for the inhabitants of Caracas and Cumaná. In a land where few travel, people enjoy exaggerating the dangers arising from the climate, animals and wild men.

The boat that took us from Cumaná to La Guaira was one of those that trade between the coasts and the West Indies Islands. They are 30 feet long, and not more than 3 feet above the water, without decks. Although the sea is extremely rough from Cape Coderà to La Guaira, and although these boats have large triangular sails, not one of them has been lost at sea in a storm. The skill of the Guaiquerí pilots is such that voyages of 120 to 150 leagues in open sea, out of sight of land, are done without charts or compasses, as with the ancients. The Indian pilot guides himself by the polar star or the sun.

·When we left the Cumaná coast we felt as if we had been living there for a long time. It was the first land that we had reached in a world that I had longed to know from my childhood. The impression produced by nature in the New World is so powerful and magnificent that after only a few months in these places you feel you have been here years. In the Tropics everything in nature seems new and marvellous. In the open plains and tangled jungles all memories of Europe are virtually effaced as it is nature that determines the character of a country. How memorable the first new country you land at continues to be all your life! In my imagination I still see Cumaná and its dusty ground more intensely than all the marvels of the Andes.

As we approached the shoal surrounding Cape Arenas we admired the phosphorescence of the sea. Bands of dolphins enjoyed following our boat. When they broke the surface of the water with their broad tails they diffused a brilliant light that seemed like flames coming from the depths of the ocean. We found ourselves at midnight between some barren, rocky islands in the middle of the sea, forming the Caracas and Chimanas groups. The moon lit up these jagged, fantastic rocks, which had not a trace of vegetation. All these islands are uninhabited, except one where large, fast, brown goats can be found. Our Indian pilot said they tasted delicious. Thirty years back a family of whites settled here and grew maize and cassava. The father outlived his children. As he had become rich he bought two black slaves, who murdered him. Thus the goats ran wild, but not the maize. Maize appears to survive only if looked after by man. Birds destroy all the seeds needed to reproduce. The two slaves escaped punishment, as nothing could be proved. One of the blacks is now the hangman at Cumaná. He betrayed his companion, and obtained pardon by accepting being hangman.

We landed on the right bank of the Neveri and climbed to the little fort of El Morro de Barcelona, built some 60 to 70 toises above sea-level. We remained five hours in this fort guarded by the provincial militia. We waited in vain for news about English pirates stationed along the coast. Two of our fellow travellers, brothers of the Marquis of Toro in Caracas, came from Spain. They were highly cultivated men returning home after years abroad. They had more reason to fear being captured and taken as prisoners to Jamaica. I had no passport from the Admiralty, but I felt safe in the protection given by the English Government to those who travel for the progress of science.

The shock of the waves was felt in our boat. My fellow travellers all suffered. I slept calmly, being lucky never to suffer seasickness. By sunrise of the 20th of November we expected to double the cape in a few hours. We hoped to arrive that day at La Guaira, but our Indian pilot was scared of pirates. He preferred to make for land and wait in the little harbour of Higuerote[65] until night. We found neither a village nor a farm but two or three huts inhabited by mestizo fishermen with extremely thin children, which told us how unhealthy and feverish this coast was. The sea was so shallow that we had to wade ashore. The jungle came right down to the beach, covered in thickets of mangrove. On landing we smelled a sickly smell,[66] which reminded me of deserted mines.

Wherever mangroves grow on the seashore thousands of molluscs and insects thrive. These animals love shade and half light, and in the scaffolding of the thick intertwined roots find shelter from the crashing waves, riding above the water. Shellfish cling to the network of roots; crabs dig into the hollow trunks, and seaweeds, drifting ashore, hang from branches and bend them down. Thus, as the mud accumulates between the roots, so dry land moves further and further out from the jungly shores.

When we reached the high seas my travelling companions got so scared from the boat's rolling in a rough sea that they decided to continue by land from Higuerote to Caracas, despite having to cross a wild and humid country in constant rain and flooding rivers. Bonpland also chose the land way, which pleased me as he collected numerous new plants. I stayed alone with the Guaiquerí pilot as I thought it too dangerous to lose sight of the precious instruments that I wanted to take up the Orinoco.

La Guaira is more a bay than a harbour; the sea is always rough, and boats are exposed to dangerous winds, sandbanks and mist. Disembarking is very difficult as large waves prevent mules from being taken ashore. The negroes and freed mulattos who carry the goods on to the boats are exceptionally muscular. They wade into the water up to their waists and, surprisingly, are not scared of the sharks that teem in the harbour. The sharks are dangerous and bloodthirsty at the island opposite the coast of Caracas, although they do not attack anybody swiming in the harbour. To explain physical phenomena simply people have always resorted to marvels, insisting that here a bishop had blessed the sharks in the port.

We suffered much from the heat, increased by the reverberation from the dry, dusty ground. However, the excessive effect of the sun held no harmful consequences for us. At La Guaira sunstroke and its effects on the brain are feared, especially when yellow fever is beginning to appear. One day I was on the roof of our house observing the meridian point and the temperature difference between the sun and shade when a man came running towards me and begged me to take a drink he had brought along with him. He was a doctor who had been watching me for half an hour out in the sun from his window, without a hat on my head, exposed to the sun's rays. He assured me that coming from northern climes such imprudence would undoubtedly lead that night to an attack of yellow fever if I did not take his medicine. His prediction, however seriously argued, did not alarm me as I had had plenty of time to get acclimatized. But how could I refuse his argument when he was so polite and caring? I swallowed his potion, and the doctor must now have included me in the list of people he had saved from fever that year.[67]

From La Venta the road to Caracas rises another 150 toises to El Guayabo, the highest point; but I continued to use the barometer until we reached the small fort of Cuchilla. As I did not have a pass — for over five years I only needed it once, when I first disembarked — I was nearly arrested at an artillery post. To placate the angry soldiers I transformed the height of the mountains into Spanish *varas*. They were not particularly interested in this, and if I had anyone to thank for my release it was an Andalusian who became very friendly the moment I told him that the Sierra Nevada of his home were far higher than any of the mountains around Caracas.

When I first travelled the high plateaux towards Caracas I met many travellers resting mules at the small inn of Guayabo. They lived in Caracas, and were arguing over the uprising that had recently taken place concerning the independence of the country. Joseph España had died on the scaffold.[68] The excitement and bitterness of these people, who should have agreed on such questions, surprised me. While they argued about the hate mulattos have for freed blacks, about the wealth of monks, and the difficulties of owning slaves, a cold wind, which seemed to blow down from La Silla, enveloped us in a thick mist and ended the animated discussion. Once inside the inn, an old man who before had spoken with great equanimity, said to the others that it was unwise to deal with political matters at a time when spies could be lurking around, as much in the mountains as in the cities. These words, spoken in the emptiness of the sierra, deeply impressed me; I was to hear them often during our journeys.

Caracas is the capital of a country almost twice the size of Peru and only a little smaller than Nueva Granada (Colombia). This country is officially called in Spanish the Capitanía-General de Caracas or the Capitanía-General de las Provincias de Venezuela, and has nearly a million inhabitants, of whom some 60,000 are slaves. The copper-coloured natives, the *indios*, form a large part of the population only where Spaniards found complex urban societies already established. In the Capitanía-General the rural Indian population in the cultivated areas outside the missions is insignificant. In 1800 I calculated that the Indian population was about 90,000, which is one ninth of the total population, while in Mexico it rose to almost 50 per cent.

Among the races making up the Venezuelan population blacks are important – seen both compassionately for their wretched state, and with fear due to possible violent uprisings – because they are concentrated in limited areas, not so much because of their total number. Of the 60,000 slaves in the Venezuelan provinces, 40,000 live in the province of Caracas. In the plains there are only some 4,000 to 5,000, spread around the haciendas and looking after the cattle. The number of freed slaves is very high as Spanish legislation and custom favour emancipation. A slave-owner cannot deny a slave his freedom if he can pay 300 piastres,[69] even if this would have cost the slave-owner double because of the amount of work the slave might have done.

After the blacks I was interested in the number of white *criollos*, who I call Hispano-Americans,[70] and those whites born in Europe. It is difficult to find exact figures for such a delicate issue. People in the New World, as in the Old, hate population censuses because they think they are being carried out to increase taxation. The number of white *criollos* may reach some 200,000 to 210,000 people.[71]

I remained two months in Caracas. Bonpland and I lived in a large virtually isolated house in the elevated part of the city. From the gallery we could see the La Silla peak, the serrated crest of the Galipano, and the cheerful Guaire valley whose leafy fields contrasted with the curtain of the mountains around. It was the dry season. To improve the land the savannah and grass on the rocks were set on fire. Seen from far off, these great fires created surprising light effects.

Wherever the savannah climbed up the slopes and filled the gorges cut by torrential waters these strips of land on fire seemed at night like lava hanging above the valley.

If we had reasons to be pleased with the location of our house we had even more for the way we were welcomed by people from all classes. I have had the advantage, which few Spaniards can share with me, of having successively visited Caracas, Havana, Bogotá, Quito, Lima and Mexico, and of making contact with men of all ranks in these six capitals. In Mexico and Bogotá it seemed to me that interest in serious scientific studies predominated; in Quito and Lima people seemed more inclined to literature and all that flatters a lively imagination; in Havana and Caracas, there predominated a broader culture in political matters, more open criteria about the state of the colonies and metropolis. Intense commerce with Europe and the Caribbean Sea have powerfully influenced the social evolution of Cuba and the beautiful provinces of Venezuela. Nowhere else in Spanish America does civilization appear so European.

In the colonies skin colour is the real badge of nobility. In Mexico as well as in Peru, at Caracas as in Cuba, a barefoot man with a white skin is often heard to say: 'Does that rich person think himself whiter than I am?' Because Europe pours so many people into America, it can easily be seen that the axiom 'Todo blanco es caballero' (All whites are gentlemen) must wound the pretensions of many ancient and aristocratic European families. We do not find among the people of Spanish origin that cold and pretentious air which modern civilization has made more common in Europe than in Spain. Conviviality, candour and great simplicity of manner unite the different classes in the colonies.[72]

In several families I found a feeling for culture. They know about the great works of French and Italian literature; music pleases them, and is played with talent, which like all of the arts unites the different social classes. The exact sciences, and drawing and painting, are not as well established here as they are in Mexico and Bogotá, thanks to the liberality of the government and the patriotism of the Spanish people.

In a country with such ravishing views I hoped to find many people who might know about the high mountains in the region; and yet we could not find one person who had climbed to La Silla's peak.

Hunters do not climb high enough, and in these countries nobody would dream of going out to look for alpine plants, or to study rock strata, or take barometers up to high altitudes. They are used to a dull domestic life, and avoid fatigue and sudden changes in climate as if they live not to enjoy life but to prolong it.

The Captain–General, Sr Guevara, lent us guides; they were negroes who knew the way that led to the coast along the sierra ridge near the western peak. It is the path used by smugglers, but neither our guides nor the most experienced militia, formed to chase the clandestine traffickers, had ever climbed to the eastern La Silla peak.

We set off before sunrise, at five in the morning, with the slaves carrying our instruments. Our party consisted of eighteen people, and we advanced in Indian file along a narrow path on a steep grassy slope. From La Puerta the path becomes steep. You have to lean forward to climb. The thick grass was very slippery because of the prolonged drought. Cramp-irons and iron-tipped sticks would have been very useful. Short grass covers the gneiss rocks; it is impossible to grip it or dig steps into it as in softer soil. More tiring than dangerous, the climb soon disheartened the men accompanying us who were not used to mountain climbing. We wasted a lot of time waiting for them, and did not decide to continue alone until we saw them returning down the mountain instead of climbing up after us. Bonpland and I foresaw that we would soon be covered in thick fog. Fearing that our guides would use the fog to abandon us we made those carrying the instruments go ahead of us. The familiar chatting of the negroes contrasted with the taciturn seriousness of the Indians who had accompanied us up to then. They joked about those who had spent hours preparing for the ascent, and then abandoned it straightaway.

After four hours walking through savannah we reached a little wood composed of shrubs called *el pejual*, perhaps because of the amount of *pejoa* (*Gaultheria odorata*) there, a plant with strong-smelling leaves. The mountain slope became more gentle and we could pleasurably study the plants of the region. Perhaps nowhere else can so many beautiful and useful plants be discovered in such a small space. At 1,000 toises high the raised plains of La Silla gave place to a zone of shrubs that reminded one of the *páramos* and *punas*.

Even when nature does not produce the same species in analogous climates, either in the plains of isothermal parallels or on tablelands whose temperature resembles that of places nearer the poles,[73] we still noticed a striking resemblance of appearance and physiognomy in the vegetation of the most distant countries. This phenomenon is one of the most curious in the history of organic forms. I say history, for reason cannot stop man forming hypotheses on the origin of things; he will always puzzle himself with insoluble problems relating to the distribution of beings.

A grass from Switzerland grows on the granitic rocks of the Magellan Strait.[74] New Holland contains more than forty European phanerogamous plants. The greater amount of these plants, found equally in the temperate zones of both hemispheres, are completely absent in the intermediary or equinoctial regions, on plains and on mountains. A hairy-leafed violet, which signifies the last of the phanerogamous plants on Tenerife, and long thought specific to that island, can be seen 300 leagues further north near the snowy Pyrenean peaks. Grasses and sedges of Germany, Arabia and Senegal have been recognized among plants collected by Bonpland and myself on the cold Mexican tablelands, on the burning Orinoco banks and on the Andes, and at Quito in the Southern hemisphere. How can one believe that plants migrate over regions covered by sea? How have the germs of life, identical in appearance and in internal structure, developed at unequal distances from the poles and from the oceans, in places that share similar temperatures? Despite the influence of air pressure on the plants' vital functions, and despite the greater or lesser degree of light, it is heat, unequally distributed in different seasons, that must be considered vegetation's most powerful stimulus.

The amount of identical species in the two continents and in the two hemispheres is far less than early travellers once led us to think. The high mountains of equinoctial America have their plantains, valerians, arenarias, ranunculuses, medlars, oaks and pines, which from their features we could confuse with European ones, but they are all specifically different. When nature does not present the same species, she repeats the same genera. Neighbouring species are often found at enormous distances from each other, in low regions of a temperate zone, and on mountains on the equator. And, as we found on La Silla at Caracas, they are not the European genera that have colonized mountains of the torrid zone, but genera of the same tribe, which have taken their place and are hard to distinguish.

The more we study the distribution of organized life on the globe, the more we tend to abandon the hypothesis of migration. The Andes chain divides the whole of South America into two unequal longitudinal parts. At the foot of this chain, on both east and west, we found many plants that were specifically identical. The various passes on the Andes would not let any vegetation from warm regions cross from the Pacific coast to the Amazon banks. When a peak reaches a great height, whether in the middle of low mountains and plains, or in the centre of an archipelago raised by volcanic fires, its summit is covered with alpine plants, many of which are also found at immense distances on other mountains under similar climates. Such are the general phenomena of plant distribution.

There is a saying that a mountain is high enough to reach the rhododendron and befaria limit, in the same way one says one has reached the snow limit. In employing this expression it is tacitly assumed that under identical temperatures a certain kind of vegetation must grow. This is not strictly true. The pines of Mexico are absent in the Peruvian Andes. The Caracas La Silla is not covered with the same oaks that flourish in New Granada at the same height. Identity of forms suggests an analogy of climate, but in similar climates the species may be very diversified.

The attractive Andean rhododendron, or befaria, was first observed by Mutis[75] near Pamplona and Bogotá, in the 4th and 7th degree of latitude. It was so little known before our expedition up La Silla that it was not to be found in any European herbal. The learned editors of *The Flora of Peru* had even described it under another name. The two species of befaria we brought down from La Silla are specifically different from those at Pamplona and Bogotá. Near the equator the Andean rhododendrons cover the mountains right up to 1,600 and 1,700 toises. Going further north on La Silla we find them lower, below 1,000 toises. Befaria recently discovered in Florida, in latitude 30, grow on low hills. Thus, within 600 leagues in latitude, these shrubs descend towards the plains in proportion as their distance from the equator increases.

Due to the thickness of the vegetation, made up of a plant of the Musaceae family, it was hard to find a path. We had to make one through that jungle of musaceous plants; the negroes led us, cutting a path with machetes. We saw the peak at intervals through breaks in the cloud, but soon we were covered in a thick mist and could only proceed using the compass; with each step we risked finding ourselves at the edge of a precipice, which fell 6,000 feet down to the sea. We had to stop, surrounded by cloud down to the ground, and we began to doubt if we would reach the eastern peak before sunset. Luckily the negroes carrying the water and the food had arrived, so we decided to eat something. But the meal did not last long because either the Capuchin father had not calculated our numbers properly or the slaves had already eaten everything. We found only olives and some bread. We had been walking for nine hours without stopping or finding water. Our guides seemed to lose heart, and wanted to go back. Bonpland and I had difficulty in persuading them to stay with us.

To reach the peak we had to approach as near as possible to the great cliff that falls to the coast. We needed three quarters of an hour to reach the top. While sitting on the peak observing the inclination of the magnetic needle I saw a great number of hairy bees, somewhat smaller than the northern European ones, crawling all over my hands. These bees nest in the ground and rarely fly. Their apathy seemed to derive from the cold mountain air. Here they are called *angelitos* (little angels) because they hardly ever sting. Until you are sure about the harmlessness of these *angelitos* you remain suspicious. I confess that often during astronomic observations I almost dropped my instruments when I realized my face and hands were covered with these hairy bees. Our guides assured us that these bees only attacked when you annoyed them by picking them up by their legs. I did not try.

It was half past four in the afternoon when we finished our observations. Satisfied with the success of our journey we forgot that there might be dangers descending steep slopes covered with a smooth, slippery grass in the dark. We did not arrive at the valley bottom until ten at night. We were exhausted and thirsty after walking for fifteen hours, practically without stopping. The soles of our feet were cut and torn by the rough, rocky soil and the hard, dry grass stalks, for we had been forced to pull our boots off as the ground was too slippery. We spent the night at the foot of La Silla. Our friends at Caracas had been able to follow us on the summit with binoculars. They liked hearing our account of the expedition but were not happy with the result of our measurements, for La Silla was not as high as the highest mountains in the Pyrenees.

CHAPTER 12

Earthquake in Caracas – Departure from Caracas – Gold mines –
Sugar plantations

We left Caracas on the 7th of February, on a fresh afternoon, ready to begin our journey to the Orinoco. The memory of this period is today more painful than it was years ago. In those remote countries our friends have lost their lives in the bloody revolutions that gave them freedom and then alternatively deprived them of it.[76] The house where we lived is now a heap of rubble. Terrible earthquakes have transformed the shape of the ground; the city I described has disappeared. On the same spot, on the fissured ground, another city is slowly being built. The ruins, tombs for a large population, have already turned into shelter for human beings.

I reckoned that it was my duty in this book to record all the data obtained from reliable sources concerning the seismic shocks that on the 26th of March 1812 destroyed the city of Caracas; in all the province of Venezuela more than 20,000 people perished. As a historian of nature, the traveller should note down the moment when great natural calamities happen, and investigate the causes and relations, and establish fixed points in the rapid course of time, in the transformations that succeed each other ceaselessly so that he can compare them with previous catastrophes.[77]

On my arrival at Terra Firma I was struck by the correlation between two natural phenomena: the destruction of Cumaná on the 14th of December 1797 and volcanic eruptions in the smaller West Indian Islands. Something similar happened at Caracas on the 26th of March 1812. In 1797 the volcano on Guadeloupe Island, on the Cumaná coast, seemed to have reacted; fifteen years later another volcano on San Vincente also reacted, and its effects were felt as far as Caracas and the banks of the Apure. Probably both times the centre of the eruption was at an enormous depth in the earth, equidistant from the points on the earth's surface that felt the movement. The shock felt at Caracas in December 1811 was the only one that preceded the terrible catastrophe of the 26th of March 1812. In Caracas, and for 90 leagues around, not one drop of rain had fallen for five months up to the destruction of the capital. The 26th of March was a very hot day; there was no wind and no cloud. It was Ascension Day and most people had congregated in the churches. Nothing suggested the horrors to come. At seven minutes past four the first shock was felt. 'It was so violent that the church bells rang, and lasted five to six seconds. It was followed immediately by another lasting ten to twelve seconds when the ground seemed to ripple like boiling water. People thought the quake was over when an infernal din came from under the ground. It was like thunder but louder and longer than any tropical storm. Following this there was a vertical movement lasting three seconds followed by undulations. The shocks coming from these contrary movements tore the city apart. Thousands of people were trapped in the churches and houses.'[78]

On the 8th of February we set off at sunrise to cross Higuerote, a group of tall mountains separating the valleys of Caracas and Aragua. Descending the woody slopes of Higuerote towards the south-west we reached the small village of San Pedro, 584 toises high, located in a basin where several valleys meet. Banana trees, potatoes and coffee grow there. In an inn (*pulpería*) we met several European Spaniards working at the Tobacco Office. Their bad temper contrasted with our mood. Tired by the route, they vented their anger by cursing the wretched country ('estas tierras infelices') where they were doomed to live, while we never wearied of admiring the wild scenery, the fertile earth and mild climate. From Las Lagunetas we descended into the Tuy river valley. This western slope is called Las Cocuyzas, and is covered with two plants with agave leaves; the maguey of Cocuzza and the maguey of Cocuy. The latter belongs to the *Yucca* genus. Its sweet fermented juice is distilled into an alcohol, and I have seen people eat its young green leaves. The fibres of the full-grown leaves are made into extremely long cords. At Caracas cathedral a maguey cord has suspended the weight of a 350-pound clock for fifteen years. We spent two very agreeable days at the plantation of Don José de Manterola who, when young, had been attached to the Spanish Legation in Russia. Brought up and protected by Sr de Xavedra, one of the more enlightened administrators in Caracas, de Manterola wanted to leave for Europe when that famous man became minister. The governor of the province, fearing de Manterola's prestige, arrested him in the harbour and when the order from Spain finally arrived to release him from such an unjust arrest the minister had fallen from grace.

The farm we lodged at was a fine sugar-cane plantation. The ground is smooth like the bed of a dried lake. The Tuy river winds through land covered with banana trees and a little wood of *Hura crepitans, Erythrina corallodrendon*, and figs with nymphae leaves. The river is formed with quartz pebbles. I can think of no more pleasant bathe than that in the Tuy. The crystal-clear water remains at 18.6 °C. This is cool for the climate; the sources of the river are in the surrounding mountains. The owner's house is situated on a hillock surrounded by huts for the negroes. Those who are married provide their own food. They are given, as everywhere in the Aragua valleys, a plot of land to cultivate, which they work on their Saturdays and Sundays, the free days of the week. They have chicken, and sometimes a pig. The owner boasts of their contentment in the same way that northern European landowners boast about the happy peasants on their land. The day we arrived three runaway negroes had been captured; newly bought slaves. I dreaded witnessing those punishments that ruin the charm of the countryside wherever there are slaves. Luckily, the blacks were treated humanely.

In this plantation, as in all the provinces of Venezuela, you can distinguish, from afar, three kinds of sugar cane by the colour of their leaves; the old Creole cane, Otaheite cane and Batavia cane. The first has a darker green leaf, a thinner stalk with knots close together. It was the first sugar cane introduced from India to Sicily, the Canaries and the West Indies. The second is lighter green; its stalk is fatter, more succulent. The whole plant seems more luxuriant. It arrived thanks to the voyages of Bougainville, Cook and Bligh. Bougainville brought it to Mauritius, where it went to Cayenne, Martinique and from 1792 to the rest of the West Indies. Otaheite sugar cane, the *to* of the islanders, is one of the most important agricultural acquisitions due to the voyages of naturalists. On the same plot of land it gives a third of *vezou* (juice) more than Creole cane, but due to the thickness of its stalk and strength of its ligneous fibres furnishes much more fuel. This is an advantage in the West Indian Islands where the destruction of the forests has forced planters to use the bagasse as fuel for their furnaces. The third species, the violet sugar cane, is called Batavia or Guinea cane, and certainly comes from Java. Its leaves are purple and large and it is preferred in Caracas for making rum.[79] At Tuy they were busy finishing a ditch to bring irrigation water. This enterprise had cost the owner 7,000 piastres to build and 4,000 piastres in lawsuits with his neighbours. While the lawyers argued over the canal, which was only half finished, de Manterola had already begun to doubt the worth of his project. I took the level of the ground with a *lunette d'épreuve* placed on an artificial horizon and found that the dam had been placed 8 feet too low. What sums of money have not been uselessly spent in the Spanish colonies founding constructions on poor levelling!

The Tuy valley has its 'gold mine', as do nearly all the places near mountains inhabited by white Europeans. I was assured that in 1780 foreign gold seekers had been seen extracting gold nuggets and had set up a place for washing the sand. The overseer of a nearby plantation had followed their tracks and after his death a jacket with gold buttons was found among his belongings, which according to popular logic meant that they came from the gold seam, later covered by a rock fall. It was no use my saying that from simply looking at the ground, without opening up a deep gallery, I would not be able to decide if there once had been a mine there – I had to yield to my host's entreaties. For twenty years the overseer's jacket had been the talking-point of the area. Gold dug out from the ground has, in the people's eyes, a special lure unrelated to the diligent farmer harvesting a fertile land under a gentle climate.

Our guides led us to the 'mine'. We turned west, and finally reached the Quebrada de Oro. On the hillside there was hardly a trace of a quartz seam. The landslide, caused by rain, had so transformed the ground that we could not even think of exploring it. Huge trees now grew where twenty years before gold seekers had worked. It is likely that there are veins in the mica-slate containing this venerable metal, but how could I judge if it was worth exploiting or if the metal was to be found in nodules? To compensate our efforts, we set to botanizing in the thick wood around the Hato.

We left the Manterola plantation on the 11th of February at sunrise. A little before reaching Mamon we stopped at a farm belonging to the Monteras family. A negress, more than a hundred years old, was sitting outside a mud-and-reed hut. Her age was known because she had been a creole slave. She seemed to enjoy amazing good health. 'I keep her in the sun' (*La tengo al sol*), said her grandson. 'The heat keeps her alive.' This treatment seemed rather harsh as the sun's rays fell vertically on to her. Blacks and Indians reach very advanced ages in the torrid zone. Hilario Pari, a native of Peru, died at the extraordinary age of one hundred and forty-three, having been married ninety years.

Beyond the village of Turmero, towards Maracay, you can observe on the distant horizon something that seems to be a tumulus covered in vegetation. But it is not a hill, nor a group of trees growing close together, but one single tree, the famous *zamang de Guayre*, known through the country for the enormous extent of its branches, which form a semi-spherical head some 576 feet in circumference. The zamang is a fine species of the mimosa family whose twisted branches are forked. We rested a long time under this vegetable roof. The branches extend like an enormous umbrella and bend towards the ground. Parasitical plants grow on the branches and in the dried bark. The inhabitants, especially the Indians, venerate this tree, which the first conquerors found in more or less the same state as it is in today. We heard with satisfaction that the present owner of the zamang had brought a lawsuit against a cultivator accused of cutting off a branch. The case was tried and the man found guilty.

We reached Maracay late. The people who had been recommended to us were away, but no sooner had the inhabitants realized our worries than they came from everywhere to offer us lodging for our instruments and mules. It has been said a thousand times, but the traveller always feels the need to repeat that the Spanish colonies are the authentic land of hospitality, even in places where industry and commerce have created wealth and a little culture. A Canarian family warmly invited us to stay, and cooked an excellent dinner. The master of the house was away on a business trip and his young wife had just given birth. She was wild with joy when she heard that we were due to pass through Angostura where her husband was. Through us he would learn about the birth of his first child. As we were about to leave we were shown the baby; we had seen her the night before, asleep, but the mother wanted us to see her awake. We promised to describe her features one by one to the father, but when she saw our instruments and books the good woman worried: 'On such a long journey, and with so many other things to think about, you could easily forget the colour of my baby's eyes!'

We spent seven agreeable days at the Hacienda de Cura in a small hut surrounded by thickets; the house itself, located in a sugar plantation, was infected with bubos, a skin disease common among slaves in the valleys. We lived like the rich; we bathed twice a day, slept three times and ate three meals in twenty-four hours. The lake water was warm, some 24 °C to 25 °C. The coolest bathing place was under the shade of ceibas and zamangs at Toma in a stream that rushes out of the granite Rincón del Diablo mountains. Entering this bath was fearsome, not because of the insects but because of the little brown hairs covering the pods of the *Dolichos pruriens*. When these small hairs, called *pica pica*, stick to your body they cause violent irritations. You feel the sting but cannot see what stung you.

During our stay at Cura we made numerous excursions to the rocky islands in the middle of Lake Valencia, to the hot springs at Mariara, and the high mountain called El Cucurucho de Coco. A narrow, dangerous path leads to the port of Turiamo and the famous coastal cacao plantations. Throughout all our excursions we were surprised not only by the progress of culture but also by the increase in the numbers of the free, hard-working population, used to manual work and too poor to buy slaves. Everywhere whites and mulattos had bought small isolated farms. Our host, whose father enjoyed an income of 40,000 piastres a year, had more land than he could farm; he distributed plots in the Aragua valley to poor families who wanted to grow cotton. He tried to surround his enormous plantation with free working men, because they wanted to work for themselves, or for others. Count Tovar was busy trying to abolish slavery and hoped to make slaves less necessary for the important estates, and to offer the freed slaves land to become farmers themselves. When he left for

Europe he had broken up and rented land around Cura. Four years later, on returning to America, he found fine cotton fields and a little village called Punta Samuro, which we often visited with him. The inhabitants are all mulatto, *zambo*[80] and freed slaves. The rent is ten piastres a *fanega* of land; it is paid in cash or cotton. As the small farmers are often in need, they sell their cotton at modest prices. They sell it even before harvest, and this advance is used by the rich landowners to make the poor dependent on them as day workers. The price of labour is less than it is in France. A free man is paid five piastres a month without food, which costs very little as meat and vegetables are abundant. I like quoting these details about colonial agriculture because they prove to Europeans that there is no doubt that sugar, cotton and indigo can be produced by free men, and that the miserable slaves can become peasants, farmers and landowners.

CHAPTER 13

The Aragua valleys form a basin, closed between granitic and calcareous mountain ranges of unequal height. Due to the land's peculiar configuration, the small rivers of the Aragua valleys form an enclosed system and flow into a basin blocked off on all sides; these rivers do not flow to the ocean but end in an inland lake, and thanks to constant evaporation lose themselves, so to speak, in the air. These rivers and lakes determine the fertility of the soil and agricultural produce in the valleys. The aspect of the place and the experience of some fifty years show that the water-level is not constant; that the balance between evaporation and inflow is broken. As the lake lies 1,000 feet above the neighbouring Calabozo steppes, and 1,332 feet above sea-level, it was thought that the water filtered out through a subterranean channel. As islands emerge, and the water-level progressively decreases, it is feared the lake might completely dry out.

Lake Valencia, called Tacarigua by the Indians, is larger than Lake Neuchâtel in Switzerland; its general form resembles Lake Geneva, situated at about the same altitude. Its opposite banks are notably different: the southern one is deserted, stripped of vegetation and virtually uninhabited; a curtain of high mountains gives it a sad, monotonous quality; in contrast, the northern side is pleasant and rural, and has rich plantations of sugar cane, coffee and cotton. Paths bordered with cestrum, azedaracs, and other perpetually flowering shrubs cross the plain and link the isolated farms. All the houses are surrounded by trees. The ceiba (*Bombax hibiscifolius*), with large yellow flowers, and the erythrina, with purple ones, whose overlapping branches give the countryside its special quality. During the season of drought, when a thick mist floats above the burning ground, artificial irrigation keeps the land green and wild. Every now and then granite blocks pierce through the cultivated ground; large masses of rocks rise up in the middle of the valley. Some succulent plants grow in its bare and cracked walls, preparing mould for the coming centuries. Often a fig tree, or a clusia with fleshy leaves, growing in clefts, crowns these isolated little summits. With their dry withered branches they look like signals along a cliff. The shape of these heights betrays the secret of their ancient origins; for when the whole valley was still submerged and waves lapped the foot of the Mariara peaks (El Rincón del Diablo) and the coastal chain, these rocky hills were shoals and islands.

But the shores of Lake Valencia are not famed solely for their picturesque beauties: the basin presents several phenomena whose interpretation holds great interest for natural historians and for the inhabitants. What causes the lowering of the lake's water-level? Is it receding faster than before? Will the balance between the flowing in and the draining out be restored, or will the fear that the lake might dry up be proved justified?

I have no doubt that from remotest times the whole valley was filled with water. Everywhere the shape of the promontory and their steep slopes reveals the ancient shore of this alpine lake. We find vast tracts of land, formerly flooded, now cultivated with banana, sugar cane and cotton. Wherever a hut is built on the lake shore you can see how year by year the water recedes. As the water decreases, you can see how islands begin to join the land while others form promontories or become hills. We visited two islands still completely surrounded by water and found, under the scrub, on small flats between 4 and 8 toises above the water-level, fine sand mixed with helicites deposited by waves. On all these islands you will discover clear traces of the gradual lowering of the water.

The destruction of the forests, the clearing of the plains, and the cultivation of indigo over half a century has affected the amount of water flowing in as well as the evaporation of the soil and the dryness of the air, which forcefully explains why the present Lake Valencia is decreasing. By felling trees that cover the tops and sides of mountains men everywhere have ensured two calamities at the same time for the future: lack of fuel, and scarcity of water. Trees, by the nature of their perspiration, and the radiation from their leaves in a cloudless sky, surround themselves with an atmosphere that is constantly cool and misty. They affect the amount of springs by sheltering the soil from the sun's direct actions and reducing the rainwater's evaporation. When forests are destroyed, as they are everywhere in America by European planters, with imprudent haste, the springs dry up completely, or merely trickle. River beds remain dry part of the year and are then turned into torrents whenever it rains heavily on the heights. As grass and moss disappear with the brushwood from the mountainsides, so rainwater is unchecked in its course. Instead of slowly raising the river level by filtrations, the heavy rains dig channels into the hillsides, dragging down loose soil, and forming sudden, destructive floods. Thus, the clearing of forests, the absence of permanent springs, and torrents are three closely connected phenomena. Countries in different hemispheres like Lombardy bordered by the Alps, and Lower Peru between the Pacific and the Andes, confirm this assertion.

Until the middle of the last century the mountains surrounding the Aragua valley were covered in forests. Huge trees of the mimosa, ceiba and fig families shaded the lake shore and kept it cool. The sparsely populated plain was invaded by shrubs, fallen tree trunks and parasitical plants, and was covered in thick grass so that heat was not lost as easily as from cultivated ground, which is not sheltered from the sun's rays. When the trees are felled, and sugar cane, indigo and cotton are planted, springs and natural supplies to the lake dry up. It is hard to form a fair idea of the enormous amount of evaporation taking place in the torrid zone, especially in a valley surrounded by steep mountains where maritime breezes blow, and whose ground is completely flat as if levelled by water. The heat prevailing on the lake shore is comparable to that in Naples and Sicily.

Lake Valencia is full of islands, which embellish the countryside with the picturesque form of their rocks and by the kind of vegetation that covers them. Tropical lakes have this advantage over alpine ones. The islands, without counting Morro and Cabrera, which are already joined to the mainland, are fifteen in number. They are partially cultivated, and very fertile due to the vapours rising from the lake. Burro, the largest island, some 2 miles long, is inhabited by mestizo families who rear goats. These simple people rarely visit the Mocundo coast. The lake seems gigantic to them: they produce bananas, cassava, milk and fish. A hut built of reeds, some hammocks woven with cotton grown in neighbouring fields, a large stone on which they build their fires, and the ligneous fruit of the *tutuma* to draw water with are their sole household needs. The old mestizo who offered us goat's milk had a lovely daughter. We learned from our guide that isolation had made him as suspicious as if he lived in a city. The night before our arrival some hunters had visited the island. Night surprised them and they preferred to sleep out in the open rather than return to Mocundo. This news spread alarm around the island. The father forced his young daughter to climb a very tall zamang or mimosa, which grows on the plain at some distance from the hut. He slept at the foot of this tree, and didn't let his daughter down until the hunters had left.

The lake is usually full of fish; there are three species with soft flesh, which are not very tasty: the *guavina*, the *bagre* and the *sardina*. The last two reach the lake from streams. The *guavina*, which I sketched on the spot, was some 20 inches long and 3 to 5 inches wide. It is perhaps a new species of Gronovius's *Erythrina*. It has silver scales bordered with green. This fish is extremely voracious and destroys other species. Fishermen assured us that a little crocodile, the *bava*, which often swam near as we bathed, contributed to the destruction of the fish. We never managed to catch this reptile and examine it close up. It is said to be very innocent; yet its habits, like its shape, clearly resemble the alligator or *Crocodilus acutus*. It swims so that only the tips of its snout and tail show: it lies at midday on deserted beaches.

The island of Chamberg is a granitic outcrop some 200 feet high, with two peaks linked by a saddle. The sides of the rock are bare; only a few white flowering clusia manage to grow there. But the view of the lake and surrounding plantations is magnificent, especially at sunset when thousands of heron, flamingo and wild duck fly over the water to roost on the island.

It is thought that some of the plants that grow on the rocky islands of Lake Valencia are exclusive to them because they have not been discovered elsewhere. Among these are the papaw tree of the lake (*papaya de la laguna*), and a tomato[81] from Cura Island; this differs from our *Solanum lycopersicum* in that its fruit is round and small but very tasty. The papaw of the lake is common also on Cura Island and at Cabo Blanco. Its trunk is slenderer than the ordinary papaw, but its fruit is half the size and completely round, without projecting ribs. This fruit, which I have often eaten, is extremely sweet.

The areas around the lake are unhealthy only in the dry season when the water-level falls and the mud bed is exposed to the sun's heat. The bank, shaded by woods of *Coccoloba barbadensis* and decorated with beautiful lilies, reminds one, because of the similar aquatic plants found there, of the marshy banks of our European lakes. Here we find pondweed (potamogeton), chara and cat's-tails 3 feet high, hardly different from the *Typha angustifolia* of our marshes. Only after very careful examination do we recognize each plant to be a distinct species, peculiar to the New World. How many plants from the Strait of Magellan to the cordilleras of Quito have once been confused with northern temperate ones owing to their analogy in form and appearance!

Some of the rivers flowing into Lake Valencia come from thermal springs, worthy of special note. These springs gush out at three points from the coastal granitic chain at Onoto, Mariara and Las Trincheras. I was only able to carefully examine the physical and geological relations of the thermal waters of Mariara and Las Trincheras. All the springs contain small amounts of sulphuretted hydrogen gas. The stink of rotten eggs, typical of this gas, could only be smelled very close to the spring. In one of the puddles, which had a temperature of 56.2 °C, bubbles burst up at regular intervals of two to three minutes. I was not able to ignite the gas, not even the small amounts in the bubbles as they burst on the warm surface of the water, nor after collecting it in a bottle, despite feeling nausea caused more by the heat than by the gas. The water, when cold, is tasteless and quite drinkable.

South of the ravine, in the plain that stretches to the lake shore, another less hot and less gassy sulphureous spring gushes out. The thermometer reached only 42 °C. The water collects in a basin surrounded by large trees. The unhappy slaves throw themselves in this pool at sunset, covered in dust after working in the indigo and sugar-cane fields. Despite the water being 12 °C to 14 °C warmer than the air the negroes call it refreshing. In the torrid zone this word is used for anything that restores your strength, calms nerves or produces a feeling of well-being. We also experienced the salutary effects of this bath. We had our hammocks slung in the trees shading this pond and spent a whole day in this place so rich in plants. Near this *băno de Mariara* we found the *volador* or gyrocarpus. The winged fruits of this tree seem like flying beings when they separate from the stem. On shaking the branches of the *volador*, we saw the air filled with its fruits, all falling together. We sent some fruit to Europe, and they germinated in Berlin, Paris and Malmaison. The numerous plants of the *volador*, now seen in hothouses, owe their origin to the only tree of its kind found near Mariara.

While following the local custom of drying ourselves in the sun after our bath, half wrapped in towels, a small mulatto approached. After greeting us in a serious manner, he made a long speech about the properties of the Mariara waters, the many sick people who over the years have come here, and the advantageous position of the spring between Valencia and Caracas, where morals became more and more dissolute. He showed us his house, a little hut covered with palm leaves in an enclosure near by, next to a stream that fed the pool. He assured us that we would find there all the comforts we could imagine; nails to hang our hammocks, oxhides to cover reed beds, jugs of fresh water, and those large lizards (iguanas) whose flesh is considered to be a refreshing meal after a bathe. From his speech we reckoned that this poor man had mistaken us for sick people wanting to install themselves near the spring. He called himself 'the inspector of the waters and the *pulpero* of the place'. He stopped talking to us as soon as he saw we were there out of curiosity – 'para ver no más' as they say in these colonies, 'an ideal place for lazy people'.

On the 21st of February, at nightfall, we left the pretty Hacienda de Cura and set off for Guacara and Nueva Valencia. As the heat of the day was stifling we travelled by night. We crossed the village of Punta Zamuro at the foot of Las Viruelas mountain. The road is lined with large zamangs, or mimosa trees, reaching some 60 feet high. Their almost horizontal branches meet at more than 150 feet distance. I have never seen a canopy of leaves so thick and beautiful as these. The night was dark: the Rincón del Diablo and its dentated rocks appeared every now and then, illuminated by the brilliance of the burning savannahs, or wrapped in clouds of reddish smoke. In the thickest part of the brush our horses panicked when they heard the howl of an animal that seemed to be following us. It was an enormous jaguar that had been roaming these mountains for three years. It had escaped from the most daring hunters. It attacked horses and mules, even when they were penned in, but not lacking food had not yet attacked human beings. Our negro guide screamed wildly to scare off the beast, which he obviously did not achieve.

We spent the 23rd of February in the marquis of Toro's house, in the village of Guacara, a large Indian community. The Indians live a life of ease because they have just won a legal case restoring lands disputed by whites. An avenue of carolineas leads from Guacara to Mocundo, a rich sugar plantation belonging to the Moro family. We found a rare garden there with an artificial clump of trees, and, on top of a granitic outcrop near a stream, a pavilion with a *mirador* or viewpoint. From here you see a splendid panorama over the west of the lake, the surrounding mountains and a wood of palm trees. The sugar-cane fields with their tender green leaves seem like a great plain. Everything suggests abundance, although those who work the land have to sacrifice their freedom.

The preparation of sugar, its boiling, and the claying, is not well done in Terra Firma because it is made for local consumption. More *papelón* is sold than either refined or raw sugar. *Papelón* is an impure sugar in the form of little yellowish-brown loaves. It is a blend of molasses and mucilaginous matter. The poorest man eats *papelón* the way in Europe he eats cheese. It is said to be nutritious. Fermented with water it yields *guarapo*, the favourite local drink.

The city of New Valencia occupies a large area of ground, but its population is of some 6,000 to 7,000 souls. The roads are very wide, the market place (*plaza mayor*) is disproportionately large. As the houses are few the difference between the population and the land they occupy is greater even than at Caracas. Many of the whites of European stock, especially the poorest, leave their town houses and live for most of the year in their cotton and indigo plantations. They dare to work with their own hands, which, given the rigid prejudices in this country, would be a disgrace in the city. The industriousness of the inhabitants has greatly increased after freedom was granted to business in Puerto Cabello, now open as a major port (*puerto mayor*) to ships coming directly from Spain.

Founded in 1555, under the government of Villacinda, by Alonso Díaz Moreno, Nueva Valencia is twelve years older than Caracas. Some justifiably regret that Valencia has not become the capital of the country. Its situation on the plain, next to a lake, recalls Mexico City. If you consider the easy communications offered by the Aragua valleys with the plains and rivers entering the Orinoco; if you accept the possibility of opening up navigation into the interior through the Pao and Portuguesa rivers as far as the Orinoco mouth, the Casiquiare and the Amazon, you realize that the capital of the vast Venezuelan provinces would have been better placed next to the superb Puerto Cabello, under a pure, serene sky, and not next to the barely sheltered bay of La Guaira, in a temperate but always misty valley.

Only those who have seen the quantity of ants that infest the countries of the torrid zone can picture the destruction and the sinking of the ground caused by these insects. They abound to such a degree in Valencia that their excavations resemble underground canals, which flood with water during the rains and threaten buildings. Here they have not used the extraordinary means employed by the monks on the island of Santo Domingo when troops of ants ravaged the fine plains of La Vega. The monks, after trying to burn the ant larvae and fumigate the nests, told the inhabitants to choose a saint by lot who would act as an Abogado contra las Hormigas. The choice fell on Saint Saturnin, and the ants disappeared as soon as the saint's festival was celebrated.

On the morning of the 27th of February we visited the hot springs of La Trinchera, 3 leagues from Valencia. They flow more fully than any we had seen until then, forming a rivulet, which in the dry season maintains a depth of some 2 feet 8 inches of water. The carefully taken water temperature was 90.3 °C. We had breakfast near the spring: our eggs were cooked in less than four minutes in the hot water. The rock from which the spring gushes is of real coarse-grained granite. Whenever the water evaporates in the air, it forms sediments and incrustations of carbonate of lime. The exuberance of the vegetation around the basin surprised us. Mimosas with delicate pinnate leaves, clusias and figs send their roots into the muddy ground, which is as hot as 85 °C. Two currents flow down on parallel courses, and the Indians showed us how to prepare a bath of whatever temperature you want by opening a hole in the ground between the two streams. The sick, who come to La Trinchera to take steam baths, build a kind of framework with branches and thin reeds above the spring. They lie down naked on this frame, which, as far as I could see, was not very strong, perhaps even dangerous.

As we approached the coast the heat became stifling. A reddish mist covered the horizon. It was sunset but no sea breeze blew. We rested in the lonely farm called both Cambury and House of the Canarian (Casa del Isleño). The hot-water river, along whose bank we travelled, became deeper. A 9-foot-long crocodile lay dead on the sand. We wanted to examine its teeth and the inside of its mouth, but having been exposed to the sun for weeks it stank so bad we had to climb back on to our horses.

More than 10,000 mules are exported every year from Puerto Cabello. It is curious to see these animals being embarked. They are pulled down with lassos and lifted on board by something akin to a crane. In the boat they are placed in double rows, and with the rolling and pitching of the boat can barely stand. To terrify them, and keep them docile, a drum is beaten day and night.

From Puerto Cabello we returned to the Aragua valley, and stopped again at the Barbula plantation through which the new road to Nueva Valencia will pass. Weeks before we had been told about a tree whose sap is a nourishing milk. They call it the 'cow tree', and assured us that negroes on the estates drank quantities of this vegetable milk. As the milky juices of plants are acrid, bitter and more or less poisonous, it seemed hard to believe what we heard, but during our stay in Barbula we proved that nobody had exaggerated the properties of *palo de vaca*. This fine tree is similar to the *Chrysophyllum cainito* (broad-leafed star-apple). When incisions are made in the trunk it yields abundant glutinous milk; it is quite thick, devoid of all acridity, and has an agreeable balmy smell. It was offered to us in *tutuma*-fruit – or gourd – bowls, and we drank a lot before going to bed, and again in the morning, without any ill effects. Only its viscosity makes it a little disagreeable. Negroes and free people who work on the plantations dip their maize and cassava bread in it. The overseer of the estate told us that negroes put on weight during the period that the *palo de vaca* exudes milk. This notable tree appears to be peculiar to the cordillera coast. At Caucagua the natives called it the 'milk tree'. They say they can recognize the trunks that yield most juice from the thickness and colour of the leaves. No botanist has so far known this plant.

Of all the natural phenomena that I have seen during my voyages few have produced a greater impression than the *palo de vaca*. What moved me so deeply was not the proud shadows of the jungles, nor the majestic flow of the rivers, nor the mountains covered with eternal snows, but a few drops of a vegetable juice that brings to mind all the power and fertility of nature. On a barren rocky wall grows a tree with dry leathery leaves; its large woody roots hardly dig into the rocky ground. For months not a drop of rain wets its leaves; the branches appear dry, dead. But if you perforate the trunk, especially at dawn, a sweet nutritious milk pours out.[82]

It was Carnival Tuesday, and everywhere people celebrated. The amusements, called *carnes tollendas* (or 'farewell to the flesh'), became at times rather wild: some paraded an ass loaded with water, and whenever they found an open window pumped water into the room; others carried bags full of hair from the *pica pica* (*Dolichos pruriens*), which greatly irritates skin on contact, and threw it into the faces of passers-by.

From La Guaira we returned to Nueva Valencia, where we met several French *émigrés*, the only ones we saw in five years in the Spanish colonies. In spite of the blood links between the Spanish and French royal families, not even French priests could find refuge in this part of the New World, where man finds it so easy to find food and shelter. Beyond the Atlantic Ocean, only the United States of America offers asylum to those in need. A government that is strong because it is free, and confident because it is just, has nothing to fear in granting refuge to exiles.

Before leaving the Aragua valleys and its neighbouring coasts, I will deal with the cacao plantations, which have always been the main source of wealth in this area. The cacao-producing tree does not grow wild anywhere in the forests north of the Orinoco. This scarcity of wild cacao trees in South America is a curious phenomenon, yet little studied. The amount of trees in the cacao plantations has been estimated at more than 16 million. We met no tribe on the Orinoco that prepared a drink with cacao seeds. Indians suck the pulp of the pod and chuck the seeds, often found in heaps in places where Indians have spent the night. It seems to me that in Caracas cacao cultivation follows the examples of Mexico and Guatemala. Spaniards established in Terra Firma learned how to cultivate the cacao tree – sheltered while young by the leaves of the erythrina and banana, making *chocolatl* cakes, and using the liquid of the same name, thanks to trade with Mexico, Guatemala and Nicaragua whose people are of Toltec and Aztec origin.

As far back as the sixteenth century travellers have greatly differed in their opinions about *chocolatl*. Benzoni said, in his crude language, that it is a drink 'fitter for pigs than humans'. The Jesuit Acosta asserts that 'the Spaniards who inhabit America are fond of chocolate to excess . . .' Fernando Cortez highly praised chocolate as being an agreeable drink if prepared cold and, especially, as being very nutritious. Cortez's page writes: 'He who has drunk one cup can travel all day without further food, especially in very hot climates.' We shall soon celebrate this quality in chocolate in our voyage up the Orinoco. It is easily transported and prepared: as food it is both nutritious and stimulating.[83]

CHAPTER 14

Mountains situated between the Aragua valleys and the Caracas plains – Villa de Cura – Parapara – Llanos or steppes – Calabozo

The chain of mountains limited on the south by Lake Tacarigua forms, you could say, the northern boundary of the great basin of the plains or savannahs of Caracas. From the Aragua valleys you reach the savannahs over the Guigue and Tucutenemo mountains. Moving from a region peopled and embellished by agriculture you find a vast desert. Accustomed to rocks and shaded valleys, the traveller contemplates with astonishment those plains without trees, those immense tracts of land that seem to climb to the horizon.[84]

We left the Aragua valleys before sunset on the 6th of March. We crossed a richly cultivated plain, bordering the south-westerly banks of Lake Valencia, along ground recently uncovered by receding water. The fertility of the earth, planted with gourds, water melons and bananas, amazed us. The distant howling of monkeys announced dawn. Opposite a clump of trees in the middle of the plain we caught sight of several bands of araguatoes (*Simia ursina*) who, as if in procession, passed very slowly from one branch to another. After the male followed several females, many with young on their backs. Due to their life-style howling monkeys all look alike, even those belonging to different species. It is striking how uniform their movements are. When the branches of two trees are too far apart, the male that guides his troop hangs on his prehensile tail and swings in the air until he reaches the nearest branch. Then all the band repeat the same operation in the same place. It is almost superfluous to add how dubious Ulloa's[85] assertion is that the araguatoes form a kind of chain in order to reach the opposite bank of a river. During five years we had ample opportunity to observe thousands of these animals: for this reason we have no confidence in statements possibly invented by Europeans themselves, although missionary Indians repeat them as if they come from their own traditions. The further man is from civilization, the more he enjoys astonishing people while recounting the marvels of his country. He says he has seen what he imagines may have been seen by others. Every Indian is a hunter and the stories of hunters borrow from the imagination the more intelligent the hunted animal appears to be. Hence so many fictions in Europe about the foxes, monkeys, crows and condors in the Andes.

The Indians claim that when howler monkeys fill the jungles with their howls there is always one that leads the howling. Their observation is correct. You generally hear one solitary and intense voice, replaced by another at a different pitch. Indians also assert that when an araguato female is about to give birth, the chorus of howling stops until the new monkey is born. I was not able to prove this, but I have observed that the howling ceases for a few minutes when something unexpected happens, like when a wounded monkey claims the attention of the troop. Our guides seriously assured us that 'To cure asthma you must drink out of the bony drum of the araguato's hyoid bone.' Having such a loud voice this animal is thought to impart a curing effect from its larynx to the water drunk out of it. Such is the people's science, which sometimes resembles the ancients'.

We spent the night in the village of Guigue. We lodged with an old sergeant from Murcia. To prove he had studied with the Jesuits he recited to us the history of the creation in Latin. He knew the names of Augustus, Tiberius and Diocletian, and while enjoying the agreeably cool nights on his banana plantation interested himself in all that had happened in the times of the Roman emperors. He asked us for a remedy for his painful gout. 'I know,' he said, 'that a *zambo* from Valencia, a famous *curioso*, could cure me, but the *zambo* would expect to be treated as an equal, and that I cannot do with a man of his colour. I prefer to remain as I am.'

San Luis de Cura or, as it is more usually called, Villa de Cura, lies in a very barren valley. Apart from a few fruit trees the region is without vegetation. The *meseta* is dry and several rivers lose themselves in cracks in the ground. Cura is more a village than a town. We lodged with a family that had been persecuted by the government after the 1797 revolution in Caracas. After years in prison, one of their sons had been taken to Havana, where he lived locked in a fort.

How pleased his mother was when she heard that we were bound for Havana after visiting the Orinoco. She handed me five piastres – 'all her savings'. I tried to hand them back, but how could I wound the delicacy of a woman happy with her self-imposed sacrifice! All the society in the village met in the evening to look at a magic lantern showing sights of the great European cities; the Tuileries palace and the statue of the Great Elector in Berlin. How odd to see our native city in a magic lantern some 2,000 leagues away!

After bathing in the fresh clear water of the San Juan river at two in the morning, we set off on the road for Mesa de Paja. The llanos at that time were infested with bandits, so other travellers joined us to form a kind of caravan. The route was downhill for several hours.

At Mesa de Paja we entered the basin of the llanos. The sun was almost at its highest point. On the ground we recorded a temperature of 48 °C to 50 °C in the sterile parts without vegetation. At the height of our heads, as we were riding the mules, we did not feel the slightest breath of air; but in the midst of that apparent calm small dust whirls were continually raised by air currents arising from the difference in temperature between the bare sand and the grass. These sand winds increased the suffocating heat. The plains surrounding us seemed to reach the sky and looked to us like an ocean covered with seaweed. Sky and land merged. Through the dry mist and vapours you could make out, in the distance, trunks of palm trees. Stripped of their leaves these trunks looked like ship masts on the horizon.

The monotony of these steppes is imposing, sad and oppressive. Everything appears motionless; only now and then from a distance does the shadow of a small cloud promising rain move across the sky. The first glimpse of the plains is no less surprising than that of the Andean chain. It is hard to get accustomed to the views on the Venezuelan and Casanare plains, or to the pampas of Buenos Aires and the *chaco* when, for twenty to thirty days without stopping, you feel you are on the surface of an ocean. The plains of eastern and northern Europe can give only a pallid image of the immense South American llanos.

The llanos and pampas of South America are really steppes. During the rainy season they appear beautifully green, but in the dry season they look more like deserts. The grass dries out and turns to dust; the ground cracks, crocodiles and snakes bury themselves in the dried mud waiting for the first rains of spring to wake them from prolonged lethargy.

Rivers have only a slight, often imperceptible fall. When the wind blows, or the Orinoco floods, the rivers disemboguing in it are pushed backward. In the Arauca you often see the current going the wrong way. Indians have paddled a whole day downstream when in reality they have been going upstream. Between the descending and ascending waters lie large stagnant tracts, and dangerous whirlpools are formed.

The most typical characteristic of the South American savannahs or steppes is the total absence of hills, the perfect flatness of the land. That is why the Spanish conquistadores did not call them deserts, savannahs or meadows but plains, *los llanos*. Often in an area of 600 square kilometres no part of the ground rises more than 1 metre high.

Despite the apparent uniformity of the ground the llanos offer two kinds of inequalities that cannot escape the attentive traveller. The first are called *bancos* (banks); they are in reality shoals in the basin of the steppes, rising some 4 to 5 feet above the plains. These banks can reach some 3 to 4 leagues in length; they are completely smooth and horizontal, and can only be recognized when you examine their edges. The second inequality can only be detected by geodesical or barometric measurements, or else by the flow of a river; they are called *mesa*, or tables. They are small flats, or convex elevations, that rise imperceptibly some metres high to divide the waters between the Orinoco and the northern Terra Firma coast. Only the gentle curvature of the savannah forms this division.

The infinite monotony of the llanos; the extreme rarity of inhabitants; the difficulties of travelling in such heat and in an atmosphere darkened by dust; the perspective of the horizon, which constantly retreats before the traveller; the few scattered palms that are so similar that one despairs of ever reaching them, and confuses them with others further afield; all these aspects together make the stranger looking at the llanos think they are far larger than they are.[86]

After spending two nights on horseback, and having vainly looked for shade under tufts of the mauritia palms, we arrived before nightfall at the small farm called Alligator (El Cayman), also called La Guadalupe. It is a *hato de ganado*, that is, an isolated house on the steppes, surrounded by small huts covered in reeds and skins. Cattle, oxen, horses and mules are not penned in; they wander freely in a space of several square leagues. Nowhere do you see any enclosures. Men, naked to the waist, and armed with lances, ride the savannahs to inspect the animals, to bring back those that have strayed too far off, and to brand with a hot iron those still not branded with the owner's mark. These coloured men, called *peones llaneros*, are partly freed and partly enslaved. There is no race more constantly exposed to the devouring fire of the tropical sun than this one. They eat meat dried in the sun, and barely salted. Even their horses eat this. Always in the saddle, they do not ever try to walk a few paces. On the farm we found an old negro slave in charge while his master was away. We were told about herds of several thousand cows grazing the steppes, and yet it was impossible to get a bowl of milk. We were offered a yellowish, muddy and fetid water drawn from a nearby stagnant pool in bowls made of *tutuma* fruit. The laziness of the llano inhabitants is such that they cannot be bothered to dig wells, even though they know that 9 feet down you can everywhere find fine springs under a stratum of conglomerate or red sandstone. After suffering half a year of flooding, you are then exposed to another half of painful drought. The old negro warned us to cover the jug with a cloth and to drink the water through a filter so as not to smell the stink, and not to swallow the fine yellowish clay in the water. We did not know then that we would follow his instructions for months on end. The Orinoco waters are just as charged with particles of earth, and are even fetid in creeks, where dead crocodiles rot on sandbanks, half buried in the slime.

We had hardly unpacked our instruments before we freed our mules and let them, as is said here, 'find water on the savannah'. There are small pools around the farm and animals find them guided by instinct, by the sight of scattered tufts of mauritia palms, by the sensation of humidity that gives rise to small air currents in an otherwise calm atmosphere. When these stagnant ponds are far off, and the farm-hands are too lazy to lead the animals to their natural watering-holes, they are locked for five or six hours in a very hot stable, and then released. Excessive thirst increases their instinctive cleverness. As soon as you open the stable doors you see the horses, and especially the mules, far more intelligent than horses, rush off into the savannah. Tails in the air, heads back, they rush into the wind, stopping for a while to explore around them, following less their sight than their sense of smell, until they finally announce by neighing that water has been found. All these movements are more successfully carried out by horses born on the llanos who have enjoyed the freedom of wild herds than by those coming from the coast, descendants of domestic horses. With most animals, as with man, the alertness of the senses diminishes after years of work, after domestic habits and the progress of culture.

We followed our mules as they sought one of these stagnant ponds that give muddy water, which hardly satisfied our thirst. We were covered in dust, and tanned by the sand wind, which burns the skin more than the sun. We were desperate to have a bathe but we found only a pool of stagnating water surrounded by palms. The water was muddy, but to our surprise cooler than the air. Used as we were on this long journey to bathing every time we could, often several times a day, we did not hesitate to throw ourselves into the pool. We had hardly begun to enjoy the cool water when we heard a noise on the far bank that made us leap out. It was a crocodile slipping into the mud. It would have been unwise to spend the night in that muddy place.

We had gone scarcely more than a quarter of a league away from the farm, yet we walked for more than an hour on our way back without reaching it. Too late we saw that we had been going in the wrong direction. We had left as the day ended, before the stars had come out, and had proceeded haphazardly into the plains. As usual we had our compass. It would have been easy to find our direction from the position of Canopus and the Southern Cross; but the means were useless because we were uncertain whether we had gone east or south when we left the small farm. We tried to return to our bathing place, and walked for another three quarters of an hour without finding the stagnant pond. We often thought we saw fire on the horizon; it was a star rising, its image magnified by vapours. After wandering for a long time on the savannah we decided to sit down on a palm trunk in a dry place surrounded by short grass; for

Europeans who have recently arrived fear water snakes more than they do jaguars. We did not fool ourselves into believing that our guides, whose indolence we well knew, would come looking for us before preparing and eating their food. The more unsure we were about our situation, the more pleasing it was eventually to hear horse hooves approaching from afar. It was an Indian, with his lance, doing his *rodeo*, that is, rounding up cattle. The sight of two white men saying they were lost made him think it was a trick. It was hard to convince him of our sincerity. He eventually agreed to lead us to the Alligator farm, but without slowing down his trotting horse. Our guides assured us that 'they were already getting worried about us', and to justify their worry had made a long list of people who had been lost in the llanos and found completely worn out. It is clear that danger exists only for those far from any farm or, as had happened recently, for those robbed by bandits and tied to a palm tree.

To avoid suffering the heat of day we left at two in the morning, hoping to reach Calabozo, a busy little town in the middle of the llanos, by midday. The appearance of the countryside remained always the same. There was no moon, but the great mass of stars decorating the southern skies lit up part of our path. This imposing spectacle of the starry vault stretching out over our heads, this fresh breeze blowing over the plains at night, the rippling of the grass wherever it is long, all reminded us of the surface of an ocean. This illusion increased especially (and we did not tire of the repetition of this sight) when the sun's disc showed on the horizon, doubling itself through refraction, and soon losing its flattened form, rising quickly towards the zenith.

As the sun rose the plains came alive. Cattle, lying down at night by ponds or at the foot of moriche and rhopala palms, regrouped, and the solitudes became populated with horses, mules and oxen that live here not like wild animals but free, without fixed abode, scorning man's care. In this torrid zone the bulls, although of Spanish pedigree like those on the cold tablelands of Quito, are tame. The traveller is never in danger of being attacked or chased, contrary to what often happened during our wanderings in the Andes. Near Calabozo we saw herds of roebucks grazing peacefully with the horses and oxen. They are called *matacanes*; their meat is very tasty. They are larger than our deer and have a very sleek skin of a dark brown with white spots. Their horns seem to be simple points and they are not shy. We saw some completely white ones in the groups of thirty to forty that we observed.

Besides the scattered trunk of the *palma de cobija* we found real groves (*palmares*) in which the corypha is mixed with a tree of the proteaceous family called *chaparro* by the Indians, which is a new species of rhopala, with hard, crackling leaves. The little groves of rhopala are called *chaparrales* and it is easy to see that in a vast plain where only two or three kinds of tree grow that the *chaparro*, which gives shade, is deemed of great value. South of Guayaval other palms predominate: the *piritu* (*Bactris speciosa*) and the mauritia (*Mauritia flexuosa*), celebrated as the *árbol de la vida*. This last is the sago tree of America: it gives flour, wine, fibres to weave hammocks, baskets, nets and clothes. Its fruit, shaped like a pine-cone and covered in scales, tastes rather like an apple, and when ripe is yellow inside and red outside. Howler monkeys love them, and the Guaramo Indians, whose existence is closely linked to this palm, make a fermented liquor that is acid and refreshing.

On the La Mesa road, near Calabozo, it was extremely hot. The temperature of the air rose considerably as soon as the wind blew. The air was full of dust, and when there were gusts the thermometer reached 40 °C and 41 °C. We moved forward slowly as it would have been dangerous to leave the mules transporting our instruments behind. Our guides advised us to line our hats with rhopala leaves to mitigate the effect of the sun's rays on our heads. In fact it was quite a relief, and later we bore this in mind.

It is hard to formulate exactly how many cattle there are on the llanos of Caracas, Barcelona, Cumaná and Spanish Guiana. Monsieur Depons, who has lived longer in Caracas than I have, and whose statistics are generally correct, calculates that in these vast plains, from the mouth of the Orinoco to Lake Maracaibo, there are 1,200,000 oxen, 180,000 horses and 90,000 mules. He worked out a value of 5 million francs for the produce of these herds, including exportation and the price of leather in the country. In the Buenos Aires pampas there are, so we believe, some 12 million cows and 3 million horses, not counting the animals without owners.

I shall not hazard any general evaluations as they are too vague by nature; but I will observe that in the Caracas llanos owners of the great *hatos* have no idea how many animals they have. They count only the young animals branded every year with the sign of their herd. The richer owners brand up to 14,000 animals a year, and sell 5,000 to 6,000. According to official documents the export of leather in all the Capitanía-General of Caracas reaches 174,000 oxhides and 11,500 goat hides. When one remembers that these figures come from custom registers and do not include contraband one is tempted to think that the calculation of 1,200,000 oxen wandering in the llanos is far too low.

In Calabozo, in the middle of the llanos, we found an electric machine with great discs, electrophori, batteries and electrometers; an apparatus as complete as any found in Europe. These objects had not been bought in America but made by a man who had never seen any instruments, who had never been able to consult anybody, and who knew about electricity only from reading Sigaud de la Fond's *Traité* and Franklin's *Mémoires*. Carlos del Pozo, this man's name, had begun by making cylindrical electrical machines using large glass jars, and cutting off their necks. Years later he managed to get two plates from Philadelphia to make a disc machine to obtain greater electric effects. It is easy to guess how difficult it must have been for Sr Pozo to succeed once the first works on electricity fell into his hands, and how he managed to work everything out for himself. Up to then he had enjoyed astonishing uneducated people with his experiments, and had never travelled out of the llanos. Our stay in Calabozo gave him altogether another kind of pleasure. He must have set some value on two travellers who could compare his apparatus with European ones. With me I had electrometers mounted in straw, pith-balls and gold leaf, as well as a small Leyden jar that could be charged by rubbing, following Ingenhousz's method, which I used for physiological tests. Pozo could not hide his joy when for the first time he saw instruments that he had not made but which appeared to copy his. We also showed him the effects of the contact of different metals on the nerves of frogs. The names of Galvani and Volta had not yet echoed in these vast solitudes.

After the electric apparatus, made by a clever inhabitant of the llanos, nothing interested us more in Calabozo than the gymnoti, living electric apparatuses. I had busied myself daily over many years with the phenomenon of Galvanic electricity and had enthusiastically experimented without knowing what I had discovered; I had built real batteries by placing metal discs on top of each other and alternating them with bits of muscle flesh, or other humid matter, and so was eager, after arriving at Cumaná, to obtain electric eels. We had often been promised them, and had always been deceived. Money means less the further from the coast you go, and there was no way to shake the imperturbable apathy of the people when even money meant nothing!

Under the name of *tembladores* ('which make you tremble') Spaniards confuse all electric fish. There are some in the Caribbean Sea, off the Cumaná coast. The Guaiquerí Indians, the cleverest fishermen in the area, brought us a fish that numbed their hands. This fish swims up the little Manzanares river. It was a new species of ray whose lateral spots are hard to see, and which resembles Galvani's torpedo. The Cumaná torpedo was very lively, and energetic in its muscular contractions, yet its electric charges were weak. They became stronger when we galvanized the animal in contact with zinc and gold. Other *tembladores*, proper electric eels, live in the Colorado and Guarapiche rivers and several little streams crossing the Chaima Indian missions. There are many of them in the great South American rivers, the Orinoco, Amazon and Meta, but the strength of the currents and the depths prevent Indians from catching them. They see these fish less often than they feel their electric shocks when they swim in the rivers. But it is in the llanos, especially around Calabozo, between the small farm of Morichal and the *missions de arriba* and *de abaxo*, that the stagnant ponds and tributaries of the Orinoco are filled with electric eels. We wanted first to experiment in the house we lived in at Calabozo but the fear of the eel's electric shock is so exaggerated that for three days nobody would fish any out for us, despite our promising the Indians two piastres for each one. Yet they tell whites that they can touch *tembladores* without shock if they are chewing tobacco.

Impatient of waiting, and having only obtained uncertain results from a living eel brought to us, we went to the Caño de Bera to experiment on the water's edge. Early in the morning on the 19th of

March we left for the little village of Rastro de Abaxo: from there Indians led us to a stream, which in the dry season forms a muddy pond surrounded by trees, clusia, amyris and mimosa with fragrant flowers. Fishing eels with nets is very difficult because of the extreme agility with which they dive into the mud, like snakes. We did not want to use *barbasco*, made with roots of *Piscidia erythrina*, *Jacquinia armillaris* and other species of phyllanthus which, chucked into the pond, numbs fish. This would have weakened the eel. The Indians decided to fish with their horses, *embarbascar con caballos*.[87] It was hard to imagine this way of fishing; but soon we saw our guides returning from the savannah with a troop of wild horses and mules. There were about thirty of them, and they forced them into the water.

The extraordinary noise made by the stamping of the horses made the fish jump out of the mud and attack. These livid, yellow eels, like great water snakes, swim on the water's surface and squeeze under the bellies of the horses and mules. A fight between such different animals is a picturesque scene.[88] With harpoons and long pointed reeds the Indians tightly circled the pond; some climbed trees whose branches hung over the water's surface. Screaming and prodding with their reeds they stopped the horses leaving the pond. The eels, dazed by the noise, defended themselves with their electrical charges. For a while it seemed they might win. Several horses collapsed from the shocks received on their most vital organs, and drowned under the water. Others, panting, their manes erect, their eyes anguished, stood up and tried to escape the storm surprising them in the water. They were pushed back by the Indians, but a few managed to escape to the bank, stumbling at each step, falling on to the sand exhausted and numbed from the electric shocks.

In less than two minutes two horses had drowned. The eel is about 5 feet long and presses all its length along the belly of the horse, giving it electric shocks. They attack the heart, intestines and the *plexus coeliacus* of the abdominal nerves. It is obvious that the shock felt by the horse is worse than that felt by a man touched on one small part. But the horses were probably not killed, just stunned. They drowned because they could not escape from among the other horses and eels.

We were sure that the fishing would end with the death of all the animals used. But gradually the violence of the unequal combat died down, and the tired eels dispersed. They need a long rest and plenty of food to recuperate the lost galvanic energy. The mules and horses seemed less frightened; their manes did not stand on end, and their eyes seemed less terrified. The eels timidly approached the shore of the marshy pond where we fished them with harpoons tied to long strings. While the string is dry the Indians do not feel any shocks. In a few minutes we had five huge eels, only slightly wounded. Later, more were caught.

The water temperature where these animals live is 26 °C to 27 °C. We are assured that their electric energy decreases in colder water. It is remarkable that these animals with electromotive organs are found not in the air but in a fluid that conducts electricity.

The eel is the largest of the electric fish; I have measured one that is 5 feet 3 inches long. Indians say they have seen even longer. A fish 3 feet 6 inches weighed 12 pounds. The eels from the Caño de Bera are of a pretty olive green, with a yellow mixed with red under their heads. Two rows of small yellow stains are placed symmetrically along their backs from the head to the tail. Each stain has an excretory opening. The skin is constantly covered with a mucus, which, as Volta has shown, conducts electricity twenty to thirty times more efficiently than pure water. It is odd that none of the electric fish discovered here are covered in scales.

It would be dangerous to expose yourself to the first shocks from a large excited eel. If by chance you get a shock before the fish is wounded, or exhausted by a long chase, the pain and numbness are so extreme that it is hard to describe the nature of the sensation. I do not remember ever getting such shocks from a Leyden jar as when I mistakenly stepped on a gymnotus just taken out of the water. All day I felt strong pain in my knees and in all my joints. Torpedoes and electric eels cause a twitching of the tendon in the muscle touched by the electric organ, which reaches one's elbow. With each stroke you feel an internal vibration that lasts two or three seconds, followed by a painful numbness. In the graphic language of the Tamanac Indians the electric eel is called *arimna*, which means 'something that deprives you of movement'.

While European naturalists find electric eels extremely interesting, the Indians hate and fear them. However, their flesh is not bad, although most of the body consists of the electric apparatus, which is slimy and disagreeable to eat. The scarcity of fish in the marshes and ponds on the llanos is blamed on the eels. They kill far more than they eat, and Indians told us that when they capture young alligators and electric eels in their tough nets the eels do not appear to be hurt because they paralyse the young alligators before they themselves can be attacked. All the inhabitants of the waters flee the eels. Lizards, turtles and frogs seek ponds free of eels. At Uritici a road had to be redirected as so many mules were being killed by eels as they forded a river.

On the 24th of March we left Calabozo. At about four in the afternoon we found a young naked Indian girl stretched out on her back in the savannah; she seemed to be around twelve or thirteen. She was exhausted with fatigue and thirst, with her eyes, nose and mouth full of sand, and breathing with a rattle in her throat. Next to her there was a jar on its side, half full of sand. Luckily we had a mule carrying water. We revived her by washing her face and making her drink some wine. She was scared when she found herself surrounded by so many people, but she slowly relaxed and talked to our guides. From the position of the sun she reckoned she had fainted and remained unconscious for several hours. Nothing could persuade her to mount one of our mules. She wanted to return to Uritici where she had been a servant on a hacienda whose owner had sacked her after she had suffered a long illness because she could not work as well as before. Our threats and requests were useless; she was hardened to suffering, like all of her race, and lived in the present without fear of the future. She insisted on going to one of the Indian missions near Calabozo. We emptied her jar of sand and filled it with water. Before we had mounted our mules she had set off, and was soon a cloud of sand in the distance.

During the night we forded the Uritici river, home of numerous voracious alligators. We were told that we should not let our dogs drink from the river as alligators often leave the banks and chase dogs. We were shown a hut, or a kind of shed, where our host in Calabozo had had an extraordinary adventure. He was sleeping with a friend on a bench, covered with skins, when at dawn he was woken by a noise and violent shaking. Bits of earth flew about the hut, and suddenly a young alligator climbed up from under their bed and tried to attack a dog sleeping in the doorway; but it could not catch it, and ran to the bank and dived into the water. When they examined the ground under their bed they found it excavated; it was hardened mud where the alligator had spent its summer asleep, as they all do in the llano dry season. The noise of the men and horses, and the smell of dogs, had woken it up. The Indians often find enormous boas,[89] which they call *uji*, or water snakes, in a similar state of lethargy. To revive them they sprinkle the boas with water. They kill them and hang them in a stream, and after they have rotted they make guitar strings from the tendons on their dorsal muscles, which are far better than strings made from howler-monkey guts.

CHAPTER 15

San Fernando de Apure – Connections and bifurcations of the
Apure and Arauca rivers – Journey up the Apure river

Until the second half of the eighteenth century the great Apure, Payare, Arauca and Meta rivers were hardly known in Europe by their names, and were obviously far less known than in preceding centuries when the valiant Felipe de Urre[90] and the conquerors of Tocayo crossed the llanos seeking the great city of El Dorado and the rich country of Omagua, the Timbuktu of the New World, beyond the Apure river. Such daring expeditions could take place only on a war footing. The weapons meant to protect the new colonizers were ceaselessly turned against the unhappy Indians. Following that period of violence and misery two Indian tribes, the Cabres and the Orinoco Caribs, became masters of those parts no longer being devastated by the Spaniards. Only poor monks were allowed to advance south of the steppes. The Venezuelan coast became isolated and the slow conquest of the Jesuit missionaries followed the banks of the Orinoco. It is hard to believe that the city of San Fernando de Apure, some 50 leagues from the coast, was not founded until 1789.

The position of San Fernando on a great navigable river, near the mouth of another river that crosses the whole province of Varinas, is extremely useful for trade. All that is produced in this province, the leathers, cocoa, cotton and top-quality Mijagual indigo, is washed down past this town to the Orinoco mouth. During the rainy season big ships come upstream from Angostura to San Fernando de Apure and along the Santo Domingo river as far as Torunos, the harbour for the town of Barinas. During this season the flooded rivers form a labyrinth of waterways between the Apure, Arauca, Capanaparo and Sinaruco rivers, covering a country of roughly 400 square leagues. At this point the Orinoco, deviating from its course, due not to neighbouring mountains but to the rising counter-slopes, turns east instead of following its ancient path in the line of the meridian. If you consider the surface of the earth as a polyhedron formed of variously inclined planes you will see by simply consulting a map that between San Fernando de Apure, Caycara and the mouth of the Meta the intersection of three slopes, higher in the north, west and south, must have caused a considerable depression. In this basin the savannahs can be covered by 12 to 14 feet of water and turned into a great lake after the rains. Villages and farms look as though they are on shoals, rising barely 2 to 3 feet above the water surface. The flooding of the Apure, Meta and Orinoco rivers is also periodic. In the rainy season horses that roam the savannah do not have time to reach the plateaux and they drown in their hundreds. You see mares followed by foals, barely sticking up out of the water, swimming part of the day to eat grass. While swimming they are chased by crocodiles, and some carry crocodile tooth marks on their hides. Horse, mule and cow carcasses attract numberless vultures.

San Fernando is infamous for its suffocating heat throughout most of the year. This western part of the llanos is the hottest because the air from all the arid steppes reaches here. During the rainy season the heat of the llanos increases considerably, especially in July when the sky is covered with cloud. The thermometer reached 39.5 °C in the shade.

On the 28th of March I was on the river bank trying to measure the width of the Apure river, which was 206 toises. It was thundering everywhere; the first storm and rains of the rainy season. The river was whipped up by an east wind into large waves, then it suddenly calmed down, and then many large cetaceans, resembling the dolphins of our seas, began to play in long lines on the river surface. The slow and lazy crocodiles seemed to fear these noisy and impetuous animals as they dived underwater when these animals approached. It is extraordinary to find these mammals so far from the coast. The mission Spaniards call them *toninas*, as they do dolphins; their Tamanaco name is *orinucna*. They are 3 to 4 feet long, and on bending their backs and whipping the water with their tails they reveal part of their back and dorsal fins. I did not succeed in catching any of them, though I often paid Indians to shoot at them with arrows.

The electrometer gave no sign of electricity. As the storm gathered the blue of the sky changed to grey. The thermometer rose 3 °C, as is usual in the Tropics, and a heavy rain fell. Being sufficiently adapted to the climate not to fear the effect of a tropical downpour we stayed on the shore to observe the electrometer. I held it more than twenty minutes in my hand, 6 feet above the ground. For several minutes the electric charge remained the same, and then I noticed that the electricity in the atmosphere was first positive, then nil, then negative. I have gone into these details on the electric charge in the atmosphere because newly arrived European travellers usually describe just their impressions of a tropical storm. In a country where the year is divided into two halves, the dry and the wet season, or as the Indians say in their expressive language, 'of sun and rain', it is interesting to follow meteorological phenomena as one season turns into the next.

The look of the sky, the movement of electricity, and the downpour of the 28th March announced the start of the rainy season: we were still advised to go to San Fernando de Apure by San Francisco de Capanaparo, along the Sinaruco river and the San Antonio *hato* to the Otomac village recently founded on the banks of the Meta river, and to embark on the Orinoco a little above Carichana. This land road crosses an unhealthy, fever-ridden country. An old farmer, Don Francisco Sanchez, offered to lead us. His clothes revealed how simply people live in these far-off countries. He had made a fortune of 100,000 piastres yet he rode on horseback barefoot with large silver spurs. We knew from several weeks' experience how sad and monotonous the llanos are and so we chose the longer route along the Apure river to the Orinoco. We chose one of the long pirogues that the Spaniards call *lanchas*. A pilot and four Indians were sufficient to drive it. On the poop a cabin covered with corypha leaves was built in a few hours. It was so spacious that it could have held a table and benches. They used oxhides stretched and nailed to frames of Brazil-wood. I mention these minute details to prove that our life on the Apure river was very different from the time when we were reduced to the narrow Orinoco canoes. We packed the pirogue with provisions for a month. You find plenty of hens, eggs, bananas, ·cassava and cacao at San Fernando. The good Capuchin monk gave us sherry, oranges and tamarinds to make fresh juices. We could easily tell that a roof made of palm leaves would heat up excessively on the bed of a large river where we would be always exposed to the sun's perpendicular rays. The Indians relied less on our supplies than on their hooks and nets. We also brought some weapons along, whose use was common as far as the cataracts. Further south the extreme humidity prevents missionaries from using guns. The Apure river teems with fish, manatees[91] and turtles whose eggs are more nourishing than tasty. The river banks are full of birds, including the *pauxi* and *guacharaca*, that could be called the turkey and pheasant of this region. Their flesh seemed harder and less white than our European gallinaceous family as they use their muscles more. We did not forget to add to our provisions fishing tackle, firearms and a few casks of brandy to use as exchange with the Orinoco Indians.

We left San Fernando on the 30th of March at four in the afternoon. The heat was suffocating; the thermometer marked 34 °C in the shade despite a strong south-east wind. This wind prevented us from setting our sails. During our journey along the Apure, the Orinoco and the Río Negro we were accompanied by the brother-in-law of the governor of the Barinas province, Don Nicolás Soto, recently arrived from Cádiz. To get to know land worthy of a European's curiosity he decided to spend seventy-four days with us in a narrow *lancha*, invaded by mosquitoes. The right bank of the Apure is somewhat better cultivated than the left bank where the Yaruro Indians have built huts with reeds and palm-leaf stalks. They live from hunting and fishing, and are skilled in hunting the jaguar whose skins, called 'tiger skins', reach Spain thanks to them. Some of these Indians have been baptized, but they never go to church. They are considered to be wild because they want to remain independent. Other Yaruro tribes accept missionary discipline. The people of this tribe look like a branch of the Mongol family. Their look is serious; their eyes elongated, their cheek-bones high and with a prominent nose.

During our voyage from San Fernando to San Carlos on the Río Negro, and from there to the town of Angostura, I made the effort to note down in writing, every day, whether in the canoe or at night camps, anything that happened which was worthy of note. The heavy rain and incredible amount of mosquitoes crowding the air on the Orinoco and Casiquiare obviously left gaps in my chronicle, but I always wrote it up a few days later. The following pages are taken from this journal. What is noted down while actually viewing the described objects keeps a semblance of truth (dare I say 'individuality'), which gives charm even to insignificant things.

March 31st.[92] A contrary wind forced us to stay on the river bank until midday. We saw a part of the cane fields devastated by a fire spreading from a nearby forest. Nomadic Indians set the forest alight everywhere they set up camp for the night; during the dry season vast provinces would be in flames if it was not for the extreme hardness of the wood, which does not completely burn. We found trunks of desmanthus and mahogany (*cahoba*) that were hardly burned more than 2 inches deep.

Only after Diamante do you enter territory inhabited by tigers, crocodiles and *chiguires*, a large species of Linnaeus's genus *Cavia* (capybara). We saw flocks of birds pressed against each other flash across the sky like a black cloud changing shape all the time. The river slowly grew wider. One of the banks is usually arid and sandy due to flooding. The other is higher, covered with full-grown trees. Sometimes the river is lined with jungle on both sides and becomes a straight canal some 150 toises wide. The arrangement of the trees is remarkable. First you see the *sauso* shrubs (*Hermesia castaneifolia*), a hedge some 4 feet high as if cut by man. Behind this hedge a brushwood of cedar, Brazil-wood and *gayac*. Palms are rare; you see only scattered trunks of corozo and thorny *piritu*. The large quadrupeds of these regions, tigers, tapirs and peccaries, have opened passages in the *sauso* hedge. They appear through these gaps to drink water. They are not frightened of the canoes, so we see them skirting the river until they disappear into the jungle through a gap in the hedge. I confess that these often repeated scenes greatly appeal to me. The pleasure comes not solely from the curiosity a naturalist feels for the objects of his studies, but also to a feeling common to all men brought up in the customs of civilization. You find yourself in a new world, in a wild, untamed nature. Sometimes it is a jaguar, the beautiful American panther, on the banks; sometimes it is the hocco (*Crax alector*) with its black feathers and tufted head, slowly strolling along the *sauso* hedge. All kinds of animals appear, one after the other. 'Es como en el paraíso' ('It is like paradise') our old Indian pilot said. Everything here reminds you of that state of the ancient world revealed in venerable traditions about the innocence and happiness of all people; but when carefully observing the relationships between the animals you see how they avoid and fear each other. The golden age has ended. In this paradise of American jungles, as everywhere else, a long, sad experience has taught all living beings that gentleness is rarely linked to might.

Where the shore is very wide, the line of *sausos* remains far from the river. In the intermediate zone up to ten crocodiles can be seen stretched out in the sand. Immobile, with their jaws wide open at right angles, they lie next to each other without the least sign of sociability, unlike those animals that live in groups. The troop separates as soon as it leaves the shore; however, it consists probably of one male and numerous females as males are rare due to the rutting season when they fight and kill each other. There were so many of these great reptiles that all along the river we could always see at least five or six of them, although the fact that the Apure had not yet flooded meant that hundreds more of these saurians remained buried in the savannah's mud. The Indians told us that not a year went by without two or three people, mainly women going to fetch water, being torn apart by these carnivorous lizards. They told us the story of an Indian girl from Uritici who by her intrepidity and presence of mind had saved herself from the jaws of one of those monsters. As soon as she felt herself seized she poked her fingers so violently into the animal's eyes that pain forced it to drop its prey after slicing off one arm. Despite the copious bleeding the little Indian girl swam ashore with her remaining arm. In those lonely places where man lives in constant struggle with nature he must resort to any means to fight off a jaguar, a boa (*tragavenado*) or a crocodile; everyone is prepared for some sort of danger. 'I knew,' said the young Indian girl coolly, 'that the crocodile would let go when I stuck my fingers in its eyes.'

The Apure crocodiles find enough food eating *chiguires* (*Cavia capybara*), which live in herds of fifty to sixty on the river banks. These unhappy animals, as big as our pigs, cannot defend themselves. They swim better than they run, but in the water they fall to crocodiles and on land to jaguars. It is difficult to understand how, exposed to such formidable enemies, they remain so numerous; it can be explained only by how quickly they reproduce.

We stopped by the mouth of the Caño de la Triguera, in a bay called Vuelta de Jobal, to measure the speed of the current, which was 2.56 feet an hour. We were again surrounded by *chiguires*, who swim like dogs with their heads and necks out of the water. On the beach opposite we saw an enormous crocodile sleeping among these rodents. It woke when we approached and slowly slipped into the water without disturbing the rodents. Indians say that their indifference is due to stupidity, but perhaps they know that the Apure and Orinoco crocodile does not attack prey on land, only when it comes across one in its way as it slips into the water.

Near the Jobal nature takes on a more imposing and wild character. It was there we saw the largest tiger we have ever seen. Even the Indians were surprised by its prodigious size; it was bigger than all the Indian tigers I have seen in European zoos. The animal lay under the shade of a great zamang. It had just killed a *chiguire*; but it had not yet touched its victim, over which it rested a paw. *Zamuros*, a kind of vulture, had gathered in flocks to devour what was left over from the jaguar's meal. It was a strange scene, mixing daring with timidity. They hop to within 2 feet of the jaguar, but the slightest movement and they rush away. To observe their movements more closely we climbed into the small canoe accompanying our pirogue. It is very rare for a tiger to attack a canoe by swimming out to it, and it will only do this if it has been deprived of all food for a long time. The noise of our oars made the animal slowly get up and hide behind the *sauso* shrub along the bank. The vultures wanted to profit from this momentary absence to devour the dead *chiguire*. But the tiger, despite our proximity, jumped into their midst; and in a fit of anger, expressed by the movement of its tail, dragged his prey into the jungle. The Indians lamented not having their lances to leap ashore and attack the tiger with. They are used to this weapon and did not trust our rifles, which in the humidity refused to fire.

Going on down the river we met the large herd of *chiguires* that the tiger had scattered after choosing his victim. These animals watched us come ashore without panicking. Some sat and stared at us like rabbits, moving their upper lips. They did not seem to fear man, but the sight of our big dog put them to flight. As their hindquarters are higher than their front they run with little gallops but so slowly that we managed to capture two of them. The *chiguire*, who swims well, lets out little groans when it runs as if it had difficulty breathing. It is the largest of the rodents; it defends itself only when it is surrounded or wounded. As its grinding teeth, particularly those at the back, are very strong and long it can, simply by biting, tear the paw off a tiger or the leg off a horse. Its flesh smells disagreeably of musk, yet local ham is made from it. That explains the name, 'water pig', given to it by ancient naturalists. Missionary monks do not hesitate to eat this ham during Lent. According to their classification they place the armadillo, the *chiguire* and the manatee near the turtles; the first because it is covered with a hard armour, like a kind of shell; the other two because they are amphibious. On the banks of the Santo Domingo, Apure and Arauca rivers, and in the marshes of the flooded savannahs, the *chiguires* reach such numbers that the pasture lands suffer. They graze the grass that fattens the horses, called *chiguirero*. They also eat fish. These animals, scared by the approach of our boat, stayed for eight to ten minutes under water.

We spent the night as usual in the open air, though we were in a plantation whose owner was hunting tigers. He was almost naked, and brownish-black like a *zambo*; this did not stop him believing that he was from the caste of whites. He called his wife and daughter, as naked as he was, Doña Isabela and Doña Manuela. Without ever having left the Apure river bank they took a lively interest 'in news from Madrid, of the unending wars, and that kind of thing from over there (*todas las cosas de allá*)'. He knew that the King of Spain would soon come and visit 'the great Caracas country', yet he added pleasingly, 'As people from the court eat only wheat bread they would never go beyond the town of Victoria so we would never see them here.' I had brought a *chiguire* with me that I wanted to roast; but our host assured me that '*Nosotros caballeros blancos* (white men like he and I) were not born to eat Indian game.' He offered us venison, killed the evening before with an arrow, as he did not have powder or firearms.

We supposed that a small wood of banana trees hid the farm hut; but this man, so proud of his nobility and the colour of his skin, had not bothered to build even an *ajupa* with palm leaves. He invited us to hang our hammocks near his, between two trees; and promised us, in a satisfied way, that if we returned up river during the rainy season we would find him under a roof. We would soon be complaining of a philosophy that rewards laziness and makes man indifferent to life's comforts. A furious wind rose after midnight, lightning crossed the sky, thunder groaned, and we were soaked to the bone. During the storm a bizarre accident cheered us up. Doña Isabela's cat was perched on the tamarind tree under which we were spending the night. He let himself fall into the hammock of one of our companions who, wounded by the cat's claws and woken from deepest sleep, thought he had been attacked by a wild animal. We ran up to him while he was screaming, and with embarrassment told him of his confusion. While the rain poured down on our hammocks and instruments Don Ignacio congratulated us on the good fortune of not having slept on the beach but on his land with well-bred white people, 'entre gente blanca y de trato'. As we were soaked it was hard to convince ourselves of this better situation, and we listened impatiently to the long story that our host told of his expedition to the Meta river, the bravery he had displayed in a bloody battle with the Guahibo Indians, and of the 'favours he had rendered to God and his King in kidnapping children (*los indiecitos*) from their parents to distribute them around the missions'. What an odd experience it was to find ourselves in these vast solitudes with a man who believed he was European, with all the vain pretensions, hereditary prejudices and mistakes of civilization, but whose only roof was a tree.

April 1st. At sunrise we said goodbye to Don Ignacio and Doña Isabela, his wife. We passed a low island where thousands of flamingoes, pink pelicans, herons and moorhens nested, displaying the most varied colours. These birds were so packed together that they gave the impression that they could not move. The island was called Isla de Aves.

We stopped on the right bank in a small mission inhabited by Indians of the Guamo tribe. There were some eighteen to twenty huts made of palm leaves, but in the statistics sent annually to the court by the missionaries this grouping of huts was registered under the name Pueblo de Santa Bárbara de Arichuna. The Guamo tribe refuse to be tamed and become sedentary. Their customs have much in common with the Achagua, Guahibo and Otomac, especially their dirtiness, their love for vengeance and their nomadic life-style, but their languages are completely different. These four tribes live principally from fishing and hunting on the often flooded plains between the Apure, Meta and Guaviare rivers. Nomadic life has been imposed by the physical conditions. The Indians of the Santa Bárbara mission could not offer us supplies as they grow only a little cassava. However, they were friendly, and when we entered their huts they gave us dried fish and water kept in porous jars where it stayed fresh.

We spent the night on a dry, wide beach. The night was silent and calm and the moon shone marvellously. The crocodiles lay on the beach so that they could see our fire. We thought that maybe the glow of the fire attracted them, as it did fish, crayfish and other water creatures. The Indians showed us tracks in the sand from three jaguars, two of them young; doubtless a female with cubs come to drink water. Finding no trees on the beach we stuck our oars in the sand and hung our hammocks. All was peaceful until about eleven when a dreadful noise began in the jungle around us that made sleep impossible. Among the many noises of screeching animals the Indians could recognize only those that were heard separately; the fluted notes of the *apajous*, the sighs of the alouate apes, the roar of the jaguar and puma; the calls of the pecarry, sloth, hocco, *parraka* and other gallinaceous birds. When the jaguars approached the edge of the jungle our dog, who up to then had been barking continuously, began to growl and hid under our hammocks. Sometimes, after a long silence, we again heard the tiger's roar from the tops of trees, and then the din of monkeys' whistles as they fled from danger.

The confidence of the Indians helped to make us feel braver. One agrees with them that tigers fear fire, and never attack a man in his hammock. If you ask the Indians why jungle animals make such a din at certain moments of the night they say, 'They are celebrating the full moon.' I think that the din comes from deep in the jungle because a desperate fight is taking place. Jaguars, for example, hunt tapir and peccaries, who protect themselves in large herds, trampling down the vegetation in their way.

April 3rd. Since leaving San Fernando we had not met one boat on the beautiful river. Everything suggested the most profound solitude. In the morning the Indians had caught with a hook the fish called *caribe* or *caribito* locally as no other fish is more avid for blood.[93] It attacks bathers and swimmers by biting large chunks of flesh out of them. When one is slightly wounded it is difficult to leave the water without getting more wounds. Indians are terrified of the *caribe* fish and several showed us wounds on their calfs and thighs, deep scars made by these little fish that the Maypure call *umati*. They live at the bottom of rivers, but as soon as a few drops of blood are spilled in the water they reach the surface in their thousands. When you consider the numbers of these fish, of which the most voracious and cruel are but 4 to 5 inches long, the triangular shape of their sharp, cutting teeth, and the width of their retractile mouths you cannot doubt the fear that the *caribe* inspires in the river inhabitants. In places on the river when the water was clear and no fish could be seen we threw bits of bloodied meat in, and within minutes a cloud of *caribes* came to fight for their food. I described and drew this fish on the spot. The *caribito* has a very agreeable taste. As one does not dare bathe when it is around you can regard it as the greatest scourge of this climate where mosquito bites and skin irritation make a bath so necessary.

At midday we stopped at a deserted spot called Algodonal. I left my companions while they beached the boat and prepared the meal. I walked along the beach to observe a group of crocodiles asleep in the sun, their tails, covered with broad scaly plates, resting on each other. Small herons, as white as snow, walked on their backs, even on their heads, as if they were tree trunks. The crocodiles were grey-green, their bodies were half covered in dried mud. From their colour and immobility they looked like bronze statues. However, my stroll almost cost me my life. I had been constantly looking towards the river, and then, on seeing a flash of mica in the sand, I also spotted fresh jaguar tracks, easily recognizable by their shape. The animal had gone off into the jungle, and as I looked in that direction I saw it lying down under the thick foliage of a ceiba, eighty steps away from me. Never has a tiger seemed so enormous.

There are moments in life when it is useless to call on reason. I was very scared. However, I was sufficiently in control of myself to remember what the Indians had advised us to do in such circumstances. I carried on walking, without breaking into a run or moving my arms, and thought I noted that the wild beast had its eye on a herd of capybaras swimming in the river. The further away I got the more I quickened my pace. I was so tempted to turn round and see if the cat was chasing me! Luckily I resisted this impulse, and the tiger remained lying down. These enormous cats with spotted skins are so well fed in this country well stocked with capybara, peccaries and deer that they rarely attack humans. I reached the launch panting and told my adventure story to the Indians, who did not give it much importance.

In the evening we passed the mouth of the Caño del Manati, named after the immense amount of manatees caught there every year. This herbivorous animal of the Cetacea family is called by the Indians *apcia* and *avia*, and reaches 10 to 12 feet long. The manatee is plentiful in the Orinoco. We dissected one that was 9 feet long while at Carichana, an Orinocan mission. The manatee eats so much grass that we found its stomach, divided into several cavities, and its intestines (108 feet long) filled with it. Its flesh is very savoury, though some prejudice considers it to be unwholesome and fever-producing. Its flesh when dried can last for a year. The clergy consider this mammal a fish, so they eat it at Lent.

We spent the night on Isla Conserva. The Indians had lit a camp-fire near the water. Again we confirmed that the glow of the flames attracted crocodiles and dolphins (*toninas*) whose noise stopped us sleeping until we decided to put the fire out. That night we had to get up twice. I mention this as an example of what it means to live in the jungle. A female jaguar approached our camp-site when it brought a cub to drink water. The Indians chased it away, but we heard its cub's cries, like a cat's, for hours. A little later our large dog was bitten, or stung as the Indians say, by some enormous bats[94] that flew around our hammocks. The wound in its snout was tiny and the dog howled more from fear than pain.

April 4th. It was our last day on the Apure river. During several days a plague of insects had been torturing our hands and faces. They were not mosquitoes but *zancudos*, which are really gnats. They appear after sunset; their proboscises are so long that they can pierce your hammock, your canvas and your clothes from the other side.

CHAPTER 16

Confluence of the Apure and Orinoco – Encaramada mountains

On leaving the Apure river we found ourselves in a vastly different countryside. An immense plain of water stretched out in front of us like a lake as far as the eye could see. White-topped waves rose several feet high from the clash between the breeze and the current. We no longer heard the cries of the herons, flamingoes and spoonbills flying in long lines from one bank to the other. We vainly looked out for those diving birds whose busy tricks vary according to their species. Nature herself seemed less alive. Only now and then did we see between waves some large crocodiles breaking the water with their tails. The horizon was lined with a ribbon of jungle; but nowhere did the jungle reach the river. Vast beaches burned by the sun were as deserted and arid as sea beaches and, thanks to mirages, resembled stagnant marshes from afar. Rather than limiting the river these sandy banks blurred it. The banks drew near or receded according to the play of the sun's rays.

These scattered features of the countryside, this trait of solitude and grandeur, characterizes the course of the Orinoco, one of the greatest New World rivers. Everywhere water, like land, displays its unique characteristics. The Orinoco bed has no similarities with the Meta, Guaviare, Río Negro or Amazon beds. These differences do not depend solely on the width or speed of the current; they derive from a combination of relations easier to grasp on the spot than to define precisely. In the same way, the shape of the waves, the colour of the water, the kind of sky and clouds, all help a navigator guess whether he is in the Atlantic, the Mediterranean or in the equinoctial part of the Pacific.

A fresh east-north-east wind blew, allowing us to sail up the Orinoco towards the Encaramada mission. Our pirogue rode the waves so badly that the rocking of the boat caused those who suffered from seasickness to feel sick on the river. The lapping of the waves arises from two rivers meeting. We passed the Punta Curiquima, an isolated mass of quartzite granite, a small promontory composed of rounded blocks. It is there, on the right bank of the Orinoco, that Father Rotella founded a mission for the Palenka and Viriviri or Guire Indians. During flooding the Curiquima rock and village at its foot are completely surrounded by water. This serious inconvenience, and the innumerable mosquitoes and *niguas*,[95] made the suffering missionaries abandon their damp site. It is entirely deserted today while on the left bank the low Coruato mountains have become the retreat for those nomadic Indians either expelled from missions or from tribes not subject to the monks.

In the port of Encaramada we met some Caribs of Panapa with their cacique on their way up the Orinoco to take part in the famous fishing of turtle eggs. His pirogue was rounded towards the bottom like a *bongo*, and followed by a smaller canoe called a *curiara*. He was sitting under a kind of tent (*toldo*) built, like the sails, of palm leaves. His silent, cold reserve, and the respect others gave him, denoted an important person. The cacique was dressed like his people. All were naked, armed with bows and arrows, and covered in annatto, the dye made from *Bixa orellana*. The chief, the servants, the furniture, the sail and boat were all painted red. These Caribs are almost athletic in build and seemed far taller than any Indians we had seen up to now. Smooth, thick hair cut in a fringe like choir boys', eyebrows painted black, and a lively and gloomy stare give these Indians an incredibly hard expression. Having seen only skulls of these Indians in European collections we were surprised to see that their foreheads were more rounded than we had imagined. The fat, disgustingly dirty women carried their children on their backs. Their thighs and legs were bound by knotted cotton ligatures, leaving space for flesh to bulge out between the strands. It is noticeable that the Caribs are as careful about their exterior and dress as naked, painted men can be. They attach great importance to the shapes of certain parts of their bodies. A mother would be accused of indifference to her children if she did not artificially bind their calves in the fashion of the country. As none of our Apure Indians spoke the Carib language we could not ask the chief where he was going to camp to gather the turtle eggs.

The Indians of this area have preserved the belief that 'during the great flood, when their ancestors had to take to the canoes to escape, the sea waves beat against the Encaramada rocks'. This tradition is found in nearly all the tribes of the Upper Orinoco. When the Tamanaco are asked how the human race survived that great catastrophe they answer: 'A man and a woman saved themselves on a high mountain called Tamanacu and there threw seed from the mauritia palm over their heads, and little men and women were born from the seeds who repopulated the world.' Among wild tribes we find a simple version of a legend that the Greeks had embellished with their great imagination! A few leagues from Encaramada a rock called Tepu-mereme (Painted Rock) rises in the middle of the savannah. It is covered with animal drawings and symbolic signs. The representations that we have found on rocks in uninhabited places – stars, suns, jaguars, crocodiles – do not seem to be related to religious cults. These hieroglyphic figures are frequently carved so high up that only scaffolding could reach them. When we asked the Indians how they could have carved those images, they answered, smiling, as if only whites could ignore such an obvious answer: 'During *the great waters*, their ancestors reached those rocks in their canoes.'

The fresh north-east wind blew us at full sail towards the *boca de la tortuga*. At eleven in the morning we landed on an island, which the Indians of the Uruana mission regard as their own, situated in the middle of the river. This island is famous for the fishing of turtles or, as is said here, the *cosecha*, or annual harvest of eggs. We found a group of Indians camping in palm-leaf huts. This camp-site had over 300 people in it. As we had been used, since San Fernando de Apure, to seeing only deserted beaches, we were struck by the bustle. Apart from Guamos and Otomacs, seen as two wild and untamed tribes, there were Caribs and other Indians from the Lower Orinoco. Each tribe camped separately, and could be recognized only by the different paints on their skins. We also found, among this noisy reunion, some white men, mainly *pulperos*, the small traders from Angostura, who had come upstream to buy turtle-egg oil from the Indians. The Uruana missionary, from Alcalá de Henares, came to meet us, extremely surprised to see us there. After inspecting our instruments, he exaggeratedly described the hardships we would suffer going further upstream beyond the cataracts. The purpose of our journey seemed very mysterious to him. 'How is anyone to believe,' he said, 'that you left your homeland to come up this river to be eaten by mosquitoes and measure lands that do not belong to you?' Luckily we were armed with recommendations from the guardian father of the Franciscan missions, while the brother-in-law of the Barinas governor accompanying us soon resolved the doubts that the whites there had about our dress, accent and arrival on the island. The missionary invited us to share a frugal meal of bananas and fish with him. He told us he had come to camp with the Indians during the harvesting of the eggs 'to celebrate open-air mass every day, to get oil for the lights in his church, and above all to govern this Republica de Indios y Castellanos where individuals wanted to profit selfishly with what God had given to everybody'.

We walked round the island with the missionary and a *pulpero* who boasted that he had been visiting the Indians' camp and the *pesca de tortugas* for over ten years. People come to this part of the Orinoco in the same way we visit fairs in Frankfurt or Beaucaire. We were on a plain of perfectly smooth sand. 'As far as the eye can see,' they told us, 'a layer of sand covers the turtle eggs.' The missionary had a long pole in his hand. He showed us that by sounding with this pole (*vara*) he could determine the depth of the stratum of eggs in the same way a miner discovers the limits of a bed of marl, bog iron or coal. By thrusting the pole perpendicularly into the sand he immediately feels, by the lack of resistance, that he has penetrated into the cavity hiding the eggs. We saw that the stratum is generally spread with such uniformity that the pole finds it everywhere in a radius of 10 toises around any given spot. People speak of 'square poles of eggs'; it is like a minefield divided into regularly exploited lots. The stratum of eggs is far from covering the whole island; it is no longer found where land rises abruptly because the turtles cannot climb to these plateaux. I reminded my guides that Father Gumilla's vivid descriptions assured us that the Orinoco beaches have less grains of sand than turtles, and that they were so numerous that if men and tigers did not annually kill thousands of them the turtles would stop boats sailing upstream. 'Son cuentos de frailes,' the *pulpero* from Angostura whispered; for the only travellers in these lands are poor missionaries and what one calls monks' tales here are what in Europe would be called travellers' tales.

Indians assured us that upstream on the Orinoco, from its mouth to its junction with the Apure, not one island nor one beach could be found to harvest eggs. The large *arrau* turtle fears inhabited places where there are many boats. It is a shy and suspicious animal, which raises its head above the water and hides on hearing the slightest noise. The beaches where nearly all the Orinoco turtles seem to annually gather is situated between the junction of the Orinoco and Apure and the Great Cataracts or Raudales between Abruta and the Atures mission. It seems that *arrau* turtles cannot climb up the cataracts, and that beyond Atures and Maypures you only find *terekay* turtles.

The three camps formed by the Indians are set up during the end of March and first days of April. The harvesting of the eggs is carried out in the regular way that characterizes all monastic institutions. Before the arrival of the monks up the river Indians profited far less from an abundant harvest supplied by nature. Each tribe dug in the beach wherever they felt like it and broke innumerable eggs because they did not dig carefully, and they unearthed more eggs than they needed. It was like amateurs exploiting a mine. Jesuit fathers have the merit of having regularized the exploitation, and although the Franciscans, who succeeded the Jesuits, boast that they follow their predecessors' examples they do not do all that prudence dictates. Jesuits did not allow the whole beach to be dug up; they kept a small part intact, for fear of seeing the race of *arrau* turtles destroyed or diminished. Today the whole beach is dug up. It has been noticed that the harvests are getting smaller and smaller each year.

Once the camp has been set up the Uruana missionary designates his representative or superintendent, who divides the beach into lots according to the number in each tribe who are to harvest. They are all mission Indians, as naked and stupid as jungle Indians: they are called *reducidos* and *neofitos* because they attend church when the bells toll, and kneel during Communion. With a long pole made of wood or bamboo, he examines the extent of the stratum of eggs. According to our calculations this reaches 120 feet from the shore, and 3 feet deep. The Indians dig with their hands, put the harvested eggs in baskets called *mappiri*, and bring them to the camp to throw them into great wooden troughs filled with water. The eggs are smashed with sticks, shaken about and exposed to the sun until the yolk, the oily floating part, thickens out. This oily substance collecting on the surface is scooped off and cooked on a hot fire. The animal oil turns into what is called *manteca de tortuga* by the Spaniards (turtle fat), and keeps better the longer it is cooked. If it is well done it is completely clear, without smell and barely yellow. Missionaries compare it with the best olive oil and not only use it for burning in lamps but also for cooking, as its taste does not spoil good food. However, we could never obtain the pure oil. Generally it stinks because the eggs are mixed up with the already formed but dead baby turtles.

I acquired some statistical notions on the spot by consulting the Uruana missionary and the traders. The three beaches furnish annually some 5,000 *botijas*, or jars of oil. Two hundred eggs yield enough oil to fill a bottle, and 5,000 eggs to fill the jar. If we estimate the number of eggs laid by each turtle as 116, and reckon that one third are destroyed, we can calculate that 330,000 *arrau* turtles must lay 33 million eggs on the three shores. But this calculation is far too low. For example, the number of eggs that hatch before the *cosecha* is so prodigious that near the Uruana camp I saw the whole beach swarming with little turtles escaping from the Indian children.

The Indians who go harvesting take thousands of dried or lightly cooked eggs away to their villages. Our rowers always had some in baskets or cotton bags. When they are well preserved the taste is not too bad. They showed us large turtle shells emptied by jaguars, who wait for the turtles on the beach where the eggs are laid. They attack them on the sand. To eat them they turn them upside down so that the undershell is right-side up. In this position the turtles cannot right themselves, and as jaguars turn many more over than they can eat in one night the Indians avail themselves of the cats' greed and cunning. If you think how hard it is for a travelling naturalist to pull the turtle's body out without separating it from the cuirass of the shell you can only admire the litheness of the jaguar's paw as it empties the two-sided shield of the *arrau* as if the muscular ligaments had been severed by a surgeon. The jaguar chases turtles into the water, even digs up the eggs, and, along with the crocodile, heron and gallinazo vulture, is one of the cruellest enemies of the newborn turtles. When the first rains come – called 'turtle rains' (*peje canepori*) – the wild Indians go along the Orinoco banks with their poisoned arrows and kill the turtles as they warm themselves in the sun.

Our pilot had tied up the pirogue at the Playa de Huevos to buy provisions as our stores were running out. We found fresh meat, Angostura rice and even biscuits made of wheat. Our Indians filled the boat with live young turtles and sun-dried eggs for their own use. After saying goodbye to the missionary who had been so friendly to us we continued our journey upstream. There was a fresh wind that turned into squalls. Since we had entered the mountainous part of the country we had begun to notice that our boat sailed poorly, but the pilot wanted to show the Indians gathered on the bank that by sailing close to the wind he could reach the middle of the stream without tacking. Just as he was boasting of his skill and the daring of his manoeuvre the wind gusted against the sail with such violence that we nearly sank. One of the boat's sides was submerged. Water poured in so suddenly that we were soon knee-deep in water. It washed over a table I was writing on in the stern. I just managed to rescue my diary, and then saw our books, dried plants and papers floating away. Bonpland was sleeping in the middle of the boat. Woken by the flooding water and the shrieking Indian he immediately took control of the situation with that coolness which he always showed in danger.[96] As one side of the boat rose up out of the water he did not think the boat would sink. He thought that if we had to abandon boat we could swim ashore as there were no crocodiles about. Then the ropes holding the sails broke, and the same gust of wind that almost sank us now helped us recover. We baled the water out with gourds, mended the sail, and in less than half an hour we were able to continue our journey. When we criticized our pilot for having sailed too close to the wind he resorted to that typical Indian phlegmatic attitude: 'that the whites would find plenty of sun on the beaches to dry their papers'. We had lost only one book overboard – the first volume of Schreber's *Genera plantarum*. Such losses are particularly painful when you are able to take so few scientific books.

As night fell we camped on a deserted island in the middle of the river. We dined in the moonlight sitting on scattered empty turtle shells. How pleasing it was to be safe and together! We imagined how it would be if one man had saved himself alone, wandering these deserted banks, meeting more and more tributaries and unable to swim because of the crocodile and *caribe* fish. We pictured this sensitive man never knowing what had happened to his companions, more worried about them than himself. If you like surrendering to these sad thoughts it is because escaping from danger makes you feel the need for strong emotions.

We landed in the middle of the Strait of Baraguan to measure the river's breadth. In this excessively hot place we looked in vain for plants in the clefts of rocks. The stones were covered with thousands of iguanas and geckos with spreading, membranous fingers. The thermometer placed against the rock rose to 50.2 °C. The ground appeared to undulate in the mirages, without a breath of wind in the air. How vivid is the calm of nature at midday in these burning zones. The wild animals retire to the thickets; birds hide under leaves. Yet in this silence, if you listen carefully, you hear slight sounds, a dull vibration, a hum of insects. Nothing makes you sense the extent and power of organic life more keenly than this.

We spent the night on the left bank of the Orinoco, at the foot of a granite hill. In this deserted place there had once stood the San Regis mission. We dearly wanted to find a spring in Baraguan for the river water smelled of musk and had a sweetish, unpleasant taste. The Indians said, 'It is due to the bark' – they meant coriaceous skin – 'of the rotting crocodiles. The older they are, the more bitter their bark is.'

April 9th. We reached the Pararuma beach early in the morning where we found a camp of Indians, like those we had seen before. They had come to dig up the sand and harvest turtle eggs for their oil but unluckily they had arrived several days too late. The young turtles had broken out of their eggs before the Indians had set up camp. Crocodiles and *garzas*, a kind of white heron, had benefited from this mistake because they devour quantities of these young. They hunt at night as the young turtles do not break the surface of the sand until it is dark.

Among the Indians gathered at Pararuma we found some whites who had come from Angostura to buy turtle butter. After wearying us with their complaints about the 'poor harvest' and about the harm done by the jaguars as the turtles laid their eggs, they led us under an *ajupa* raised in the middle of the Indian camp. There we found the missionary monks from Carichana and the cataracts sitting on the ground playing cards and smoking tobacco in long pipes. These poor priests received us in a very friendly manner. They had been suffering from tertiary fever for months. Pale and emaciated, they had no trouble convincing us that the countries we were about to visit were dangerous for our health.

The Indian pilot who had led us from San Fernando de Apure up to the Pararuma beach did not know his way through the Orinoco rapids, and no longer wanted to sail our boat. We had to accept his decision. Luckily the Carichana missionary agreed to loan us a fine pirogue quite cheaply. Father Bernardo Zea, missionary from Atures and Maypures near the Great Cataracts, even offered to accompany us himself to the Brazilian border. The number of Indians willing to carry the canoes along the cataracts was so few that without this monk's presence we risked waiting weeks in that humid and unhealthy area. Father Zea hoped to recover his health by visiting the Río Negro missions. He talked of those places with the enthusiasm that all those in the colonies feel when talking about far-off places.

The gathering of Indians at Pararuma again afforded a fascinating chance for civilized men to study the development of our intellectual faculties in savages. It is hard to recognize in this infancy of society, in this gathering of dull, silent, impassive Indians, the primitive origins of our species. We do not see here a human nature that is sweet and naïve as described by our poets. We would like to persuade ourselves that these Indians, squatting by the fire, or sitting on huge turtle shells, their bodies covered in mud and grease, fixing their eyes stupidly for hours on the drink they are preparing, belong to a degenerate race rather than being a primitive type of our own species that, having been dispersed for ages in jungles, have fallen back into barbarism.

Red paint is – we could say – the only clothing the Indians use. Two kinds may be distinguished according to how prosperous they are. The common decoration of the Caribs, Otomacs and Yaruros is annatto, which Spaniards call *achote*. It is the colouring matter extracted from the pulp of *Bixa orellana*. To prepare this annatto Indian women throw the seeds of the plant into a tub filled with water. They beat this for an hour and then leave the mixture to deposit the colouring fecula, which is an intense brick-red. After pouring off the water they take out the fecula, dry it in their hands and mix it with turtle oil, after which it is shaped into rounded cakes. Another more precious pigment comes from a plant of the Bignoniaceae family, which Bonpland has made known by the name *Bignonia chica*. It climbs up the tallest trees by attaching its tendrils. Its bilabiate flowers are an inch long and of a pretty violet colour. The fruit is a pod filled with winged seeds, some 2 feet long. This bignonia grows wild and abundantly near Maypures. The red chica dye does not come from the fruit but from the leaves when soaked in water. The colouring matter separates itself as a light powder. It is gathered, without being mixed with turtle oil, into little loaves. When heated they give off a pleasant smell of benzoin. Chica, which was not known until our voyage, could even be used in the arts. The chemistry practised by the savage is essentially the preparation of pigments and poisons, and the neutralization of amylaceous roots.

Most missionaries on the Upper and Lower Orinoco let their Indians paint their skin. It is painful to say that some missionaries make a profit from the nakedness of Indians. Unable to sell them cloth or clothes the monks trade in red pigment. I have often seen in their huts, pompously called *conventos*, stores of chica cakes, sold for up to four francs. To give an exact idea of what Indians mean by luxury I would say that here a man of large stature hardly earns for two weeks' work enough chica to paint himself red. Just as in temperate climates we say of a poor man that 'he does not earn enough to dress himself' so I have heard Indians say that 'a man is so miserable he cannot even paint half his body'.

Some Indians are not content with colouring themselves evenly all over. They sometimes imitate European clothes by painting them on. We saw one at Parurama who had painted a blue jacket with black buttons on to his skin.

We were struck to see in the Parurama camp that old women were more preoccupied in painting themselves than young ones. We saw an Otomac woman having her hair rubbed with turtle oil and her back painted with annatto by her two daughters. The ornaments consisted of a kind of lattice-work in crossed black lines on a red background. It was work needing incredible patience. We came back from a long herborization and the painting was still only half done. It is all the more amazing that this research into ornament does not result in tattooing, for the painting done so carefully washes off if the Indian exposes herself to a downpour. Some nations paint themselves to celebrate festivals; others are covered in paint all year round. With these Indians annatto is seen as so indispensable that men and women have less shame in appearing without a *guayuco*[97] than without paint. The Orinoco *guayucos* are made from bark and cotton. Men wear larger ones than women who, according to the missionaries, seem to feel less shame than men. Shouldn't we attribute this indifference, this lack of shame in the women in tribes that are not depraved, to the state of numbness and slavery to which the female sex has been reduced in South America by the injustice and power of men?

When one speaks in Europe of a Guianan Indian we imagine a man whose head and waist are decorated with beautiful macaw, toucan and hummingbird feathers. Our painters and sculptors have for a long time seen these ornaments as typical of the native Americans. We were surprised not to find, on any of the Orinoco and Casiquiare banks, these fine feathers that travellers so frequently reported from Cayenne and Demerara. Most of the Guianan Indians, even those with the most developed intellectual faculties, who cultivate food and weave with cotton, are naked and poor. Extreme heat and sweating make clothes unbearable.

In the Pararuma camp we saw for the first time some live animals that we had only previously seen stuffed in European cabinets. Missionaries trade with these little animals. They exchange tobacco, a resin called *mani*, chica pigment, *gallitos* (cock-of-the-rocks), titi monkeys, capuchin monkeys, and other monkeys appreciated on the coast, for cloth, nails, axes, hooks and needles. These Orinoco animals are bought at disgustingly low prices from the Indians who live in the monks' missions. These same Indians then have to buy from the monks at very high prices what they need for fishing and farming with the money they get from the egg harvest. We bought various little animals, which travelled with us for the rest of our voyage up-river, enabling us to study their way of life.

The *gallitos*, or cock-of-the-rocks, sold at Pararuma in pretty cages woven from palm leaves, are far rarer on the Orinoco banks and in all northern and western tropical America than in French Guiana. They have been spotted only here in the Raudales. This bird chooses its nest in hollows in the granite rocks of the cataracts. We saw it a few times in the middle of the foaming river, calling its females and fighting like our cocks while folding back the mobile double crest on top of its head.

The titi of the Orinoco (*Simia sciurea*) is very common south of the cataracts. Its face is white, with a blue-black spot covering its mouth and the tip of its nose. No other monkey reminds you more of a child than the titi; the same innocent expression, the same cheeky smile, the same sudden shifts from joy to sadness. Its large eyes fill with tears the moment it is frightened. It is avid for insects, especially spiders. The cleverness of this little monkey is such that one we brought in our boat could perfectly distinguish different plates in Cuvier's *Tableau élémentaire d'histoire naturelle*.[98] Though the engravings are not coloured yet the titi tried to catch a grasshopper or a wasp with its small hand every time we showed a plate with these insects represented. When several of these little monkeys are shut up in the same cage and exposed to rain they twist their tails round their necks and hug each other to warm themselves. The titis are delicate and timid little animals. They become sad and dejected when they leave the jungle and enter the llanos.

The *macavahu*, called by the missionaries *viuditas*, or 'widows in mourning', has soft glossy black hair. Its face is a kind of whitish-blue square mask, which contains its eyes, nose and mouth. Its ears have an edge; are small, pretty and hairless. Its neck has a white area in two rings. Its feet, or hind legs, are black like its body, but its forehands are white outside and black inside. These white spots led the missionaries to recognize a veil, a neck scarf and the gloves of a widow in mourning. The character of this little monkey, which sits up on its hind legs to eat, is not related to its appearance. It has a wild and shy air, and often refuses food even when ravenous. We have seen it remain motionless for hours without sleeping, attentive to everything happening around it. The *viudita*, when alone, becomes furious at the sight of a bird, and climbs and runs with astonishing speed, and, like a cat, leaps on to its prey and eats all it can. The *viuditas* accompanied us throughout our entire voyage on the Casiquiare and Río Negro. It is an advantage to study animals for several months in the open air, and not indoors where they lose their natural vivacity.

We began to load the new pirogue. It was, like all Indian canoes, made from one tree trunk, hollowed out by axe and fire. It was 40 feet long and 3 feet wide. Three people could not squeeze together from one side to the other. These pirogues are so unstable that the weight must be distributed very equally and if you want to stand up for a second you must warn the rowers (*bogas*) to lean over the other side. Without this precaution water would pour in on the lopsided side. It is difficult to form an idea of the inconveniences of these miserable boats.

The missionary from the Raudales looked after the preparations for our journey rather too well. He worried that there might not be enough Maco and Guahibo Indians on hand who knew the labyrinth of small canals and rapids that form the *raudales* and cataracts, so at night he put two Indians in the *cepo*, that is, they were tied to the ground and fastened together between two pieces of wood with a padlock. In the morning we were awoken by the shouts of a young Indian who was being brutally beaten with a whip of manatee skin. His name was Zerepe, an extremely intelligent Indian who later served us well, but at the time refused to travel with us. He had been born in the Atures mission; his father was from the Maco tribe and his mother from the Maypure; he had run off to the jungle (*al monte*) and lived with wild Indians for years. He had learned several languages, and the missionary used him as an interpreter. Not without difficulty did we obtain his pardon. 'Without severity,' we were told, 'you would get nothing.'

April 10th. We were unable to set sail until ten in the morning. It was hard to adapt to the new pirogue, which we saw as a new prison. To make it wider at the back of the boat we made branches into a kind of trellis, which stuck out on both sides. Unfortunately the leaf roof of this lattice-work was so low that you either had to lie down, and consequently saw nothing, or you had to stay hunched over. The need to transport pirogues across rapids, and even from one river to another, and the fear of giving too much hold to the wind by raising the *toldo* made this construction necessary for the little boats going up the Río Negro. The roof was designed for four people stretched out on the deck or lattice-work, but your legs stuck far out, and when it rained half your body got wet. Worse still, you lie on oxhides or tiger skins, and the branches under the skins hurt you when you lie down. The front of the boat was filled with the Indian rowers, armed with 3-foot-long paddles in the form of spoons. They are all naked, sitting in twos, and row beautifully together. Their songs are sad and monotonous. The little cages with our birds and monkeys, increasing as we went on, were tied to the *toldo* and the prow. It was our travelling zoo. Despite losses due to accidents and sunstroke, we counted fourteen little animals when we came back from the Casiquiare. Every night when we established camp, our zoo and instruments occupied the middle; around them we hung our hammocks, then the Indians' hammocks and, outside, the fires we thought indispensable to scare off jaguars. At sunrise our caged monkeys answered the cries of the jungle monkeys.

In the overloaded pirogue, which was only 3 feet deep, there was no other room for the dried plants, trunks, sextant, compass and meteorological instruments but under the lattice of branches on which we were obliged to lie down for most of our trip. To take the smallest object from a trunk, or to use an instrument, we had to moor up and get ashore. To these inconveniences can be added the torment of mosquitoes that accumulate under the low roof, and the heat coming from the palm leaves continually exposed to the burning sun. We tried everything to improve our situation, without any results. While one of us hid under a sheet to avoid insects, the other insisted on lighting greenwood under the *toldo* to chase off the mosquitoes with the smoke. Pain in our eyes and increasing heat in a climate that was already asphyxiating made both these means impractical. With some gaiety of temper, with looking after each other and taking a lively interest in the majestic nature of these great river valleys, the travellers put up with the evils that became habitual. I have entered into such minute details in order to describe how we navigated on the Orinoco, and to show that despite our goodwill,

Bonpland and I were not able to multiply our observations during this section of the journey.

April 11th. To avoid the effect of flooding, so harmful to health, the Carichana mission was installed some three quarters of a league from the river. The Indians belonged to the Saliva tribe, and speak with a disagreeable nasal pronunciation. They are mild, shy and sociable, easier to discipline than other tribes on the Orinoco. To escape the dominating Caribs the Saliva readily congregated in the early Jesuit missions. These fathers praised the intelligence of these tribes, and their keenness to learn. The Saliva show a natural talent for music; from remote times they have played a trumpet, some 4 or 5 feet long, made of baked earth, with several large globular cavities joined by narrow pipes. The sound is mournful. Since the dispersion of the Jesuits missionaries have continued to stimulate their beautiful religious music. Not long ago a traveller was surprised to see how Indians played the violin, violoncello, guitar and flute.

Among the Saliva Indians we found a white woman, the sister of a Jesuit from New Granada. After having lived with people who did not understand us, it is hard to describe the joy we felt on meeting somebody with whom we could converse without an interpreter. Each mission has at least two interpreters, *lenguarazes*. These Indians are rather less stupid than the others through whom the missionaries, who do not bother to learn the languages any more, communicate with neophytes. These interpreters accompanied us when we went out botanizing; they understood Spanish but spoke it badly. With their usual apathy they would arbitrarily answer any questions with a smiling 'yes father' or 'no father'. You will understand that after months of this kind of dialogue you lose patience without managing to get the information that you urgently require. It was not rare for us to use several interpreters, and sometimes we had to translate several times the same sentence in order to begin to understand the Indians. 'After leaving my mission,' said the goodly monk at Uruana, 'you will be travelling as mutes.' This prediction was exact. To get something even from the most primitive Indians we met, we turned to sign language. As soon as the Indian realizes you do not need him as an interpreter but are asking him something directly by pointing it out, he drops his usual apathy and shows a special skill in making himself understood. He varies his signs, pronounces his words slowly, and seems flattered by your interest.

April 12th. We left Carichana at about two in the afternoon and found our way obstructed with granite blocks that break the river current. We passed close to the great reef called Piedra del Tigre. The river is so deep that sounding with a line of 22 fathoms did not touch the bottom. Towards the evening the sky covered over and squalls of wind announced a coming storm. It began to pour so hard with rain that our leafy roof hardly protected us. Luckily the rain scared off the mosquitoes that had been tormenting us all day. We were opposite the Cariven cataract, and the current was so strong that we had great difficulty in reaching land. Time and time again we were pushed back to the middle of the river until two Salivas, excellent swimmers, threw themselves into the water and swam ashore, pulling the boat in until it could be tied to a rock where we spent the night. Thunder rolled all night; the river swelled under our eyes, and we often worried that the furious waves would sink our fragile boat.

From the mouth of the Meta, the Orinoco seemed freer of shoals and rocks. We navigated in a canal 500 toises wide. The Indians stayed in the pirogue, rowing without towing or pushing it with their hands, tiring us with their wild screams. It was already dark when we found ourselves by the Raudal de Tabaje. The Indians did not want to risk crossing the cataract and so we spent the night on land on a site that was extremely uncomfortable, on a rock bench with a steep slope sheltering a cloud of bats in crevices. All night we heard the cries of jaguars. Our dog answered by howling back. The deafening noise of the Orinoco waterfalls contrasted with the thunder grumbling over the jungle.

April 13th. Early in the morning we passed the Tabaje rapids and landed again. Father Zea, who accompanied us, wanted to say mass in the new San Borja mission established two years before. We found six huts inhabited by uncatechized Indians. They were no different from wild Indians. Only their large black eyes showed more liveliness than those living in older missions. They refused our brandy without even trying it. The young girls had their faces marked with round black spots. The rest of their bodies were not painted. Some of the men had beards, and they seemed proud. Holding our chins they showed through signs that they were made like us. I was again struck by how similar all the Orinoco Indians are. Their look is sombre and sad, not hard or ferocious. Without any notions about the practices of the Christian religion they behaved quite decently in the church. Indians like representations; they submit themselves momentarily to any nuisance provided they are sure of being stared at. Just before the moment of communion they make signs to show that the priest was about to bring the chalice to his lips. Apart from this gesture they stay immobile, in their imperturbable apathy.

CHAPTER 17

Mouth of the Anaveni river – Uniana peak – Atures mission –
Cataract or raudal of Mapara – Islets

As the Orinoco runs from south to north it crosses a chain of granite
mountains. Twice checked in its course the river breaks furiously
against rocks that form steps and transversal dykes. Nothing can be
grander than this countryside. Neither the Tequendama Falls[99] near
Bogotá, nor the magnificent cordilleras surpassed my first impressions
of the Atures and Maypures rapids. Standing in a position that
dominates the uninterrupted series of cataracts it is as if the river, lit
by the setting sun, hangs above its bed like an immense sheet of foam
and vapours. The two great and famous cataracts of the Orinoco are
formed as the river breaks through the Parima mountains. Indians call
them Mapara and Quituna, but missionaries have substituted these
names with Atures and Maypures, named after tribes living in two
villages near by. On the Caracas coast the two Great Cataracts are
simply called the two Raudales, from the Spanish *raudo*, 'rushing'.[100]

Beyond the Great Cataracts an unknown land begins. This partly
mountainous and partly flat land receives tributaries from both the
Amazon and the Orinoco. No missionary writing about the Orinoco
before me has passed beyond the Maypures *raudal*. Up river, along
the Orinoco for a stretch of over 100 leagues, we came across only
three Christian settlements with some six to eight whites of European
origin there. Not surprisingly, such a deserted territory has become
the classic place for legends and fantastic histories. Up here serious
missionaries have located tribes whose people have one eye in the
middle of their foreheads, the heads of dogs, and mouths below their
stomachs. It would be wrong to attribute these exaggerated fictions
to the inventions of simple missionaries because they usually come by
them from Indian legends. From his vocation, a missionary does not
tend towards scepticism; he imprints on his memory all that the
Indians have repeated and when back in Europe delights in astonishing

people by reciting facts he has collected. These travellers' and monks' tales (*cuentos de viajeros y frailes*) increase in improbability the further you go from the Orinoco forests towards the coasts inhabited by whites. When at Cumaná you betray signs of incredulity, you are silenced by these words, 'The fathers have seen it, but far above the Great Cataracts *más arriba de los Raudales*.'

April 15th. At dawn we passed the Anaveni river, a tributary river that comes down from mountains in the east. The heat was so excessive that we stayed for a long time in a shaded place, fishing, but we could not carry off all the fish we hooked. Much later we reached the foot of the Great Cataract in a bay, and took the difficult path – it was night by then – to the Atures mission, a league away. We found this mission in a deplorable state. At the time of Solano's boundary expedition[101] it contained 320 Indians. Today it has only forty-seven. When it was founded Atures, Maypures, Meyepures, Abanis and Uirupas tribes lived there, but now there were only Guahibos and a few families from the Macos left. The Atures have completely disappeared; the little known about them comes from burial caves in Ataruipe.

Between the 4th and 8th degrees of latitude the Orinoco not only divides the great jungles of Parima from the bare savannahs of the Apure, Meta and Guaviare but also separates tribes of very different customs. On the west the Guahibo, Chiricoa and Guamo tribes wander through treeless plains. They are filthy, proud of their independence, wild, and hard to settle in a fixed place to do regular work. Spanish missionaries call them *indios andantes* (wandering Indians). On the east of the Orinoco live the Maco, Saliva, Curacicana and Pareca tribes; they are tame, peaceful farmers who easily adapt to missionary discipline.

In the Atures mission both types of tribe can be found. With the missionary we visited huts of the Macos. The independent Macos are orderly and clean. They have their *rochelas*, or villages, two or three days' journey away. They are very numerous and like all wild Indians cultivate cassava, not maize. Thanks to these peaceful relations some *indios monteros*, or nomadic Indians, had established themselves in the mission a short time before. They insistently asked for knives, hooks and coloured glass beads, which they sewed on to their *guayucos (perizomas).* Once they got what they wanted they slipped back to the jungle because missionary discipline was not to their liking. Epidemics of fever, so common at the start of the rainy season, contributed to the desertion. Jungle Indians have a horror of the life of civilized man and desert when the slightest misfortune befalls them in the mission.

Smallpox, which has so devastated other areas of America that Indians burn their huts, kill their children and avoid any grouping of tribes, is not one of the reasons for the depopulation of the Raudales. In the Upper Orinoco this plague is almost unknown. Desertion from Christian missionaries must be sought more in the Indian's hate for the discipline, the poor food, the awful climate, and the unpardonable custom that Indian mothers have of using poisonous herbs to avoid pregnancy. Many of the women do not want to have babies. If they do have children they are not only exposed to jungle dangers but also to absurd superstitions. When twins are born family honour demands that one be killed. Indians say: 'To bring twins into the world is to be exposed to public scorn, it is to resemble rats, sarigues and the vilest animals.' And, 'Two children born at the same time cannot belong to the same father.' If a newborn child shows some physical deformity the father kills it immediately. They want only well-formed, robust children because deformities indicate some evil spell. Among the Orinoco Indians the father returns home only to eat or sleep in his hammock; he shows no affection for his children or his wife, who are there only to serve him.

While we unloaded the pirogue we investigated the impressive spectacle of a great river squeezed and reduced to foam. Instead of just describing my own sensations I shall try to paint an overall view of one of the most famous spots in the New World. The more imposing and majestic a scene, the more important it is to capture it in its smallest details, to fix the outline of the picture that you want to present to the reader's imagination, and to simply describe the particular characteristics of the great monuments of nature.

Throughout his entire journey through the Lower Orinoco the traveller faces only one danger: the natural rafts formed by drifting trees uprooted by the river. Woe to the canoes that at night strike one of these rafts of tangled lianas and tree trunks! When Indians wish to attack an enemy by surprise they tie several canoes together and cover them with grass to make it seem like a tangle of trees. Today Spanish smugglers do the same to avoid customs in Angostura.

Above the Anaveni river, between the Uniana and Sipapu mountains, you reach the Mapara and Quituna cataracts, commonly called by missionaries the Raudales. These natural weirs crossing from one side to the other offer the same picture: one of the greatest rivers in the world breaks into foam among many islands, rocky dykes and piles of granite blocks covered in palms.[102]

April 16th. Towards evening we heard that our boats had passed both rapids in less than six hours, and arrived in good condition at the Puerto de Arriba. 'Your boat will not be wrecked because you are not carrying goods, and you travel with the monk of the Raudales,' a little brown man said to us bitterly. By his accent we recognized him as a Catalan. He traded in tortoise oil with the mission Indians, and was not a friend of the missionaries. 'The frail boats belong to us Catalans who, with permission from the Guianan Government, but not from the president of the mission, try to trade above the Atures and Maypures. Our boats are wrecked in the Raudales, key to all the missions beyond, and then Indians take us back to Carichana and try to force us to stop trading.' What is the source of this deep hatred of the missions in the Spanish colonies? It cannot be because they are rich in the Upper Orinoco. They have no houses, no goats and few cows. The resentment is aimed at the ways the missionaries obstinately close their territories off to white men.

In the little Atures church we were shown remains of the Jesuits' wealth. A heavy silver lamp lay half buried in sand. This object did not tempt the Indians; the Orinoco natives are not thieves, and have a great respect for property. They do not even steal food, hooks or axes. At Maypures and Atures locks on doors are unknown.

The missionary told us a story about the jaguars. Some months before our arrival a young jaguar had wounded a child while playing with him. I have verified the facts on the spot; it should interest those who study animal behaviour. Two Indian children, a boy and a girl of about eight and nine years of age, were sitting on the grass near the village when a jaguar came out from the jungle and ran round the children, jumping and hiding in the high grass, like our cats. The little boy sensed danger only when the jaguar struck him with its paw until blood began to flow. The little girl chased it off with branches from a tree. The intelligent little boy was brought to us. The jaguar's claw had ripped skin from his forehead. What did this playfulness mean in the jaguar? If the jaguar was not hungry, why did it approach the children? There is something mysterious in the sympathies and hatreds of animals.

In this area there are several species of peccaries, or pigs with lumbar glands, only two of which are known to naturalists in Europe. The Indians call the little peccary a *chacharo*. Reared in their houses they become tame like our sheep and goats. Another kind is called the *apida*, which is also domesticated and wanders in large herds. These animals announce themselves from a long way off because they break down all the shrubs in their way. During a botanical excursion Bonpland was warned by his Indian guides to hide behind a tree trunk as these *cochinos*, or *puercos del monte*, passed by. The flesh of the *chacharo* is flabby and disagreeable, but the Indians hunt them nevertheless, with small lances tied to cords. We were told at Atures that jaguars dread being surrounded by herds of wild pigs and climb trees to save themselves. Is this a hunters' tale, or a fact?

Among the monkeys we saw at the Atures mission we found one new species, which the creoles call *machis*. It is the *ouavapavi*,[103] with grey hair and a bluish face. This little animal is as tame as it is ugly. Every day in the missionary courtyard it would grab a pig and sit on its back all day. We have also seen it riding a large cat brought up in Father Zea's house.

It was at the cataracts that we first heard talk about the hairy man of the jungle, called *salvaje*, who rapes women, builds huts, and sometimes eats human flesh. Neither Indians nor missionaries doubt the existence of this man-shaped monkey, which terrifies them. Father Gili seriously related the story of a lady from San Carlos who praised the gentle character of the man of the jungle. She lived several years with him in great domestic harmony, and only asked hunters to bring her back home because she and her children (rather hairy also) 'were tired of living far from a church'. This legend, taken by missionaries, Spaniards and black Africans from descriptions of the orang-utang, followed us for the five years of our journey. We annoyed people everywhere by being suspicious of the presence of a great anthropomorphic ape in the Americas.

After two days near the Atures cataract we were happy to load the canoe again and leave a place where the temperature was usually 29 °C by day and 26 °C at night. All day we were horribly tormented by mosquitoes and *jejenes*, tiny venomous flies (or *simuliums*), and all night by *zancudos*, another kind of mosquito feared even by the Indians. Our hands began to swell, and this swelling increased until we reached the banks of the Temi. The means found to escape these insects are often quite original. The kind missionary Father Zea, all his life tormented by mosquitoes, had built a small room near his church, up on a scaffolding of palm trunks, where you could breathe more freely. At night we climbed up a ladder to dry our plants and write our diary. The missionary had correctly observed that the insects preferred the lower levels, that is, from the ground up to some 15 feet. At Maypures the Indians leave their villages at night and sleep near the cataracts because the mosquitoes seem to avoid air loaded with vapours.

Those who have not travelled the great rivers of tropical America, like the Orinoco or the Magdalena, cannot imagine how all day long, ceaselessly, you are tormented by mosquitoes that float in the air, and how this crowd of little animals can make huge stretches of land uninhabitable. However used to the pain you may become, without complaining; however much you try to observe the object you are studying, the mosquitoes, *jejenes* and *zancudos* will tear you away as they cover your head and hands, pricking you with their needle-like suckers through your clothes, and climbing into your nose and mouth, making you cough and sneeze whenever you try to talk. In the Orinoco missions the *plaga de las moscas*, or plague of mosquitoes, is an inexhaustible subject of conversation. When two people meet in the morning the first questions they ask each other are, 'Que le han parecido los zancudos de anoche?' and 'Como estamos hoy de mosquitos?' ('How were the *zancudos* last night?' and 'How are we for mosquitoes today?').

The lower strata of air, from the ground to some 20 feet up, are invaded by poisonous insects, like thick clouds. If you stand in a dark place, such as a cave formed by granite blocks in the cataracts, and look towards the sunlit opening you will see actual clouds of mosquitoes that get thicker or thinner according to the density of insects. I doubt that there is another country on earth where man suffers more cruelly during the rainy season than here. When you leave latitude 5 the biting lessens, but in the Upper Orinoco it becomes more painful because it is hotter, and there is absolutely no wind so your skin becomes more irritated. 'How good it would be to live on the moon,' a Saliva Indian said. 'It is so beautiful and clear that it must be free of mosquitoes.'[104]

Whoever lives in this region, whether white, mulatto, black or Indian, suffers equally from insect stings. People spend their time complaining of the *plaga, del insufrible tormento de las moscas*. I have mentioned the curious fact that whites born in the Tropics can walk about barefoot in the same room where a recently arrived European runs the risk of being bitten by *niguas*, or chigoes (*Pulex penetrans*). These hardly visible animals dig under toenails and soon reach the size of a pea as they develop their eggs, situated in little sacs under their abdomens. It seems as if the *nigua* is able to distinguish the cellular membrane and blood of a European from those of a white *criollo*, something that the most detailed chemical analysis has been unable to do. It is not the same with mosquitoes, despite what is said on South American coasts. These insects attack Indians as much as Europeans; only the consequences of the bites vary with race. The same venomous liquid applied to the skin of a copper-coloured Indian and to a recently arrived white does not cause inflammations to the first, while to the second it causes hard, inflamed blisters that last for various numbers of days.

All day, even when rowing, Indians continually slap each other hard with the palm of the hand to scare off mosquitoes. Brusque in all their movements they continue to slap each other mechanically while they sleep. At Maypures we saw young Indians sitting in a circle, cruelly scratching each other's back with bark dried by the fire. With that patience only known in the copper-coloured race, some Indian women busied themselves by digging small lumps of coagulated blood from each bite with a sharp, pointed bone. One of the wildest Orinoco tribes, the Otomacs, use mosquito nets woven from fibre from the moriche palm. In villages on the Magdalena river Indians often invited us to lie down on oxhides near the church in the middle of the *plaza grande* where they had herded all the cattle, as the proximity of cattle gives you some respite from bites. When Indians saw that Bonpland was unable to prepare his plants because of the plague of mosquitoes they invited him into their 'ovens' (*hornitos*), as they call these small spaces without doors or windows, which they slide into on their bellies through a low opening. Thanks to a fire of greenwood, which gives off plenty of smoke, they expel all the insects and then block the 'oven' door. Bonpland, with a praiseworthy courage and patience, dried hundreds of plants shut up in these Indian *hornitos*.

The trouble an Indian takes to avoid the insects proves that despite his different skin colour he is just as sensitive to mosquito bites as any white. Irritability is increased by wearing warm clothes, by applying alcoholic liquors, by scratching the wounds, and – and this I have observed myself – by taking too many baths. By bathing whenever we could Bonpland and I observed that a bath, though soothing for old bites, made us more sensitive to new ones. If you take a bath more than twice a day the skin becomes nervously excited in a way nobody in Europe could understand. It seems as if all one's sensitivity has become concentrated in the epidermic layers. Today the dangers that prevent Spaniards navigating up the Orinoco do not come from wild Indians or snakes or crocodiles or jaguars but, as they naïvely say, from 'el sudar y las moscas' (sweating and mosquitoes).

I have shown that winged insects which live in society and whose suckers contain a liquid that irritates skin make vast territories virtually uninhabitable. Other insects, just as small, called termites (*comején*) create insuperable obstacles to the progress of civilization in several hot countries. They rapidly devour paper, cardboard and parchment, and thus destroy archives and libraries. Whole provinces of Spanish America do not have any document that dates back more than a hundred years.

CHAPTER 18

*Garcita cataract – Maypures – Quituna cataract – Confluence of
the Vichada and Zama – Aricagua rock – Siquita*

Our boat was waiting for us in the Puerto de Arriba above the Atures
cataract. On the narrow path that led to the *embarcadero* we were
shown the distant rocks near the Ataruipe caves. We did not have
time to visit that Indian cemetery though Father Zea had not stopped
talking about the skeletons painted red with *onoto* inside the great
jars. 'You will hardly believe,' said the missionary, 'that these skeletons
and painted vases, which we thought unknown to the rest of the
world, have brought me trouble. You know the misery I endure in
the Raudales. Devoured by mosquitoes, and lacking in bananas and
cassava, yet people in Caracas envy me! I was denounced by a white
man for hiding treasure that had been abandoned in the caves when
the Jesuits had to leave. I was ordered to appear in Caracas in person
and journeyed pointlessly over 150 leagues to declare that the cave
contained only human bones and dried bats. However, commissioners were appointed to come up here and investigate. We shall wait a
long time for these commissioners. The cloud of mosquitoes (*nube de
moscas*) in the Raudales is a good defence.'

April 17th. After walking for three hours we reached our boat at
about eleven in the morning. Father Zea packed provisions of clumps
of bananas, cassava and chicken with our instruments. We found the
river free of shoals, and after a few hours had passed the Garcita *raudal*
whose rapids are easily crossed during high water. We were struck by
a succession of great holes, more than 180 feet above the present
water-level, that appeared to have been caused by water erosion. The
night was clear and beautiful but the plague of mosquitoes near the
ground was such that I was unable to record the level of the artificial
horizon and lost the opportunity of observing the stars.

April 18th. We set off at three in the morning in order to reach the
cataracts known as the Raudal de Guahibos before nightfall. We

moored at the mouth of the Tomo river, and the Indians camped on the shore. At five in the afternoon we reached the *raudal*. It was extremely difficult to row against the current and the mass of water rushing over a bank several feet high. One Indian swam to a rock that divided the cataract in two, tied a rope to it, and began hauling our boat until, halfway up, we were able to get off with our instruments, dried plants and bare provisions. Surprisingly we found that above the natural wall over which the river fell there was a piece of dry land. Our position in the middle of the cataract was strange but without danger. Our companion, the missionary father, had one of his fever fits, and to relieve him we decided to make a refreshing drink. We had taken on board at Apures a *mapire*, or Indian basket, filled with sugar, lemons and grenadillas, or passion-fruit, which the Spaniards call *parchas*. As we had no bowl in which to mix the juices we poured river water into one of the holes in the rock with a *tutuma*, and then added the sugar and acid fruit juices. In a few seconds we had a wonderfully refreshing juice, almost a luxury in this wild spot, but necessity had made us more and more ingenious. After quenching our thirst we wanted to have a swim. Carefully examining the narrow rocky dyke on which we sat, we saw that it formed little coves where the water was clear and still. We had the pleasure of a quiet bathe in the midst of noisy cataracts and screaming Indians. I enter into such detail to remind those who plan to travel afar that at any moment in life pleasures can be found.

After waiting for an hour we saw that our pirogue had safely crossed the *raudal*. We loaded our instruments and provisions and left the Guahibo rock. We began a journey that was quite dangerous. Above the cataract the river is some 800 toises wide and must be crossed obliquely at the point where the waters start rushing towards the fall. The men had been rowing for over twenty minutes when the pilot said that instead of advancing we were drifting back to the falls. Then there was a storm and heavy rain fell. Those anxious moments seemed to last for ever. The Indians whisper as they always do when in danger; but they rowed very hard and we reached the port of Maypures by nightfall.

The night was very dark and it would take us two hours to reach the village of Maypures. We were soaked to the skin, and after it

stopped raining the *zancudos* returned. My companions were unde-
cided as to whether to camp in the harbour or walk to the village.
Father Zea insisted on going to the village where, with help from
Indians, he had begun to build a two-floored house. 'You will find
there,' he said naïvely, 'the same comforts as you have out of doors.
There are no tables or chairs but you will suffer less from mosquitoes
because in the mission they are not as shameless as down by the river.'
We followed the missionary's advice. He ordered torches of copal to
be lit. These are tubes of bark filled with copal resin. At first we
passed beds of slippery rock, then a thick palm grove. We twice had
to cross streams over tree trunks. The torches burned out. They give
off more smoke than light, and easily extinguish. Our companion,
Don Nicolas Soto, lost his balance in the dark crossing a marsh and
fell off a tree trunk. For a while we had no idea how far he had fallen,
but luckily it was not far and he was not hurt. The Indian pilot, who
spoke Spanish quite well, did not stop saying how easy it would be to
be attacked by snakes or jaguars. This is the obligatory topic of
conversation when you travel at night with Indians. They think that
by frightening European travellers they will become more necessary
to them, and will win their confidence.

The Maypures cataracts[105] appear like a cluster of little waterfalls
following each other, as if falling down steps. The *raudal*, the name
given by Spaniards to these kind of cataracts, is made up of a
veritable archipelago of small islands and rocks which narrow the
river so thoroughly that there is often less than 18 to 21 feet for boats
to navigate through.

At the confluence of the Cameji and Orinoco we unloaded our
baggage, and the Indians, familiar with all the shoals in the *raudal*, led
the empty pirogue to the mouth of the Toparo river where the water
is no longer dangerous. Each rock forming the falls of the *raudal* has a
different name. As long as they are not more than 1.5 to 2 feet above
water the Indians do not mind letting the current take their canoes;
but to go up river they swim ahead and after much struggling tie
cables to rocks and pull the boats up.

Sometimes, and it's the only accident the Indians fear, the canoes
break against rocks. Then, their bodies bloodied, the Indians try to
escape the whirlpools and swim ashore. In those places where the

rocks are very high, or the embankment they are going up crosses the whole river, they roll the boat up on tree trunks.

The most famous cataracts, with the most obstacles, are called Purimarimi and Manimi and are about 3 metres wide. The difficulties involved in reaching these places, and the foul air filled with millions of mosquitoes, made it impossible to take a geodesical levelling, but with the aid of a barometer I was amazed that the whole fall of the *raudal* from the mouth of the Cameji to the Toparo was only some 27 to 30 feet. My surprise was related to the terrible din and foam flying from the river.

From the Manimi rock there is a marvellous view. Your eyes survey a foaming surface that stretches away for almost 2 leagues. In the middle of the waves rocks as black as iron, like ruined towers, rise up. Each island, each rock, is crowned by trees with many branches; a thick cloud floats above the mirror of the water and through it you see the tops of tall palms. What name shall we give these majestic plants? I guess that they are *vadgiai*, a new species, more than 80 feet high. Everywhere on the backs of the naked rocks during the rainy season the noisy waters have piled up islands of vegetation. Decorated with ferns and flowering plants these islands form flower-beds in the middle of exposed, desolate rocks. At the foot of the Manimi rock, where we had bathed the day before, the Indians killed a 7.5-foot snake, which we examined at leisure. The Macos called it a *camudu*. It was beautiful, and not poisonous. I thought at first that it was a boa, and then perhaps a python. I say 'perhaps' for a great naturalist like Cuvier appears to say that pythons belong to the Old World, and boas to the New. I shall not add to the confusions in zoological naming by proposing new changes, but shall observe that the missionaries and the latinized Indians of the mission clearly distinguish the *tragavenado* (boa) from the *culebra de agua*, which is like the *camudu*.

In the time of the Jesuits the Maypures *raudal* mission was well known and had as many as 600 inhabitants including several families of whites. Under the government of the fathers of the Observance this has shrunk to some sixty. Those who still live there are mild and moderate, and very clean. Most of the wild Indians of the Orinoco are not excessively fond of strong alcohol like the North American Indian. It is true that Otomacs, Yaruros, Achaguas and Caribs often get drunk on *chicha* and other fermented drinks made from cassava, maize and sugared palm-tree fruit. But travellers, as usual, have generalized from the habits of a few villages. We often could not persuade the Guahibos who worked with us to drink brandy even when they seemed exhausted.[106]

They grow banana and cassava, but not maize. Like the majority of Orinoco Indians, those in Maypures also make drinks that could be called nutritious. A famous one in the country is made from a palm called the *seje*, which grows wild in the vicinity. I estimated the number of flowers on one cluster at 44,000; the fruit that fall without ripening amount to 8,000. These fruit are little fleshy drupes. They are thrown into boiling water for a few minutes to separate the pulp, which has a sweet taste, from the skin, and are then pounded and bruised in a large vessel filled with water. Taken cold, the infusion is yellowish and tastes like almond milk. Sometimes *papelón* (unrefined sugar) or sugar cane is added. The missionary said that the Indians become visibly fatter during the two or three months when they drink this *seje* or dip their cassava cakes in it. The *piaches*, or Indian shamans, go into the jungle and sound the *botuto* (the sacred trumpet) under *seje* palm trees 'to force the tree to give a good harvest the following year'.

'Tengo en mi pueblo la fábrica de loza' (I have a pottery works in my village), Father Zea told us and led us to the hut of an Indian family who were baking large earthenware vessels, up to 2.5 feet high, out in the open on a fire of shrubs. This industry is characteristic of the diverse branches of the Maypures tribes, cultivated since time immemorial. Wherever you dig up the ground in the jungle, far from any human habitations, you find bits of painted pottery. It is noteworthy that the same motifs are used everywhere. The Maypures Indians painted decorations in front of us that were identical to those we had seen on the jars from the Ataruipe caves, with wavy lines, figures of crocodiles, monkeys and a large quadruped that I did not recognize but which was always crouched in the same position.

With the Maypures Indians, it is the women who decorate the vessels, clean the clay by washing it several times; then they shape it into cylinders and mould even the largest jars with their hands. The American Indians never discovered the potter's wheel.

It was fascinating to see *guacamayos*, or tame macaws, flying around the Indian huts as we see pigeons in Europe. This bird is the largest and most majestic of the parrot species. Including its tail it measures 2 feet 3 inches. The flesh, which is often eaten, is black and rather tough. These macaws, whose feathers shine with tints of purple, blue and yellow, are a grand ornament in Indian yards, and are just as beautiful as the peacock or golden pheasant. Rearing parrots was noticed by Columbus when he first discovered America.

Near the Maypures village grows an impressive tree some 60 feet high called by the colonists the *fruta de burro*. It is a new species of annona. The tree is famous for its aromatic fruit whose infusion is an efficient febrifuge. The poor missionaries of the Orinoco who suffer tertian fevers most of the year rarely travel without a little bag of *fruta de burro*.

April 21st. After spending two and a half days in the little village of Maypures near the Great Cataracts, we embarked in the canoe that the Carichana missionary had got for us. It had been damaged by the knocks it had received in the river, and by the Indians' carelessness. Once you have passed the Great Cataracts[107] you feel you are in a new world; that you have stepped over the barriers that nature seems to have raised between the civilized coasts and the wild, unknown interior. On the way to the landing-stage we caught a new species of tree frog on the trunk of a hevea. It had a yellow belly, a back and head of velvety purple, and a narrow white stripe from its nose to its hind parts. This frog was 2 inches long; probably allied to the *Rana tinctoria* whose blood, so it is said, makes the feathers that have been plucked out of a parrot grow again in frizzled yellow and red if poured on to its skin.

The Indians told us that the jungles which cover the banks of the Sipapo abound in the climbing plant called *bejuco de maimure*. This species of liana is very important for the Indians as they weave baskets and mats from it. The Sipapo jungles are completely unknown. It is there that the missionaries place the Rayas tribe, whose mouths are said to be in their navels, perhaps due to the analogy with rays, whose mouths appear to be halfway down their bodies. An old Indian we met at Carichana, who boasted that he had often eaten human flesh, had seen these headless people 'with his own eyes'.

At the mouth of the Zama river we entered into a fluvial network worthy of attention. The Zama, Mataveni, Atabapo, Tuamini, Temi and Guianai rivers have *aguas negras*, that is, seen as a mass they appear brown like coffee, or greenish-black. These waters are, however, beautifully clear and very tasty. I have observed that crocodiles and mosquitoes, but not the *zancudos*, tend to avoid the black waters.

April 24th. A violent rainstorm forced us to embark before dawn. We left at two in the morning and had to abandon some books, which we could not find in the dark. The river runs straight from south to north, its banks are low and lined with thick jungle.

*San Fernando de Atabapo – San Baltasar – The Temi and
Tuamini rivers – Javita – Journey on foot from the Tuamini river
to the Río Negro*

During the night we had left the Orinoco waters almost without
realizing it. At sunrise we found ourselves in a new country, on the
banks of a river whose name we had hardly heard mentioned, and
which would lead us after a foot journey over Pimichín to the Río
Negro on the Brazilian frontier. The father superior of the San
Fernando mission said to us: 'First you must go up the Atabapo, then
the Temi, and finally the Tuamini. If the black-water current is too
strong to do this the guides will take you over flooded land through
the jungle. In that deserted zone between the Orinoco and the Río
Negro you will meet only two monks established there. In Javita you
will find people to carry your canoe over land in four days to Caño
Pimichín. If the canoe is not wrecked go straight down the Río
Negro to the fort of San Carlos, then go up the Casiquiare and in a
month you will reach San Fernando along the Upper Orinoco.' That
was the plan drawn up for us, which we carried out, without danger,
in thirty-three days. The bends are such in this labyrinth of rivers that
without the map which I have drawn it would be impossible to
picture the route we took. In the first part of this journey from east
to west you find the famous bifurcations that have given rise to so
many disputes, and whose location I was the first to establish through
astronomic observations. One arm of the Orinoco, the Casiquiare,[108]
running north to south, pours into the Guainia or Río Negro, which
in turn joins the Marañon or Amazon.

No astronomical instruments had been brought along during the
frontier expedition in this region, so with my chronometer, and by
the meridional height of the stars, I established the exact location of
San Baltasar de Atabapo, Javita, San Carlos de Río Negro, the
Culimacarai rock and the Esmeralda mission. The map I drew has
resolved any doubts about the reciprocal distances between the Christ-

ian outposts. When there is no other road but the tortuous and intricate river; when little villages lie hidden in thick jungle; when in a completely flat country with no mountains visible, you can read where you are on earth only by looking up to the sky.

The San Fernando missionary, with whom we stayed two days, lived in a village that appears slightly more prosperous than others we had stayed in on our journey, yet still had only 226 inhabitants.[109] We found some traces of agriculture; every Indian has his own cacao plantation, which gives a good crop by the fifth year but stops fruiting earlier than in the Aragua valleys. Around San Fernando there are some savannahs with good pasture but only some seven or eight cows remain from a vast herd left behind by the frontier expedition. The Indians are a little more civilized than in the other missions. Surprisingly, we came across an Indian blacksmith.

In San Fernando we were most struck by the *pihiguado* or *pirijao* palm, which gives the countryside its peculiar quality. Covered with thorns, its trunk reaches more than 60 feet high. The fruit of this tree is extraordinary; each bunch has some fifty to eighty; they are yellow, like apples, but turn purple on ripening, when they are 2 or 3 inches thick. Generally they fall off before the kernel develops. Of the eighty to ninety palm trees peculiar to the New World that I have described in my *Nova Genera plantarum aequinoctialem* (1815–25) none has such a fleshy fruit. The *pirijao* fruit yields a substance rather like flour, as yellow as egg yolk, slightly sweet and very nutritious. It is eaten like banana or sweet potato, cooked or baked in ashes, and is as healthy as it tastes good. Indians and missionaries vie in praising this magnificent palm, which could be called the peach palm. In these wild regions I was reminded of Linnaeus's assertion that the country of palm trees was man's first abode, and that man is essentially palmivorous.[110] When we examined what food the Indians stored in their huts we noticed that their diet depends as much on the fruit of the *pirijao* as on cassava and banana.

At San Fernando, and in the neighbouring villages of San Baltasar and Javita, the missionaries live in attractive houses, covered in liana and surrounded by gardens. The tall *pirijao* were the most decorative part of the plantation. In our walks the head of the mission told us about his incursions up the Guaviare river. He reminded us how these

journeys, undertaken for the 'conquest of souls', are eagerly anticipated by the Indians. All the Indians enjoy taking part, even old men
and women. Under the pretext of recovering neophytes who have
deserted the village, children of eight to ten are kidnapped and
distributed among the missionary Indians as serfs, or *poitos*.

As soon as you enter the basin of the Atabapo river everything
changes: the air, the colour of the water, the shape of the river-side
trees. By day you no longer suffer the torment of mosquitoes; and
their long-legged cousins the *zancudos* become rare at night. Beyond
the San Fernando mission these nocturnal insects disappear altogether.
The Orinoco waters are turbid, full of earthy matter, and in the coves
give off a faint musky smell from the amount of dead crocodiles and
other putrefying animals. To drink that water we had to filter it
through a linen cloth. The waters of the Atabapo, on the other hand,
are pure, taste good, are without smell, and appear brownish in
reflected light and yellow under the sun.

The extreme purity of the black waters is confirmed by their
transparency, and by the way they clearly reflect all the surrounding
objects. The minutest fish are visible at a depth of 20 or 30 feet. It is
easy to see the river bottom, which is not muddy but composed of a
dazzlingly white granite or quartz sand. Nothing can be compared to
the beauty of the Atabapo river banks, overloaded with vegetation,
among which rise the palms with plumed leaves, reflected in the river
water. The green of the reflected image seems as real as the object
seen with your eyes.

Contrary to geographers, the Indians of San Fernando claim that
the Orinoco rises from two rivers, the Guaviare and the Paragua.
This latter name they give to the Upper Orinoco. Following their
hypothesis they say the Casiquiare is not a branch of the Orinoco, but
of the Paragua. If you look at my map you will see these names are
quite arbitrary. It does not matter if you do not call the Orinoco the
Paragua as long as you trace the rivers as they actually are in nature
and do not separate rivers that form part of the same river system
with mountain chains. The Paragua, or that part of the Orinoco east
of the mouth of the Guaviare, has clearer, purer, more transparent
water than the part of the Orinoco below San Fernando. The waters
of the Guaviare are white and turbid and have the same taste,

according to the Indians whose sense organs are very delicate and well tested, as the Orinoco waters near the Great Cataracts. 'Give me water from three or four great rivers of this country,' an old Indian from the Javita mission said, 'and I will tell you by tasting them where they come from; whether it is a white or black river, whether it is the Atabapo, Paragua or Guaviare.' European geographers are wrong not to admit to seeing things as Indians do, for they are the geographers of their own country.

April 26th. We advanced only 2 or 3 leagues, and spent the night on a rock near the Indian plantations or *conucos* of Guapasoso. As the river floods and spills over into the jungle, you lose sight of the banks and can moor only to a rock or small tableland rising above the water. In these granite rocks I found no cavity (druse), no crystallized substance, not even rock crystal, and no trace of pyrites or other metallic substances. I mention this detail on account of the chimerical ideas that have spread following Berrio's and Raleigh's voyages about 'the immense riches of the great and fine empire of Guiana'.[111]

In the Atabapo, above San Fernando, there are no longer any crocodiles; every now and then you come across some *bavas*, numerous freshwater dolphins, but no manatees. You would not find tapirs, nor araguato monkeys, nor howler monkeys, *zamuros*, or *guacharacas*, a kind of crested pheasant. However, enormous water snakes similar to boas are very common and endanger Indian bathers. From the first day we saw them swimming past our canoes, reaching 14 feet in length.

April 27th. The night was beautiful; black clouds crossed the sky with surprising speed. Guapasoso's latitude was 3.53′ 55″. The black waters served as my horizon. I was all the more delighted to make this observation as in the white-water rivers from the Apure to the Orinoco we had been cruelly bitten by mosquitoes, as Bonpland recorded the hours with the chronometer, and I myself adjusted the horizon. At two we left the Guapasoso *conucos*, going south and upstream as the river, at least that part of it free of trees, began to narrow. At sunrise it started to rain. In these forests we no longer heard the cries of the howler monkeys. Dolphins, or *toninas*, played by the side of our boat. At about midday we passed the mouth of the Ipurichapano river, and a little later the granite rock called Piedra del

Tigre. We later regretted not resting near this rock as we had some problems trying to find a spot of dry land large enough upon which to light a fire and set up our hammocks and instruments.

April 28th. It poured with rain as soon as the sun set and we were worried about the damage to our collections. The poor missionary suffered one of his fever attacks and begged us to leave before midnight. After passing the Guarinuma rapids the Indians pointed out the ruins of the Mendaxari mission, abandoned some time back. On the east bank of the river, near the little rock of Kemarumo in the middle of Indian plantations, we saw a gigantic ceiba (the *Bombax ceiba*). We landed to measure it; it was some 120 feet high, with a diameter of 14 or 15 feet.

April 29th. The air was cooler, and without *zancudos*, but the clouds blocked out all the stars. I begin to miss the Lower Orinoco as the strong current slowed our progress. We stopped for most of the day, looking for plants. It was night when we reached the San Baltasar mission or, as the monks call it, *la divina pastora de Baltasar de Atabapo*. We lodged with a Catalan missionary, a lively and friendly man who, in the middle of the jungle, displayed the activities of his people. He had planted a wonderful orchard where European figs grew with persea, and lemon trees with mamey. The village was built with a regularity typical of Protestant Germany or America. Here we saw for the first time that white and spongy substance which I have made known as *dapicho* and *zapis*. We saw that this stuff was similar to elastic resin. But through sign language the Indians made us think that it came from under ground so we first thought that maybe it was a fossil rubber. A Poimisano Indian was sitting by a fire in the missionary hut transforming *dapicho* into black rubber. He had stuck several bits on to thin sticks and was roasting it by the fire like meat. As it melts and becomes elastic the *dapicho* blackens. The Indian then beat the black mass with a club made of Brazil-wood and then kneaded the *dapicho* into small balls some 3 to 4 inches thick, and let them cool. The balls appear identical to rubber though the surface remains slightly sticky. At San Baltasar they are not used for the game of pelota that Indians play in Uruana and Encaramada but are cut up and used as more effective corks than those made from cork itself. In front of the Casa de los Solteros – the house where unmarried men lived – the missionary showed us a drum made from a hollow cylinder of wood. This drum was beaten with great lumps of *dapicho* serving as drumsticks. The drum has openings that could be blocked by hand to vary the sounds, and was hanging on two light supports. Wild Indians love noisy music. Drums and *botutos*, the baked-earth trumpets, are indispensable instruments when Indians decide to play music and make a show.

April 30th. We continued upstream on the Atabapo for 5 miles, then instead of following this river to its source, where it is called the Atacavi, we entered the Temi river. Before reaching this tributary, near the Guasacavi mouth, a granite outcrop on the west bank fixed our attention: it is called the rock of the Guahiba Indian woman, or the Mother Rock, the Piedra de la Madre. Father Zea could not explain its bizarre name, but a few weeks later another missionary told us a story that stirred up painful feelings. If, in these deserted places, man leaves hardly any traces behind him, it is doubly humiliating for a European to see in the name of a rock a memory of the moral degradation of whites that contrasts the virtue of a wild Indian with the barbarity of civilized men!

In 1797 the San Fernando missionary had led his men to the banks of the Guaviare river on one of those hostile incursions banned both by religion and Spanish law. They found a Guahiba mother with three children in a hut, two of whom were not yet adults. They were busy preparing cassava flour. Resistance was impossible; their father had gone out fishing, so the mother tried to run off with her children. She had just reached the savannah when the Indians, who hunt people the way whites hunt blacks in Africa, caught her. The mother and children were tied up and brought back to the river bank. The monks were waiting for this expedition to end, without suffering any of the dangers. Had the mother resisted the Indians would have killed her; anything is allowed in this hunting of souls (*conquista espiritual*), and it is especially children that are captured and treated as *poitos* or slaves in the Christian missions. They brought the prisoners to San Fernando, hoping that the mother would not find her way back by land to her home. Separated from those children who had gone fishing with their father the day she was kidnapped, this poor woman began to show signs of the deepest despair. She wanted to bring those children in the power of the missionaries back home, and several times ran off with them from the San Fernando village but the Indians hunted her down each time. After severely punishing her the missionary took the cruel decision of separating the mother from her two infants. She was led alone to a mission on the Río Negro, up the Atabapo river. Loosely tied up, she sat in the bow of the boat. She had not been told where she was going; but she guessed by the sun's position that she was being taken away from her house and native land. She managed to break her bonds and jumped into the water and swam to the river bank. The current pushed her to a bank of rock, which is named after her today. She climbed up and walked into the jungle. But the head of the mission ordered his Indians to follow and capture her. She was again caught by the evening. She was stretched out on the rock (the Piedra de la Madre) where she was beaten with manatee whips. Her hands tied up behind her back with the strong cords of the *mavacure*, she was then dragged to the Javita mission and thrown into one of the inns called *casas del rey*. It was the rainy season and the night was very dark. Impenetrable forests separate the Javita and San Fernando missions some 25 leagues apart in a straight line. The only known route was by river. Nobody ever tried to go by land from one mission to another, even if only a few leagues away. But this did not prevent a mother separated from her children. Her children were at San Fernando so she had to find them, rescue them from Christians, and bring them back to their father on the Guaviare. The Guahiba woman was not closely supervised in the inn. As her hands were bloodied the Javita Indians had loosened her bindings. With her teeth she managed to break the cords, and she disappeared into the night. On the fourth day she was seen prowling round the hut where her children were being kept at the San Fernando mission. 'This woman had just carried out,' added the monk telling us this sad story, 'something that the toughest Indian would not have even considered.' She had crossed the jungle in a season when the sky is continuously covered with cloud, when the sun appears only for a few minutes for days on end. Had she followed the flow of water? But flooding had forced her to walk far from the river, in the middle of jungles where the river is imperceptible. How many times must she have been blocked by thorny liana growing round trees! How many times must she have swum across streams! What on earth could this luckless woman have eaten during her four days' walk? She said that she had eaten only those large black ants called *vachacos* that climb up trees and hang resinous nests from branches. We pressed the missionary to tell us whether the Guahiba woman had finally enjoyed peace and happiness with her family. He did not want to satisfy our curiosity. But on our return from the Río Negro we learned that this Indian woman was not even left to recover from her wounds before she was again separated from her children, and sent to a mission on the Upper Orinoco. She died by refusing to eat food, as do all Indians when faced with great calamities.[112]

Such is the memory attached to this fatal rock called the Piedra de la Madre. If I have dawdled over this touching story of maternal love in an often vilified race, it is because I wanted to make public this story heard from monks to prove that even missions should obey laws.

Wherever the Temi forms bays the jungle is flooded for more than half a square league. To avoid the bends and shorten our journey the Indians leave the river bed and go south along paths or *sendas*, that is, canals, some 4 or 5 feet wide. The depth of the water rarely exceeds half a fathom. These *sendas* are formed in the flooded jungle like paths in dry land. Whenever they could the Indians crossed from one mission to another along the same path in their pirogues. But as the passage is narrow the thick vegetation sometimes leads to surprises. An Indian stands in the bow with his machete, incessantly cutting branches blocking the canal. In the thickest part of the jungle we heard an odd noise. As the Indian cut at some branches a school of *toninas* – freshwater dolphins – surrounded our boat. The animals had hidden under branches of a ceiba and escaped through the flooded jungle, squirting up water and compressed air, living up to their name of 'blowers'. What a strange sight, inland, 300 to 400 leagues from the Orinoco and Amazon mouths!

May 1st. The Indians wanted to leave long before sunrise. We got up before them because we had hoped to see some stars, but in this humid, thick-jungled zone the nights were getting darker and darker as we approached the Río Negro and the interior of Brazil. We stayed in the river until dawn, fearing to get lost in the trees. But as soon as the sun rose we went through the flooded jungle to avoid the strong current. We reached the confluence of the Temi and Tuamini and went upstream on the latter south-west, reaching the Javita mission on the banks of the Tuamini at about eleven in the morning. It was at this Christian mission that we hoped to find help in carrying our pirogue to the Río Negro. A minor accident shows how fearful the little sagouin monkeys are. The noise of the 'blowers' scared one of them and it fell into the water. These monkeys can hardly swim, and we just managed to save it.

At Javita we had the pleasure of meeting a cultured, reasonable monk. We had to stay in his house the four or five days it took to carry our canoe along the Pimichín portage. Delay allowed us to visit the region, as well as rid us of an irritation that had been annoying us for the last two days: an intense itching in the articulations of our fingers and the backs of our hands. The missionary said this came from *aradores* (literally, 'ploughers') encrusted under our skin. With the aid of a magnifying glass we saw only lines, or whitish parallel furrows, which show why it is called an *arador*. The monks called for a mulatta who knew how to deal with all the little insects that burrow into human skin, from *niguas*, *nuches* and *coyas* to the *arador*. She was the *curandera*, the local doctor. She promised to remove all the insects irritating us, one by one. She heated the tip of a little stick on the fire and dug it into the furrows in our skin. After a long examination she announced, with that pedantic gravity peculiar to coloured people, that she had found an *arador*. I saw a little round bag that could have been the egg of the acaride. I should have been relieved when this clumsy mulatta poked out three or four more of these *aradores*. But as my skin was full of acarides I lost all patience with an operation that had already lasted until well into the night. The next day a Javita Indian cured us incredibly quickly. He brought a branch of a shrub called *uzao*, which had little shiny leathery leaves similar to the cassia. With its bark he prepared a cold bluish infusion that smelled of liquorice. When he beat it it became very frothy. Thanks to a washing with this *uzao* infusion the itching caused by the *aradores* disappeared. We were never able to find flowers or fruit of this *uzao*; the shrub seemed to belong to the leguminous family. We dreaded the pain caused by these *aradores* so much that we took various branches with us right up to San Carlos.

The mission of San Antonio was usually named after its Indian founder Javita. This captain, Javita, was still living when we arrived at the Río Negro. He was an Indian with a lively mind and body, and spoke Spanish with great ease. As he accompanied us on all our herborizations we obtained very useful information directly from him. In his youth he had seen all the Indian tribes of the region eat human flesh, and the Daricavanos, Puchirinavis and Manitibitanos seemed to him to be the greatest cannibals.[113] He believed that cannibalism was the effect of a system of vengeance; they only eat enemies captured in battle. It was very rare for an Indian to eat a close relation like a wife or an unfaithful mistress.

The climate of the Javita mission is extremely rainy. Rains fall all year round and the sky is constantly clouded. The missionary assured us that he had seen it rain for four and five months without stopping. I measured the rainfall on the 1st of May over five hours and registered 46.4 millimetres.

The Indians in Javita number about 160 and come from the Poimisano, Echinavis and Paraganis tribes. They make canoes out of the trunks of sassafras (*Ocotea cymbarum*), hollowing them out with fire and axes. These trees grow over 100 feet high, their wood is yellow, resinous, and never rots in water. It gives off a rich smell.

The jungle between Javita and Caño Pimichín holds a quantity of gigantic trees: ocoteas, laurels, *curvana*, *jacio*, *iacifate*, with a red wood like Brazil-wood, *guamufate*, the *Amyris caraña* and the *mani*. All these trees top 100 feet. As their trunks throw out branches more than 100 feet high we had trouble getting flowers and leaves. Though the ground was strewn with foliage we could not rely on the Indians to tell us from which tree or liana they came. In the midst of such natural riches, our herborizations caused us more regret than satisfaction. What we managed to collect seemed without interest in comparison with what we might have collected. It rained without a break for several months and Bonpland lost the greater part of the specimens he had dried with artificial heat. Usually Indians name trees by chewing the bark. They distinguish leaves better than flowers or fruit. Busy in locating timber for canoes they are inattentive to flowers. 'None of those tall trees have flowers or fruit,' they continually repeated. Like the botanists of antiquity, they denied what they had not bothered to observe. Tired by our questions they, in turn, made us impatient.

Every day we went into the jungle to see how our canoe was advancing over land. Twenty-three Indians were dragging it by placing logs as rollers. Usually this takes a day and a half, but our canoe was very large. As we also had to pass the cataracts a second time it was necessary to be very careful about not scraping it on the ground.

In this same jungle we at last were able to solve the problem of the supposed fossil rubber that the Indians call *dapicho*. The old Indian captain Javita led us to a small stream that runs into the Tuamini. He showed us how to dig some 2 to 3 feet deep into the muddy ground between the roots of two trees: the *jacio* and the *curvana*. The first is the hevea or siphonia of modern botany, which yields rubber; the second has pinnate leaves; its juice is milky but very diluted and barely sticky. It appears that *dapicho* is formed when the latex oozes out from the roots, especially when the tree is very old and begins to decay inside its trunk. The bark and sapwood crack to achieve naturally what man himself must do to gather latex.

Four days had passed and our boat still had not reached the Pimichín river landing-stage. 'There is nothing you lack in my mission,' Father Cerezo said to us. 'There are bananas and fish; at night mosquitoes do not bite; and the longer you stay the more likely it is that you will be able to observe stars. If your boat is wrecked during the portage we will get you another one and I will enjoy living a few more weeks *con gente blanca y de razón* (with white and rational people).' Despite our impatience, we listened with interest to this missionary's stories confirming all that we had been told about the spiritual state of the Indians in that region. They live in isolated clans of forty to fifty people under a chief. They recognize a common cacique only in times of war with neighbours. Between these clans mutual mistrust is great, as even those who live near each other speak different languages. Such is the labyrinth of these rivers that families settled themselves without knowing what tribe lived nearest to them. In Spanish Guiana a mountain or a jungle just half a league wide separates clans who would need two days navigating along rivers to meet. In the impenetrable jungle of the torrid zone rivers increase the dismemberment of great nations, favour the transition of dialects into separate languages, and nourish distrust and national hatred. Men avoid each other because they do not understand each other, and hate because they fear.

When we carefully examine this wild part of America we imagine how it was in primitive times when the land was peopled in stages, and seem to be present at the birth of human societies. In the New World we do not see the progressive developments of civilization, those moments of rest, those stations in the lives of a people. Such is the wonderful fertility of nature that the Indian's field is a patch of land. To clear it means setting fire to branches. To farm means dropping a few seeds into the ground. However far back in time you go in thought in these dense jungles the Indians have got their food from the earth, but as this earth produces abundantly on a small patch, without much work, these people often change their homes along the river banks. Still today, the Orinoco Indians travel with their seeds, transporting what they cultivate (*conucos*), like the Arab does his tents.

The tribes of the Upper Orinoco, the Atabapo and the Inirida, worship only the forces of nature. The principle of good is called Cachimana; it is the *manitu*, the great spirit, that controls the seasons and ripens fruit. Next to Cachimana there is the principle of evil, Jolokiamo, less powerful but more astute and, especially, more dynamic. When the jungle Indians go to missions it is difficult for them to conceive of a church or an image. 'These good people,' said our missionary, 'like only outdoor processions. Recently when I celebrated the village's saint's day the Inirida Indians came to mass. They told me: "Your god is locked into a house as if he was old and sick; our god is in the jungle, in fields, in the Sipapu mountains from where the rains come."' In the larger, and thus more barbarous tribes, peculiar religious societies are formed. Some of the older Indians claim to be better initiated in divine matters and guard the famous *botuto* that they play under palm trees to make the fruit ripen. On the Orinoco banks no images or idols can be found, but the *botuto*, the sacred trumpet, is worshipped. To be initiated into the mysteries of the *botuto* you must be pure and celibate. The initiated are subject to flagellations, fasting and other disciplinarian practices. There are few sacred trumpets. The most famous is found on a hill at the confluence of the Tomo and Guainia rivers. It is said it can be heard at a distance of 10 leagues. Father Cerezo assured us that Indians talk of this *botuto* as the object of a cult common to several neighbouring tribes. Fruit and alcoholic drinks are placed round this sacred trumpet. Sometimes the great spirit Cachimana himself blows the *botuto*, sometimes he speaks through whoever guards the instrument. As these tricks are very ancient (the fathers of our fathers, the Indians say) you should not be surprised that there are many believers. Women are not allowed to see the marvellous trumpet, and are excluded from all religious service. If one has the misfortune to see it she is mercilessly killed. The missionary told us that in 1798 he was lucky enough to save a young girl whom a jealous lover had accused of having followed the Indians who sounded the *botuto*. 'They would have murdered her publicly,' said Father Cerezo. 'How could she have protected herself from Indian fanaticism, in a country where it is so easy to be poisoned? I sent her away to one of the missions on the Lower Orinoco.'

On the evening of the 4th of May we were told that an Indian carrying our boat by the Pimichín portage had been bitten by a poisonous snake. The tall, strong man was brought to the mission, seriously ill. He had lost consciousness; nausea, giddiness and headaches followed his collapse. Many Indians ran to the sick man's hut, and gave him infusions of *raiz de mato*. We cannot say exactly what plant is used for this antidote. I really regret that travelling botanists are often unable to see the fruit or flower of plants useful to man when so many other plants can be seen daily in flower. This root is probably an apocynacea, perhaps the *Cerbera tevethia* that people in Cumaná call *lengua de mato* or *contra-culebra*, used against snake bites.

In the snake-bitten Indian's hut we found balls, some 2 to 3 inches thick, of an earthy, dirty salt called *chivi*, which Indians prepare meticulously. In Javita they make salt by burning the spadix and fruit of the *seje* palm. As well as this they also distil the ashes of the famous *cupana*, a liana. A missionary seldom travels without seeds prepared from the *cupana*. This preparation requires great care. The Indians break up the seeds and mix them with cassava flour wrapped in banana leaves and leave the mixture to ferment in water until it becomes a saffron-yellow colour. This yellow paste is dried in the sun and taken in the morning as a tea. The drink is bitter and stomachic, though I found it repulsive.

May 5th. We set off on foot following our boat, which had reached Caño Pimichín by portage. We had to wade through numerous streams. This journey demands caution because water snakes teem in the marshes. Indians pointed out tracks in the wet clay left by the small black bears that are so common on the Temi banks. They are different in size from the *Ursus americanus*: missionaries call them *oso carnicero* to differentiate them from the *oso palmero* or tamanoir (*Myrmecophaga jubata*) and the *oso hormiguero* or tamandua ant-eater. Two of these animals, which are good to eat, defend themselves by rising up on to their hind legs. Buffon's tamanoir is called *uaraca* by the Indians: they are irascible and brave, which is strange given that they are without teeth. As we advanced we came across some accessible clearings in the jungle. We picked new species of *coffea*, a *Galega piscatorum*, which Indians use like the jacquinia, and a composite plant of the Temi river, as a kind of *barbasco* to stun fish; and a large liana known locally as *bejuco de mavacure*, which gives the famous curare poison.

Towards night we reached a small farm in the port of Caño Pimichín. We were shown a cross near the river, which marked a spot 'where a poor Capuchin missionary had been killed by wasps'. Here people talk a lot about poisonous wasps and ants, but we were not able to find any. It is well known that in the torrid zone tiny bites bring on intense fevers. The death of the luckless monk was more likely the result of exhaustion and dampness than the poison in the wasps' stings, which the Indians also dread.

The Pimichín landing-stage is surrounded by a small cacao plantation. The trees are very robust and loaded with fruit all year round. When you think that the cacao tree is native to the Parima jungle, south of latitude 6, and that the humid climate of the Upper Orinoco suits this precious tree far more than the Caracas and New Barcelona air, which each year gets drier, then one regrets that this beautiful part of the world is in monks' hands as they discourage agriculture. We spent the night in a recently abandoned hut. An Indian family had left behind fishing tackle, earthen jars, mats woven with palm-tree petioles: all the household goods of these carefree people who are indifferent to property. Large amounts of *mani* (a mixture of the resins *moronobea* and *Amyris caraña*) lay in piles around the hut. This is used by Indians to pitch their canoes and to fix the bony ray spines on to their arrows. We found several jars filled with a vegetable milk, which is used as a varnish, called in the missions *leche para pintar* (milk for painting). They coat their furniture with this viscous juice. It leaves it a fine white; it thickens in contact with air to appear glossy. The more we study vegetable chemistry in the torrid zone the more we shall discover in remote spots still accessible to European trade, and already half prepared by the plants themselves, products that we believed belonged to the animal kingdom. These discoveries will be multiplied when, as the political state of the world now seems to show, European civilization flows towards the equinoctial regions of the New World.

As I have already written, the marshy plains between Javita and the Pimichín landing-stage are infamous for the quantity of poisonous snakes inhabiting them. Before we installed ourselves in the hut some Indians killed two *mapanares* snakes, about 5 feet long. It is a beautiful animal, with a white belly and red and black spots on its back, and very poisonous. As we could not hang our hammocks, and as there was lots of grass inside the hut, we were nervous about sleeping on the floor. In the morning as we lifted up a jaguar skin that one of our servants had slept on, another large snake appeared. Indians say these reptiles move slowly while not being chased, and approach man seeking his heat. I do not want to defend snakes, but I can assure you that if these poisonous animals were as aggressive as some think, in some places in America, like the Orinoco and the damp mountains of Choco, man would long ago have died out faced with the infinite number of snakes.

May 6th. We set off at dawn after inspecting the bottom of our canoe. We counted on our boat surviving another 300 leagues of navigation down the Río Negro, up the Casiquiare and back down the Orinoco again to Angostura. The Pimichín is about as wide as the Seine in Paris but little trees that like water narrow the river so much that only a canal of some 15 to 20 toises remains. This *caño* is navigable all year round. After following it for four hours we at last reached the Río Negro.

The morning was fresh and beautiful. For thirty-six days we had been locked up in a narrow canoe which was so unsteady that standing up suddenly from your seat would have capsized it. We had cruelly suffered from insect bites, but we had survived this unhealthy climate, and had crossed the many waterfalls and dykes that block the rivers and make the journey more dangerous than crossing the seas, without sinking. After all that we had endured, it gives me pleasure to speak of the joy we felt in having reached a tributary of the Amazon, of having passed the isthmus that separates the two great river systems. The uninhabited banks of the Casiquiare, covered in jungle, busied my imagination. In this interior of a new continent you get used to seeing man as not essential to the natural order. The earth is overloaded with vegetation: nothing prevents its development. An immense layer of mould manifests the uninterrupted action of organic forces. Crocodile and boa are the masters of the river; jaguar, peccary, the dante and monkeys cross the jungle without fear or danger, established there in an ancient heritage. This view of a living nature where man is nothing is both odd and sad. Here, in a fertile land, in an eternal greenness, you search in vain for traces of man; you feel you are carried into a different world from the one you were born into.

CHAPTER 20

The Río Negro – The frontier with Brazil – The Casiquiare –
The Orinoco bifurcation

If you compare the Río Negro with the Amazon, the River Plate or the Orinoco it is but a river of the second order. Possessing it has been, for centuries, of great political interest for the Spanish Government because it affords its rivals, the Portuguese, easy access into the Guianan missions to worry the Capitanía-General of Caracas in its southern limits. Three hundred years have passed in pointless territorial disputes. In different times, according to their degree of civilization, people have leaned either on papal authority or on astronomy. As they have generally been keener to prolong this dispute rather than solve it, only nautical science and geography have gained anything. When the affairs of Paraguay and the possession of the Sacramento colony became important for the two Courts of Madrid and Lisbon, commissioners were sent out to study the boundaries of the Orinoco, Amazon and River Plate. Besides the idle, who filled archives with their complaints and lawsuits, there were a few educated engineers and some naval officers acquainted with the means of determining the position of a place. The little we knew up to the end of the last century about the geography of the interior of the New Continent is due to these hard-working men. It is pleasing to remind ourselves that the sciences gained accidentally from these border commissions, often forgotten by the states that sent them out.

When one knows how unreliable the maps of America are, and when one has closely seen these uncultivated lands between the Jupura, the Río Negro, the Madeira, the Ucayale, the Branco river and the Cayenne coast that have been seriously disputed in Europe up until today, one is surprised how these litigations over who owns a few square leagues have so perseveringly dragged on.

The Río Negro and the Jupura are two tributaries of the Amazon, comparable in length to the Danube, whose upper parts belong to

Spain and whose lower reaches are occupied by Portugal. In these majestic rivers people have gathered in those places where civilization is most ancient. The banks of the Upper Jupura or Caqueta have been cultivated by missionaries who came down from the mountains of Popayan and Neiva. From Mocoa to the confluence with Caguan there are many Christian settlements, while in the Lower Jupura the Portuguese have founded hardly a few villages. Along the Río Negro, on the other hand, the Spaniards have not been able to rival their neighbours. How can they rely on a people so distanced from the province of Caracas? Steppes and virtually deserted jungle some 160 leagues thick separate the cultivated parts of the river bank from the four missions of Maroa, Tomo, Davipe and San Carlos.

When I was in Spanish Río Negro the conflict between the Courts of Lisbon and Madrid – even in peaceful times – had heightened the mistrust of the commanders of petty neighbouring forts. A commander with sixteen to eighteen soldiers tired 'the garrison' with his measures for safety, dictated by 'the important state of affairs'. If he were attacked he hoped 'to surround the enemy'. A people who have preserved a national hatred through the ages loves any excuse to vent it. We enjoy all that is passionate and dynamic, as much in our feelings as in the rival hatreds built up on age-old prejudices. On the banks of the Río Negro the Indians in the neighbouring Portuguese and Spanish villages hate each other. These poor people speak only their Indian languages and have no idea what happens 'on the other bank of the ocean, beyond the great salt pond', but the gowns of the missionaries are of different colours and this enrages them.

The rivalry between Spain and Portugal has contributed to the poor geographical knowledge about the tributary rivers of the Amazon. The Indians are excellent geographers and can outflank the enemy despite the limits on the maps and the forts. Each side prefers to conceal what it knows, and the love of what is mysterious, so common among ignorant people, perpetuates doubt. It is also known that different Indian tribes in this labyrinth of rivers give rivers different names that all mean 'river', 'great water' and 'current'. I have often been puzzled trying to determine synonyms after examining the most intelligent Indians through an interpreter. Three or four languages are spoken in the same mission, it is hard to make witnesses agree. Our maps are full of arbitrary names. The desire to leave no void in maps in order to give them an appearance of accuracy has caused rivers to be created whose names are not synonymous.[114]

After entering the Río Negro by the Pimichín, and passing the small cataract at the confluence of the two rivers, we saw the mission of Maroa a quarter of a league off. This village of 150 Indians appeared prosperous and cheerful. We bought some beautiful live toucans (*piapoco*); birds whose 'intelligence' can be trained, like our ravens. Above Maroa we passed the mouths of the Aquio and of the Tomo. We did not enter the Tomo mission, but Father Zea told us with a smile that the Indians of Tomo and Maroa had been in full insurrection because monks had tried to force them to dance the famous 'dance of the devils'. The missionary had wanted to hold the ceremony in which the *piastres* (who are shamans, doctors and conjurors) evoke the evil spirit Jolokiamo, but in a burlesque way. He thought that the 'dance of the devils' would show the neophytes that Jolokiamo no longer had any power over them. Some young Indians, believing the missionary's promises, agreed to act as devils; they were decked out in black and yellow feathers and jaguar skins with long tails. The church square had been surrounded by soldiers from other missions to make the missionary more redoubtable. Indians who were unsure about the dance and the impotence of the evil spirits were brought along. But the oldest of the Indians managed to imbue all the younger ones with a superstitious dread and they decided to flee *al monte*. The missionary had to postpone his project of mocking the Indian demon.

After two hours' navigation we reached the mouth of the Tomo and the small mission of Davipe, founded in 1755 by an army lieutenant, and not by monks. Father Morillo, the missionary on the spot, with whom we stayed a few hours, received us with great hospitality, and even offered us some Madeira wine. As far as luxury foods go we would have preferred wheat bread; the absence of bread is felt far more over a long time than any alcoholic drink. Every now and then the Portuguese bring small quantities of Madeira wine to the Río Negro. But the word *madera* in Spanish means 'wood', so some monks, poorly versed in geography, were reluctant to celebrate mass with Madeira wine; they took it for a fermented liquor from some local tree, like palm-tree wine, and asked the superior of their order to decide if the *vino de Madera* was in fact a wine made from grapes or the sweet juice from a tree (*de algún palo*). Already, from the beginning of the conquest, the question of whether priests could celebrate mass with another fermented liquor similar to wine had been raised. The question, predictably, was decided negatively.

[margin handwritten note: all these explorers religions]

At Davipe we bought provisions, including chicken and a pig. This purchase greatly interested the Indians, who had not eaten meat for ages. They urged us to leave for Dapa Island where the pig was to be killed and roasted overnight. In the convent we just had time to examine great piles of the *mani* resin and rope from the *chiquichiqui* palm, which deserves to be better known in Europe.

A little above the Davipe mission the Río Negro receives a branch of the Casiquiare whose existence is a remarkable phenomenon in the history of river branching. This branch emerges from the Casiquiare, north of Vasiva, under the name Itinivi; and after crossing a flat, virtually uninhabited country some 25 leagues long, pours into the Río Negro under the name of Río Conorichite. It seemed to me, near its mouth, to be 120 toises wide, and added large quantities of white waters to the black waters. Even though the Conorichite current is very fast, you shorten the journey from Davipe to Esmeralda by three days using this canal. It is not surprising to find a double communication between the Casiquiare and the Río Negro when you recall that so many American rivers form deltas when they meet other rivers. In this way the Branco and the Jupura pour into the Río Negro and Amazon through many branches. At the confluence with the Jupura there is another more extraordinary phenomenon. Before joining the Amazon this river, which is its main recipient, sends three branches called Uaranapu, Manhama and Avateprana to the Jupura, which is none other than its tributary. The Amazon thus sends its waters into the Jupura before receiving the waters of the latter back.

The Río Conorichite played an important role in the time when the Portuguese traded in slaves in Spanish territory. The slave-traders went up the Casiquiare and the Caño Mee to Conorichite; then they carried their canoes over land to the Rochuelas de Manuteso, and thus reached the Atabapo. This abominable trade lasted until about 1756. The Caribs, a warrior and trading people, received knives, hooks, mirrors and glass objects from the Dutch and Portuguese. In exchange, they urged Indian caciques to fight each other, and then bought their prisoners of war, or cunningly grabbed them, or used force to get them. These Carib incursions covered an enormous region.

We left the Conorichite mouth and the Davipe mission and at sunset reached the island of Dapa, picturesquely situated in the middle of the river. We were amazed to find cultivated ground and, on top of a hill, an Indian hut. Four Indians sat round a small brushwood fire eating a kind of white paste spotted with black that aroused our curiosity. These black spots proved to be *vachacos*, large ants, whose abdomen resemble lumps of grease. They had been dried and blackened by smoking. We saw several bags of ants hanging above the fire. These good people paid little attention to us, yet there were more than fourteen Indians lying completely naked in hammocks hung one above the other in the hut. When Father Zea arrived they received him joyously. Two young Indian women came down from their hammocks to make cassava cakes for us. Through an interpreter we asked them if the land on the island was fertile. They answered saying that cassava grew poorly but that it was a good place for ants. *Vachacos* were the subsistence diet of Río Negro and Guianan Indians. They are not eaten out of greed but because, in the missionary's terms, the fat is very nutritious. When the cakes were ready, Father Zea, whose fever seemed to increase rather than decrease his appetite, asked for a bag of smoked ants to be brought to him. Then he mixed these crushed insects into the cassava flour and urged us to taste. It tasted rather like rancid butter mixed with breadcrumbs. The cassava was not acid, but vestiges of our European prejudices restrained us from praising what the missionary called 'an excellent ant pâté'.

As rain was pouring down we had to sleep in the overcrowded hut. The Indians slept only from eight at night to two in the morning; the rest of the time they chatted and prepared their bitter *cupana* drink, poking the fire and complaining of the cold, even though the temperature was 21 °C. This custom of staying awake, even of getting up four or five hours before dawn, is common to the Guiana Indians.

Despite the speed of the current and the effort of our rowers it took us twelve hours on the river to reach the San Carlos fort on the Río Negro. We left the mouth of the Casiquiare on our left, and the little island of Cumarai on our right. Here they believe that the fort lies on the equator itself, but after my observations made on the Culimacari rock, it lies on 1.54′ 11″.

At San Carlos we lodged with the fort commander, a lieutenant in the militia. From a gallery in the house we enjoyed an agreeable view on to three long islands covered in thick vegetation. The river lies straight from north to south, as if it had been dug by man. The constantly covered sky gives these countries a solemn, sombre quality. In the village we found some *juvia* trunks: it is the majestic tree that gives what in Europe are called Brazil-nuts. We made it known under the name *Bertholletia excelsa*.[115] The trees reach 30 feet in eight years.

The military establishment of this frontier consists of seventeen soldiers, ten of whom are detached in neighbouring missions. The humidity is such that hardly four rifles work. The Portuguese have twenty-five better-dressed and better-armed men in the fort of San Jose de Maravitanos. In the San Carlos mission we found a *garita*, or square house, built with unbaked bricks, with six rooms. The fort, or as they prefer to call it, the Castillo de San Felipe, is on the right bank of the Río Negro, *vis-à-vis* San Carlos. The commander showed some scruples, and refused to allow Bonpland and myself to visit the fort as our passports clearly stated we could measure mountains and perform trigonometric operations on land, but we could not see inside fortified places. Our fellow traveller, Don Nicolás Soto, a Spanish officer, was luckier, and was allowed to cross the river.

The passage from the mouth of the Río Negro to Grand Para took only twenty to twenty-five days, so we could have gone down the Amazon as far as the Brazilian coast just as easily as returning by the Casiquiare to Caracas. We were told at San Carlos that political circumstances made it difficult to cross from Spanish to Portuguese colonies, but we did not know until our return to Europe what danger we would have been exposed to had we gone as far as Barcellos. It was known in Brazil, probably through newspapers, whose indiscretion is not helpful for travellers, that I was going to visit the Río Negro missions and examine the natural canal uniting the two river systems. In these deserted jungles the only instruments ever seen had been carried by the boundary commissioners. The Portuguese Government agents could not conceive how a sensible man could exhaust himself 'measuring lands that did not belong to him'. Orders had been issued to arrest me, seize my instruments, and especially my astronomical observations, so dangerous to the safety of the State. We were to be led along the Amazon to Grand Para, and then back to Lisbon. Fortunately, the Lisbon Government instantly ordered that I should not be disturbed but rather encouraged.

In the lands of the Río Negro Indians we found several of those green stones known as 'Amazon stones' because Indians claim that they come from a country of 'women without men', or 'women living alone'. Superstition attaches great importance to these stones, which are worn as amulets round the neck as popular belief claims they protect wearers from nervous diseases, fevers and poisonous snake bites. Because of this they have for centuries been traded between the Indians of the northern Orinoco and those in the south. The Caribs made them known on the coast. Up to a few years ago during debates about quinine these green stones were considered an efficient febrifuge in enlightened Europe; if we can count on the credulity of Europeans, there is nothing odd about Spanish colonizers appreciating these amulets as much as the Indians, or that these stones are sold at high prices. Usually they are shaped into cylinders with holes down the sides, and covered in inscriptions and figures. But it is not today's Indians who have perforated holes in such hard stones or carved animals and fruit. This work suggests another, older culture. The actual inhabitants of the torrid zone are so ignorant of how to carve hard stone that they think the green stone comes from soft earth, and that it hardens when carved.

The history of the jade, or green Guianan stones, is intimately linked with that of the warlike women named Amazons by sixteenth-century travellers. La Condamine has produced many testimonies in favour of this tradition. Since returning from the Orinoco and Amazon I have often been asked in Paris if I agreed with that learned man, or thought that he said what he said to satisfy a public eager for novelties. A taste for the marvellous and a wish to describe the New World with some of the tones of antiquity no doubt contributed to the reputation of the Amazons. But this is not enough to reject a tradition shared by many isolated tribes. I would conclude that women, tired of the state of slavery in which men have held them, united together and kept their independence as warriors. They received visits once a year from men, and probably killed off their male babies. This society of women may have been quite powerful in one part of Guiana. But such is the disposition of man's mind that, in the long succession of travellers discovering and writing about the marvels of the New World, each one readily declared that he had seen what earlier ones had announced.

We passed three nights in San Carlos. I counted the nights because I stayed awake hoping to be able to observe stars. But I had to leave the place without ever once being able to effect a trusty observation of the geographical latitude of the place.

May 10th. Overnight our canoe was loaded and we set off a little before dawn to go up the Río Negro to the mouth of the Casiquiare and begin our researches on the true course of this river linking the Orinoco and Amazon. The morning was beautiful, but as the heat rose the sky began to cloud over. The air is so saturated with water in these forests that water bubbles become visible at the slightest increase of evaporation on the earth's surface. As there is no breeze the humid strata are not replaced and renewed by drier air. This clouded sky made us gloomier and gloomier. Through this humidity Bonpland lost the plants he had collected; for my part I feared finding the same Río Negro mists in the Casiquiare valley. For more than half a century nobody in the missions has doubted the existence of communications between the two great river systems: the important aim of our journey was reduced to fixing the course of the Casiquiare by astronomic means, especially at its point of entry into the Río Negro, and its bifurcation with the Orinoco. Without sun or stars this aim would have been frustrated, and we would have been uselessly exposed to long, weary deprivations. Our travelling companions wanted to return by the shortest journey, along the Pimichín and its small rivers; but Bonpland preferred, like myself, to persist in the original plan we had traced out while crossing the Great Cataracts. We had already travelled by canoe from San Fernando de Apure to San Carlos along the Apure, Orinoco, Atabapo, Temi, Tuamini and Río Negro for over 180 leagues. In entering the Orinoco by the Casiquiare we still had some 320 leagues to cover from San Carlos to Angostura. It would have been a shame to let ourselves be discouraged by the fear of a cloudy sky and the Casiquiare mosquitoes. Our Indian pilot, who had recently visited Mandavaca, promised us sun and 'those great stars that eat up clouds' once we had left the black waters of the Guaviare. So we managed to carry out our first plan and returned to San Fernando along the Casiquiare. Luckily for our researches the Indian's prediction was fulfilled. The white waters brought us a clear sky, stars, mosquitoes and crocodiles.

Having reached the south of the Caravine *raudal* we saw that the winding Casiquiare again approached San Carlos. By land the distance from the San Francisco Solano mission, where we slept, is only 2.5 leagues, but by river it was 7 or 8. I spent part of the night outside, vainly waiting for stars to appear.

The San Francisco mission, situated on the left bank of the Casiquiare, was named after one of the leaders of the boundary expedition, Don Joseph Solano. This educated officer never got any further than San Fernando de Atabapo; he had never seen the Río Negro waters or the Casiquiare, or the Orinoco east of the Guaviare. Ignorance of the Spanish language drove geographers to locate erroneously on the famous La Cruz Olmedilla map the 400-league route made by Joseph Solano to the sources of the Orinoco. The San Francisco mission was founded not by monks but by military authorities. Following the boundary expedition, villages were built wherever an officer or a corporal stopped with his soldiers. Some of the Indians withdrew and remained independent; others, whose chiefs were caught, joined the missions. Where there was no church they were happy to raise a great red wooden cross, and to build a *casa fuerte*, that is, a house with long beams placed horizontally on top of each other, next to it. This house had two floors; upstairs were placed small cannons; downstairs two soldiers lived, served by Indian families. Tamed Indians established themselves around the *casa fuerte*. In the event of an attack soldiers would gather the Indians together by sounding the horn, or the baked-earth *botuto*. These were the nineteen so-called Christian establishments founded by Don Antonio Santos. Military posts had no effect in civilizing the Indians living there. They figured on maps and in mission works as *pueblos* (villages) and as *reducciones apostólicas*.

The Indians we found at San Francisco Solano belong to two different tribes: the Pacimonales and the Cheruvichanenas. The latter came from a prestigious tribe living on the Tomo river, near the Manivas of the Upper Guiana, so I tried to find out from them about the upper course of the Río Negro, and where I could find its sources; but my interpreter could not make them understand the true sense of my question. They just repeated over and over again that the sources of the Río Negro and the Inirida were as close together as 'two fingers on a hand'. In one of the Pacimonales's huts we bought two great, beautiful birds: a toucan (*piapoco*), similar to the *Ramphastos erythrorynchos*, and an *ana*, a kind of macaw, with purple feathers like the *Psittacus macao*. In our canoe we already had seven parrots, two cock-of-the-rocks (*pipra*), a motmot, two guans or *pavas del monte*, two *manaviris* (cercoleptes or *Viverra caudivolvula*), and eight monkeys, of which three were new species. Father Zea was not too happy about the rate our zoological collection increased day by day, although he kept that to himself. The toucan resembles the raven in its habits and intelligence; it is a brave creature and easy to tame. Its long, strong beak serves as its defence. It becomes master of the house; steals whatever it can, frequently takes a bath, and likes fishing on the river bank. The one we bought was very young, yet throughout our journey it took malicious delight in molesting the sad, irritable monkeys. The structure of the toucan's beak does not oblige it to swallow food by throwing it into the air as some naturalists claim. It is true that it does have problems lifting food from the ground, but once food is seized in its long beak it throws back its head so that it swallows perpendicularly. When this bird wants to drink it makes an odd gesture; monks say it makes the sign of the cross over the water. Because of this creoles have baptized the toucan with the strange name of Diostedé (May God give it to you).

Most of our animals were locked in small reed cages, but some ran freely about the boat. When it threatened to rain the macaws started a terrible racket, the toucan tried to fly to the shore to fish, and the titi monkeys ran to hide under Father Zea's long sleeves. These spectacles were common, and allowed us to forget the torment of mosquitoes. To camp at night we built a kind of leather box (*petaca*), which held our provisions; next to it we placed our instruments and the animal cages; around this we hung our hammocks and a little further out the Indians' hammocks. Around the outside we lit fires to scare off jungle jaguars. The Indians often spoke of a small nocturnal animal with a long snout, which traps young parrots in their nests and uses its hands to eat like monkeys. They call it *guachi*; it is doubtless a coati. Missionaries forbid the eating of *guachi* flesh. Superstition claims that it is an aphrodisiac.

May 11th. We went on shore. A few steps from the beach Bonpland discovered an *almendrón*, a majestic *Bertholletia excelsa*. The Indians assured us that this tree on the Casiquiare banks was unknown at San Francisco Solano, Vasiva and Esmeralda. They did not think that this 60-foot-high tree could have been accidentally planted by some traveller. Experiments made at San Carlos have shown how rare it is to make a bertholletia germinate because of its ligneous pericarp, and the oil in the nut, which turns the seed rancid. Perhaps this was part of a forest of inland bertholletia.[116]

May 12th. We set off from the Culimacari rock at half past one in the morning. The plague of mosquitoes was intensifying as we left the Río Negro. In the Casiquiare valley there are no *zancudos*, but insects from the Simulium and the Tipulary families are all the more numerous and poisonous. Before reaching the Esmeralda mission we still had eight more nights to spend out in the open in this unhealthy, humid country. Our pilot was happy to count on the hospitality of the Mandavaca missionary and shelter in the village of Vasiva. We struggled against the current, which flowed at some 8 miles an hour. Where we aimed to rest was only some 3 leagues away, yet we took fourteen hours to make this short journey, despite the effort of our rowers.

We crossed some violent rapids before reaching the Mandavaca mission. The village, also called Quirabuena, has only sixty inhabitants. Most of these Christian settlements are in such a deplorable condition that over a stretch of 50 leagues we counted barely 200 people. The river banks were more populated before the arrival of the missionaries. The Indians retreated into the jungle towards the east as the plains on the west are uninhabited. They live for part of the year off the large ants I have already described. In Mandavaca we met a good missionary who had spent 'over twenty years of mosquitoes in the Casiquiare jungles' and whose legs were so spotted by mosquito bites that you could hardly see he was a white. He spoke of his isolation, and the sad necessity that forced him to witness how the most atrocious crimes went unpunished. In Vasiva a few years before an Indian chief had eaten one of his wives after taking her from her *conuco* and fattening her up with plenty of food. If the Guiana Indians eat human flesh it is not because of privations, or during rituals, but out of vengeance after a victory or, as the missionaries say, 'out of their perverted greed'. Victory over an enemy horde is celebrated with a feast where parts of prisoners' corpses are eaten. During the night an enemy family is attacked, or an enemy found by chance in the jungle is killed by a poisoned arrow. The corpse is cut up and brought home like a trophy. Civilization has led man to sense the unity of the human race, the bonds that link him to customs and languages which he does not know. Wild Indians hate all those who do not belong to their tribe or family. Indians who are at war with a neighbouring tribe hunt them as we would animals in the wood. When they see unknown jungle Indians arrive at their mission they say: 'They must be related to us as we understand what they say.' They recognize only their own family: a tribe is but a reunion of relations. They recognize family and kin ties, but not those of humanity in general. No feelings of compassion prevent them from killing women or children of an enemy tribe. These latter are their favourite food after a skirmish or ambush.

The hate that Indians show for nearly all human beings who speak another language, and are considered to be barbarians of an inferior race, often erupts in the missions after years of slumber. A few months before our arrival at Esmeralda, an Indian born in the jungle behind the Duida was travelling with another who previously, having been captured by the Spaniards on the banks of the Ventuario, had lived peacefully in the village or, as they say, 'under the sound of a bell' *(debajo de la campana)*. This latter Indian had to walk slowly because of a fever he had caught in the mission, usually due to a sudden change in diet. Annoyed by this delay his companion killed him and hid the corpse under some thickets near Esmeralda. The crime, like so many others committed among the Indians, would not have been discovered if the murderer had not proposed to celebrate a feast the following day. He tried to persuade his sons, who were born in the mission and were Christians, to accompany him to the jungle and fetch bits of the corpse to eat. The boys had difficulty in stopping him. The family squabble alerted a soldier who found out what the Indians had tried to conceal.

'You cannot imagine,' said the old Mandavaca missionary, 'how perverse this *familia de indios* (family of Indians) is. You accept individuals from another tribe into your mission; they seem tame, honest, good workers; you let them out on a foray (*entrada*) to capture wild Indians and you can scarcely stop them throttling all they can and hiding pieces of the corpses.' We had with us in our pirogue an Indian who had escaped from the Guaisia river. In a few weeks he had become very civilized. At night he helped us prepare our astronomical instruments. He was as cheerful as he was intelligent, and we were ready to employ him. Imagine our disappointment when through an interpreter we heard him say that 'Marimonda monkey meat, although blacker, had the same taste as human meat.' He assured us that 'his *relations* – that is, his tribal brothers – preferred to eat the palms of human hands, as well as those of bears'. As he spoke he gestured to emphasize his brutal greed. We asked this young, pacifistic man through our interpreter if he still felt a desire to 'eat a Cheruvichanena Indian' and he answered calmly that 'in the mission he would eat only what he saw *los padres* (the fathers) eating'. It is no point reproaching Indians about this abominable practice. In the eyes of a Guaisia Indian, a Cheruvichanena Indian is totally alien to him; to kill one was not morally very different from killing a jaguar. Eating what the fathers ate in the mission was simply convenience. If Indians escape to rejoin their tribes, or are driven by hunger, they quickly fall back into cannibalism.

The Casiquiare Indians, though easily reverting to barbaric customs, show some intelligence in the missions, work well and learn Spanish. As most missions have two or three tribes speaking different languages the language of the missionaries lets them communicate with each other. I saw a Poignave Indian talk in Castilian with a Guahibo, though both had left the jungle only three months before. Every quarter of an hour one spoke a carefully prepared phrase in which the verb, following the grammar of their own languages, was always a gerund ('When me seeing the father, the father me saying . . .').

Both here and in the Río Negro the humidity and consequent quantity of insects make all agriculture impossible. Everywhere you see large ants, which march in packed columns and devour all cultivated plants that are soft and juicy, while in the jungle they can find only woody stalks. If a missionary wants to plant lettuce, or any other European vegetable, he has to hang his garden in the air. He fills an old canoe with good earth and hangs it 4 feet above the ground with rope made from *chiquichiqui* palm or, more commonly, rests it on some scaffolding.

May 13th. We left Mandavaca at half past two in the morning. After six hours of travelling we passed the mouth of the Idapa or Siapa on the east. It rises on the Uturan mountain. It has white waters. Its upper course has been strangely misrepresented on La Cruz's and Surville's maps, which all later maps have imitated. We stopped near the Cunuri *raudal*. The noise of the little cataract got much louder during the night. Our Indians said that meant certain rain. It fell before sunrise. However, the araguato monkeys' continuous wails had warned us that rain was approaching.

May 14th. Mosquitoes and ants chased us from the river bank before two in the morning. We thought that ants could not climb the ropes on which we hung our hammocks; but whether this was inexact, or whether they fell on top of us from branches, we struggled to rid ourselves of these annoying insects. The more we advanced the narrower the river became. Its banks were so muddy that Bonpland could only reach the trunk of a *Carolinea princeps* covered with enormous purple flowers with extreme effort. This tree is the most beautiful in these jungles.

From the 14th to the 21st of May we slept out in the open air; but I cannot point out where exactly we camped. This country is so wild and so deserted that, apart from a few rivers, the Indians could not name anything from my compass bearings. No observations of stars could reassure me about our latitude. After passing the place where the Itinivini separates from the Casiquiare to go west towards the granite Daripabo hills, we found the muddy banks covered with bamboo. These arborescent *gramina* rise up to 20 feet; their stalks arch towards the top. It is a new species of long-leafed bamboo. Bonpland rejoiced to find one in flower. Nothing is more rare in the New World than seeing these gigantic *gramina* in flower. Mutis[117] herbalized for over twenty years without ever finding one in flower.

Our first camp, above the Vasiva, was easily set up. We found a corner of dry land free from shrubs at the south of the *caño* Curamuni in a place where we saw capuchin monkeys, so easily identified with their black beards and sad, wild look, as they climbed along horizontal branches of a genipap. The next five nights became more and more uncomfortable as we approached the Orinoco bifurcation. The exuberance of the vegetation increases to such a point that it is hard to imagine, even when you have got used to the Tropics. There is no beach; a palisade of bunched trees becomes the river bank. You see a channel some 200 toises wide bordered with two enormous walls carpeted with leaves and liana. We tried to get ashore but could not even get out of the canoe. Sometimes at sunset we would follow the bank for an hour to reach, not a clearing, but a less overgrown patch where our Indians with their machetes could cut down enough to let thirteen or fourteen people camp. We could not spend the night in the pirogue. The mosquitoes that tormented us during the day crowded towards evening under the *toldo*, that is, the roof made of palm leaves that sheltered us from rain. Never were our hands or faces more swollen. Even Father Zea, boasting that in his cataract missions he had the biggest and bravest (*los más valientes*) mosquitoes, agreed that these Casiquiare bites were the most painful he had ever felt. In the middle of thick jungle it was difficult to find any wood to light our fire; the branches are so full of sap in this equatorial region where it always rains that they hardly burn. Where there are no arid beaches we hardly ever came across that old wood which Indians say has been 'cooked in the sun'. A fire was only necessary to scare away jungle animals: we had such a low stock of food that we did not need wood to cook.

On the evening of the 18th of May we reached a place on the bank where wild cacao trees grew. The seed of these cacao trees is small and bitter; the Indians suck the pulp and throw away the seed, which is then picked up by mission Indians who sell it to those who are not too fussy about how to prepare cocoa. 'This is Puerto del Cacao

(Cacao Port)', said our pilot. 'Here the Fathers sleep on their way to Esmeralda to buy *sarbacans* (blowpipes to shoot poison arrows) and *juvias* (Brazil-nuts).' Only five boats a year pass along the Casiquiare. Since Maypures, that is, for a month, we had not met anyone on the rivers outside the missions. We spent the night south of Lake Duractumuni in a forest of palm trees. It poured with rain, but the pothoses, arums and lianas made such a thick trellis that we sheltered underneath.

Of all body complaints those that persist without change are the worst; against them the only cure is patience. It is likely that the emanations of the Casiquiare jungle infected Bonpland with such a serious disease that he almost died when we reached Angostura. Luckily neither he nor I suspected this at the time. The view of the river and the hum of insects became monotonous; but our natural good temper did not snap, and helped us survive this long journey. We discovered that eating small bits of dry cacao ground without sugar and drinking a lot of river water appeased our hunger for several hours. Ants and mosquitoes annoyed us more than hunger and humidity.

We passed the night of the 20th of May, the last on the Casiquiare, near the bifurcation with the Orinoco. We hoped to make some astronomical observations as we saw extraordinary shooting stars visible through the mist. Indians, who do not embellish their imagination through words, call shooting stars the 'piss of the stars', and dew the 'spit of the stars'. But the clouds thickened and prevented us from seeing both meteors and stars.

We had been warned that we would find the insects at Esmeralda 'even more cruel and voracious' than in this branch of the Orinoco; despite this we looked forward to sleeping in an inhabited place, and botanizing a little at last. At our last camp on the Casiquiare we had quite a fright. I presume to describe something that might not greatly interest a reader, but should be part of a journal of incidents on a river in such wild country. We slept on the edge of the jungle. At midnight the Indians warned us that they had heard a jaguar growl very close to us; it seemed to be up a nearby tree. The jungle is so thick here that only animals who climb trees exist. As our fires gave off plenty of light, and as we had become hardened to fear, we did not worry too much about the jaguar's cries. The smell and barking of one of our dogs had attracted the jaguar. This dog, a large mastiff, had barked at the start, but when the jaguar approached the dog howled and hid under our hammocks. Since the Apure we had been used to this alternating bravery and fear in a young, tame and affectionate dog. We had a terrible shock the next morning. When getting ready to leave, the Indians told us that our dog had disappeared! There was no doubt that the jaguar had killed it. Perhaps when it no longer heard the roars it had wandered off along the shore, or perhaps we slept so deeply we never heard the dog's yelps. We were often told that on the Orinoco and the Magdalena old jaguars were so clever that they hunted their prey in the very camps, and twisted their victims' necks so that they could not shout. We waited a long while in case the dog was merely lost. Three days later we returned to the same place and again heard a jaguar roar. So the dog, which had been our companion from Caracas, and had often swum away from crocodiles, had ended up being devoured in the jungle.

On the 21st of May we again entered the bed of the Orinoco, 3 leagues above the Esmeralda mission. It had been a month since we had left this river near the mouth of the Guaviare. We still had 750 leagues to navigate as far as Angostura, but it was downstream, and this made the thought less painful. Going downstream you follow the middle of the river bed where there are less mosquitoes. Going upstream you are forced to stick close to the banks, to benefit from eddies and counter-currents, where the jungle and organic detritus thrown up on the beaches attract insects of the Tipulary family. The point where the Orinoco bifurcates is incredibly imposing. High granitic mountains rise on the northern shore, among them the Maraguaca and the Duida. There are no mountains at all on the left bank, or to the west or east as far as the mouth of the Tamatama.[118]

CHAPTER 21

The Upper Orinoco from its confluence with the Guaviare –
Second crossing of the Atures and Maypures cataracts – The
Lower Orinoco between the mouth of the Apure river and
Angostura, capital of Spanish Guiana

I still have to refer to the most isolated of the Christian colonies of the Upper Orinoco. Opposite the point where the Orinoco bifurcates there is a granite mass called Duida, in the form of an amphitheatre. The missionaries call this mountain of nearly 8,000 feet a volcano. Because its slopes on the south and west are very steep it looks grand. The peak is bare and stony; but everywhere else in the less steep slopes earth has collected and jungles seem to hang from the air. At the foot of the Duida lies the Esmeralda mission, a small village of eighty people, surrounded by a lovely plain, and fed by little black-watered but limpid streams; a proper prairie with groups of mauritia palms, the American breadfruit. As you approach the mountain the marshy plain becomes a savannah that stretches along the lower reaches of the chain. There you find enormous, delicious pineapples. These bromelia always grow solitary among the grasses.

There is no missionary at Esmeralda: the monk appointed to celebrate mass here lives in Santa Bárbara, some 50 leagues away. To come upstream takes him four days and he only appears five or six times a year. An old soldier welcomed us in a friendly way; he took us for Catalan shopkeepers come to trade with the missions. When he saw our wads of paper for drying plants he laughed at our naïve ignorance: 'You have come to a land where nobody is going to buy such a thing. Here few write. We use dried maize, banana and *vijaho* (heliconia) leaves, as you do paper in Europe, to wrap up small objects like needles, hooks and other things you have to look after carefully.' This old soldier was both the civil and spiritual authority. He taught children, if not the catechism, then at least how to say the rosary, and he tolled the bells as a hobby. Sometimes he used the sacristan's stick in ways that did not amuse the Indians.

Despite the size of the Esmeralda mission three languages are spoken: Catarpen, Idapaminare and Maquiritare. This last is the dominant language of the Upper Orinoco, like Carin in the Lower, Otomac near the Apure, and Tamanac and Maypure at the Great Cataracts. It was strange to see many *zambos*, mulattos and other coloured people who, through vanity, call themselves Spaniards, and think that they are white because they are not red like the Indians. These people lead a miserable life; most of them had been banished to here (*desterrados*). To found a territory in the interior as quickly as possible, in order to keep the Portuguese out, Solano had rounded up as many vagabonds and criminals as he could and sent them to the Upper Orinoco where they lived with the unhappy Indians lured from the jungle. A mineralogical error had made Esmeralda famous. The Duida and Maraguaca granite holds superficial seams of a pretty rock crystal, sometimes quite transparent and sometimes coloured by chlorite or mixed with actonite and mistaken for diamonds and emeralds. In those mountains, so close to the sources of the Orinoco, everybody dreamed of El Dorado, which could not be far off, with Lake Parime and the ruins of the great city of Manoa.

The vagabonds of the plains had as little interest in working as the Indians, who were obliged to live 'under the sound of the church bell'. The former used their pride to justify their indolence. In the missions every coloured person who is not completely black like an African, or copper-coloured like an Indian, calls himself a Spaniard; belongs to the *gente de razón*, that is, gifted with reason, and this 'reason', which is both arrogant and lazy, tells the whites and those who think themselves white that agriculture is work for slaves, *poitos* and newly converted Indians. As these American colonists were separated from their homelands by jungles and savannahs they soon dispersed, some going north to Caura and Caroní, and others south to the Portuguese possessions. Thus, the fame of the emerald mines of Duida died out, and Esmeralda became a cursed place of banishment for monks where the dreadful cloud of mosquitoes darkens the atmosphere all year round. When the father superior of the mission wants to upbraid his monks he threatens to send them to Esmeralda: 'That is,' say the monks, 'to be condemned to mosquitoes, to be devoured by *zancudos gritones* (shouting flies), which God seems to have created to punish man.'

Esmeralda is the most famous place on the Orinoco for the making of the active poison that is used in war, out hunting and, surprisingly, as a remedy against gastric illnesses. The poison of the Amazonian Tikuna, the *upas-tieuté* of Java and the Guianan curare are the most poisonous substances known. Already by the sixteenth century Raleigh had heard the word *urari* spoken, signifying a vegetable substance used to poison arrows. However, nothing was known for sure in Europe about this poison.[119]

When we arrived in Esmeralda, most of the Indians were returning from an excursion they had made beyond the Padamo river to pick *juvias*, the fruit of the bertholletia, and a liana that gives curare. Their return was celebrated with a feast called in this mission the *fiesta de las juvias*, which resembles our harvest festivals. Women had prepared plenty of alcohol and for two days you met only drunk Indians. Among people who attach importance to palm-tree fruits and other useful trees, the period when these are harvested is marked by public celebrations. We were lucky to find an Indian slightly less drunk than others, who was making curare with the recently picked plants. He was the chemist of the locality. Around him we saw large clay boilers used to cook the vegetable juices, as well as shallow vessels used for evaporation, and banana leaves rolled into filters to separate the liquid from the fibres. The Indian who was to teach us was known in the mission as master of the poison, *amo del curare*; he had that same formal and pedantic air that chemists were formerly accused of in Europe. 'I know,' he said, 'that whites have the secret of making soap, and that black powder which scares away the animals you hunt when you miss. But the curare that we prepare from father to son is superior to all that you know over there. It is the sap of a plant that "kills silently", without the victim knowing where it comes from.'

The chemical operation, whose importance is exaggerated by the master of the curare, seemed to us very simple. The *bejuco* used to make the poison in Esmeralda has the same name as in the Javita jungles. It is the *bejuco de mavacure*, which is found in abundance east of the mission on the left bank of the Orinoco. Although the bundles of *bejuco* that we found in the Indian's hut were stripped of leaves, there was no doubt that they came from the same plant of the *Strychnos* genus that we examined in the Pimichín jungles. They use either fresh *mavacure* or *mavacure* that has been dried for several weeks. The sap of a recently cut liana is not considered as poisonous; perhaps it only really works when it is very concentrated. The bark and part of the sapwood contain this terrible poison. With a knife they grate some *mavacure* branches; the bark is crushed and reduced to thin filaments with a stone like those used to make cassava flour. The poisonous sap is yellow, so all this matter takes on that colour. It is thrown into a funnel some 9 inches high and 4 inches wide. Of all the instruments in the Indian's laboratory, this funnel is the one he was most proud of. He several times asked if *por allá* (over there, in Europe) we had seen anything comparable to his *embudo*. It was a banana leaf rolled into a trumpet shape, and placed into another rolled trumpet made of palm leaves; this apparatus was held up by a scaffolding made of palm-leaf stalks. You begin by making a cold infusion, pouring water on the fibrous matter that is the crushed bark of the *mavacure*. A yellow water filters through the leafy funnel, drop by drop. This filtered water is the poisonous liquid; but it becomes strong only when concentrated through evaporation, like molasses, in wide clay vessels. Every now and then the Indian asked us to taste the liquid. From its bitterness you judge whether the heated liquid has gone far enough. There is nothing dangerous about this as curare only poisons when it comes into contact with blood. The steam rising from the boiler is not noxious, whatever the Orinoco missionaries might say.

The most concentrated sap from the *mavacure* is not thick enough to stick on arrows. It is thus only to thicken the poison that another concentrated infusion of vegetable sap is added. This is an extremely sticky sap taken from a tree with long leaves called *kiracaguero*. As this tree grows a long way off, and at this period is without flowers or fruit like the *bejuco de mavacure*, we were not able to name it botanically. I have often spoken of the ill fate that prevents travellers from studying the most interesting plants. When you travel quickly you hardly see an eighth of the trees that offer the essential parts of their fructification, even in the Tropics where flowers last so long.

The moment the sticky sap of the *kiracaguero* tree is poured into the poisonous and concentrated liquid, kept boiling, it blackens and coagulates to become rather like tar or a thick syrup. This mass is the curare that is sold inside crescentia fruit; but as its preparation is in the hands of a few families, first-class curare from Esmeralda and Manda-vaca is sold at high prices. When dried this substance looks like opium, but it attracts humidity if exposed to air. It tastes agreeably bitter, and Bonpland and I have often swallowed little bits. There is no danger as long as you make sure your gums and lips are not bleeding. The Indians regard curare taken by mouth as an excellent stomachic. The way the poison is made is rather similar everywhere, but there is no certainty that different poisons sold under the same name in the Orinoco and Amazon are identical or from the same plant.

In the Orinoco the curare made from the *raíz* (root) is differentiated from that made from the *bejuco* (the liana or bark from branches). We saw only the latter prepared; the former is weaker and less sought after. On the Amazon we learned to identify poisons made by the Tikuna, Yagua, Pevas and Jibaros tribes, which, coming from the same plant, differ only due to more or less care spent in their elaboration. The Tikuna poison, made famous in Europe by M. de la Condamine, and which is becoming known as *tikuna*, is taken from a liana that grows on the Upper Marañon. This poison is partly due to the Tikuna Indians, who have remained independent in Spanish territory, and partly to Indians of the same tribe in missions. As poisons are indispensable to hunters in this climate, the Orinoco and Amazon missionaries have not interfered with their production. The poisons just named are completely different from those made by the Peca, the Lamas and Moyobambas. I convey such details because the fragments of plants that we examined have proved (contrary to common opinion) that the three poisons of the Tikuna, Peca and Moyobambas do not come from the same species, not even the same family. Just as curare is simple in its composition, so the fabrication of the Moyobamba poison is long and complicated. You mix the sap of the *bejuco de ambihuasca*, the main ingredient, with pepper (capsicum), tobacco, *barbasco* (*Jacquinia armillaris*), *sanango* (*Tabernae montana*) and the milk of some apocyneae. The fresh sap of the *ambihuasca* is poisonous if it touches blood; the sap of the *mavacure* is deadly only when it is concentrated by heating, and boiling eliminates the poison from the root of the *Jatropha manihot* (*Yucca amarca*). When I rubbed the liana, which gives the cruel poison of the Peca, for a long time between my fingers on a very hot day, my hands became numb.

I will not go into further details about the physiological properties of these New World poisons that kill so quickly without ever making you sick if taken in the stomach, and without warning you of death by violently exciting the marrow in your spine. On the Orinoco river banks you cannot eat chicken that has not been killed by a poison arrow. Missionaries claim that animal flesh is only worth eating if killed in this way. Though ill with tertiary fever Father Zea insisted every morning that a poison arrow and the live chicken due to be eaten by us be brought to his hammock. He did not want anybody else to kill the bird, despite his weakness. Large birds like the guan (*pava de monte*) or the curassow (*alector*), pricked in their thighs, die in two to five minutes; but it takes ten to twelve minutes for a pig or peccary to die. Bonpland found that the same poison bought in different villages revealed enormous differences.

I placed very active curare on the crural nerves of a frog without noticing any change, measuring the degree of its organs' irritability with an arc formed of heterogeneous metals. But these Galvanic experiments hardly worked on birds a few minutes after they had been shot with poison arrows. Curare works only when the poison acts on the vascular system. At Maypures, a coloured man (a *zambo*, a cross between Indian and negro) was preparing one of those poison arrows that are shot in blowpipes, to kill small monkeys or birds for M. Bonpland. He was a carpenter of extraordinary strength. He stupidly rubbed the curare beween slightly bleeding fingers and fell to the ground, dizzy for half an hour. Luckily it was a weak curare (*destemplado*), used for small animals, which may be revived later by placing muriate of soda in the wound. During our journey back from Esmeralda to Atures I escaped from danger myself. The curare had attracted humidity and become liquid and spilled from a poorly closed jar on to our clothes. We forgot to check the inside of a sock filled with curare when washing our clothes. Just touching this sticky stuff with my hand I realized I should not pull on the poison sock. The danger was all the greater as my toes were bleeding from chigoe wounds.

There is exciting chemical and physiological work to be done in

Europe with the effects of New World poisons once we are sure that different poisons from different areas are properly distinguished. As far as our botanical knowledge about these poisonous plants is concerned we could sort out the differences only very slowly. Most Indians who make poison arrows completely ignore the nature of poisonous substances used by other tribes. A mystery surrounds the history of toxics and antidotes. Among wild Indians the preparation is the monopoly of *piaches*, who are priests, tricksters and doctors all at once; it is only with Indians from the missions that you can learn anything certain about such problematic matters. Centuries passed before any Europeans learned, thanks to Mutis's researches, that the *bejuco del guaco* is the most powerful antidote to snake bites, and which we were the first to describe botanically.

It is well established in the missions that there is no cure for curare that is fresh and concentrated and that has remained long enough in the wound for it to enter the bloodstream. Indians who have been wounded in wars by arrows dipped in curare described to us symptoms that resembled those of snake bites. The individual feels a congestion in his head, and giddiness makes him sit down. He feels nausea, vomits several times, and is tortured by thirst as the area around his wound becomes numb.

The old Indian called 'master of the poison' was flattered by our interest in his chemical procedures. He found us intelligent enough to think that we could make soap; for making soap, after making curare, seemed to him the greatest of human inventions. Once the poison was poured into its jars, we accompanied the Indian to the *juvias* fiesta. They were celebrating the Brazil-nut harvest, and became wildly drunk. The hut where the Indians had gathered over several days was the strangest sight you could imagine. Inside there were no tables or benches, only large smoked and roasted monkeys lined up symmetrically against the wall. These were marimondas (*Ateles belzebuth*) and the bearded capuchins. The way these animals, which look so like human beings, are roasted helps you understand why civilized people find eating them so repulsive. A little grill made of a hard wood is raised about a foot from the ground. The skinned monkey is placed on top in a sitting position so that he is held up by his long thin hands; sometimes the hands are crossed over his shoulders. Once it is fixed to the grill a fire is lit underneath; flames and smoke cover the monkey, which is roasted and smoked at the same time.[120] Seeing Indians eat a leg or arm of a roasted monkey makes you realize why cannibalism is not so repugnant to Indians. Roasted monkeys especially those with very round heads, look horribly like children. Europeans who are forced to eat them prefer to cut off the head and hands before serving up the rest of the monkey. The flesh of the monkey is so lean and dry that Bonpland kept an arm and a hand, roasted in Esmeralda, in his Paris collections. After many years it did not smell in the least.

We saw the Indians dancing. These dances are all the more monotonous as women do not dare take part. The men, both young and old, hold hands, form a circle, and for hours turn around to the right, then the left, in utter silence. Usually the dancers themselves are the musicians. Weak notes blown from reeds of different sizes make it all seem slow and sad. To mark the time the leading dancer bends both knees rhythmically. The reeds are tied together in rows. We were surprised to see how quickly young Indians could cut reeds and tune them as flutes when they found them on the banks.

In the Indian huts we found several vegetable productions brought from the Guiana mountains that fascinated us. I will mention only the fruit of the *juvia* or Brazil-nut, some extremely long reeds, and shirts made from marima bark. The *almendrón* or *juvia*, one of the most impressive trees in the New World jungles, was virtually unknown before our journey to the Río Negro.

This Brazil-nut tree is usually not more than 2 to 3 feet in diameter, but reaches up to 120 feet in height. The fruit ripens at the end of May and, as they are as big as a child's head, make a lot of noise when they fall from so high up. I usually found between fifteen and twenty-two nuts in one fruit. The taste is very agreeable when the nuts are fresh; but its copious oil – its main use – quickly goes rancid. In the Upper Orinoco we often ate quantities of these nuts for want of food, and no harm came to us. According to trustworthy Indians only small rodents can break into this fruit, thanks to their teeth and incredible tenacity. But once the fruit have fallen to the ground all kinds of jungle animals rush to the spot: monkeys, *manaviris*, squirrels, cavies, parrots and macaws fight over the booty.

All are strong enough to break the woody seed case, pick out the nut and climb back up the trees. 'They too have their fiestas,' the Indians say as they return from the harvest. To hear them complain about these animals you would think that the Indians alone are masters of the jungle.[121]

One of the four canoes that the Indians had used for their expedition was filled with a kind of reed (*carice*) used to make blowpipes. The reeds measured 15 to 17 feet without a sign of a knot for leaves and branches. They are quite straight, smooth and cylindrical. Known as 'reeds of Esmeralda' they are very sought after beyond the Orinoco. A hunter keeps the same blowpipe all his life; he boasts of its lightness, precision and shine as we might our firearms. What monocotyledonous plant do these magnificent reeds come from? I was unable to answer this question, as I was unable to say what plant was used in making the marima shirts. On the slopes of the Duida mountain we saw trunks of this tree reaching 50 feet high. The Indians cut off cylindrical pieces 2 feet in diameter and peel off the red fibrous bark, careful not to make longitudinal incisions. This bark becomes a kind of garment, like a sack, of a coarse material without seams. You put your head through a hole at the top and your arms through two holes cut in the sides. Indians wear these marima shirts when it rains; they look like cotton ponchos. In these climates the abundance and beneficence of nature are blamed for the Indians' laziness. Missionaries do not miss the opportunity of saying: 'In the Orinoco jungles clothes are found readymade on trees.'

In the fiesta women were excluded from dancing and other festivities; their sad role was reduced to serving men roast monkey, fermented drinks and palm-tree hearts, which tasted rather like our cauliflowers. Another more nutritious substance comes from the animal kingdom: fish flour (*mandioca de pescado*). Throughout the Upper Orinoco Indians roast fish, dry them in the sun and crush them into powder, along with the bones. When eaten it is mixed with water into a paste.

In Esmeralda, as in all missions, the Indians who refuse to be baptized but who live in the villages have remained polygamous. The number of wives differs according to the tribe; those who have most are the Caribs and those tribes that still carry young girls off from enemy tribes. Women live as slaves. As men exert absolute authority no women dare to complain in their presence. In the homes an apparent peace reigns, and the women vie to anticipate the whims of their demanding and bad-tempered master. They look after children, whether their own or another's. Missionaries say that this peace, the result of collective fear, breaks down when the master is away for a long time. The squabbling does not end until he returns and silences them just with the sound of his voice, or with a simple gesture, or by some other more violent means. As these unhappy women do all the work, it is not strange that in some tribes there are few women. Then you find a sort of polyandry. With the Avanos and Maypures several brothers share one wife. When an Indian with several wives becomes a Christian the missionaries force him to choose the one he wants to keep and to reject the others. The moment of separation is critical: the new convert finds that each wife has some special quality: one knows about plants, another how to make *chicha*, the drink made from cassava root. Sometimes an Indian would rather keep his wives than become a Christian; but usually the man lets the missionary choose for him, as part of his fate.

According to my careful trigonometric calculations the Duida mountain rises 2,179 metres above the Esmeralda plain, some 2,530 metres, more or less, above sea-level. I say more or less because I had the bad luck to break my barometer before our arrival in Esmeralda. The rain had been so heavy that we could not protect this instrument from the damp and, with the unequal expansion of the wood, the tubes snapped. This accident especially annoyed me as no barometer had ever lasted so long on such a journey. The granite summit of the Duida falls so steeply that Indians have not managed to climb it. Though the mountains are not as high as people think, it is the highest point of the chain that stretches from the Orinoco to the Amazon.

Between the mouths of the Padamo and the Mavaca the Orinoco receives the Ocamo from the north, into which flows the Matacona river. At the source of this last river live the Guainare Indians, far less copper-coloured or brown than others in this region. This tribe belongs to what missionaries call 'fair Indians' or *Indios blancos*. Near the mouth of the Ocamo travellers are shown a rock that is the local marvel. It is granite passing into gneiss, characterized by its black mica, which forms little ramified veins. Spaniards call this rock Piedra Mapaya (Map Rock). I chipped off a bit.[122]

We left the Esmeralda mission on the 23rd of May. We were not exactly ill, but emaciated and weak thanks to the torment of mosquitoes, the bad food and the long journey on that narrow and damp pirogue. We did not go further up the Orinoco than the mouth of the Guapo; had we wanted to reach the Orinoco sources we would have gone beyond this point, but private travellers are not authorized to leave pacified areas. From the Guapo river to the Guaharibo cataract there are only 15 leagues. But the cataract is crossed by a liana bridge where Indians armed with bows and arrows stop whites from entering their lands. Up to the present time the Orinoco posed two distinct problems for geographers: its sources, and the nature of its communications with the Amazon. This latter was the aim of our journey.

Our canoe was not ready until nearly three in the afternoon. During our trip up the Casiquiare countless ants had nested in its *toldo* and hulk where we would have to lie for another twenty-two days, and it was difficult to clear them out. We spent the morning trying again to find out from those who lived in Esmeralda whether they knew about a lake towards the east. When shown maps the old soldiers laughed at the idea of a supposed link between the Orinoco and Iapa, as much as they laughed at the idea of its being linked to the 'white sea'. What we politely call geographers' fictions they call *mentiras de por allá* ('Lies from over there, the Old World'). These good men could not understand how people could draw maps of unseen countries and know precise things without ever having visited the country, things that even those who do live there have never heard about.

On the point of leaving we were surrounded by those inhabitants who called themselves whites and Spaniards. They begged us to ask the Angostura Government to let them return to the llanos, or at least to the Río Negro missions. 'However serious our crimes,' they said, 'we have expiated them after twenty years of hell in this swarm of mosquitoes.' I pleaded their case in a report to the government on the industrial and commercial state of these countries.

All I could say about our journey from Esmeralda to the mouth of the Atabapo would be merely a list of rivers and uninhabited places. From the 24th to the 27th of May we slept only twice on land; the first at the confluence with the Jao river and the second below the Santa Bárbara mission on Minisi island. As the Orinoco has no shoals the Indian pilot let the canoe drift all night with the current. It took us only thirty-five hours to reach Santa Bárbara. The Santa Bárbara mission is located a little to the west of the mouth of the Venturari river. We found in this small village of 120 inhabitants some traces of industry; but what the Indians produce is of little use to them; it is reserved for the monks or, as they say, for the church and the convent. We were told that a great silver lamp, bought at the expense of the neophytes, was expected from Madrid. Let us hope that after this lamp arrives they will think of clothing the Indians, buying them agricultural instruments, and schooling their children. The few oxen in the savannahs round the mission are not used to turn the mill (*trapiche*) to crush the juice from the sugar cane. This the Indians do and, as happens whenever Indians work for the church, they are not paid.

We spent only one day at San Fernando de Atabapo, despite the village, with its *pirijao* palms and their peach-like fruit, promising us a delightful refuge. Tame *pauxis* (*Crax alector*) ran round the Indian huts; in one of which we saw a very rare monkey that lives on the banks of the Guaviare. It is called the caparro, which I have made known in my *Observations on Zoology and Comparative Anatomy*.[123] Its hair is grey and extremely soft to touch. It has a round head, and a sweet, agreeable expression.

Over night the Orinoco had swollen and its faster current took us in ten hours the 13 leagues from the mouth of the Mataveni to the higher Maypures cataract, reminding us where we had camped coming up river. From the mouth of the Atabapo to that of the Apure we enjoyed travelling through a country in which we had long lived. We were just as squashed in the canoe and were stung by the same mosquitoes, but the certainty that in a few weeks our suffering would end kept our spirits up.

On the 31st of May we passed the Guahibo and Garcita rapids. The islands in the middle of the river were covered in a brilliant green.

The winter rains had unfolded the spathes of the *vadgiai* palms whose leaves pointed up to the sky. Just before sunset we landed on the eastern bank of the Orinoco, at the Puerto de Expedición, in order to visit the Ataruipe cavern, apparently the burial-ground of a tribe that was destroyed.

We had a tiring and dangerous climb up a bald granite hill. It would have been impossible to have kept our balance on the steep slippery surface of the rock had it not been for large feldspar crystals that stuck out and supported us. At the summit we were amazed at the extraordinary panorama. An archipelago of islands covered with palm trees filled the foamy river bed. The setting sun seemed like a ball of fire hanging over the plain. Birds of prey and goatsuckers flew out of reach above us. It was a pleasure to follow their shadows over the wall of rocks.

The most remote part of the valley is covered with thick jungle. In this shady place lies the opening to the Ataruipe cavern, less a cavern than a deep vault formed by an overhanging rock, and scooped out by water when it reached this height. This is the cemetery of an extinct race. We counted some 600 well-preserved skeletons, lined in rows. Each skeleton is enclosed in a basket made of palm-leaf petioles. These baskets, called *mapires* by the Indians, are a kind of square sack whose dimensions vary according to the age of the dead. Children who die at birth also have their *mapires*. The skeletons are so intact that not even a rib or a phalanx is missing.

The bones are prepared in three different ways; they are whitened, or coloured red with annatto, a dye from *Bixa orellana*, or varnished with a scented resin and wrapped like mummies in banana leaves. Indians insisted that as soon as somebody died the corpse was left for months in damp earth so that the flesh rotted away; then it was dug up and the remains of the flesh scraped off with a sharp stone. Some tribes in Guiana still practise this method. Next to the baskets or *mapires* we also found half-baked clay urns with the remains of whole families. The largest urns are almost 3 feet high and 5.5 feet wide. They are greenish, and of a pleasing oval shape. Some have crocodiles and snakes drawn on them. The top edges are decorated with meanders and labyrinths. These are very similar to the decorations covering the walls of the Mexican palace at Mitla; they are found everywhere, even among the Greeks and Romans, as on the shields of the Tahitians and other Pacific Islanders.

Our interpreters could give us no details about the age of these baskets and vessels. However, the majority of the skeletons did not seem to be more than a hundred years old. Among the Guareca Indians there is a legend that the brave Atures, chased by the cannibalistic Caribs, hid in the cataract rocks, where they died out, leaving no trace of their language. The last survivor of the Atures could not have lasted much longer, for at Maypures you can still see an old parrot that 'nobody understands because', so the Indians say, 'it speaks the language of the Atures'.[124]

Despite the indignation of our guides we opened various *mapires* to study the skulls. They were all typical of the American race, with one or two Caucasian types. We took several skulls with us, as well as a skeleton of a six- or seven-year-old child, and two Atures adults. All these bones, partly painted red, and partly covered in resin, lay in the baskets already described. They made up the whole load of one mule and, as we knew all about the superstitious aversions that Indians have about corpses once they have been buried, we covered the baskets with newly woven mats. But nothing could fool the Indians and their acute sense of smell. Wherever we stopped Indians ran to surround our mules and admire the monkeys we had bought on the Orinoco. But hardly had they touched our luggage than they announced the certain death of the mule that 'carried the dead'. In vain we tried to dissuade them and said the baskets contained crocodile and manatee skeletons. They insisted that they smelled the resin that covered the bones 'of their old relations'. One of the skulls we brought from the Ataruipe cavern has been painted by my old master Blumenbach.[125] But the skeletons of the Indians have been lost with much of our collection in a storm off Africa, where our travelling companion and friend the Franciscan monk Juan Gonzalez also drowned. We left the burial-ground of this extinct race in a sad mood.

We stayed in the Atures mission just the time needed to have the canoes taken down the cataracts. The bottom of our small boat was so worn that we took great care to prevent it cracking. We said goodbye to Father Bernardo Zea who, after two months of travelling with us, sharing all our sufferings, remained in Atures. The poor man continued to have fits of tertian fever, a chronic condition that did not worry him at all. During this second stay in Atures other fevers raged. Most of the Indians could not leave their hammocks; to get some cassava bread we had to ask the independent Piraoas tribe to find some for us. Up to now we had escaped fevers, which I believe are not always contagious.

We dared to cross the last half of the Atures *raudal* in our boat. We landed every now and then on rocks, which act as dykes, forming islands. Sometimes water crashes over them, sometimes it falls into them with a deafening noise. It was here that we saw one of the most extraordinary scenes. The river rolled its waters over our heads, like the sea crashing against reefs, but in the entrance to a cavern we could stay dry as the large sheet of water formed an arch over the rocks. We had the chance to view this bizarre sight for longer than we wished. Our canoe should have passed around a narrow island on the eastern bank and picked us up after a long detour. We waited for several hours as night and a furious storm approached. Rain poured down. We began to fear that our fragile boat had smashed against some rocks and that the Indians, as indifferent as ever to the distress of others, had gone off to the mission. There were only three of us, soaked to the skin and worrying about our pirogue, as well as thinking about spending the night in the Tropics, sleeping in the din of the cataracts. M. Bonpland proposed to leave me alone on the island with Don Nicolás Soto and swim the bit of the river between the granite dykes. He hoped to reach the jungle and seek help from Father Zea at Atures. We finally managed to dissuade him. He had no idea about the labyrinth of canals that split up the Orinoco or of the dangerous eddies. Then what happened under our noses as we were discussing this proved that the Indians had been wrong to say there were no crocodiles in the cataracts. We had placed our little monkeys on the tip of our island. Soaked by the rain, and sensitive to any fall in temperature, they began to howl, attracting two very old lead-grey crocodiles. Seeing them made me realize how dangerous our swim in this same *raudal* on our way up had been. After a long wait our Indians turned up just as the sun was setting.

We continued to travel part of the night, and set up camp on Panumana island, passing the Santa Bárbara mission by without stopping. Only days later did we hear that the little colony of Guahibo Indians there had fled *al monte* because they thought we had come to capture them and sell them as *poitos* or slaves. In Carichana Bonpland was able to dissect a 9-foot-long manatee. It was a female and its meat tasted of ox. The Piraoas Indians at this mission so hate this animal that they hid so as not to have to touch its flesh as it was being carried to our hut. They claim 'that people from their tribe die if they eat its flesh'.

Our stay in Carichana let us gather our strength. Bonpland was carrying the germs of a serious illness, and needed rest. But as the delta of the rivers Horeda and Paruasi is covered with dense vegetation he could not resist a long botanical excursion and soaked himself several times a day in the water. Fortunately in the missionary's house we were supplied with bread made from maize flour, and even milk.

In two days we went down the Orinoco from Carichana to the Uruana mission, again passing the famous Baraguan Strait. The Uruana mission is situated in a very picturesque place. The little Indian village backs on to a high granite mountain. Rocks rise like pillars above the highest jungle trees. Nowhere else is the Orinoco more majestic than when viewed from Father Ramón Bueno's missionary hut. It is more than 2,600 toises wide and runs in a straight line east like a canal. The mission is inhabited by Otomacs, a barbaric tribe who offered us an extraordinary physiological phenomenon. The Otomacs eat earth; every day for several months they swallow quantities of earth to appease their hunger without any ill effect on their health. This verifiable fact has become, since my return to Europe, the object of lively disputes. Though we could stay only one day in Uruana it was sufficient to find out how the *poya* (balls of earth) are prepared, to examine the reserves of this the Indians keep, and how much is eaten in twenty-four hours. I also found traces of this perverse appetite among the Guamos, between the Meta and the Apure. Everybody speaks of earth eating or *geophagie* as anciently known. I shall limit myself to what I saw and heard from the missionary, doomed to twelve years among this wild, unruly Otomac tribe.

The Uruana inhabitants belong to those people of the savannah (*Indios andantes*), harder to civilize than those from the jungle (*Indios del monte*). They show a great aversion to agriculture and live exclusively from hunting and fishing. The men are tough, ugly, wild, vindictive and passionately fond of alcohol. They are 'omnivorous animals' in every sense. That is why other Indians consider them as barbarians and say, 'There is nothing, however disgusting it is, that an Otomac will not eat.' While the Orinoco and its waters are low the Otomacs live on fish and turtles. They kill fish with astounding skill, shooting them with arrows when they surface. The river floods stop all fishing: it becomes as hard as fishing in deep sea. During the period of floods the Otomacs eat earth in prodigious amounts. We found pyramids of earth balls in their huts. The earth they eat is a fine oily clay, of a greyish-yellow; they cook it slightly so that its hard crust turns red due to the iron oxide in it.

The Otomacs do not eat all clays indiscriminately: they choose alluvial beds where the earth is oilier and smoother to touch. They do not mix the clay with maize flour or turtle fat or crocodile fat. In Paris we analysed a ball of earth brought back from the Orinoco and found no trace of organic matter. The savage will eat anything as long as it satisfies his hunger. Earth becomes his staple diet, for it is hard to find even a lizard or a fern root or a dead fish floating on the water. Surprisingly, during the flood season, the Otomac does not get thin; in fact he remains very tough, and without a swollen belly.

The following are the true facts, which I verified. The Otomacs, over months, eat three quarters of a pound of slightly baked clay daily. Their health is not affected. They moisten the clay to swallow it. It was not possible to find out what other vegetable or animal matter the Indians ate at the same time; but it is clear that the sensation of a full stomach came from the clay, and not from whatever else they might eat. Everywhere in the torrid zone I noticed women, children, even full-grown men, show a great desire to swallow earth. Not an alkaline or calcareous earth to neutralize acid juices, but a fat, oily clay with a strong smell. They often have to tie children's hands to prevent them from eating earth when it stops raining. In the village of Banco, on the Magdalena, I saw Indian women potters continually swallowing great lumps of clay. They were not pregnant, and said, 'Earth is food that does not harm us.' It could be asked why this mania for eating earth is so rare in the cool, temperate zones, compared to the Tropics; and why in Europe it is confined to pregnant women and sick children.[126]

The little village of Uruana is harder to govern than most other missions. The Otomacs are restless, noisy, and extreme in their passions. They not only adore the fermented liquors of cassava, maize and palm wine, but also get very drunk, to the point of madness, with *niopo* powder. They gather the long pods of a mimosa, which we have made known as *Acacia niopo*; they cut them into little pieces, dampen them and let them ferment. When the macerated plants turn black they are crushed into a paste and mixed with cassava flour and lime obtained from burning the shell of a helix. They cook this mass on a grill of hardwood above a fire. The hardened pâté looks like little cakes. When they want to use it they crumble it into a powder and put it on a small plate. The Otomac holds this plate with one hand while through his nose, along the forked bone of a bird whose two extremities end up in his nostrils, he breathes in the *niopo*. I sent some *niopo* and all the necessary instruments to Fourcroy in Paris.[127] *Niopo* is so stimulating that a tiny portion produces violent sneezing in those not used to it. Father Gumilla wrote: 'The diabolic powder of the Otomacs makes them drunk through their nostrils, deprives them of reason for several hours, and makes them mad in battle.'

The proper herbaceous tobacco[128] (for missionaries call *niopo* 'tree-tobacco') has been cultivated from time immemorial by all the Orinoco tribes: from the time of the conquest smoking had spread to all the Americas. The Tamanacs and Maypures wrap their cigars in maize leaves, as the Mexicans had done when Cortés arrived. Imitating them, the Spaniards substituted maize leaf for paper. The poor Indians of the Orinoco jungles know as well as the great lords in Montezuma's Court that tobacco smoke is an excellent narcotic. They use it not only to take siestas but also to reach that quiet state they naïvely call 'a dream with your eyes open, or day-dream'.

It is neither from Virginia nor South America that Europe received in 1559 the first tobacco seeds, as is erroneously stated in most botanical books, but from the Mexican province of Yucatán. The man who boasted most about the fertility of the Orinoco banks, the famous Raleigh, also introduced smoking tobacco to the northern peoples. Already by the end of the sixteenth century there were bitter complaints in England 'of this imitation of wild Indian manners'. They thought that by smoking tobacco 'Englishmen would degenerate into a barbarous state'.

After the Otomacs of Uruana take *niopo* (their tree-tobacco), or their fermented liquors, they fall into a drunken stupor lasting days on end, and they kill each other without using weapons. The most vicious put poisonous curare on a fingernail, and according to the missionary a scratch from this fingernail can kill if the curare is very active. At night, after a brawl, when they murder someone they chuck the corpse into the river in case signs of violence can be seen on the body. 'Each time,' Father Bueno said, 'I see women fetching water from a part of the river bank that is not their usual place I guess that someone has been murdered.'

In the Uruana huts we found that vegetable substance called *yesca de hormigas* (ant tinder) already seen at the cataracts, used to stop bleeding. This tinder, which should be called 'ant's nest', is much needed in a region where there is so much violence. A new species of ant (*Formica spinicollis*), of a pretty emerald green, gathers this soft cotton-like down from the leaves of a melastomacea to make its nest.

On the 7th of June we sadly left Father Ramón Bueno. Alone among all the missionaries we met he cared for the Indians. He hoped to return to Madrid to publish the result of his researches into the figures and characters that cover the Uruana rocks. In this area between the Meta, Arauca and Apure, Alonso de Herrera,[129] during the first 1535 expedition to the Orinoco, found mute dogs (*perros mudos*). We cannot doubt that this dog is indigenous to South America. Different Indian languages have words for this dog that cannot be related to European languages. Early historians all speak of mute dogs, and this same dog was eaten in Mexico and on the Orinoco.

We took nine days to travel the 95 leagues from the island of Cucuruparu to the capital of Guiana, commonly called Angostura. We rarely spent the night on land, but the plague of mosquitoes was diminishing. On the morning of the 9th of June we met many boats filled with merchandise going up the Orinoco by sail towards the Apure. It is a much frequented trade route between Angostura and Torunos. Our travelling companion, Don Nicolás Soto, brother-in-law of the governor of Barinas, took this route to return to his family. During the great floods months are lost struggling against the currents. Boatmen are forced to moor to tree trunks and haul themselves up river. In this winding river they can take days just to advance 200 to 300 toises.

How hard it is to express the pleasure we felt arriving at Angostura, capital of Spanish Guiana. The discomforts felt at sea in small boats cannot be compared to those felt under a burning sky, surrounded by swarms of mosquitoes, cramped for months on end in a pirogue that does not let you budge an inch because of its delicate balance. In seventy-five days we had travelled along the five great rivers of the Apure, the Orinoco, the Atabapo, the Río Negro and the Casiquiare for 500 leagues, rarely sighting inhabited places. Although, after our life in the jungle, our clothes were not in good order, we hurried to present ourselves to the provincial governor Don Felipe de Ynciarte. He received us in the most considerate way, and lodged us in the house of the Secretary of the Intendencia. Coming from such deserted places we were struck by the bustle of a town of only 6,000 people. We appreciated what work and trade can do to make life more civilized. Modest houses seemed luxurious: anybody who spoke to us seemed witty. Long deprivations make small things pleasurable: how can I express the joy we felt on seeing wheat bread on the governor's table. I may be wrong in repeating what all travellers feel after long journeys. You enjoy finding yourself back in civilization, though it can be short-lived if you have learned to feel deeply the marvels of tropical nature. The memory of what you endured soon fades; as you reach the coasts inhabited by European colonists you begin to plan to make another journey into the interior.

A dreadful circumstance forced us to stay a whole month in Angostura. The first days after our arrival we felt tired and weak, but completely healthy. Bonpland began to study the few plants that he had managed to protect from the humidity while I was busy determining the longitude and latitude of the capital and observing the dip of the magnetic needle. All our work was interrupted. On almost the same day we were struck by an illness that took the form of a malignant typhus in my travelling companion. At that time the air in Angostura was quite healthy and, as the only servant we had brought from Cumaná showed the same symptoms, our generous hosts were sure that we had caught the typhus germs somewhere in the damp Casiquiare jungles. As our mulatto servant had been far more exposed to the intense rains, his illness developed with alarming speed. He got so weak that after eight days we thought he was dead. However, he had only fainted, and he later recovered. I too was attacked by a violent fever; I was given a mixture of honey and quinine from the Caroní river (*Cortex angosturae*), a medicine recommended by the Capuchin monks. My fever continued to rise, but vanished the following day. Bonpland's fever was more serious, and for weeks we worried about his health. Luckily he was strong enough to look after himself; and took medicines that suited him better than the Caroní river quinine. The fever continued and, as is usual in the Tropics, developed into dysentery. During his illness Bonpland maintained his strength of character and that calmness which never left him even in the most trying circumstances. I was tortured by premonitions. It was I who had chosen to go up-river; the danger to my companion seemed to be the fatal consequence of my rash choice.

After reaching an extraordinary violence the fever became less alarming. The intestinal inflammation yielded to emollients obtained from malvaceous plants. But the patient's recuperation was very slow, as happens with Europeans not thoroughly acclimatized to the Tropics. The rainy season continued. To return to the Cumaná coast meant crossing the llanos, which would be flooded. So as not to expose Bonpland to a dangerous relapse we decided to stay in Angostura until the 10th of July. We spent part of the time in a nearby plantation, which grew mangoes and breadfruit (*Artocarpus incisa*).[130]

CHAPTER 22

The llanos of Payo, or the eastern Venezuelan plains
— Carib missions — Last visit to the Nueva Barcelona, Cumaná
and Araya coasts

It was already dark when we crossed the Orinoco bed for the last time. We meant to spend the night near the small San Rafael fort and begin the journey across the Venezuelan steppes at dawn. Nearly six weeks had passed since our arrival at Angostura; we dearly wanted to reach the Cumaná or Nueva Barcelona coasts to find a boat to take us to Cuba and then on to Mexico. After several months on mosquito-infested rivers in small canoes, a long sea journey excited our imaginations.

Our mules waited for us on the left bank of the Orinoco. The plant collections and geological specimens brought from Esmeralda and the Río Negro had greatly increased our baggage. It would have been dangerous to leave our herbals behind, but this added weight meant we now faced a tediously slow journey across the llanos. The heat was excessive due to the bare ground's reverberations. The thermometer by day recorded between 30 °C and 34 °C, and at night 27 °C to 28 °C. Like everywhere in the Tropics it was less the actual degree of heat than its duration that affected our bodies. We spent thirteen days crossing the steppes, resting a little in the Carib missions and in the village of Payo.

Soon after entering the Nueva Barcelona llanos we spent the night in a Frenchman's house. He welcomed us very cordially. He came from Lyon, and had left home when still very young. He seemed quite indifferent to all that was happening across the ocean or, as they scornfully say here, 'del otro lado del charco' ('on the other side of the pond'). He was busy sticking large bits of wood together with a glue called *guayca*, used by carpenters in Angostura. It is as good as any glue made from animal matter. It is found ready-made between the bark and sap of a creeper of the Combretaceae family (*Combretum guayca*). It resembles birdlime made from mistletoe berries and the inner bark of the holly. An astonishing amount of this glue pours out from the twining branches of the *bejuco de guayca* when they are cut.

It took us three days to reach the Cari Carib missions. The ground was not as cracked by the drought as in the Calabozo plains. A few showers had revived the vegetation. We saw a few fan palms (*Corypha tectorum*), rhopalas (*Chaparro*) and malpighias with leathery, shiny leaves growing far apart from each other. From far off you recognize where there might be water from groups of mauritia palms. It was the season in which they are loaded with enormous clusters of red fruit looking like fir-cones. Our monkeys loved this fruit, which tasted like overripe apples. The monkeys were carried with our baggage on the backs of mules and did all they could to reach the clusters hanging over their heads. The plains seemed to ripple from the mirages. When, after travelling for an hour, we reached those palms standing like masts on the horizon, we were amazed to realize how many things are linked to the existence of one single plant. The wind, losing its force as it strikes leaves and branches, piles sand round the trunks. The smell of fruit and the bright green of the leaves attract passing birds that like to sway on the arrow-like branches of the palms. All around you hear a murmur of sound. Oppressed by the heat, and used to the bleak silence of the llanos, you think you feel cooler just by hearing the sound of branches swaying. Insects and worms, so rare in the llanos, thrive here so that even one stunted tree, which no traveller would have noticed in the Orinoco jungles, spreads life around it in the desert.

On the 13th of July we reached the village of Cari, the first of the Carib missions dependent on the Observance monks from the Piritu college. As usual we stayed in the convent, that is, with the parish priest. Apart from passports issued by the Captain-General of the province, we also carried recommendations from bishops and the director of the Orinoco missions. From the coasts of New California to Valdivia and the mouth of the River Plate, along 2,000 leagues, you can overcome all obstacles by appealing to the protection of the American clergy. Their power is too well entrenched for a new order of things to break out for a long time. Our host could hardly believe how 'people born in northern Europe could arrive in his village from the frontiers with Brazil by the Río Negro, and not by the Cumaná coast'. Although affable, he was also extremely curious, like everyone who meets travellers who are not Spanish. He was sure that the minerals we carried contained gold, and that the plants we had dried were medicinal. Here, as in many parts of Europe, sciences interest people only if they bring immediate and practical benefit.

We counted more than 500 Caribs in the Cari village; and many more in the surrounding missions. It is curious to meet a once nomadic tribe only recently settled, whose intellectual and physical powers make them different from other Indians. Never have I seen such a tall race (from 5 feet 9 inches to 6 feet 2 inches). As is common all over America the men cover their bodies more than the women, who wear only the *guayuco* or *perizoma* in the form of narrow bands. The men wrap the lower part of their bodies down to their hips in a dark blue, almost black, cloth. This drapery is so ample that when the temperature drops at night the Caribs use it to cover their shoulders. Seen from far off against the sky, their bodies, dyed with annatto, and their tall, copper-coloured and picturesquely wrapped figures, look like ancient statues. The way the men cut their hair is typical: like monks or choirboys. The partly shaved forehead makes it seem larger than it is. A tuft of hair, cut in a circle, starts near the crown of the head. The resemblance of the Caribs with the monks does not come from mission life, from the false argument that the Indians wanted to imitate their masters, the Franciscan monks. Tribes still independent like those at the source of the Caroní and Branco rivers can be distinguished by their *cerquillo de frailes* (monks' circular tonsures), which were seen from the earliest discovery of America. All the Caribs that we saw, whether in boats on the Lower Orinoco or in the Piritu missions, differ from other Indians by their height and by the regularity of their features; their noses are shorter and less flat, their cheekbones not so prominent, their physiognomy less Mongoloid. Their eyes, blacker than is usual among the Guiana hordes, show intelligence, almost a capacity for thought. Caribs have a serious manner and a sad look, common to all the New World tribes. Their severe look is heightened by their mania for dyeing their eyebrows with sap from the *caruto*, then lengthening and joining them together. They often paint black dots all over their faces to make themselves look wilder. The local magistrates, governors and mayors, who alone are authorized to carry long canes, came to visit us. Among these were some young Indians aged between eighteen and twenty, appointed by the missionaries. We were struck to see among these Caribs painted in annatto the same sense of importance, the same cold, scornful manners that can be found among people with the same positions in the Old World. Carib women are less strong, and uglier than the men. They do nearly all the housework and fieldwork. They insistently asked us for pins, which they stuck under their lower lips; they pierce their skin so that the pin's head remains inside the mouth. It is a custom from earlier savage times. The young girls are dyed red and, apart from their *guayuco*, are naked. Among the different tribes in the two continents the idea of nakedness is relative. In some parts of Asia a woman is not allowed to show a fingertip, while a Carib Indian woman wears only a 2-inch-long *guayuco*. Even this small band is seen as less essential than the pigment covering her skin. To leave her hut without her coat of annatto dye would be to break all the rules of tribal decency.

The Indians of the Piritu mission intrigued us because they belonged to a tribe whose daring, and warrior and mercantile skills, have exerted a big influence on a vast part of the land. All along the Orinoco we came across records of the hostile excursions of the Caribs. Also the Carib language is one of the more widely spread.

The fine Carib tribes inhabit only a small part of the country they once occupied before the discovery of America. European cruelty ensured that they completely vanished from the West Indies and Darien coasts. Once subdued they lived in populous villages in Nueva Barcelona province and Spanish Guiana. I think you could count more than 35,000 Caribs living in the Piritu llanos and on the banks of the Caroní and Cuyuni. If you add the independent Caribs living in the Cayenne and Pacaraymo mountains between the Essequibo and Branco river sources they would reach a total of 40,000 pure-blooded Indians. I linger on this point because the Caribs, before my voyage, had been supposed to have become extinct.

I first found the word 'Carib' in a letter from Pierre Martyr d'Anghiera.[131] It derives from 'Calina' and 'Caripuna', the l and p transformed into r and b. It is noteworthy that this word, heard by Columbus from people on Haiti, is also found on other islands and on the mainland. From Carina, or Calina, Galibi (Caribi) was formed. This is how a tribe in French Guiana are still known, though they are shorter and speak a Carib dialect. Those on the islands called themselves in men's language Calinago; and in women's language Callipinan. This difference between the languages of the two sexes is more marked than among other American tribes. This is possibly due to the women living so cut off from men that they have adopted ways of speaking that men refuse to follow. But the contrast in Carib tribes between the dialects of the two sexes is so great, and surprising, that a more satisfying explanation must be sought. It could be found in the Caribs' barbarous custom of killing all male prisoners and making the women slaves. When the Caribs burst into the archipelago of the smaller West Indian Islands they arrived as warriors, not as colonizers with their families. The female language was formed slowly by these conquerors living with foreign women, learning words alien to Carib.

The Caribs on the mainland admit that the smaller West Indian Islands were inhabited by Arowaks, a warlike tribe still found on the unhealthy banks of the Surinam and Berbice rivers. They say that all the Arowaks were exterminated by Caribs coming from the Orinoco mouth, except for the women. They quote as evidence the similarities between Arowak and Carib women's languages.

The Caribs have so dominated such a large part of the continent that the memory of their ancient grandeur has left them with a dignity and national superiority that is obvious in their manners and way of speaking. 'We alone are a tribe,' they say proverbially, 'the others (*oquili*) are here to serve us.' This scorn that Caribs have for their old enemies is so accentuated that I have seen a ten-year-old child froth with rage when called a Cabre or a Cavere. Yet he had never seen anyone from such a tribe, decimated by the Caribs after a long resistance. Among half-civilized tribes, as much as in civilized Europe, we find similar deep-seated hates where the names of enemy people have passed into language as the worst kind of insult.

The missionary led us into several ordered and extremely clean Indian huts. It was painful to see how Carib mothers forced their children from the earliest age to enlarge the calves of their legs, as well as mould their flesh in stripes from the ankle to the top of the thigh. Bands of leather or cotton are tied tightly 2 inches apart and pulled hard so that the muscles in between swell out. Our swaddled children suffer far less than the Carib children, who are meant to be closer to nature. The monks, ignorant of Rousseau's works[132] and even of his name, are unable to prevent this ancient physical education; man from the jungle, whom we believed to be so simple in customs, is far from docile when it comes to his dress and ideas about beauty and well-being. I was also surprised to see that the torture imposed on these children in no way hindered their blood circulation or their muscular movements. There is no tribe that is stronger or runs faster than the Caribs.

When you travel through Carib missions and observe the order and submission there it is hard to remind yourself that you are among cannibals. This American word, of doubtful origin, probably comes from the Haitian or Puerto Rican language. It passed into European languages from the fifteenth century as a synonym for anthropophagy. I do not doubt that the conquering island Caribs were cruel to the Ygneris and other West Indian inhabitants, who were so weak and unwarlike; but their cruelty has been exaggerated because the first discoverers listened only to stories from conquered tribes. All the missionaries that I asked assured me that the Caribs are perhaps the least cannibalistic of the New World tribes. Perhaps the desperate way in which the Caribs fought the Spaniards, which led in 1504 to a royal decree declaring them to be slaves, contributed to their fame for ferocity. It was Christopher Columbus who first decided to attack the Caribs and deny them their freedom and natural rights; he was a fifteenth-century man, and less humane than is thought today. In 1520 Rodrigo de Figueroa was appointed by the Spanish Court to decide which South American tribes were Caribs, or cannibals, and which were Guatiaos, or peaceful and friendly to Spain. His ethnographic piece, called *El auto de Figueroa*, is one of the most curious records of the early conquistadores' barbarism. Without paying attention to languages, any tribe that was accused of eating prisoners was called Carib. All the tribes that Figueroa called Carib were condemned to slavery; they could be sold at will or exterminated. It was after these bloody wars, and the death of their husbands, that Carib women, d'Anghiera says, became known as Amazons.

On feast days, after celebrating mass, the whole community assembles in front of the church. Young girls leave bundles of firewood, maize, bananas and other foodstuff at the missionary's feet. At the same time the governor, mayor and other municipal officers, all pure Indians, exhort the Indians to work, arrange who will do what, scold the lazy and, it has to be said, cruelly beat those who refuse to obey. These strokes are received with the same impassivity with which they are given. These acts of justice last a long time and are frequently seen by any traveller who crosses the llanos. It would be better if the priest did not impose corporal punishment as soon as he left the altar; he should not witness the punishment of men and women in his priestly robes; but his abuse arises from the bizarre principles on which missions are based. The most arbitrary civil powers are tightly linked to the rights exercised by priests; yet, though the Caribs are not cannibals, and you would like them to be treated gently, you do realize that some violence is necessary to maintain order in a new society.

When we were about to leave the Cari mission we had an argument with our Indian muleteers. To our amazement they had discovered that we were transporting skeletons from the Ataruipe caves, and were sure that the mule carrying 'the corpses of our ancient relatives' would die on the journey. All our precautions to hide the bones had been useless; nothing escapes the Carib's sense of smell. We needed the missionary's authority to be able to leave. We had to cross the Cari river in a boat and ford, or perhaps I should say swim, the Río de Agua Clara. Quicksand on the bottom made the crossing during the floods very tiring. You are surprised to find such strong currents in flat land. We spent unpleasant nights out at Matagorda and Los Riecitos. Everywhere we saw the same things: small huts made of reed and roofed with leather, men on horseback with lances, guarding the cattle, semi-wild herds of horned cattle all the same colour, fighting for grass with horses and mules. Not a goat or a sheep in these immense steppes!

On the 15th of July we reached the fundación, or the Villa de Pao, established in 1744 and well situated as a depot between Nueva Barcelona and Angostura. Many geographers have mistaken its position, confusing it with other small towns. Though it was cloudy I was able to determine the latitude and the longitude from the sun. The astronomical fixing of Calabozo and Concepción del Pao are very important to the geography of this country where there are so few fixed points in the savannahs. Around about we saw some fruit trees, quite rare in the steppes. We also noticed coconut palms, despite the distance from the sea. I insist on this observation as some have doubted the veracity of travellers describing coconut palms, a coastal plant, in Timbuktu and in the heart of Africa.

It took us five long days from the Villa de Pao to the port of Nueva Barcelona. As we got closer the sky became clearer, the ground more dusty and the air more burning hot. This oppressive heat does not arise from the temperature but from fine sand floating in the air, which irradiates heat in all directions, and whips your face and the ball of the thermometer. In fact I never saw the mercury rise above 45.8 °C once in this sand wind in America.

We spent the night of the 16th of July in the Indian village of Santa Cruz de Cachipo, founded in 1749 when several Carib families from the unhealthy, flooding Orinoco gathered together. We lodged in the missionary's house. In the parish register we discovered how rapidly the mission had progressed thanks to his zeal and intelligence. From the middle of the plains the heat had become almost unbearable so we thought of travelling by night; but we were not armed and the llanos were infested with numberless robbers who murdered all whites who fell into their hands in atrociously cunning ways. Nothing can be worse than the administration of justice in these colonies. Everywhere we found the prisons filled with criminals who had waited up to eight years for a trial. About one third escape from prison and find refuge in the llanos, where nobody but cattle live. They attack on horseback, like Bedouin Arabs. The dirt in the prisons would be intolerable if prisoners were not allowed to escape every now and then. It is also common that the death penalty cannot be carried out because there are no executioners. When this happens they pardon one of the guilty if he agrees to hang the others. Our guides told us about a *zambo*, famous for his violence, who, just before our arrival at Cumaná, chose to avoid his execution by turning executioner. The preparations broke his will, and he was horrified at what he was about to do, preferring death to the shame of saving his own life. He asked for his irons to be put back on. He did not stay in prison much longer, as cowardice in another prisoner saw that he was executed. This awakening of honour in a murderer is psychologically very interesting. A man who has spilled so much blood robbing travellers on the steppes hesitates to inflict a punishment that he feels he himself has deserved.

If in the peaceful times when Bonpland and myself travelled through both Americas the llanos were the refuge of criminals from the Orinoco missions, or who had escaped from coastal prisons, how much worse it must be following the bloody Independence struggles! Our wastes and heaths are but a poor image of the New World savannahs, which for over 8,000 to 10,000 square leagues are as smooth as the sea. Their immensity makes it easy for vagabonds to remain free.

After three days' journey we finally glimpsed the Cumaná mountains between the llanos or, as they say here, 'the great sea of green' ('los llanos son como un mar de yerbas'), and the Caribbean coast. Although some 800 toises high, the Brigantín is visible from over 27 leagues away; however, the atmosphere prevented us from seeing that attractive curtain of mountains. At first it appeared as a layer of mist; gradually this mass of mist turned blue and took on its fixed outline. What a sailor sees on approaching new land is what a traveller experiences on the borders of the llano. A *llanero*, or llano inhabitant, only feels at ease when, so the popular saying goes, 'he can see all around him'. What appears to us as covered in vegetation, a rolling land with slight hills, is for him a terrible region bristling with mountains. After having lived for months in the thick Orinoco jungles where you see stars as if from a well, a gallop across the steppes is quite agreeable. The novelty of all you feel strikes you, and like a *llanero* you too feel happy 'to see everywhere around you'. But this new pleasure (which we ourselves experienced) does not last long. To contemplate an immense horizon is imposing whether from Andean summits or the Venezuelan plains. Limitless space reflects a similar quality inside us (as poets in all languages have written); it suggests higher matters, and elevates the minds of those who enjoy solitary meditation. However, there is also something sad and monotonous about the dusty and cracked steppes. After eight to ten days' journey you get used to the mirages and the brilliant green of the tufts of mauritia palms, and seek more variety, like seeing tall jungle trees or wild cataracts or cultivated lands.

On the 23rd of July we entered the town of Nueva Barcelona, less affected by the heat on the llanos than by the sand wind that painfully chapped our skin. We were well received at the house of Don Pedro Lavié, a wealthy French merchant. He had been accused of hiding the unfortunate España[133] on the run in 1796. He was arrested by order of the *audiencia*. But his friendship with the Cumaná governor, and his services as a merchant, got him released. We had visited him in prison before and now found him back with his family, but very ill. He died without seeing the independence of America that his friend Don José España had predicted just before his execution.

The climate of Nueva Barcelona is not as hot as that of Cumaná, but it is humid and unhealthy during the rainy season. Bonpland had survived the crossing of the llanos and had recovered his strength to work as hard as before. I myself felt worse in Nueva Barcelona than I had in Angostura after our long river trip. One of those tropical downpours, with those enormous raindrops that fall far apart from each other, made me so ill I thought I had typhus. We spent a month in Neuva Barcelona, enjoying all the comforts of the town.

Two leagues south-east of Nueva Barcelona there is a high chain of mountains backing on the Cerro Brigantín known as the Aguas Calientes (Hot Waters). When I felt my health had returned we made an excursion there. This trip ended with an unfortunate accident. Our host had lent us his best saddle horses. We had been warned not to cross the Narigual river on horseback so we crossed on a kind of bridge made of tree trunks; the animals swam across as we held the bridles. Suddenly my horse disappeared and struggled under water. There was no way I could find out what had pulled it under. Our guides guessed that it must have been a cayman, common in this region, that had seized its legs.

The mail-boats (*correos*) that cross from La Coruña to Havana and Mexico had been due for over three months. It was thought they had been attacked by English ships near by. I was in a hurry to reach Cumaná and cross to Veracruz so on the 26th of August I hired an open boat called a *lancha*. This *lancha* smuggled cocoa to the island of Trinidad, so its owner was not afraid of the enemy ships blockading the Spanish ports. We loaded our plants, instruments and monkeys and hoped that it would be but a short journey from the mouth of the Neveri river to Cumaná. But no sooner were we in the narrow canal that separates the mainland from the rocky islands of Borracha and Chimanas than we bumped into an armed ship, which ordered us to stop, and fired a round at us from far off. The boat belonged to a pirate from Halifax. By his accent and build I recognized a Prussian from Memel among his crew. Since I had been in America I had not once spoken my mother tongue, and would have preferred a more peaceful opportunity to do so. But my protests were to no avail, and we were led aboard the pirate ship. They ignored the passports issued by the governor of Trinidad allowing cocoa smuggling, and considered us a lawful prize. As I spoke English fairly well I was able to bargain with the captain, and stopped him from taking us to Nova Scotia by persuading him to put us ashore on the nearest coast. While I was arguing about our rights in the cabin I heard a noise on deck. A sailor rushed in and whispered something to the captain, who left quite upset. Luckily for us an English warship (the *Hawk*) was also passing by. It had signalled the pirate boat, but on receiving no answer had shot a round of artillery and sent a midshipman aboard. He was a polite young man who led me to hope that our *lancha* with its cocoa would be released. He invited me to accompany him, assuring me that Captain John Garnier of the Royal Navy could offer better accommodation than the ship from Halifax.

I accepted, and was very politely welcomed by Captain Garnier. He had been as far to the north-west as Vancouver, and was fascinated by all that I told him about the great Atures and Maypures cataracts, about the Orinoco bifurcation and its link with the Amazon. He had followed my progress from reading English newspapers.[134] He introduced me to several of his officers. For over a year I had not met so many well-informed people in one gathering. I was very well treated, and the captain gave me his state room. When you have come from the Casiquiare jungles, with nothing but the company of a narrow circle of missionaries for months, it is a joy to talk to men who have travelled round the world and broadened their minds by seeing so many different things. I left the boat, blessing the career I had devoted my life to.

It was moving to see the beach where we had first arrived, and where Bonpland had nearly lost his life. Among the cacti stood the Guaiquerí Indian huts. Every part of the landscape was familiar to us, from the forest of cacti to the huts and the giant ceiba, which grew near where we had swum every evening. Our Cumaná friends came to meet the *lancha*; botanizing had enabled us to meet people from all social classes. They were relieved as there had been news that Bonpland had died of fever on the banks of the Orinoco, and that we had sunk in a storm near the Urana mission.

The port of Cumaná was closely blockaded, and we had to wait there two and a half months longer. We spent our time completing our collection of the flora of Cumaná, geologizing along the eastern part of the Araya peninsula, and observing numerous planetary eclipses. The live animals we had brought from the Orinoco intrigued all the Cumaná inhabitants. We wanted to send them to the zoo in Paris. The arrival of a French squadron gave us an unexpected opportunity to send the monkeys and birds on, but they all died in Guadeloupe.

Having given up hope of the mail-boat from Spain we boarded an American ship loaded with salt for Cuba. We had spent sixteen months on this coast and in the interior of Venezuela. On the 16th of November we left our Cumaná friends to cross the Gulf of Cariaco for Nueva Barcelona for the third time. The sea breeze was strong and after six hours we anchored off the Morro of Nueva Barcelona, where a ship was waiting to take us to Havana.[135]

CHAPTER 23

Cuba to Cartagena

I twice visited the island of Cuba, living there first for three months, and then for six weeks. Bonpland and I visited the neighbourhood of Havana, the beautiful Guines valley, and the coast between Batabanó and the port of Trinidad.

The way Havana looks as you enter the port makes it one of the most pleasant and picturesque places on the American equinoctial coasts.[136] Celebrated by travellers from all over the world, this site is not like the luxurious vegetation along the Guayaquil banks, nor the wild majesty of Rio de Janeiro's rocky coasts, but the charms that in our climates embellish cultivated nature are here joined to the power and organic vigour of tropical nature. In this sweet blend of impressions, the European forgets the dangers that threaten him in crowded West Indian cities; he tries to seize all the diverse elements in this vast countryside and contemplate the forts that crown the rocks to the east of the port, the inland basin surrounded by villages and farms, the palm trees reaching amazing heights, a town half hidden by a forest of ships' masts and sails. You enter Havana harbour between the Morro fort (Castillo de los Santos Reyes) and the San Salvador de la Punta fort: the opening is barely some 170 to 200 toises wide, and remains like this for one fifth of a mile. Leaving this neck, and the beautiful San Carlos de la Cabaña castle and the Casa Blanca to the north, you reach the basin shaped like a clover whose great axis, stretching south-south-west to north-north-east, is about 2.2 miles long. This basin links up with three creeks, one of which, the Atares, is supplied with fresh water. The city of Havana, surrounded by walls, forms a promontory limited to the south by the arsenal; to the north by the Punta fort. Passing some sunken ships, and the Luz shoals, the water becomes some 5 to 6 fathoms deep. The castles defend the town from the west. The rest of the land is filled with suburbs (*arrabales* or *barrios extra muros*), which year by year shrink the Field of Mars (Campo de Marte). Havana's great buildings, the cathedral, the Casa del Gobierno, the admiral's house, the arsenal, the *correo* or post office, and the tobacco factory are less remarkable for their beauty than for their solidity; most of the streets are very narrow and are not yet paved. As stones come from Veracruz, and as transporting them is expensive, someone had recently come up with the strange idea of using tree trunks instead of paving-stones. This project was quickly abandoned, though recently arrived travellers could see fine *cahoba* (mahogany) tree trunks sunk into the mud. During my stay, few cities in Spanish America could have been more unpleasant due to the lack of a strong local government. You walked around in mud up to your knees, while the amount of four-wheeled carriages or *volantes* so typical of Havana, carts loaded with sugar cane, and porters who elbowed passers-by made being a pedestrian annoying and humiliating. The stench of *tasajo*, or poorly dried meat, stank out the houses and tortuous streets. I have been assured that the police have now remedied these inconveniences, and cleaned up the streets. Houses are more aerated; but here, as in ancient European cities, correcting badly planned streets is a slow process.

There are two fine walks, one (the Alameda) between the Paula hospital and the theatre, redecorated by an Italian artist in 1803 in fine taste; the other between the Punta fort and the Puerta de la Muralla. This last one, also called the Paseo Extra Muros, is a deliciously fresh walk: after sunset many carriages come here. Near the Campo de Marte there is a botanical garden, and something else, which disgusts me – the huts in front of which the slaves are put to be sold. It is along this walk that a marble statue of Charles III was meant to be erected. Originally this site was meant for a monument to Columbus, whose ashes were brought from Santo Domingo to Cuba. Fernando Cortés's ashes had been transferred the same year to Mexico from one church to another. At the end of the eighteenth century the two greatest men in the history of the conquest of America were given new tombs.

The most majestic palm tree of its tribe, the *palma real*, gives the countryside around Havana its special character. It is the *Oreodoxa regia* in our description of American palms; its tall trunk, swelling slightly in the middle, rises 60 to 80 feet high; its upper part shines with a tĕnder green, newly formed by the closing and dilation of the petioles, and contrasts with the rest, which is whitish and fissured. It looks like two columns, one on top of the other. The Cuban *palma real* has feathery leaves rising straight up towards the sky, curving only at the tips. The form of this plant reminded us of the *vadgiai* palm covering the rocks on the Orinoco cataracts, balancing its long arrows above the mist of foam. Here, like everywhere, as the population increases so vegetation diminishes. Around Havana, in the Regla amphitheatre, these palms that so delighted me are now disappearing year by year. The marshy places covered with bamboos have been cultivated and are drying out. Civilization progresses; and today I am told that the land offers only a few traces of its former savage abundance. From the Punta to San Lázaro, from the Cabaña to Regla, from Regla to Atares, everything is covered with houses: those circling the bay are lightly and elegantly built. The owners draw a plan and order a house from the United States, as if ordering furniture. As long as yellow fever rages in Havana, people will retire to their country houses and enjoy fresher air. In the cool nights, when ships cross the bay and leave long phosphorescent tracks in the water, these rural sites become a refuge for those who flee a tumultuous, over-populated city.[137]

At the end of April Bonpland and I had completed the observations we intended to make at the northern extreme of the torrid zone and were about to leave for Veracruz with Admiral Ariztizabal's fleet. But we were misled by false information concerning Captain Baudin's journey and decided to forgo our plan of passing Mexico on our way to the Philippine Islands. A newspaper announced that the two French sloops, the *Géographie* and the *Naturaliste*, had set sail for Cape Horn and would call in at Chile and Peru on their way to New Holland. This news shook me. I was reminded of my original intention in Paris when I had asked the Directorate to hasten Captain Baudin's departure.[138]

On leaving Spain I had promised to join his expedition wherever I could reach it. Bonpland, as active and optimistic as usual, and I immediately decided to split our herbals into three lots to avoid the risk of losing what had taken so much trouble to collect on the banks of the Orinoco, Atabapo and Río Negro. We sent one collection by way of England to Germany, another via Cádiz to France, and the third we left in Havana. We had reason to congratulate ourselves on this prudence. Each collection contained virtually the same species; if the cases were taken by pirates there were instructions to send them to Sir Joseph Banks or to the natural history museum in Paris. Luckily I did not send my manuscripts to Cádiz with our friend and fellow traveller Father Juan Gonzalez, who left Cuba soon after us but whose vessel sank off Africa, with the loss of all life. We lost duplicates of our herbal collection, and all the insects Bonpland had gathered. For over two years we did not receive one letter from Europe; and those we got in the following three years never mentioned earlier letters. You may easily guess how nervous I was about sending a journal with my astronomical observations and barometrical measurements when I had not had the patience to make a copy. After visiting New Granada, Peru and Mexico I happened to be reading a scientific journal in the public library in Philadelphia and saw: 'M. de Humboldt's manuscripts have arrived at his brother's house in Paris via Spain.' I could scarcely suppress an exclamation of joy.

While Bonpland worked day and night dividing our herbal collections, thousands of obstacles prevented our departure from Havana. No ship would take us to Porto Bello or Cartagena. People seemed to enjoy exaggerating the difficulties faced crossing the isthmus and the time it takes to go by ship from Guayaquil to Lima. They reproached me for not continuing to explore those vast rich Spanish American lands that for over fifty years had not been open to any foreign travellers. Finding no boat I had to hire a Catalonian sloop anchored at Batabanó to take me to Porto Bello or Cartagena, depending on how the Santa Marta gales might blow. The prosperity of Havana, and its mercantile links with pacific ports, allowed me to procure funds for several years. I was able to exchange my revenues in Prussia for a part of General Don Gonzalo O'Farrill's, who was Minister to the Spanish Court in Prussia. On the 6th of March the sloop I had hired was ready to sail.

The road from Río Blanco to Batabanó crossed uncultivated land, half covered in jungle, with wild indigo and cotton trees in the clearings. Several friends, including Señor de Mendoza, captain of

Valparaíso harbour, and brother of the famous astronomer who had lived so long in London, accompanied us to Potrero de Mopox. While herborizing we found a new palm tree with fan leaves (*Corypha maritima*).

Batabanó was then a poor village, and its church had only just been finished. The *ciénaga* begins about half a league from the village, a marsh stretching about 60 leagues from west to east. At Batabanó it is thought that the sea is encroaching on the land. Nothing is sadder than these marshes. Not even a shrub breaks the monotony; a few stunted palm trees rise like broken masts among tufts of reeds. As we stayed only one night there I regretted not being able to investigate the two species of crocodile, or *cocodrilo*, infesting the *ciénaga*. One the locals call a cayman. The crocodile is said to be very daring, and even climbs into boats when it can. It often wanders a league inland just to devour pigs. It reaches some 15 feet long, and even chases (so they say) men on horseback, while the caymans are so shy that people can bathe in the water when they are around.

On my second visit to Havana in 1804[139] I could not return to the Batabanó *ciénaga* and so I had these two species brought to me at great expense. Two crocodiles arrived alive. The eldest was 4 feet 3 inches long. They were captured with great difficulty and arrived on mules with their snouts muzzled and bound. They were lively and ferocious. In order to observe them we let them loose in a great hall, and from high pieces of furniture watched them attack large dogs. Having lived on the Orinoco, the Apure and the Magdalena for six months among crocodiles we enjoyed observing this strange animal before leaving for Europe, as they change from immobility to frenzied action quite suddenly. I counted thirty-eight teeth in the upper jaw and thirty in the lower. In the description that Bonpland and I made on the spot we deliberately marked that the lower fourth tooth rises over the upper jaw. The cayman sent from Batabanó died on the way and stupidly was not brought to us, so we could not compare the two species.

We set sail on the 9th of March before dawn, nervous about the uncomfortable narrow boat in which we had to sleep on deck. The cabin (*cámara de pozo*) had no light or air and was merely a hold for provisions; we could only just fit our instruments in there. These inconveniences lasted only twenty days.

Batabanó Gulf, surrounded by a low marshy coast, looks like a vast desert. The sea is a greenish-brown. Our sloop was the only boat in the gulf, for this sea route is used only by smugglers or, as they are politely called here, 'traders' (*los tratantes*). One large island called Isla de Pinos, with mountains covered with pines, rises in this bay. We sailed east-south-east to clear the archipelago that Spanish pilots called Jardines (Gardens) and Jardinillos (Bowers), reaching the rocky island of Cayo de Piedras. Columbus named them the Queen's Gardens in 1494 when on his second voyage he struggled for fifty-eight days with the winds and currents between Pinos Island and the eastern cape of Cuba. A part of these so-called gardens is indeed beautiful; the scene changes all the time and the green contrasts with the white, barren sands. The sand seems to undulate in the sun's heat as if it were liquid.

Despite the small size of our boat, and the boasted skill of our pilot, we often ran aground. The bottom was soft so there was no danger of sinking. At sunset we preferred to lie at anchor. The first night was beautifully serene, with countless shooting stars all falling in the same direction. This area is completely deserted, while in Columbus's time it was inhabited by great numbers of fishermen. These Cuban inhabitants used a small fish to catch the great sea-turtles. They tied this fish to a long cord of the *revés* (the Spanish name for the echeneis). This 'fisher-fish' fixed itself on the shell of the turtle by means of its suckers. The Indians pulled both sucker fish and turtle ashore. It took three days to pass through this labyrinth of Jardines and Jardinillos. As we moved east the sea got rougher.

We visited the Cayo Bonito, which deserves its name (pretty) as it is covered with lush vegetation. On a layer of sand and shells 5 to 6 inches thick rises a forest of mangroves. From their shape and size they look from afar like laurels. What characterizes these coral islands is the wonderful *Tournefortia gnaphalioides* of jacquin, with silvery leaves, which we found here for the first time. This is a shrub some 4 to 5 feet high that gives off a pleasing scent. While we were botanizing our sailors looked for lobsters among the rocks. Irritated at not finding any they took revenge by climbing into the mangroves

and slaughtering young alcatras nesting in pairs. This alcatras builds
its nest where several branches meet, and four or five nest on the
same trunk. The younger birds tried to defend themselves with their
long beaks, while the older ones flew above our heads making hoarse,
plaintive cries. Blood streamed from the trees for the sailors were
armed with long sticks and machetes. We tried to prevent this
pointless cruelty but sailors, after years at sea, enjoy slaughtering
animals. The ground was littered with wounded birds struggling
against death. When we arrived on the scene it was strangely silent, as
if saying, 'man has passed this way'.

On the 14th of March we entered the Guaurabo river at one of
Trinidad de Cuba's two ports, to put our *práctico*, or pilot, who had
steered us through the Jardinillos and run us aground, ashore. We also
hoped to catch a *correo marítimo* (mail-boat) to Cartagena. Towards
evening I landed and began to set up Borda's azimuth compass and
the artificial horizon to observe the stars when a party of *pulperos*, or
small traders, who had dined on board a foreign ship cheerfully
invited us to accompany them into town. These good people asked us
to mount two each to a horse; as it was excessively hot we accepted
their offer. The road to Trinidad runs across a plain covered with
vegetation where the *miraguama*, a silver-leafed palm tree, stands
out. This fertile soil, although of *tierra colorada*, needs only to be tilled
to yield rich harvests. After emerging from a forest we saw a curtain
of hills whose southern slope was covered with houses. This is
Trinidad, founded in 1514 on account of the 'rich gold mines' said to
lie in the Armani river valley. The streets of Trinidad are all very
steep and again show why people complain, as they do over all
Spanish America, of how badly the conquistadores chose the sites of
new towns.

We spent a very agreeable evening in the house of Don Antonio
Padrón, one of the richest inhabitants, where we found all Trinidad
society gathered in a *tertulia*. We were again struck by how vivacious
Cuban women are. Though lacking the refinements of European
civilization, the primitive simplicity of their charms pleased us. We
left Trinidad on March the 15th. The mayor had us driven down to
the mouth of the Guaurabo river in a fine carriage lined with old
crimson damask. To add to our confusion a priest, the local poet,

dressed in a velvet suit despite the heat, celebrated our voyage to the Orinoco with a sonnet.

On the road to the harbour we were struck by the countless phosphorescent insects (*Cocuyo*, *Elater noctilucus*). The grass, the branches and the leaves of trees all shone with that reddish, flickering light. It seemed as if the stars had fallen on to the savannah! In the poorest hut in the country fifteen *cocuyos*, placed in a gourd pierced with holes, give sufficient light to look for things at night. Shaking the gourd excites the animals and increases the luminous discs on their bodies. A young woman at Trinidad told us that during a long passage from the mainland she used the phosphorescent *cocuyos* when she wanted to nurse her baby at night. The captain of the ship would use only *cocuyos* lights so as not to attract pirates.

Our journey from Cuba to the South American coast near the Sinu river took sixteen days. On the 30th of March we doubled Punta Gigantes, and made for the Boca Chica, the present entrance to Cartagena harbour. From there to our anchorage the distance is 7 or 8 miles. We took a *práctico* to pilot us but repeatedly touched sandbanks. On landing I learned with great satisfaction that M. Fidalgo's coastal surveying expedition[140] had not yet set out to sea. This enabled me to fix astronomical positions of several towns on the shore. The passage from Cartagena to Porto Bello, and the isthmus along the Chagres and Cruces rivers, is short and easy. But we were warned that we might stay in Panama a while before finding a boat for Guayaquil, and then it would take ages to sail against the winds and currents. I reluctantly gave up my plan to level the isthmus mountains with my barometer, though I never guessed that as I write today (1827) people would still be ignorant of the height of the ridge dividing the waters of the isthmus.[141] Everybody agreed that a land journey via Bogotá, Popayán, Quito and Cajamaraca would be better than a sea journey, and would enable us to explore far more. The European preference for the *tierras frías*, the cold, temperate climate of the Andes, helped us make our decision. The distances were known, but not the time we finally took. We had no idea it would take us eighteen months to cross from Cartagena to Lima. This change in our plan and direction did allow me to trace the map of the Magdalena river, and astronomically determine eighty points inland, collect several thousand new plants and observe volcanoes.

The result of my labours have long since been published. My map of the Magdalena river appeared in 1816. Till then no traveller had ever described New Granada, and the public, except in Spain, knew how to navigate the Magdalena only from some lines traced by Bouguer.[142] Travel books have multiplied, and political events have drawn travellers to countries with free institutions who publish their journals too hurriedly on returning to Europe. They have described the towns they visited and stayed in, as well as the beautiful landscape; they give information about the people, the means of travel in boat, on mule or on men's backs. Though these works have familiarized the Old World with Spanish America, the absence of a proper knowledge of Spanish and the little care taken to establish the names of rivers, places and tribes have led to extraordinary mistakes.[143]

During our six-day stay at Cartagena, our most interesting excursions were to the Boca Grande and the Popa hill with its fine view. The port, or *bahía*, is 9.5 miles long. The unhealthiness of Cartagena comes from the great marshes surrounding the town on the east and north. The Ciénaga de Tesca is more than 15 miles long. A sad vegetation of cactus, *Jatropha gossypifolia*, croton and mimosa covers the arid slopes of Cerro de la Popa. While botanizing on these wild spots our guides pointed out a thick *Acacia cornigera* bush infamous for a deplorable event. This acacia is armed with very sharp thorns, and extraordinarily large ants live on it. A woman, annoyed by her husband's well-founded jealousy, planned a barbarous revenge. With the help of her lover she tied her husband up with rope, and at night chucked him into this *Acacia cornigera* bush. The more violently he struggled the more the sharp thorns tore his skin. His screams were heard by some passers-by who found him after several hours covered with blood and dreadfully stung by ants. This crime is without example in the history of human perversion; the violence of its passion derives from the coarseness of manners, not from the Tropics. My most important work at Cartagena was comparing my observations with the astronomical positions fixed by Fidalgo's officers.

We prolonged our stay in Cartagena as long as our work and my comparisons with Fidalgo's astronomical observations demanded. The company of this excellent sailor and Pombo and Don Ignacio Cavero (once Secretary to Viceroy Góngora) taught us a lot about statistics. I often quoted Pombo's notes about trade in *quinquina* and the state of the province of Cartagena's population and agriculture. We also came across a curious collection of drawings, machine models and minerals from New Granada in an artillery officer's house. The Pascua (Easter) processions enabled us to see how civilized the customs of the lower classes are. The temporary altars are decorated with thousands of flowers, including the shiny *Plumeria alba* and *Plumeria rubra*. Nothing can be compared with the strangeness of those who took the main parts in the procession. Beggars with crowns of thorns asked for alms, with crucifixes in their hands. They were covered in black cloth and went from house to house having paid the priest a few piastres for the right to collect. Pilate was dressed in a suit of striped silk; the apostles sitting round a long table laid with sweet foods were carried on the shoulders of *zambos*. At sunset you saw dummies of Jews dressed as Frenchmen, filled with straw and rockets, hanging from strings like our own street lights. People waited for the moment when these *judíos* (Jews) would be set on fire. They complained that this year the Jews did not burn as well as they had in others because it was so damp. These 'holy recreations' (the name given to this barbarous spectacle) in no way improves manners.

Frightened about being exposed too long to the unhealthy Cartagena airs we moved to the Indian village of Turbaco (once called Tarasco) on the 6th of April. It is situated in a delicious place where the jungle begins some 5 leagues south-south-east of Pipa. We were happy to leave a foul inn (*fonda*) packed with soldiers left over from General Rochambeau's unfortunate expedition.[144] Interminable discussions about the need to be cruel to the blacks of Santo Domingo reminded me of the opinions and horrors of the sixteenth-century conquistadores. Pombo lent us his beautiful house in Turbaco, built by Archbishop Viceroy Góngora. We stayed as long as it took us to prepare for our journey up the Magdalena, and then the long land trip from Honda to Bogotá, Popoyán and Quito. Few stays in the Tropics have pleased me more. The village lies some 180 toises above sea-level. Snakes are very common and chase rats into the houses. They climb on to roofs and wage war with the bats, whose screaming annoyed us all night. The Indian huts covered a steep plateau so that everywhere you can view shady valleys watered by small streams. We especially enjoyed being on our terrace at sunrise and sunset as it faced the Sierra Nevada de Santa Marta, some 35 leagues distant. The snow-covered peaks – probably San Lorenzo – are clearly seen from Turbaco when the wind blows and brings cooler air. Thick vegetation covers the hills and plains between the Mahates dyke and the snowy mountains: they often reminded us of the beautiful Orinoco mountains. We were surprised to find, so close to the coast in a land frequented by Europeans for over three centuries, gigantic trees belonging to completely unknown species, such as the *Rhinocarpus excelsa* (which the creoles call *caracoli* because of its spiral-shaped fruit), the *Ocotea turbacensis* and the *mocundo* or *Cavanillesia platanifolia*, whose large fruit resemble oiled paper lanterns hanging at the tip of each branch.

Every day we went botanizing in the Turbaco forests from five in the morning until dark: these long walks would have been a delight in this fertile marshy soil if we had not been devoured by mosquitoes, *zancudos*, chigoes and numberless insects already described in the Orinoco part of this narrative. In the midst of these wonderful forests, smelling the flowers of the *Crinum erubescens* and *Pancratium littorale*, we often came across Indian *conucos*, little banana and maize plantations where Indians, ever ready to flee from whites, live during the rainy season. This taste for the jungle and isolation typifies the American Indian. Though the Spanish population has mixed with the Indian population in Turbaco, the latter display the same lack of culture as in the Guianan missions. Examining their farming tools, the way they build their bamboo huts, their clothes and crude arts, I ask myself what the copper race has earned by contact with European civilization.

People in Turbaco out botanizing with us often spoke of a marshy land in the middle of a palm-tree forest that they called 'little volcanoes', *los volcancitos*. A village tradition claims that this land had once been in flames but that a good priest, known for his piety, cast holy water and put the underground fire out, changing the volcano of fire into a volcano of water, *volcán de agua*. This tale reminded me of the geological disputes between Neptunists and Vulcanists of the last century. The local wise man, the Turbaco priest, assured us that the *volcancitos* were simply thermal waters swimming with sulphur, erupting during storms with 'moans'. We had been too long in the Spanish colonies not to doubt these marvellous fantasies coming more from superstitious whites than from Indians, half-castes and African slaves. We were led to the *volcancitos* in the jungle by Indians and found *salses*, or air volcanoes.

In the Turbaco forest, full of palm trees, there is a clearing about 800 square feet in size without any vegetation, bordered by tufts of *Bromelia kavatas*, whose leaf is like a pineapple's. The surface of the ground was composed of layers of cracked grey-black clay. What they call *volcancitos* are fifteen to twenty small truncated cones rising in the middle of the clearing. They are some 3 to 4 toises high. The high edges are filled with water and they periodically release large air bubbles. I counted five explosions in two minutes. The force of the rising air makes you think of a powerful pressure deep in the earth. Indian children who came with us helped us block some of the smaller craters with clay, but the gas always pushed the earth away. According to the Indians the number and shape of the cones near the path had not changed for over twenty years, and they remain full of water even in droughts. The heat of the water was the same as that of the air. With long sticks we could reach some 6 to 7 feet down inside a cone. Leaving the water in a glass it became quite clear, and tasted slightly of alum.

Our stay in Turbaco was extremely agreeable, and useful for our botanical collection. Even today those bamboo forests, the wild fertility of the land, the orchids carpeting the old ocotea and Indian fig-tree trunks, the majestic view of the snowy mountains, the light mist covering the valleys at sunrise, bunches of gigantic trees like green islands above a sea of mist, all return incessantly to my imagination. Our life at Turbaco was simple and hard-working; we were young, linked by similar tastes and characters, always full of hope in the future, on the eve of a journey that would take us to the highest Andean peaks, and volcanoes on fire in a country where earthquakes are common. We felt happier than at any other moment in our expedition. The years that have passed since then, not without bitterness and hardships, have added to the charms of these impressions; I would like to think that in his exile in the Southern hemisphere, in the isolation of Paraguay, my unfortunate friend Bonpland[145] might still recall our delightful herborizings.

As Bonpland's health had cruelly suffered during our journey on the Orinoco and Casiquiare we decided to follow the advice of the locals and supply ourselves with all the comforts possible on our trip up the Magdalena. Instead of sleeping in hammocks or lying on the ground on skins, exposed to the nightly torment of mosquitoes, we did what was done in the country, and got hold of a mattress, a country-bed that was easy to unfold, as well as a *toldo*, a cotton sheet, which could fold under the mattress and make a kind of closed-off tent that no insects could penetrate. Two of these beds, rolled into cylinders of thick leather, were packed on to a mule. I could not praise this system more; it is far superior to the mosquito net.

We had as travelling companions a Frenchman, Dr Rieux from Carcassonne, and the young son of the ill-fated Nariño. The bad luck of these two moved us, reminding us of the state of oppression in this unhappy country. Dr Rieux, a charming, educated man, had come from Europe as doctor to Viceroy Ezpeleta. He was accused of interfering in politics, dragged out of his house in Honda in 1794, clapped in irons and taken to the inquisition prison in Cartagena. This damp place caused him a chronic blindness. For more than a year his wife had no news of his whereabouts. His belongings were dispersed and, as nothing could be proved, he was sent (*bajo partido de registro*) to Cádiz prison where his case would be forgotten. He managed to escape off the African coast.

We left Turbaco on a fresh and very dark night, walking through a bamboo forest. Our muleteers had difficulty finding the track, which was narrow and very muddy. Swarms of phosphorescent insects lit up the tree-tops like moving clouds, giving off a soft bluish light. At dawn we found ourselves at Arjona where the bamboo forest ends and arborescent grasses begin.

We waited nearly the whole day in the miserable village of Mahates for the animals carrying our belongings to the landing-stage on the Magdalena river. It was suffocatingly hot; at this time of year there is not a breath of wind. Feeling depressed we lay on the ground in the main square. My barometer had broken and it was the last one I had. I had anticipated measuring the slope of the river and fixing the speed of its current and the position of different stages through astronomical observations. Only travellers know how painful it is to suffer such accidents, which continued to dog me in the Andes and in Mexico; each time this happened I felt the same. Of all the instruments a traveller should carry the barometer is the one, despite all its imperfections, that caused me the most worry and whose loss I felt the most. Only chronometers, which sometimes suddenly and unpredictably change their rates, give rise to the same sense of loss. Indeed, after travelling thousands of leagues over land with astronomical and physical instruments, you are tempted to cry out: 'Lucky are those who travel without instruments that break, without dried plants that get wet, without animal collections that rot; lucky are those who travel the world to see it with their own eyes, trying to understand it, and recollecting the sweet emotions that nature inspires!'

We saw several beautiful species of large *aras* (*guacamayos*) in the hands of Indians who had killed them in the nearby jungle to eat them. We began to dissect their enormous brains, though they are far less intelligent than parrots. I sketched the parts while Bonpland cut them apart; I examined the hyoid bone and the lower larynx, which cause this bird's raucous sounds. It was the kind of research that Cuvier had recently instigated in anatomy and it appealed to me. I began to console myself for the loss of my barometer. Night did not allow me to determine our latitude through the stars. On the 20th of April at three in the morning, while it was still delightfully fresh, we set off for the Magdalena river landing-stage in the village of Barancas Nuevas. We were still in the thick jungle of bamboos, *Palma amarga* and mimosas, especially the inga with purple flowers. Halfway between Mahates and Barancas we came across some huts raised on bamboo trunks inhabited by *zambos*. This mixture of negro and Indian is very common around here. Copper-coloured women are very attracted to African men and many negroes from Choco, Antioquia province and Simitarra, once they gained their freedom by working hard, have settled in this river valley. We have often reminded you how the wisdom of the oldest Spanish laws favoured the freeing of black slaves while other European nations, boasting of a high degree of civilization, have hindered and continue to hinder this absurd and inhuman law.[146]

NOTES

1. Relation historique: The full title in French was *Relation historique du voyage aux régions équinoxiales du nouveau continent*, which I have translated as *Personal Narrative of Travels to the Equinoctial Regions of America*.

2. *jointly published . . . our work*: See my introduction. Humboldt generously attributed all the thirty volumes to Bonpland and himself, though Bonpland actually authored only one of the two volumes of *Monographie des melastomacées* (1816).

3. *loss of dear friends*: For example, Humboldt's young aristocratic friend Carlos Montúfar and the young botanist José de Caldas (both are named in my introduction) were executed by the Spaniards in 1816.

4. *Captain Baudin*: Captain Thomas Nicolas Baudin (? 1750–1803) was sent on a scientific expedition to the West Indies and on to Australia in year VI of the French Revolutionary calendar. Humboldt wrote to Baudin from La Coruña saying that he intended to join his round-the-world voyage. In 1801 in Cuba he read in an American newspaper that Baudin had left Le Havre. So Humboldt hired a boat from Cuba to Portobello and journeyed south as far as Quito before discovering that Baudin had gone via the Cape of Good Hope. False news made Humboldt travel over 800 leagues (some 2,400 miles) out of his way. Part of Baudin's voyage was published as *Voyage dans les quatre principales îles des mers d'Afrique . . . avec l'histoire de la traversée jusqu'au Port-Louis de l'île de France* in 1804, followed by the Australian part, *Voyage de découverte aux terres australes* in 1841.

5. *Bougainville*: Louis Antoine de Bougainville (1729–1811) sailed round the world in the frigate *La Boudeuse* from 1766 to 1769 and published his influential account *Voyage autour du monde* in 1771. Humboldt met him in Paris. See Louis Constant's edition and introduction (Paris, 1980).

6. '*I was authorized . . . advance the Sciences*': Humboldt included the whole document in Spanish in a footnote, dated 7 May 1799.

7. This section is followed by Humboldt's meticulous list of instruments brought with him on his journey. It should be noted in passing that when Humboldt refers to his barometer he meant a mercury barometer with glass tubes some 30 inches long, both delicate and easily broken.

8. *Malaspina*: Alejandro Malaspina (1754–1810), a Sicilian, sailed round the world in the frigate *Astrea* from 1782 to 1784. In 1789 he was in charge of a fleet hired to map the north-western coast of America but could not find the north-west passage. In 1795 he was arrested as politically suspect and imprisoned without trial. Humboldt refers to him in his *Essai politique sur le royaume de la Nouvelle-Espagne* (1811), vol. 1,

p. 338. See Edward J. Goodman (1972), pp. 209–20; and Iris H.W. Engstrand (1981), pp. 44–75.

9. As an example of Humboldt's digressions this last passage is followed by thirty quarto pages of detailed speculation on ocean currents and their origins.

10. *Gutiérrez*: Pedro Gutiérrez, chief steward on Columbus's first voyage and formerly butler of the King's dais, was murdered by the cacique of Maguara on Hispaniola. Guanahani, named San Salvador by Columbus, was the first sight of the 'Indies', seen on 12 October 1492. It is one of the Bahamas. See Samuel Eliot Morison, *The Great Explorers: The European Discovery of America* (Oxford, 1978).

11. *archil*: Archil is a name given to various species of lichen (like *Roccella tinctoria*), which yield a violet dye and the chemical test substance litmus. It is also the colouring-matter prepared from these lichens.

12. The chapter ends with Humboldt speculating on the visibility of mountain peaks from a distance.

13. *toises*: 1 toise (a French lineal measure) = 1.946 metres or 6.25 feet. Humboldt also uses leagues: the Spanish land league = 4.2 kilometres or 2.6 miles (the English land league = *c.* 3 miles). The metric system, sometimes used by Humboldt, was introduced by a French Revolutionary decree of 1795.

14. *African heat to alpine cold*: Humboldt initiated 'plant geography', especially linking latitudinal vegetation zones with altitudinal ones as seen in his famous cross section or profile of the Andes, covered with plant names. See Malcolm Nicolson, 'Alexander von Humboldt and the Geography of Vegetation' in Andrew Cunningham and Nicholas Jardine (eds.) (1990).

15. Humboldt goes on to describe the establishing of a botanical garden at Tenerife.

16. *Franqui's dragon tree*: Humboldt's *Atlas pittoresque* (1810) includes a sketch of Franqui's dragon tree made in 1776. Marianne North painted several dragon trees, which can be seen at Kew Gardens. Humboldt saw his *Atlas* as a companion volume to his travels. In a note Humboldt describes the dragon tree's astringent juice, called dragon's blood, which nuns at La Laguna soak toothpicks in, which are praised for preserving gums.

17. *sketched a view*: In Humboldt's *Atlas pittoresque* (1810).

18. Humboldt continues: 'So as not to interrupt the narrative of my journey to the summit of the Pico I have been silent about my geological observations,' and then offers a detailed 'tableau physique' of the Canary Islands from quarto pp. 148 to 197. Clearly written, it is based on much extra reading after his return home. The basis of this section is Humboldt's boast that he has formed his ideas by actually being there on the spot to compare volcanoes in both the Old and New Worlds. Travel and new observations had changed his fixed ideas about nature. He sees himself as the first scientist to look at the whole earth 'dans son ensemble'.

19. *existence is as dubious as that of the isles of Fonseco and Saint Anne*: Humboldt's note: 'Jeffery's and Van-Keulen's charts indicate four islands, which are only imaginary dangers: Garca, Saint Anne, the Green Island and Fonseco. How is it possible to believe in the existence of four islands in latitudes crossed by thousands of ships?'

20. *passage from Dante*: Humboldt cites in Italian:

> Right-hand I turned, and, setting me to spy
> That alien pole, beheld four stars, the same
> The first men saw, and since, no living eye;
>
> Meseemed the heavens exulted in their flame –
> O widowed world beneath the northern Plough,
> For ever famished of the sight of them!
>
> Dante's *Purgatory*, Canto 1, 22–7

21. *Paul and Virginie*: As noted in my introduction, Humboldt virtually knew *Paul et Virginie* by heart.

22. *time-keeper*: Humboldt's time-keeper or chronometer was a Lewis Berthoud, No. 27, and had belonged to 'the celebrated Borda'; Jean Louis Borda (1733–99), a French sailor and mathematician who tested various measuring instruments.

23. *Terra Firma*: Terra Firma refers to the northern coasts of South America (Venezuela/Colombia) as distinct from the West Indies.

24. *this malady*: Humboldt identifies the disease in a note: '*Typhus*, Sauvages; *Febris nervosa*, Frank.'

25. Humboldt closes this chapter by saying that he has avoided interrupting the narrative of his voyage by giving detailed physical observations. He then fully explains, from quarto pp. 224 to 266, with tables and speculations, all his experiments on board ship concerning the temperature of the air, the colour of the sky and sea, the dip of the magnetic needle, and his log with time and latitudes all noted. These pages exemplify his ceaseless activity.

26. pulpero: Humboldt notes that a *pulpero* is the owner of a *pulpería*, or little shop, where food and drinks are sold.

27. charas: Humboldt notes that *chara* is corrupted from *chacra*, meaning a hut surrounded by a garden.

28. Scoparia dulcis ... *sensitive leaves*: Humboldt notes that Spaniards called these plants *dormideras* (sleeping plants) and that he and Bonpland discovered three new species previously unknown to botanists.

29. *Lope de Aguirre*: Humboldt's note:

When at Cumaná, or on the island of Margarita, people say the word 'el tirano' it is always to denote the hated Lopez d'Aguire (Lope de Aguirre), who, after taking part in the 1560 revolt led by Fernando de Guzmán against Pedro de Ursúa, governor of the Omeguas and Dorado, voluntarily took the title of *traidor*, or traitor. He descended the Amazon river with his band and reached the island of Margarita along the Guianan rivers. The port of Paraguache is still called the tyrant's port.

30. *Acosta's*: José Acosta, Jesuit priest, was born *c.* 1539 in Spain, went out to Peru in 1571, and died in 1600. He wrote *Historia natural y moral de las Indias* in Spanish in 1590, translated into English in 1604.

31. *Dollond's telescope*: Humboldt used the English-made 3-foot achromatic Dollond telescope, strong enough to see Jupiter's moons. Luigi Galvani (1737–98) was an Italian experimenter with electricity who published in 1791 his *De Viribus electricitatis in motu musculari* after discovering that electricity made a frog's legs twitch. He made a device with two different metal contacts that made muscles contract. Humboldt, with his brother Wilhelm, experimented with Galvanism in Jena in 1795; in 1797 he published a paper on his Galvanic experiments.

32. *debasing custom . . . shown in a play by Cervantes . . . Algiers*: Miguel de Cervantes Saavedra (1547–1616) was captured at sea by the Turks and taken to Algiers as a slave for five years until 1580. He wrote an early play called *El trato de Argel*, discovered in manuscript in 1784.

33. *'who save . . . harvesting'*: Humboldt quotes from La Bruyère's *Caractères* (1765).

34. *'Qué hielo! Estoy emparamado'*: In a note Humboldt translates, 'What an icy cold! I shiver as if I was on top of a mountain.' The provincial word *emparamarse* he derives from *páramo*, in Peruvian *puna*, which signifies a mountainous place covered with stunted trees, exposed to the winds, where a damp cold prevails.

35. *abundance of salt . . . Portobello*: Humboldt notes that he unearthed these facts from an archive in Cumaná; another example of his industriousness.

36. Humboldt continues with a digression over salt and its uses, especially salted beef, or *tasajo*, and then the geology of the region.

37. *across the ocean*: Humboldt's note explains the Spanish 'por allá' and 'del otro lado del charco' – 'over there' and 'across the pond' – as figurative expressions used by colonists to denote Europe.

38. *Benzoni*: According to Humboldt Benzoni was related to the Duke of Milan's assassin, Galeazzi Maria Sfonza, and could not pay back the capital advanced to him by Sevillian traders; he stayed five years at Cubagua, and died in a fit of madness.

39. *petroleum, mentioned by the first chroniclers*: Humboldt quoted from Oviedo (Fernández de Oviedo y Valdés (1478–1557), official historian of the Indies who published in 1534 his *Historia general y natural de las Indias*) who called it a 'resinous, aromatic and medicinal liquor'.

40. *Azara*: Félix de Azara (1746–1821) spent many years mapping frontiers in Paraguay, and wrote in French his *Voyage dans l'Amérique méridionale* (Paris, 1809). See Edward J. Goodman (1972), pp. 238–42.

41. quipus: The *quipu* was an Inca record knot, a mnemonic device of coloured knotted strings. The Incas had not developed writing.

42. *missions*: Humboldt notes that in the Spanish colonies a *misión*, or *pueblo de misiónes*, is a cluster of huts round a church run by a missionary monk. Indian villages, governed by priests, are called *pueblos de doctrina*. One differentiates the *cura doctrinario*, who is the priest in charge of Indians, from the *cura rector*, who is the priest of a village inhabited by whites or half-castes.

43. *Saussure's hygrometer*: Humboldt carried two instruments perfected by Horace Saussure (1740–99), a Swiss mountaineer and botanist whose *Voyage dans les Alpes* (1779–96) and *Traité d'hygrométrie* were famous in his day. The hygrometer (an instrument measuring humidity) was made of hair and whalebone. Humboldt also had Saussure's magnetometer.

44. *gramineous plant with verticillate branches*: Humboldt in his note calls it *carice*, excellent fodder for mules. He refers the reader to his forthcoming *Nova Genera et species plantarum* that he is preparing with Bonpland, though W. Kunth later replaced Bonpland. It came out in seven folio volumes between 1815 and 1825. See William T. Stearn (ed.) (1968).

45. Humboldt digresses here to explore the cinchona-cuspa found here. He describes its taste but confesses he did not see its flower, and says, 'and we know not what genus it belongs to'. He reflects on all febrifuge plants by listing them and even tries experiments to find out whether the antifebrile virtues lie in the tannin or in its resinous matter.

46. Bambusa gadua: Illustrated by Humboldt in *Plantes équinoxiales*, vol. 2 (1808–9), plate 20.

47. *Moravian Brethren*: A Protestant sect founded in Saxony by emigrants from Moravia who followed the doctrines of John Huss, a fifteenth-century Bohemian martyr and religious reformer. The Brethren were active as missionaries.

48. tambos . . . *Manco Capac's laws*: Manco Capac was the first Inca emperor from about AD 1200, a demigod, and founder of the Inca dynasty. *Tambos*, or rest houses, were built along the Inca highways and used exclusively for those travelling on official business.

49. Humboldt digresses on male animals whose breasts contain milk, like Corsican billy-goats. After numerous researches, he found two or three examples of breast-feeding men. He concludes that this ability is not confined to American Indians, and is not more common in the New World than in the Old. Lozano was of European stock. Humboldt's other examples came from Syria and Cork, Ireland. He finally speculates on the purpose of the male nipple.

50. Humboldt continues by claiming that Cumaná tobacco is the most aromatic after Cuban and Río Negran. He details its culture – the *cura seca* – as it differs from the Virginian technique.

51. *machetes*: In a note Humboldt describes a machete as a large knife with a long blade, like a hunting knife. No one enters the jungles in the torrid zone without a machete, not only to cut through liana and branches but also as defence against wild animals.

52. *Buffon*: George Louis Leclerc, known as Count Buffon (1707–88), a prestigious Enlightenment figure, was elected to the Académie Royale des Sciences in 1739 and then to Director of the Jardin du Roi. His bestselling *Histoire naturelle* began to appear in 1749 and ran to thirty-six volumes by 1788, but covered only minerals, quadrupeds and birds. Humboldt set out to correct Buffon's erroneous views about Latin America, for Buffon, never having visited the New World, had accused Latin American nature of being immature, and of producing small, weak animals (and no elephants). See Germán Arciniegas, *América en Europa* (Buenos Aires, 1975); and H.R. Hays, *Birds, Beasts and Men: A Humanist History of Zoology* (London, 1973).

53. *leaves, flowers and fruit*: Botanical nomenclature requires leaves, flowers and fruit.

54. *Cocollar* : In a note Humboldt wonders if the former name is of Indian origin. 'At Cumaná I heard it derived, in a far-fetched manner, from the Spanish *cogollo*, meaning the heart of oleraceous plants.'

55. *beautiful grass . . . which I drew*: In Humboldt's *Plantes équinoxiales*, see note 46.

56. *Feijóo's* Teatro crítico *. . . Chaptal's treatise on chemistry*: Benito Jerónimo Feijóo (1676–1764), a Spanish Benedictine 'natural philosopher' who set out to eradicate superstition. L'Abbé Nollet (1700–70), member of the Académie Royale des Sciences, famous for his work on electricity. Jean Antoine Chaptal (1756–1832), a French chemist who rose to become Interior Minister in 1800. His *Eléments de chimie* came out in 1790.

57. *Guácharo grotto*: Humboldt notes the etymology. *Guácharo* is 'one who cries and laments'. The birds in the Caripe caves and the *guacharaca* are very noisy. The Latin name today is *Steatornis caripensis*. Humboldt follows 'M. Cuvier' (see note 98) in placing this bird with the Passeres, and noted it under the genus *Steatornis* in the second volume of his *Recueil d'observations de zoologie et d'anatomie comparée* (1805–33), which Humboldt had dedicated to Cuvier in 1811.

58. Humboldt adds: 'Before leaving the grotto, let us throw a last glance on the phenomena presented by the Guácharo cave . . .' and continues for nine quarto pages.

59. *I sketched these organs*: In Humboldt, *Recueil d'observations de zoologie et d'anatomie comparée*, vol. 1 (1805), plate 4. Humboldt read a paper on the new species of monkey – *Simia leonina* – that he had found on the Orinoco to the Institut National in Paris on 21 January 1805. He published a separate paper on all the monkeys he had observed, with colour prints, in 1810, which was later included in his *Recueil d'observations de zoologie* in 1811.

60. *Mariguitar*: Humboldt notes here that in Raynal's *Geographic Atlas* a town called Verina was drawn in between Cariaco and Cumaná. 'The most recent maps of America are loaded with names of rivers, places and mountains which are erroneous, and handed down from age to age.'

61. *independent Indians . . . Ulloa . . . considerably increased*: See Mary Maples Dunn's abridged edition of John Black's 1811 translation of Humboldt's *Political Essay on the Kingdom of New Spain* and the fascinating chapter on the Indians. Minguet claimed that Humboldt was the first to calculate the Indian population in the Spanish American colonies where whites were only 19 per cent of the total population, compared to 60 per cent in the USA. Antonio de Ulloa (1716–95) was sent with Jorge Juan by the Spanish Crown to accompany and report on the French Académie Royale des Sciences expedition. Ulloa wrote his *Relación histórica del viaje a la América meridional* in 1747, translated into English as *A Voyage to South America* in 1758. He also prepared a secret report, *Noticias secretas de América*, which was suppressed but finally published in England in 1826.

62. Over the next twenty-four quarto pages Humboldt 'succinctly exposes his investigations' into the Chaima language. He lists words, tenses ('an enormous complication of tenses'), grammatical analogies and roots. He outlines other languages. He also lists American words passed into Spanish (*hamaca, tabaco*, etc.) and ends with a list of the grammar books of Indian languages he brought back with him, along with a basic word list. Humboldt brought an Indian servant back from Caripe to Europe. His elder brother Wilhelm was a celebrated philologist. See his *On*

Language: The Diversity of Human Language-Structure and Its Influence on the Mental Development of Mankind, trans. Peter Heath (Cambridge, 1988).

63. Humboldt closes the chapter with a section on the causes of bolides and shooting stars.

64. *Angostura*: Today, Ciudad Bolívar.

65. *Higuerote*: In a letter to his mentor Willdenow (21 February 1801) Humboldt complains that there were so many mosquitoes in Higuerote that he had to bury himself in the sand to sleep.

66. *mangrove . . . sickly smell*: Humboldt collected mangrove roots and branches. In Caracas, he tried to imitate the coastal tides in his room, to see what happened and what gases they gave off as they decomposed.

67. Humboldt continues with pages speculating on yellow fever – *calentura amarilla* or *vómito negro* – whose 'mysterious' cause was unknown in Humboldt's time, though he, like others, blamed miasma. In 1881, in Havana, Carlos Finlay thought the virus was transmitted by mosquitoes (*Aedes aegypti*); his view was confirmed in 1900 by Major Walter Reed; an inoculation was introduced in 1937.

68. *Joseph España had died on the scaffold*: España was executed in Caracas in 1799. He was the *corregidor* of Macuto and participated in the San Blas conspiracy in Spain in 1796, affirming the equality of races (see Charles Minguet (1969), p. 252).

69. *piastres*: A piastre, or peso, a Spanish dollar, broke down into eight *reales*, small silver coins.

70. *Hispano-Americans*: Humboldt imitated the word 'Anglo-American'. He adds that in the Spanish colonies whites born in America are called Spaniards while real Spaniards are called Europeans, *gachupines* or *chapetones*.

71. Following the excerpts about population that I have included Humboldt goes on with a physical description of Caracas, its mean temperatures, rainfall, etc.

72. *peoples of Spanish origin . . . in the colonies*: In letters home Humboldt praised their hospitality and simplicity, and did not mind their ignorance. In a letter (1800) to Baron Forrel in Madrid he wrote: 'On returning to Europe I will very reluctantly de-Spanishify myself.'

73. *analogous climates . . . the poles*: Humboldt's long note:

Plant geography does not merely examine analogies observed in the same hemispheres, like that between Pyrenean vegetation and Scandinavian plains, or that between the cordillera of Peru and Chilean coasts. It also investigates relations between alpine plants in both hemispheres. It compares plants on the Alleghanies and Mexican cordilleras with those in Chile and Brazil . . .

74. *grass from Switzerland . . . Magellan Strait*: Humboldt's note: '*Phleum alpinium*, examined by Mr Brown. The investigations of this great botanist prove that a certain number of plants are at once common to both hemispheres.' See D.J. Mabberley (1985).

75. *Mutis*: Father José Celestino Mutis, born in Cádiz in 1732, died in 1808. Appointed director of the botanical expedition to New Granada (1783–93), he was living in Bogotá from 1761, and warmly received Humboldt. He gave many of his

plates to Humboldt, who dedicated his *Plantes équinoxiales*, vol. 2 (1808–9) to him. Humboldt called Mutis 'one of the century's greatest botanists'. Mutis's monumental *Flora de Bogotá* comprised 5,393 plates (2,495 coloured); they lay forgotten until recently when a joint project by the Spanish and Colombian Governments began to reprint them. Mutis gave Humboldt one hundred plates (now in the Institut National, Paris). See Edward J. Goodman (1972), pp. 223–7.

76. *our friends . . . bloody revolutions . . . deprived them of it*: Humboldt wrote this in Paris in 1819. Bolívar was in Venezuela in 1808 when Napoleon invaded Spain. The first junta of Caracas was created in 1810, sending Bolívar to London. In 1811 independence was formally declared and a Republican constitution invoked. By 1812 Venezuela was back in Royalist hands. A year later, 1813, Bolívar, the 'libertador', was back in charge, only to lose out to the Spaniards a second time. By 1819 he was back in control. See J.F. Rippy and E.R. Brann, 'Alexander von Humboldt and Simón Bolívar', *American Historical Review*, 52 (July 1947), pp. 503–697.

77. *my duty . . . compare them with previous catastrophes*: Humboldt admits he follows M. de la Condamine's example, who wrote about the eruptions of Cotopaxi long after his departure from Quito. La Condamine's *Voyage à l'équateur* (1751) was a model for Humboldt's own narrative. La Condamine, Voltaire's friend, was a scientist, a keen observer, and remained in South America for ten years (1735–44). He travelled down the Amazon, speculated on the myth of the Amazon women, the Casiquiare canal joining the Amazon and Orinoco rivers (later proved by Humboldt), Indian languages, and back in Paris read a memoir to the Académie Royale des Sciences on the rubber trees. See Helen Minguet's edition of his 1745 *Voyage sur l'Amazone* (Paris, 1981).

78. *'It was so violent . . . churches and houses'*: Humboldt quoted from a manuscript by Delpeche, *Sur le tremblement de terre de Venezuela en 1812*, with purple passages about mothers, groaning victims in the moonlight, etc. Humboldt's Romantic sympathy for catastrophes is followed by a long 'study of volcanoes', epitomizing his comparative approach, and his meticulous lists.

79. *In this plantation . . . rum*: Humboldt repeats all this in his popular *Anschiten der Natur* (1808, in English, *Views of Nature or Contemplation on the Sublime Phenomena of Creation*, trans. E.C. Otté (London, 1850), pp. 22–4). This was Humboldt's first report back to Europe of his South American odyssey, and was immensely influential in securing his fame as far south as Argentina where this opening chapter served as Domingo Sarmiento's authority in *Facundo* (1845) for analysing the pampas in Humboldtian terms of civilization and barbarism.

80. *zambo*: *Zambos*, as Humboldt notes far later on, are descendants of Indians and negroes.

81. *papaw tree of the lake . . . tomato*: Humboldt sent the seeds of the lake's papaw and tomato to the Berlin botanical garden. Willdenow called the tomato *Solanum humboldtii*. In a later note Humboldt adds: 'They are said to lead to constipation, and are called by the locals *tapaculo*, that is, "arse blockers".'

82. *nutritious milk pours out*: Humboldt spends pages on plants that exude milky substances. He complains: 'It can scarcely be imagined in Europe how difficult it is to obtain accurate information in a country where nobody ever travels.'

83. Humboldt continues with pages of a detailed study of cacao.

84. *plains without trees . . . climb to the horizon*: Humboldt described the llanos in his popular *Anschiten der Natur* (1808).

85. *Ulloa's*: See note 61.

86. Humboldt interpolates a long description of the continent's llanos, comparing them with others in the world. He adds in these principal features 'to make the narrative of my journey across such a monotonous plain more interesting'; a touch of Humboldtian humour.

87. embarbascar con caballos: In a note Humboldt translates: 'to set to sleep, or intoxicate the eels by means of horses'.

88. *A fight . . . picturesque scene*: Humboldt had first introduced Europeans to electric eels in a paper read at the Institut de France (20 October 1806), then in his *Anschiten der Natur* (1808) where he offered the same 'picturesque' spectacle as here. The electric eel (*Electrophorus electricus*, family Gymnotidae) gives off an alternating electric current that passes from the electrically positive tail to the negative head, reaching 500 volts at 2 amperes to immobilize its prey. Humboldt had one sent back live to Paris where he continued experiments with his friend Gay-Lussac.

89. *enormous boas*: In his *Anschiten der Natur* Humboldt described the boas. The creoles call them *tragavenado*, and found one with antlers stuck in its throat after it had swallowed a stag. They supposedly attain 48 feet, though in Europe the longest actually measured reached only 23 feet.

90. *Felipe de Urre*: Humboldt refers to Philip von Hutten, known as Urre, a German born in 1511 who sailed as an adventurer to Venezuela under a concession granted by Charles V in 1528. He searched for treasure in the interior, and became Captain-General of Venezuela in 1540. He returned inland to seek gold; after having been away for five years he was captured and executed in 1541.

91. *manatees*: Humboldt's notes on the manatee can be found in his *Recueil d'observations de zoologie*, vol. 2 (1833). It is today an endangered species.

92. *March 31st*: From here Humboldt dates his entries, copying down from his actual diary.

93. caribe . . . avid for blood: *Caribe* are the carnivorous piranha of the Characidae family, genus *Serrasalmus*, with massive jaws and razor-sharp teeth. They were called *caribe* after the fierce Carib Indians, warriors from whom we derive the word 'cannibal'. According to Robin Furneaux (1969) Humboldt was the first naturalist to notice the piranha.

94. *our large dog was bitten . . . by some enormous bats*: In Humboldt's *Anschiten der Natur* (E.C. Otté's translation, 1850) we read: 'Huge bats now attack the animals during sleep and, vampire-like, suck their blood.'

95. niguas: Humboldt's note: 'The chigoe (also jigger), *Pulex penetrans*, which digs under the nails of toes in men and monkeys and lays its eggs there.'

96. *Bonpland . . . took control . . . in danger*: In a letter to his brother (17 October 1800) Humboldt praised Bonpland's 'amazing courage' and 'devotion', and tells how he calmed Humboldt down, and baled out the boat, as if he had saved his life. Humboldt did not know how to swim.

97. guayuco: A narrow loincloth usually worn by Indian women.

98. *Cuvier's* Tableau élémentaire d'histoire naturelle: There are letters extant from Humboldt to Cuvier. Georges Cuvier (1769–1832) was Professor of Natural History at Paris, and Secretary of the Académie Royale des Sciences. An important zoologist and comparative anatomist, his law of 'the correlation of parts' led to new means of classifying fossil remains. See J. Théodorides, 'Humboldt and Cuvier', *Biologie médicale*, LIX (1961), pp. 50–71; and Dorinda Outram (1984).

99. *Tequendama Falls*: Illustrated by Humboldt in his *Atlas pittoresque* (1810).

100. The following section on the rapids was first published in Humboldt's *Anschiten der Natur* (1808) in a more exaggerated way. 'Few Europeans' had visited these cataracts. Here Humboldt is explicit about how the physical world is reflected on the inner, susceptible mental world, a mysterious communion. Here also Humboldt mentions his famous parrot of Maypures; the last speaker of the language of the Atures tribe had vanished, so nobody could understand the parrot.

101. *Solano's boundary expedition*: José Solano y Boto (1726–1806), a member of the frontier expedition to the Orinoco.

102. Humboldt continues here with details on the phenomenon of cataracts. Describing the moon, Humboldt felt transported to Bernardin de Saint-Pierre's Ile de France (today Mauritius). Saint-Pierre 'knew how to depict nature, not because he had studied it scientifically, but because he felt it in all its harmonious analogies of forms, colours and inner powers'.

103. ouavapavi: Humboldt refers his reader to his monograph on the Orinoco monkeys, *Recueil d'observations de zoologie*, vol. 1 (1805). The *ouavapavi*, from the Guaiquerí language, is Humboldt's *Simia albifrons*.

104. Humboldt continues here with a discussion on the geographical distribution of venomous insects, according to white and black waters 'in this labyrinth of rivers'. He laments that an entomologist cannot live on the spot. He gives a note in Latin of the five new species of culex he found. Later H.W. Bates, an entomologist, did live there from 1848 to 1859. See his *The Naturalist on the Amazons* (London, 1863). See also Victor W. von Hagen (1948 and 1949); and Edward J. Goodman (1972).

105. *Maypures cataracts*: Humboldt sketched this *raudal* for the Governor-General of Caracas in his *Atlas géographique* (1811). He remained three days in Maypures. He describes the geography; pointing out new species. 'No traveller has yet described this place.'

106. Following this Humboldt notes down as much as he can about the Maypures language and beliefs.

107. *Once you have passed the Great Cataracts*: In a note to the Governor-General of Caracas (see note 105) Humboldt suggested building a canal bypassing the cataracts.

108. *whose location I was the first to establish . . . the Casiquiare*: Sailing down the Casiquiare was Humboldt's greatest exploratory achievement. The Casiquiare canal was known to La Condamine, but not actually explored by him. A.R. Wallace followed Humboldt's 'illustrious' trail from Brazil in 1851; see *Travels on the Río Negro* (1853), chs. 8–10. For a modern trip, accompanied by Humboldt's travelogue, see Redmond O'Hanlon, *In Trouble Again: A Journey between the Orinoco and the Amazon* (London, 1988).

109. Here Humboldt interrupts his narrative by gathering together all his observations and readings about the San Fernando mission.

110. *Linnaeus's assertion ... palmivorous*: Humboldt refers to Linnaeus, *Systema naturae*, in Latin, vol. 1 (1735), p. 24.

111. *Berrio's and Raleigh's ... Guiana*: Humboldt cites Raleigh's 'pompously' titled *The Discovery of the Large, Rich and Beautiful Empire of Guiana* (London, 1596). Raleigh sailed for the Orinoco in 1595 and again in 1616. Antonio de Berrio's first expedition up the Orinoco in search of El Dorado was in 1586. He was guided by a Spanish soldier who had been taken there blindfolded, so he could not remember the way back. In 1590 Berrio, now governor of El Dorado, tried again. See Edward J. Goodman (1972), p. 80.

112. *Piedra de la Madre ... great calamities*: Humboldt in this tale airs his age's sentimentalities about the 'sanctity of motherhood'. Redmond O'Hanlon retells this story in Helen Maria Williams's words in *In Trouble Again* (London, 1988), pp. 134–6.

113. *the greatest cannibals*: In a letter to Willdenow in 1801 back home Humboldt exaggerated these tales of cannibalism: 'We found in some huts disgusting remains of cannibalism!'

114. Humboldt digresses twenty quarto pages to research into the sources of the Río Negro, and in passing praises La Condamine, whose 'voyage has thrown so much light on different parts of America'.

115. Bertholletia excelsa: Humboldt made the *Bertholletia excelsa* (*almendrón* and *juvia* in text) known in Europe. He named the Brazil-nut after Claude Louis Berthollet, a French chemist (1748–1822) who was active on scientific committees during the Revolution, went with Napoleon to Egypt, and ran meetings of distinguished scientists from 1807 to 1817 known as the Society of Arcueil (see Maurice Crosland (1967)). Humboldt published a paper on isothermal lines in the journal *Mémoires de la société d'Arcueil* run by Berthollet. According to Helmut de Terra (1955), Berthollet said of Humboldt: 'Cet homme réunit toute une académie en lui.' The Brazil-nut tree grows straight up to some 98 feet. The fruit is the size of a croquet ball and its shell is harder than a coconut, with twenty-five to thirty seeds inside. A.R. Wallace in *Travels on the Amazon* (London, 1853) says they fall like cannon-balls, sometimes even killing people. See also Redmond O'Hanlon, *In Trouble Again* (London, 1988), pp. 33–4.

116. Humboldt continues here with details about fixing the boundary between the Spanish and Portuguese colonies. In a note he quotes from his own 1800 memoir in Spanish to Mariano de Urquijo (1768–1817; a Spanish statesman who had granted Humboldt his travel permit), arguing for free trade between the colonies. This would lessen the anger of *americanos* in their demand for natural rights. This note shows that Humboldt was aware of American grievances against the central Spanish Government.

117. *Mutis*: See note 75.

118. Humboldt moves out of his narrative at this point to consider the Orinoco, Río Negro and Amazon river systems over twenty-five quarto pages.

119. urari . . . *poison*: Humboldt was the first to accurately report back to Europe on this secret poison curare, used by Indians to hunt animals by causing neuromuscular relaxation or paralysis, although Walter Raleigh had brought a little back in the seventeenth century. Only in 1937 were the majority of plants used to make up curare identified. Charles Waterton's *wourali* is the same. See A.R. McIntyre, *Curare: Its History, Nature and Clinical Use* (Chicago, 1947).

120. *monkey . . . roasted and smoked at the same time*: Humboldt in a note describes a drawing made by Schick in Rome representing one of their camps in the Orinoco with Indians roasting monkeys.

121. Humboldt goes on to give details about the *juvia*, or the 'chestnut of Brazil' (see note 115), and traces earlier references to it in previous travellers' accounts.

122. Humboldt goes on to give details about tribes of dwarves and fair Indians.

123. *caparro . . . made known in my* Observations on Zoology and Comparative Anatomy: Vol. 1 (1805), pp. 322 and 354. According to Humboldt, Geoffroy Saint-Hilaire thought it a new genus. Humboldt wrote letters to Geoffroy Saint-Hilaire, a 'Goethian' scientist. See my introduction.

124. *parrot . . . language of the Atures*: See note 100.

125. *my old master Blumenbach*: J.F. Blumenbach (1752–1840) was Professor of Natural History at Göttingen, and a friend of Humboldt's.

126. Humboldt continues with a description of his researches into earth eating all round the world. This section caused controversy in Paris, as Humboldt notes.

127. *Fourcroy in Paris*: Fourcroy (1755–1809) was Professor of Chemistry at the Museum d'Histoire Naturelle, Paris. He was very active in education during the Revolution. Humboldt wrote at least two letters to him from South America addressing him as 'citizen'.

128. *tobacco*: In a note Humboldt derives the word 'tobacco', like the words 'savannah', 'maize', 'cacique', 'maguey' and 'manatee', from the ancient languages of Haiti. It did not refer to the plant but the tube through which it was smoked.

129. *Alonso de Herrera*: Humboldt read the historian Herrera's account of his expedition up the Orinoco with 'astonishment' and gives details of where he stayed. Herrera was killed in battle by an arrow poisoned with curare in 1535.

130. Humboldt wrote: 'I will end this chapter with a succinct description of Spanish Guiana,' and then researches into the El Dorado myth, and the search for that 'imaginary country', for over sixty quarto pages.

131. *Pierre Martyr d'Anghiera*: Pierre Martyr d'Anghiera (1455–1526), an Italian historian who wrote about Columbus in *De Rebus oceanicis et de orbe novo decades* (1494). This is a good example of how on his return to Europe Humboldt read voraciously and 'with attention the Spanish sixteenth-century authors' to document his own voyage.

132. *Carib children . . . closer to nature . . . Rousseau's works*: This is a critical reference to Jean-Jacques Rousseau, who described the Caribs as 'closest to the state of nature'. Rousseau claimed that they 'are precisely the most peaceful in their loves, and the least subject to jealousy, despite their living in the kind of hot climate that always seems to inflame those passions' (*A Discourse on Inequality*, trans. Maurice Cranston

(Harmondsworth, 1984), p. 103). Rousseau's ideas on infant education come from his novel *Émile* (1762).

133. *the unfortunate España*: See note 68.

134. *He had followed my progress from reading English newspapers*: On Humboldt in English papers see Calvin P. Jones, 'The Spanish American Works of Alexander von Humboldt as Viewed by Leading British Periodicals, 1800–1830', *The Americas*, 29 (April 1973), pp. 442–8.

135. Before continuing his narrative Humboldt adds in a long chapter (ch. 26, quarto pp. 56–321) on the political state of the Venezuelan provinces, their population, natural productions and commerce, as well as research on the difficulties of communications in the Republic of Colombia. This is followed by a brief chapter (ch. 27, quarto pp. 322–41) factually describing Bonpland's and Humboldt's crossing from New Barcelona on 24 November 1801, arriving in Havana on 19 December 1801.

136. *The way Havana looks . . . coasts*: For a modern view of Havana see Nissa Torrents, *La Habana* (Barcelona, 1989).

137. Humboldt here includes his *Essai politique sur l'île de Cuba* (quarto pp. 351–457), also published separately in Paris. It was translated in 1856 by J.S. Thrasher as *The Island of Cuba*, but Humboldt was furious that Thrasher cut out the chapter on the horror of slavery. As Louis Agassiz pointed out, Humboldt died pained that slavery (not abolished until 1865) had not been abolished in the United States during his lifetime.

138. *Captain Baudin's departure*: See note 4.

139. *On my second visit to Havana in 1804*: The travellers left Veracruz and arrived in Havana on 29 March 1804, and left for Philadelphia on the ship *La Concepción* on 29 April 1804.

140. *M. Fidalgo's coastal surveying expedition*: Joaquín Francisco Fidalgo (?–1820), a Spanish sailor in charge of measuring the Caribbean coasts.

141. *waters of the isthmus*: Humboldt was the first to seriously propose a canal across the 'isthmus of Panama'.

142. *Bouguer*: Pierre Bouguer, Professor of Hydrography, accompanied Godin and La Condamine to Peru in 1736, and published his *Traité de la figure de la terre* (1749).

143. *Travel books have multiplied . . . extraordinary mistakes*: Humboldt's writing up of his South American travels was so diversified into other disciplines that the third volume of his *Relation historique* came out in 1825, eleven years after the first. He complained to his reader: 'In the late publication of my *Personal Narrative*, which was preceded by more scientific tomes, I have been pre-empted by travellers who crossed America twenty-five years after me.' According to Miguel Wionczek, Humboldt's thirteen original diary volumes in French from his 1799–1804 trip remained unedited until 1986 when Margot Faak published *Alexander von Humboldt: Reise auf dem Rio Magdalena, durch die Anden und Mexico. Aus seinen Reisetagebuchern zusammengestellt und erlautert* (Berlin, 1986), which corresponds to the countries not covered by his *Personal Narrative*.

144. *General Rochambeau's unfortunate expedition*: Donatien Rochambeau (1750–1813) was sent out to Santo Domingo in 1792; chased the English from Martinique in

1793, and helped defeat Toussaint L'Ouverture in Haiti in 1802. But his troops were decimated by malaria and he was captured by the British in 1803 and imprisoned until 1811.

145. *in his exile . . . my unfortunate friend Bonpland*: Bonpland was imprisoned by Dr Francia in Paraguay; see my introduction and my essay, 'The Strange Fate of Aimé Bonpland', *London Magazine* (April–May 1994), pp. 36–48.

146. Humboldt's narrative ends in May 1801. He supposedly destroyed the final fourth volume, which was ready for press. A reader may follow his trip to Lima, his climbing of Chimborazo, his first sight of the Pacific in his *Anschiten der Natur* (1808), as well as in Margot Faak (1986) (see note 143).